The History Of The City Of Glasgow And Suburbs

Engraved for Denholms History of Glasgow.

Drawn by J.Denholm

Eng. by R.Scott

THE

HISTORY

OF THE

CITY OF GLASGOW

AND SUBURBS.

To which is added,

A SKETCH OF A TOUR TO THE PRINCIPAL

Scotch and English Lakes.

BY

JAMES DENHOLM,

OF THE ACADEMY, ARGYLE-STREET,

MEMBER OF THE PHILOSOPHICAL AND PHILOTECHNICAL
SOCIETIES OF GLASGOW.

Embellished with Fifteen Elegant Engravings.

THIRD EDITION.

GLASGOW:
Printed by R. Chapman,
FOR A. MACGOUN, BOOKSELLER.
1804.

TO THE

RIGHT HONOURABLE

THOMAS, EARL OF HYNDFORD,

LORD CARMICHAEL,

VICE LIEUTENANT

OF THE

COUNTY OF LANARK, &c. &c.

MY LORD,

THE many obligations which
your noble predecessor, John, Earl of Hyndford, conferred on those with whom I was
most nearly connected, and the polite atten-
tions with which you have since condescended
to honour me, very powerfully induce me to
submit these sheets to your Lordship's patronage.

Your Lordship may recollect, that some
years ago, under the flattering auspices of
your approbation, I had projected a work *
on a still-more extended scale. Since then,
however,

* The Natural and Civil History of the County of Lanark.

however, the necessary avocations in which I am engaged, have hitherto prevented me from carrying it farther. Should future leisure enable me to resume the execution of the plan, your Lordship's encouragement will add another obligation to the many which I already owe you.

I have the honour to be,

With the most distinguished respect,

Your Lordship's most obedient, and

Most humble servant,

JA. DENHOLM.

Glasgow, 28th May,
1804.

PREFACE.

PREVIOUS to the publication of the first Edition of this work, no regular historical account of Glasgow had appeared for upwards of twenty years. During that interval, the population of the city had greatly increased; and other changes had occurred, sufficiently numerous and important, to call for a more enlarged series of details.

This history was, therefore, composed and published in the year 1797; and has, since that period, passed through two very considerable editions. Encouraged by the success of the attempt, and the approbation of the discerning, I was induced to revise my juvenile performance for a third impression.

A slight glance, however, convinced me, that various alterations and additions would be necessary to adapt my narrative to the growing prosperity of the city; and to that more intimate acquaintance with its history and condition, which results from a continued residence within its precincts. Agreeably to this view of the subject, I have in several respects deviated from the original plan; and have inserted many particulars formerly omitted in the preceding editions. The ecclesiastical has been separated from the civil history; the description has been enlarged, as well as the accounts of the various public institutions; and many facts, relative to the commerce,

the

the manufactures, and present state of the city, have been incorporated with the work.

But while I am conscious that I have omitted nothing which appeared to merit attention, or which I deemed consistent with the nature of such a publication, I am at the same time sensible, that notwithstanding my care to collect every material information, some things may have escaped me; I may also have committed many errors which I have not as yet been able to detect. In either case, as well as upon the whole of the performance, I must again solicit the candour of that public, from whom I have hitherto met with much indulgence, and to whom, in other respects, I am so much indebted.

It would be improper in me to conclude, without returning my acknowledgements to the many gentlemen who favoured me with much valuable information respecting a number of facts, with which, otherwise, I could not so easily have become acquainted. To particularize their names, however, would be tedious, and to name a few, to the exclusion of others, might appear invidious. Let it therefore suffice, in general to say, that I owe much to the learned gentlemen of the University and clergymen of the city. I also am under many obligations to several individuals who are placed at the head of the municipal departments, and to many private citizens, alike distinguished by taste, literature, and talents; and by their politeness, candour, and affability.

CONTENTS.

of

CHAPTER XIII.

TOUR.

CHAP. I.

Origin and Antiquity of the City—Derivation of its Name—Its Ecclesiastical History, and the Succession of its Bishops to the Reformation.

IN tracing the origin of nations, cities, or families, that lay claim to any high degree of antiquity, we most commonly find ourselves involved in fable and conjecture. From the want of records, the low state of civilization in these distant periods, and the almost total neglect of every thing but what tended to defence, convenience, or comfort, has arisen this mist, which so effectually obscures the prospect.

To point out therefore the cause which gave rise to Glasgow is now impossible.

The vicinity of a river, a strong and healthy situation, and fertile soil uniting in one spot, have often

A   induced

induced mankind to congregate together, and thus form villages, which, in progress of time, became towns and cities.

Chance, or some accidental circumstance, has most likely, however, given rise to the city whose history is the subject of these sheets, because in many other places, and at no great distance, more eligible situations might have been found, either with respect to one or other of these advantages.

Neither can we speak with certainty as to the etymology of its name.

Glasgow hath been derived from two Gælic words, which signify a Dark Glen, and to account for such a derivation, it is said, that the banks of the Molendinar burn, on which the ancient part of the city stood, and which are steep and precipitous, were at one time covered with wood. The name is likewise derived by some from a word in the same language, signifying a Black or Gray Smith, and they think it probable, that in these early ages, when artizans were but thinly scattered over the face of the country, the name might have arisen from a person of that profession, who had settled there, and who, if we suppose his existence to have been antecedent to the cathedral, may have given origin to the city, as well as its name.

Though thus undetermined as to its origin or etymology, we can speak with more certainty as to its antiquity. Few towns in Britain can carry their history to a more remote period. That it existed in the sixth century, is a fact which we are assured of by our early historians; nay, it is probable, that it may have had its origin at a still more distant period,

period, even at the time when the Roman power extended over great part of Britain. It may have been a military station of that people, as it lies on the great Roman road running through the province of Valentia, betwixt Carlisle and Dunglass, the western termination of the wall of Hadrian.

But leaving conjecture, we now proceed to state such facts as are better founded: beginning first with the ecclesiastical department, and succession of bishops, and then proceeding in the second place, to·the civil and political history of the city.

560.

Spottiswoode, in his history of the church and state of Scotland, informs us that a religious establishment was founded at Glasgow at this early period, of which a person of the name of St. Mungo, or Kentigern, was superintendant or bishop†.

A 2   After

† He likewise (lib. i.) mentions several particulars respecting St. Kentigern, which it will not be improper to notice. According to that writer, he was the son of Thametes, daughter of Loth, king of the Picts, his father was supposed to be Eugenius III. king of Scots. St. Kentigern was born near Culross, where are still to be seen the ruins of a chapel dedicated to that saint, which though in the diocese of St. Andrew's, was under the government of the bishop of Glasgow. When a young man, he was put under the care of Servanus, bishop of Orkney. While under his charge, " he gave tokens of his rare piety, for he was in prayer more frequent than young ones are seen to be, of a spare diet, and so compassionate to the poor, that he distributed all that came into his hands amongst them. Servanus loving him beyond others, was ordinarily wont to call him *Mongab*, which signifies, dear friend.

After

601.

After his death, which took place in the beginning of this year, he was succeeded by Baldrede,
his disciple, who, amongst other acts of piety, is
said to have founded a religious house at Inchinnan.
Of the time of his death, of the person who succeeded him, or with any fact concerning the history
of the town, whether ecclesiastical or civil, downwards to the eleventh century, we are perfectly unacquainted. This may be accounted for from the situation of the kingdom at the time, which every
where presented pictures of human nature in its ru-
dest and most barbarous form. Civil wars, discord,
an utter disregard to laws and the property of societies or individuals, were the principal features of
that gloomy period. In this state was Scotland,
when

After the death of his tutor, St. Kentigern retired into
Wales, where he lived a retired life, and founded a monastery
betwixt the rivers Elwid and Edway. In this monastery, it is
said, there were daily entertained six hundred and sixty-six
people, of which number three hundred were kept at work
within the house, three hundred laboured without, the remainder were appointed for divine service, and divided in such a
manner, that day and night some were always employed in de-
votion.

St. Kentigern at length resigned his situation, and returning to Scotland, fixed upon Glasgow as the place of his residence, where, says Spottiswoode, " he laid the foundation of
a stately church, in which he was interred." It is affirmed,
says the same author, " that after he came to years of under-
standing, he did never eat flesh, or taste wine, or any strong
drink, and when he went to rest, slept on the cold ground, having a stone for his pillow." Notwithstanding he lived thus
hardily, he attained the age of *nine-score and five years.*

when David the I. then prince of Cumberland, refounded the see.

1126.

From the inquisition * or grant for this purpose,
it appears that the ancient possessions of the church
were very extensive, consisting of eighteen baronies
of land in the counties of Peebles, Selkirk, Roxburgh, Dumfries, and Stewartry of Annandale, besides other lands in Cumberland†.

This

---

* Cart. of Glasg. vol. 1. pag. 1.

† To enforce payment of the customary tithes, from these
lands, Malcolm the IV. by his charter, (Cart. vol. 1. p. 16.) ordained those residing within the diocese, to give all due reve-
rence to the bishop, and to pay their tithes and other ecclesiastical dues, viz. " of corn, lint, wool, cheese, butter, lambs,
calves, pigs, chickens, and of every thing else, not made mention of, which the Christian law enjoins to be paid."

This prelate was likewise chancellor of Scotland, while he
held the see. He appears to have been a person of great learning for these times, and had travelled into several countries, before his accession to the bishopric. He divided the diocese into
the two archdeaconries of Glasgow and Teviotdale, and established the offices of dean, subdean, chancellor, treasurer, sacrist, chanter, and succensor, and settled a prebendary upon
each of them. He died 28th May 1147.

From the space of time that has intervened betwixt the
present period and the Reformation, as well as from other causes, many are unacquainted with the system of government in
the Roman church. As Glasgow was the residence of the second church dignitary of Scotland, and a numerous retinue of
clergy, from whom for several centuries it appears to have derived its chief importance, it perhaps may not be improper in
the history of such a city, to take some notice of the principal
orders

1129.

This year John Achaius, preceptor to David I. was by that prince nominated to the bishopric. He rebuilt

orders which composed the popish establishment in this country.

The clergy were divided into two great divisions, REGU-LAR and SECULAR.

The first, or *Regular Clergy*, were so denominated because they were under an obligation to live according to certain rules prescribed them by St. Augustine, or St. Bennet. The members of each society slept under one roof.

There were several distinct societies of the regular clergy. The principal of these constituted an Abbey, of which the abbot was head. Some abbots were independent of the bishop; these were called *abottes exempti*. Some were invested with episcopal power, wore a mitre, and were called sovereign mitred abbots, and had a seat in parliament.

The second division of the regular clergy formed a Priory. —At first, the prior was only the ruler of the abbey under the abbot, who was *primus* in the monastery, and the prior was no dignitary; but afterwards, a mother-abbey detaching a party of its monks, and obtaining a settlement for them in some other place, they became a separate convent. A prior was set over them, and their house was called *cella obedientia*, denoting that they depended upon a superior monastery. This was called a conventual prior, and was a dignitary, but a prior in the abbey was only a *claustral* prior.

In general the priory lands were erected into a regality, of which the prior was lord.

The third division consisted of *Monks, Friars*, and *Nuns*.— The monks and friars differed in this respect, that the former were seldom allowed to go out of their cloisters, but the friars, who were commonly mendicants, travelled about, and preached in the neighbourhood. Every monk or friar used the tonsure, or shaved crown, an emblem, they said, of their hope of a crown of glory. They vowed chastity, poverty and obedience,

rebuilt and adorned a part of the cathedral church, which he consecrated in presence of the king, upon the 9th of July 1136.

After

dience, besides the rules of their respective orders. The principal orders of the friars were,

1. The Dominicans, or Black Friars, because they wore a black cross on a white gown, were instituted by Dominic, a Spaniard, and first brought into Scotland by William Malvoisin, bishop of Glasgow, about the year 1200.

2. The Franciscans, called Grey Friars, from their wearing a grey gown and cowl, with a rope about their waist, were established by St. Francis, an Italian, in the year 1206.

3. The Carmelite, or White Friars, like the two preceding orders, were allowed to preach abroad, and beg their subsistence. In addition may be mentioned

The Grey Sisters, or Nuns of Sienna in Italy. They wore a grey gown and a rotchet, followed St. Austin's rule, and were never allowed to go forth of their cloisters, after they had made their vows.

THE SECULAR CLERGY

Consisted of the bishops and parish ministers, &c. They lived in the world abroad, without being shut up in convents and cloisters as the regulars were.

Colleges were instituted for performing divine service, and singing masses for the souls of the founders, or their friends. They were removed sometimes to cathedrals, and sometimes to ordinary churches. In the former case, the bishop was the ruler. In the latter they were called collegiate churches, and the head or ruler was called provost or dean. The colleges consisted of canons or prebendaries, who had their stalls for orderly singing the canonical hours, and were commonly erected out of parish churches, or out of the chaplains belonging to churches.

Canons or chanons secular (so called to distinguish them from the regulars in convents) were *ministers* or *parsons* within the diocese, chosen by the bishop to be members of his chapter

ter

1147.

After the death of Achaius, Herbert, abbot of Kelso, succeeded to the see. During the incumbency of this prelate, the archbishop of York revived his pretensions of a jurisdiction over the church of

ter or council. They lived within the college, performed divine service in the cathedral, and sung in the choir, according to rules or canons made by the chapter. Prebendaries had each a *prebendum*, or portion of land, allotted to him for his service. Canons and prebendaries differed chiefly in this, that the canon had his *canonica*, or portion, merely for his being received, although he did not serve in the church; but the prebendary had his *prebendum* only when he served.

Every canonry had a vicarage annexed to it, for the better subsistence of the canon, who had the great tithes of both parishes, and was generally the patron of the annexed vicarage.

The dignified clergy, besides the bishop, were five in number, viz.

The *Dean*, who presided in the chapter, &c. during the bishop's absence.

The *Archdeacon*, who visited the diocese, examined candidates for orders, and was the bishop's vicar.

The *Chanter*, who regulated the music, and when present, presided in the choir.

The *Chancellor*, who was the judge of the bishop's court, the secretary of the chapter, and the keeper of their seal; and

The *Treasurer*, who had the charge of the common revenue of the diocese.

All these had rich livings, and deputies to officiate for them, and with the addition of some canons and prebendaries chosen by the bishop, constituted his privy-council, and in a vacancy, elected for bishop whom the king recommended.

The inferior clergy were parsons, vicars, ministers of mensal churches, and of common churches, and chaplains.

Parsons

of Scotland. The Scotch clergy resented, and the matter was referred to pope Alexander III. The bishop of Glasgow and the chancellor of the kingdom were appointed on the part of the Scotch bishops to negotiate the business at Rome. Thither

B   they

Parsons were those who had a right to the tithes, and were the ministers and rectors of parishes.

Vicars served the cure in place of the rector. To augment the revenues of the bishop, the other dignified clergy, and the canons, parish churches were annexed to the churches in which they served, and they were the rectors and parsons of such annexed churches. They had right to the tithes, and they sent vicars to serve the cure, to whom an allowance was made of a portion of the tithes as their stipend. They generally had the small tithes assigned to them. The parsons who had vicarages depending upon them, claimed the patronage of them. Hence, after the Reformation, the patron of the parsonage acted as patron of the vicarage.

Mensal Churches were such as were *de mensa episcopi*, for furnishing the table of the bishop. He was parson and titular, and employed a vicar or *stipendiary* to serve the cure.

Common Churches were so called because the tithes of them were the common good, or for the common exigencies of the diocese.

Chaplains were those clergy who officiated in chapels. These chapels were of different kinds. In parishes of great extent, chapels of ease were erected in distant corners, for convenience, and the rector of the parish maintained a curate there to read prayers and sing mass. Some chapels were called free chapels, which were not dependent on any parish, but had proper endowments for their own ministers, whose charge was called a chaplainry. Besides these there were domestic chapels, or oratories, built near the residence of great men, and almost in every parish there were private chapels, built by individuals, that mass might be celebrated for the souls of

themselves

they went and were successful. The pope, by his bull, exempting the church of Scotland from all jurisdiction whatever, excepting that of the apostolic see.

1164.

themselves or their friends. The office of saying mass in such chapels, was called chantery or chanting masses. The priest's salary was termed alterage. The service performed for the dead was the *obit*, and the register of the dead was called obituary. In the first part of the obit, are the words, *Dirge nos domine*, and hence came the dirge.

The government of the diocese was vested in the bishop: for his convenience he had officers, and courts, ecclesiastic, civil and criminal. These courts were five in number.

The chapter was the principal. The legislative power was lodged in this court, or rather in the bishop, who, with the advice of the chapter, made laws, canons, and regulations for the diocese, erected, annexed, or disjoined parishes, purchased, sold or let in tack, church lands and tithes, &c.

Diocesan Synods were called at the pleasure of the bishop, who, or the dean, in his absence, was president. Cases of discipline, and appeals from deaneries were cognosced in these synodical meetings, and from them the protestant church took the plan of provincial synods.

The *diocese* was divided into *deaneries*, which seem to have been, in some respects, what presbyteries are now.

The consistorial court was held in the bishop's name by his official. It judged in all matters of tithes, marriages, divorces, testaments, mortifications, &c. This court granted dispensations, allowing marriages betwixt persons within the degrees of consanguinity or affinity.

The bishop also seized on the effects of those who died intestate, to the exclusion of the widow, children, relations, and even creditors, under pretence of applying them for promoting the good of the soul of the deceased. This court is now succeeded by the commissary court.

The next court was that of the regality, whose jurisdiction also

11

1164.

The immediate successor of Herbert, was Ingelram Newbigging *, rector of Peebles, and as such archdeacon of Glasgow. After his death in

1174

Joceline†, abbot of Melrose, was consecrated bishop by Escelin archbishop of London, the pope's legate, he considerably enlarged the cathedral, which he dedicated, 9th July 1197. Previous to this ceremony, and it would appear the same year he attained the sacerdotal dignity, he procured a charter from William the Lyon, erecting the city of Glasgow into a royal burgh, in favour of him and his sucessors,

1199.

Hugh de Roxburgh succeeded to the see, but this dignity he held only for a few months, when he died ‡.

B 2   1200.

also extended over the diocese. The chief revenues of the clergy, though it is almost unnecessary to mention it, arose from tithes, from church lands mortified to them by the crown, and from private mortifications and donations. Such was the power and wealth of the church, it possessed no less than fifty-three votes in the Scotch parliament, previous to the Reformation.

* This prelate was chancellor of the kingdom, when Herbert was bishop; he was brother to Elias, laird of Dunsyre in Lanarkshire, and died, 2d February, 1174. Keith's Catalogue.

† Joceline, when bishop, bequeathed to the abbey of Paisley, the churches of Mearns, Cathcart, and Rutherglen, and to the monks of Melrose, the church of Hastendean. He died at Melrose, 16th April, 1199, and was interre dwithin his own cathedral church. Chronicle of Melrose.

‡ 6th July, 1199. He was rector of Tullibody, and archdeacon of St. Andrew's.

1200.

The archdeacon of St. Andrew's, William Malvoisin was next consecrated. He continued in the
office only two years, when he was translated to the
primacy; and in

1202

He was succeeded by Florentius†, son to the earl of
Holland, and nearly connected with the royal family of Scotland. Florentius resigned in a few years
thereafter his episcopal function with consent of
the pope. His successor Walter*, chaplain to the
king (William) was bishop in 1207, and consecrated in

1208.

This prelate was one of the commissioners sent
to treat of a peace with John king of England; he
likewise, with some other dignified clergy, attended
a council at Rome in the year 1215.

1233.

William de Boddington this year succeeded to
the see‡: he was chancellor of Scotland, and privy
counsel-

---

† Florentius it would appear was never consecrated, so that
he was only elect of the see. He died at Rome shortly after
his resignation.

* He is witness to a charter of Walter, second steward of
Scotland, granting to the monks of Paisley free liberty to elect
a prior and abbot to themselves, about the year 1220. He
died in the year 1231.

‡ William de Boddington was descended of an ancient family in the shire of Berwick, first rector of Edelstone, then a
prebend

counsellor to Alexander II. In a general council
held at Basil in 1240, called by pope Gregory IX.
to consider about the relief of the Holy Land, this
bishop appears to have been present. After his return, he made several reparations and additions to
the cathedral church, and in the last year of his life,
he introduced into his diocese, the use of the liturgy, as used in the church of Salisbury.

1260.

Upon the death of William de Boddington, the
qualified clergy of the diocese of Glasgow, or chapter as they are most commonly named, elected Walter Moffat, archdeacon of Teviotdale, one of their
members, to be bishop. The election was, however,
cast at Rome, and John de Cheynam*, an Englishman, consecrated and preferred to the see. This situation he retained only a few years.

1268.

This year Nicholaus de Moffat was again elected
bishop. He was never consecrated, from the strong
opposition

---

prebend of Glasgow, one of the *clericii cancellarii*, archdeacon of St. Andrew's, and a privy counsellor to Alexander II.
In his journey to Rome, it would appear, he, with some other
prelates, were stopped for some time by the emperor of Ger-
many, Frederick II. but afterwards were allowed to proceed,
He died, November 10th, 1258, and was interred on the 13th,
in the abbey church of Melrose, near the high altar.

* John de Cheynam resided mostly in foreign parts, being
disliked by the king and his diocese. He died in 1268.

opposition made against him by some of his own canons, and retained the see only two years‡.

1270.

The successor of Nicholaus de Moffat, was William Wisheart, archdeacon of St. Andrew's, and lord high chancellor of Scotland. Before his consecration he was preferred to the see of St. Andrew's, when in

1272

His nephew, Robert Wisheart*, archdeacon of Lothian, succeeded to the bishopric. This prelate was of the council of Alexander III. upon whose death he succeeded to the regency. This high office he discharged with integrity and reputation, during a very perilous time. In the war which took place when the dispute was depending betwixt Bruce and Baliol, he was taken prisoner, and kept in confinement in England, until the battle of Bannockburn, when he was exchanged for another person of rank.

1317.

The next in succession was Stephen de Dundemore,

‡ He died in 1270 of an apoplexy, at Tinningham in East Lothian.

* * At the convention which took place at Norham, betwixt the competitors for the crown of Scotland, and Edward of England as umpire; bishop Wisheart also attended, and so boldly asserted the independence of his country, as to draw upon himself the hatred of the English monarch. He died after returning from his confinement, which had very much impaired his health, in November 1316.

more, descended from an ancient family of that
name in Fife; though elected by the chapter to the
bishopric, it appears he was never consecrated. Edward II. of England, whose interest this prelate violently opposed, having had sufficient influence with
the pope to stop the performance of this ceremo-
ny†.

1319.

Upon the death of Stephen de Dundemore, John
Wisheart, archdeacon of Glasgow, was next raised
to the episcopal dignity. Like his predecessor he
was a violent enemy to the English, from whom he
suffered a long and rigorous imprisonment while he
was archdeacon; first, in the castle of Conway, and
then in the Tower of London, from which it is likely he was released after the battle of Bannockburn,
when Robert Wisheart and some others were exchanged for persons of equal rank‡.

1325.

John Wisheart was succeeded by John Lindsay*, of the house of Crawford, he was first a prebend

† He died on his way to Rome, the same year he was elected, viz. 1317.

‡ In the year 1322, this bishop with consent of his chapter,
gives to the church of the Holy Cross, Edinburgh, and to the
canons thereof, the church of Dalgarnock. He died 1325.

* This bishop was a partizan of John Baliol's, in the noted
contest about the right to the crown, and he, with the bishops
of Aberdeen and Dunkeld, are witnesses to a grant made
by king Edward Baliol, to Edward king of England, dated
12th February, 1334.

bend or canon of Glasgow, then great chamberlain of Scotland. In the year 1335, in returning home from Flanders with two vessels, aboard of which were two hundred and fifty of his countrymen, they were attacked by a superior fleet of the English under the command of the earls of Sarum and Huntington, and being overpowered by numbers, were obliged to yield. In this engagement the bishop was mortally wounded, and immediately expired.

1335.

The prelate next in order was William Rae*, to whom the city owes the erection of the bridge over the Clyde, which he first caused to be built of stone, it having been before this time constructed of timber.

Robert, lord high steward, and afterwards king of Scotland, having obtained in the year 1364, a dispensation from the pope, for contracting a marriage with Elizabeth More, notwithstanding their consanguinity, the bishop of Glasgow was appointed the pope's delegate, and as such, the dispensation was agreed to be granted, under the provision of Robert II. erecting and endowing a chaplainry in the cathedral church, which he did accordingly.

1368.

---

* There are several original writs in this bishop's name, lying among the archives of the see of Glasgow, in the Scots college at Paris, and in the monastery of the Carthusians, particularly two acquittances for the contribution of the diocese of Glasgow to the pope, in 1340 and 1341.

1368.

Walter Wardlaw, a younger brother of the family of Wardlaw of Torry, in Fifeshire, was first canon of Aberdeen, thereafter archdeacon of Lothian, and secretary to David II. He was consecrated this year, and nominated one of the ambassadors to England.

In the reign of Robert III. he, with Sir Archibald Douglas, lord of Galloway, were sent into France to renew the ancient league betwixt the two countries: in this negotiation he rendered himself so acceptable to the French court, that, at the special request of Charles VI. he was by the pope (Clement VII.) created a cardinal, anno 1384*.

1387.

This last prelate was succeeded by Matthew Glendinning, of the family of that name in Eskdale: he was a canon or prebend of Glasgow, at the time he was preferred to the see. He appears to have been a man of abilities, being much employed in the public transactions that were then carried on betwixt the two nations of Scotland and England, according to Rymer's Fœdera†.

C   1408.

* He died in 1387. His coat of arms is placed near the middle of the choir, in the cathedral church, on the right side of the high altar, and over it his name in Saxon capitals, " Walterus Cardinales."

† While he was in possession of the see, the steeple of the cathedral church which was built of timber, and covered with lead, was burnt by lightning. His death happened in the year 1408.

1408.

Upon the decease of the last mentioned prelate, William Lauder, son to Sir Allan Lauder of Hatton in Edinburghshire, was appointed bishop by pope Benedict XIII.

In the year 1444, he was preferred to be chancellor of the kingdom, and the same year, he had the honour to be employed in the negotiation which was carried on with the court of England, for the ransom of king James I. who had been detained a prisoner for about eighteen years.

This bishop laid the foundation of the vestry of the cathedral church, and built the great tower of stone, as far as the first battlement†.

1426.

William Lauder was succeeded in the see by John Cameron of the family of Lochiel, Invernessshire. Before his arrival at the episcopal dignity, he passed through several situations, being official of Lothian, then rector of Cambuslang by the presentation of the earl of Douglas, whose secretary and confessor he was: thereafter he was appointed provost of Lincluden, constituted secretary of state, and keeper of the private seal, soon after of the great seal, which he retained till he was elected bishop of Glasgow‡.

The

---

† In different places of the structure, are to be seen his arms, being a Griffen saliant,—the bearing of Lauder of Hatton. He died, 14th June, 1425.

‡ In the year 1429, he erected six churches within his diocese

The truce with England expiring about the year 1437, he was appointed one of the Scots commissioners for redressing any grievances that had taken

C 2   place

cese into prebendaries, at the desire of their respective patrons: viz. Cambuslang, at the request of Archibald earl of Douglas; Kirkmahoe, at the desire of John Forst de Castorfyne, and Maria Stewart de Dalswyntone, his wife; the other four were Tarbolton, Eaglesham, Luss, and Killearn.

The prebendaries of Glasgow were near forty in number, they formed the chapter or council of the bishop, whom they had the power of electing, though this privilege was often of little avail, from the interference of the pope.—The prebendaries belonging to this diocese, with their offices, as fixed by bishop Cameron, were as follows:

The Prebend of Hamilton, Dean of the Chapter.—The Prebend of Peebles, Archdeacon of Glasgow.—The Prebend of Ancrum, Archdeacon of Teviotdale.—The Prebend of Monkland was Subdean.—The Prebend of Cambuslang was Chancellor.—The Prebend of Carnwath was Treasurer.—The Prebend of Kilbride was Chantor.—The Prebend of Glasgow, primo, was the Bishop's Vicar.—The Prebend of Glasgow, secundo, was Sub-Chantor.—The Prebend of Campsie was Sacrist.—The Prebend of Balernock was styled Lord of Provan.—The Prebend of Carstairs.—The Prebend of Erskine.—The Prebend of Cardross.—The Prebend of Renfrew.—The Prebend of Eaglesham.—The Prebend of Kirkmahoe.—The Prebend of Calder.—The Prebend of Lanark.—The Prebend of Marbottle.—The Prebend of Moffat.—The Prebend of Govan.—The Prebend of Tarbolton.—The Prebend of Menar.—The Prebend of Eldastone.—The Prebend of Dorisdyre.—The Prebend of Ayr.—The Prebend of Killearn.—The Prebend of Douglas.—The Prebend of Askirk.—The Prebend of Alnermube.—The Prebend of Roxburgh.—The Prebend of Luss.—The Prebend of Stobo.—The Prebend of Strathblane and Polmadie.—The Prebend of Cumnock.—The Prebend

place during the time of peace; he was also chosen
one of the delegates from the church of Scotland to
the council of Basle, to which he set out with a safe
conduct from the king of England, and with a retinue of thirty persons†. He first began the building
of the great tower of the episcopal palace, and likewise carried on the vestry.

1446.

On the death of the last mentioned prelate, James
Bruce, of the family of Clackmannan, and bishop
of Dunkeld, was preferred to the see. He held the
office

bend of Sanquhar.—The Prebend of Bothwell.—The Prebend
of Hawick.

These prebendaries bishop Cameron obliged to build houses, and to reside in the town, their cures being served by the
vicars.

The diocese of Glasgow was very extensive, it extended o-
ver the shires of Dumbarton, Renfrew, Ayr, and Lanark, with
part of the counties of Roxburgh, Peebles, Selkirk, and Dumfries, including no less than two hundred and forty parishes.
When the bishop was raised to the rank of archbishop, he had
under his jurisdiction the bishoprics of Galloway, Argyle, and
the Isles.

The arms of the see of Glasgow, are *Argent*, St. Ninian
standing full faced, proper, clothed with a pontifical robe, *pur-
pure*, on his head a mitre, and in his *dexter* hand a crossier, *or*.
The archbishop took place next the lord chancellor.

† Some of our historians, particularly Buchanan, describe this
prelate as a great oppressor, they likewise say he made a very
tragical exit, at his country seat of Lochwood, five or six miles
N. E. of Glasgow, on Christmas-eve, 1446.

office of lord chancellor, and was succeeded upon his death, which happened the same year he was elected, by

. 1447

William Turnbull, of the family of Bedrule, in the county of Roxburgh. This bishop was archdeacon of St. Andrew's, and keeper of the privy seal, before he got possession of the see. He is deservedly esteemed for the services he did his country, by procuring from pope Nicholas V. a bull for erecting the university of Glasgow, which he liberally endowed: he likewise received from James II. a charter erecting the city and patrimony of the episcopal see, into a regality‡.

1455.

Andrew Muirhead was the next in succession, a son of the family of Lachop, in Lanarkshire, a man of abilities, integrity, and learning, as appears from the important transactions in which he was engaged: in particular, he was one of the commissioners appointed to negotiate a truce betwixt Scotland and England in the year 1462, which was effected at the city of York, in the month of December that year. He likewise was employed with some others of rank, to treat at the court of Denmark, about the marriage betwixt his sovereign and a princess of that court, in which he was equally successful*.

1474.

‡ Bishop Turnbull died at Rome, 3d September, 1454.

* He founded the vicars in the choir, and built houses for
them

1474.

The prelate immediately following, was John Laing, descended of the family of Redhouse, in the county of Edinburgh. His first situation in the church, was the rectory of Tannadyce, in Angus, which he held with the vicarage of Linlithgow. He was next preferred by James III. to be lord treasurer, and thereafter lord register. Finally, he attained the see of Glasgow, which he held till his death*.

1483.

The rector of Carnwath, and as such, treasurer of the bishopric, George Carmichael, was this year elected; he was a son of the ancient and now noble family of that name in Lanarkshire. His consecration never took place, he having died on his journey to Rome for that purpose. He was succeeded in

1484

By Robert Blackadder, of the house of that name in Berwickshire. He was translated to Glasgow from the bishopric of Aberdeen. From the high estimation in which he was held at Rome, he procured from pope Alexander VI. a bull erecting the see of Glasgow into an archbishopric, notwithstanding a violent opposition from the archbishop of St. Andrew's, and some others of the clergy.

Archbishop

---

them to the north of the cathedral, where there are now only gardens: they were called the vicar alleys. He also founded an hospital, which bears his name. He died, November 20th, 1473.

* This event took place 11th January, 1483.

Archbishop Blackadder, with one or two other persons of rank, were employed to negotiate the marriage between James IV. and the princess Margaret, eldest daughter to Henry VII. of England; an union, which it is well known, has proved of the greatest benefit to Britain.

Even at this period, the dawn of the Reformation appeared in Scotland. Numbers began to perceive the absurdities of the Roman church, whose basis was superstition, which, while it tended to enrich and aggrandize its clergy, equally humbled, depressed, and kept in ignorance and error, the bulk of the people. Some impressed with these sentiments, were so bold as publish them‡. In the diocese of Glasgow, upwards of thirty were called before the council, for broaching their opinions too freely: the principal persons amongst these, were, Adam Read of Barskimming, George Campbell of Cessnock, and John Campbell of Newmills, gentlemen of the districts of Kyle and Cunningham, in the county of Ayr. Instead, however, of making any concessions, they openly defended their doctrines, and that with such confidence, that for the time, it was thought the best policy to dismiss them, after an admonition to beware of their future conduct.

This prelate (archbishop Blackadder) founded and built to its present height, the great south aisle of the cathedral, upon which, in several places, his arms are still to be seen. In the latter part of his
life,

‡ They were in derision at that time called Lollards.

life, he undertook a journey to the Holy Land, which he, however, did not live to accomplish, having died on the way thither.†

1508.

James Beaton succeeded this year, having been translated from the bishopric of Galloway. He held the office of treasurer of the kingdom, which he resigned upon his accession to the see of Glasgow. He was thereafter, from the favour of John Duke of Albany, created lord chancellor, and at the same time, possessed the rich abbacies of Kilwinning and Arbroath. At the time Albany went over to France, archbishop Beaton was appointed one of the lords of the regency. After possessing the see for about fourteen years, he was translated to the primacy of St. Andrews*.

1524.

Upon the translation of archbishop Beaton, Gavin Dunbar was preferred to the archiepiscopal dignity, he was descended of the family of Mochrum in Galloway. After entering into orders, he was created dean of Murray, then prior of Whithorn. Being a man of great learning and abilities, he was pitched upon as a proper person to superintend the education of James V. This task he executed so much to the satisfaction of all, that upon the vacancy taking place in the see of Glasgow, he was appointed to fill that situation. In the year 1527, as

† His death is said to have happened 28th July, 1508.

* Archbishop Beaton died 1539.

as a farther mark of favour, he was appointed chancellor of the kingdom, on the fall of the earl of Angus, and in a few years thereafter, nominated one of the lords of the regency, on occasion of the journey which his sovereign took to France, to solemnize a marriage with Magdalene, a princess of that court.

We are now nearly arrived at that period when there took place one of the most remarkable events in the history of this or any other country, the Reformation of Religion*: the secondary causes of this change, have often been pointed out. Many years before the time we allude to, Martin Luther, a German divine, had openly attacked the superstitious rites of the Roman worship; as the attempt was bold, and almost unprecedented, the eyes of Europe

D   were

---

* This great event, like almost every other, if we believe popular tradition, was, issued in by a great many prodigies. A comet appeared in the months of November and December 1559, which alarmed many. In the summer, large rivers so overflowed their banks, as to inundate several villages, in consequence of which, many lives were loft, and numbers of cattle swept away; while again, in the season of winter, their channels were dried up, as happens in a long and continued drought; showers of hail, each stone of which equalled in size the egg of a pigeon, destroyed the corn in many places; great numbers of whales were cast ashore, and embayed in the Frith of Forth. So far, these circumstances were only such as might happen from natural causes, but what shall we say of the following: during many days and nights, a fiery dragon, of a most terrific form, was seen to fly near to the earth, it emitted flames of fire from its mouth continually, which obliged many to guard their houses and corn!!!

was directed to him. Many champions came forward to combat his assertions; unavailing, however, were their arguments, against the voice of reason and of common sense, so that the number of his proselytes, every day increased.

The noise of the contest soon reached Scotland. Numbers here, like their brethren on the continent, as if just awake from that lethargy that had so long had dominion over them, examined the opinions of this celebrated reformer; these they soon found more congenial to truth, reason, and the dignity of the Deity, than the doctrines of the Roman church. The licentiousness of the clergy afforded another great argument for the change, many of whom, by this time, had arrived to such a pitch of effrontery, as even to avow in the face of day, their profligacy and their crimes, while at the same time, from their immense riches, and spiritual dominion, they kept the higher ranks of the laity in bondage, and by the their continual, and daily increasing exactions, grinded the very faces of the poor.

Murmurs began to be heard, one communicated his opinions to another, and thus, in the progress of time, notwithstanding the most violent opposition, the torrent increased, till, gathering sufficient force, it burst its barriers, and carried all before it.

Such, perhaps, were the secondary causes of the Reformation; the great first cause was, however, undoubtedly, the will of the Deity, who thus, for reasons which we cannot fathom, relieved us from the thraldom of Rome, while many other nations, seemingly more civilized and enlightened than we

were

were at the time alluded to, continued, as they still do, the spiritual subjects of the Roman pontiff.

Many measures were resorted to, in order to stop the progress of the doctrines of the Reformation; lenient measures, as we have had occasion before to notice, were sometimes used, but more frequently, the most rigorous proceedings were adopted. In the diocese of Glasgow, where other means had no effect, it was resolved to make an example, which might strike a terror into the hearts of men, and allay their desire after new doctrines. The persons pitched upon for this purpose, were Jerome Russel, a Grey Friar, and John Kennedy, from the county of Ayr, a young man, scarcely exceeding eighteen years of age.

After their trial, which was principally carried on by some violent and inflamed papists, deputed to Glasgow for that purpose, they were condemned to the flames. When preparing for the fire, Russel, a man of uncommon fortitude, addressed his fellow-sufferer, bidding him not to " fear, for though the pain which we shall suffer is short and light, our joy and consolation shall never have an end; death cannot destroy us, for it is destroyed already by him for whose sake we suffer;-therefore, let us strive to enter in by that same straight way, which our Saviour hath taken before us*."

To the honour of archbishop Dunbar, he was averse to such rigorous proceedings, insisting, that

D 2   they

* They suffered at the east end of the cathedral church. Knox, b. i. p. 134.

they hurt the cause of the church, more than o-
therwise, and that it would be still prudent to pursue lenient measures*.

1551.

On the decease of archbishop Dunbar, James Beaton, nephew to the primate of Scotland, the archbishop of St. Andrew's, was appointed to the diocese. He was first chantor of the cathedral, and thereafter, had possession of the abbey of Aberbrothick,
which he held till he was preferred to the see.
Though placed in this high situation, he found his
power extremely limited, from the spirit of the times:
among the inferior orders of the clergy, there were
many who openly professed the doctrines of the reformed, and these, as well as the laity, increased so
quickly in number, as portended the immediate ruin
of the ancient system. To hinder, as well as he
could, the further propagation of the reformed principles, and to secure the personal safety of himself,
as well as the safety of the effects of the church, he
applied to the duke of Chatelherault. That nobleman, accordingly, by his bond, dated 6th February,
1558, agreed to defend and protect the archbishop,
and all that pertained him. By this means, and the
protection and support of some of the other gentlemen in the neighbourhood, he fortified the castle,
(into which he removed the most valuable effects of
the cathedral) in such a manner, as enabled it to hold
out against any sudden attacks. Finding, however,

at

* Archbishop Dunbar, died, 30th April, 1547, and was interred in the chancel of the cathedral church.

at length, that the doctrines of the Reformation were still gaining ground amongst all ranks, and that it would be impossible much longer to ensure safety either to himself or his property, he withdrew into France, in the year 1560, carrying with him all the writs and archives of the bishopric of Glasgow‡:
· these

‡ Besides these writs, he carried away every thing valuable belonging to the cathedral, particularly the image of our Saviour in gold, and those of the twelve apostles in silver, with the whole vestments belonging to the church, as well as the relics undermentioned. To gratify curiosity, a list of these is here inserted, translated from the original in the Chartulary of the University, viz.

A silver cross, gilded in the upper part, adorned with precious stones in the lower part, with a small part of the wood of the cross of our Lord.

Also another silver cross, gilded, adorned with precious stones, with some other small parts of the wood of the cross of Christ.

One silver casket, gilt, with the hairs of the blessed Virgin, as appears by the writing affixed.

In a square silver coffer, part of the scourges of St. Kentigern, and St. Thomas of Canterbury, and a part of the hair garment, made use of by St. Kentigern, our patron, as appears by the schedule.

In another silver casket, gilded, part of the skin of St. Bartholomew the apostle.

In another silver casket, gilded, a bone of St. Ninian.

In another silver casket, gilded, part of the girdle of the blessed Virgin Mary.

In a crystal case, a bone of some saint, and of St. Magdalene.

In a small phial of crystal, part of the milk of the blessed Virgin Mary, and a part of the manger of our Lord.

In a small phial, of the colour of saffron, what flowed of old from the tomb of St. Kentigern.

One

these he deposited in the Scotch college, and monastery of the Carthusians, at Paris‡. While residing
there, he was appointed ambassador at the court of
France, by Queen Mary, and was continued as
such, by James VI. who afterwards, in 1588, restored to him the temporalities of the see, of which
he had been deprived, from the period of his departure.

CHAP,

One other phial, with some bones of St. Eugene, and St.
Blaze.

In another silver phial, part of the tomb of St. Catherine,
the virgin.

One small hide, with a part of the cloak of St. Martin, as
appears by the writing annexed.

One precious hide, with a part of the bodies of St. Kentigern, and St. Thomas of Canterbury.

Four other hides, with bones of saints, and other relics.

A wooden chest, with many small relics.

Two linen bags, with the bones of St. Kentigern, St. Thanew, and other deceased saints.

‡Cart. vol, 2, pag, 1213.

CHAP. II.

Reformation, and Succession of Bishops downwards to the Revolution—Assembly in 1610 establishing Episcopacy—Another General Assembly held at Glasgow in 1638—Presbytery established—Overthrown by Act of Parliament in 1661—Revolution in 1688.

AT the time archbishop Beaton abdicated the see of Glasgow, the doctrines of the Reformation had made a rapid progress amongst all ranks of men, if we except the dignified clergy, and some others, whose interest suffered by the change.

In consequence of this almost general assent, the Reformation was this year, 1560, established by law, and that gloomy fabric of Roman superstition and error, which had so long confined the minds of men, at once levelled with the ground. When this great event took place, superintendents were appointed over the kingdom, who had the charge of the clergy, within certain bounds. The west of Scotland, was under the care of John Willocks, formerly a Franciscan friar, but who had embraced the opinions of the reformed. He officiated in Glasgow,

gow, as first Protestant minister, after the Reformation.

In the confusion arising from such a revolution, and the little regard paid to the supreme civil authorities, the temporalities of the church were seized by the most powerful of the nobles, and their revenues mostly applied to their own purposes. Creatures of their own, were often appointed to the bishoprics, apparently for the purpose of conveying to their patron, under some appearance of law, the property of the diocese: of this description, appears to have been the first archbishop of Glasgow, after the Reformation, John Porterfield, who obtained the title in

1571.

In the following year, he was superseded by James Boyd of Trochrigg, a man of an excellent character. He obtained the archbishopric by the treaty of Leith, settling episcopacy in 1572. In six years, thereafter, viz. 1578, when the legality of the episcopal function was called in question by the general assembly, he submitted to their decision, but retained the temporalities of the see till his death*.

1581.

Upon the decease of archbishop Boyd, the duke de Aubigne, predecessor of the family of Lennox, obtained, from the interest he had with James VI. Robert Montgomery, a minister of Stirling, to be appointed

---

* This bishop feued out the lands of Bedlay to the lord Boyd, and the lands of Gorbals to George Elphinstone, merchant in Glasgow. He died June, 1581.

appointed to the see of Glasgow, seemingly with the view of having the revenues of the benefice conveyed to him in somewhat of a legal form†. This, for the trifling consideration mentioned in the note, Montgomery agreed to do; the matter coming to be generally known, the censures of the church were levelled against him, in consequence of which he resigned the office, and afterwards became minister, at Symonton, in Ayrshire, in 1587‡.

1585.

Upon the resignation of archbishop Montgomery, the king gave the title and revenue to William Erskine, commendator of Paisley. This he retained only two years, when the archbishopric was bestowed upon Walter, commendator of Blantyre, with power to feu out the lands. This he did accordingly, in the year 1588, by converting the real rent into a feu duty.

1588.

This year, the king again took the possession of the property of the diocese, for the purpose of restoring it to archbishop Beaton, who had, since the Reformation, resided in France, where he had acted

E   in

---

† It is said, that the whole emoluments the archbishop derived from possession of the office, were one thousand pounds Scots, some horse, corn, and poultry. By the alienation of Montgomery, in favour of the family of Lennox, they came to be hereditary lords of the archbishop's castle.

‡ 7th November, 1583. The session of Glasgow was this year regularly constituted of one minister, thirty-five elders, and twenty-six deacons.

in the quality of ambassador to king James. The
temporality of the see, was accordingly restored by
act of parliament, and held possession of by archbishop Beaton, till his death in April, 1603.

1603.

At this period, John Spottiswoode, parson of
Calder, in the county of Edinburgh, was appointed
to fill the vacancy, occasioned by the decease of
archbishop Beaton. He was not, however, consecrated till 1612, the ceremony being performed, at the
same time, upon him and the bishops of Brechin
and Galloway, in London, by the bishops of London, Worcester, Rochester, and Ely. In 1615,
archbishop Spottiswoode * was translated to the
primacy of St. Andrew's; he was the same year,

1615,

Succeeded by James Law, bishop of Orkney†,
who held possession of the see, for the seventeen
succeeding years.

At the time of this prelate's accession, one John
Ogilvy, a Jesuit, from the college of Gratz, was apprehended at Glasgow, under suspicion of his being
a popish emissary, sent into the country for treason-
able purposes. After a fair trial, during which he
behaved with the most daring arrogance, he was
found guilty of endeavouring to inculcate popish
principles,

---

* Archbishop Spottiswoode, first began a new leaden roof
upon the cathedral. He wrote a small, treatise *De Regimine Eccles.*
Scotticane, and the well-known History of the Church of Scotland.

† He compleated the leaden roof of the cathedral.

principles, tending to destroy the supremacy of the king, as head of the church, and to establish that of the pope, and accordingly sentenced to suffer the penalties prescribed to a capital crime. His execution took place in the streets of Glasgow, the same day he received his doom.

On the death of archbishop Law, which happened 12th November, 1632, Patrick Lindsay, bishop of Ross, was this year,

1633,

Preferred to the see. He was descended of the family of Edzel, a branch of the family of Crawford, and was first ordained minister of St. Vigean's, in Angus. In the year 1613, he obtained the bishopric of Ross, which he held till he succeeded to that of Glasgow. His character is by some of our historians represented as amiable and praise-worthy in the highest degree, moderate in the exercise of power, lenient to those who differed in opinion from him, and charitable to all.

During the time of archbishop Lindsay, a general assembly was held at Glasgow of the clergy and nobles of the realm, convened for the purpose of determining the future form of church government.

Before saying any thing concerning its proceedings, it may not be improper to state, that from the period of the Reformation, to the year 1610, presbytery was established, and even although church dignitaries were named by the crown, during that period, yet their power was very limited, notwithstanding they had a seat in parliament. At the period last mentioned, an assembly was held at Glasgow,

E 2 which,

which, it is said, principally, through the influence of archbishop Spottiswoode, abolished presbytery, and established the government of the church, by episcopacy. This was by no means agreeable to the bulk of the people; various means, of a gentle nature, were fallen upon to conciliate them; these had no effect, and others were determined upon of a contrary nature.

1637.

Accordingly, a liturgy or service-book of the church of England, arranged under the direction of Laud, archbishop of Canterbury, was ordered this year to be read as the common form of worship. The attempt was first made in St. Giles's church in Edinburgh, in presence of the archbishops of St. Andrew's and Glasgow; but a riot ensuing, the service was interrupted. It was afterwards repeatedly tried, but with as ill success; and the more the crown seemed bent upon its introduction, the more were the people inflamed against it. To such a pitch indeed did the popular zeal arise, that combinations were formed, entituled the *Tables*, whose sole aim was declared to be the abolition of the liturgy. Representatives from these different bodies throughout the kingdom, having met at Edinburgh, they, for their greater security, entered into a bond, entituled the *Covenant*, which all persons well-affected to the presbyterian form of worship were invited to subscribe.

Such a combination could not fail to alarm the legislature—concessions were offered, but they were rejected, and though afterwards a proclamation was issued, abolishing the use of the service-book, the

cove-

covenanters were not satisfied; being persuaded that
the mask was only put on till a more convenient season. Some of the ministers of Glasgow, however, do
not appear to have fallen in with the general opinion.
They wrote a letter of thanks, expressed in a strain of
the most servile adulation, to the king's commissioner,
" for the proclamation, which was received," they
said, " with acclamations universally joyful, that they
" praised God for inspiring their dread sovereign
" with such wisdom, piety, clemency, and fatherly
" care of the church and commonwealth, as is abun-
" dantly manifested in the said proclamation; so
" they would gladly testify, by every means in their
" power, their thankfulness to his majesty, *their
" crown of rejoicing, and the breath of their nostrils* ."

The king afterwards granted warrant for a general assembly, to meet at Glasgow, which we have
just now noticed.

This assembly which met on Wednesday, 21st
November, 1638, consisted of a vast concourse of
people, almost all the nobility and gentry of any
family or interest being present, either as elders or
assessors. As the presbyterians had taken particular care that few should be admitted but those
of their own party, every thing they wished they
carried almost *unanimously.* All the acts of assembly, passed since the accession of James to the throne
of England, were declared null and void, although
many of them had been confirmed by parliament.
Afterwards,

<hr>

* Arnot's History, b. i. chap. iii.

Afterwards, the whole bishops were deposed and excommunicated, episcopacy and the liturgy abolished, and every one ordered to subscribe the covenant, under pain of excommunication. They proceeded to such lengths as made it evident, that the abolition of the service-book was not the only object they had in view; they wished to establish the independency of the ecclesiastical upon the civil power, and *conscious* that this proposition would never be admitted by the king, they found it necessary to support their tenets by military force. Accordingly, after the parliament met in the beginning of the year 1639, which, like the assembly, was almost wholly composed of covenanters, war was resolved upon, and their operations immediately began against the adherents of Charles.

In consequence of the proceedings of this assembly, and the universal dislike which the people had conceived against the archiepiscopal function, archbishop Lindsay withdrew into England, and fixed his residence, by the king's order, at Newcastle: there he remained, with several others of his brethren, till his death in 1641.

During the space which elapsed from the sitting of the memorable assembly in 1638, to the year 1661, the presbyterian form of church government was established in Scotland. At the last mentioned period, and about the time of his restoration, Charles II. contrary to his most solemn engagements, determined its overthrow; and, heedless of the ruin which his unfortunate father had plunged himself into, by prosecuting similar measures, he set every engine at work, in order to bring about the end he so much desired. In a short time, having gained over a complaisant parliament, it rescinded, at one stroke, the whole acts passed since A. D. 1633, in favour of presbytery, and in its stead, episcopacy was re-established.

In the space of time just now alluded to, the see of Glasgow was vacant*. At its termination, and in the year

1661

Andrew Fairfowl, a native of Anstruther, in Fifeshire, and at the time of his appointment, minister of Dunse, was appointed to the see by Charles II. He was consecrated the following year, but did not long thereafter enjoy his situation, having been seized with sickness, the very day of riding the parliament, in 1663. He died a few days thereafter, and was interred on the 11th day of the same month, in the abbey-church of Holyroodhouse.

1664.

The next prelate in succession, was Alexander Burnet, son of a clergyman at Lauder, in Berwickshire: his first situation in the church, was that of a rector, in the county of Kent, which he was under the necessity of abdicating, from his loyalty in 1650. He then retired to the continent, and was employed by Charles II. in procuring intelligence for

---

* The pastoral charge at this time, of the city and barony, was under the care of three ministers, who officiated severally in the high church, the tron church, and the black friars or college church. In 1691, a fourth minister was added, who was fixed in the wynd church.

for him, from England, and other places. Upon the restoration, he became chaplain to general Rutherford, governor of Dunkirk, and in a few years thereafter, his sovereign promoted him to the bishopric of Aberdeen, upon the death of bishop Mitchel, in 1663. This charge he did not retain long, having been the following year translated to the archbishopric of Glasgow.

Bishop Burnet continued in office, till December 1669, at which time, a dispute having arisen between him and the duke of Lauderdale, the prime minister, he was turned out of office. Matters were, however, adjusted in the course of a few years, and he was restored to his see†, which he possessed till he was translated to the primacy of St. Andrew's, where he died on the 24th of August, 1684. His character is variously estimated, according to the opinion of men with respect to the great questions which then agitated the people; some applaud him as a person of abilities, and good intentions; others possess quite different sentiments, regarding him as narrow-minded and illiberal, and the chief cause of much bloodshed and oppression.

1671.

At the period of archbishop Burnet's dismission, Robert Leighton, son of Alexander Leighton, descended of a family in Angus, was preferred to the see. He first was ordained as a minister of the church at Newbottle, in Mid Lothian: thereafter he was promoted to the see of Dumblane, where he continued

† 7th September, 1674.

continued eight years, till the time of his being appointed first commendator, and then archbishop of Glasgow, in the year 1669. He resigned this situation in five years afterwards, when he retired into Sussex, where he died in 1685.

1679.

Upon the translation of archbishop Burnet, Arthur Ross, bishop of Argyle, was nominated to the vacant archbishopric. He was a native of Aberdeenshire, and descended of the family of Kilravock, in the county of Ross. In 1665, he was made parson of Glasgow*, and thereafter, upon the death of the person who held possession of the see of Argyle, he was preferred to that situation, from whence he was translated to Glasgow, as has been just now mentioned. Upon the death of the primate of St. Andrew's, Dr. Burnet, archbishop Ross succeeded to the office, where he continued till the period of the Revolution†.

1684.

At the period of the translation of the last mentioned prelate, Alexander Cairncross, bishop of Brechin, was appointed his successor, through the interest of the Duke of Queensberry. In two years thereafter, Dr. Cairncross and his patron, having shewn themselves averse to the annulling the penal statutes and tests relative to religious matters, he was, in virtue of the king's letter to the privy coun-

F   cil,

---

* The parson of Glasgow, had under his charge the barony parish. The church where he officiated was the cathedral.

† He died, 13th June, 1704.

cil, deprived of his office. He however, thereafter, obtained the bishopric of Raphoe, in Ireland, where he continued till the year 1701, the period of his death.

1687.

The last of this numerous race of prelates that filled the episcopal chair in Glasgow, was John Paterson, bishop of Edinburgh, a son of John Paterson, bishop of Ross. The first situation he held in the church, was that of dean of Edinburgh, from whence he was removed to the see of Galloway, and in 1679, to the bishopric of Edinburgh, where he continued till the deprivation of Dr. Cairncross, that he was translated to the archbishopric of Glasgow. This office he did not long enjoy, the Revolution having taken place the year after his appointment, which deprived him and the rest of his brethren, of their official situations, by the re-establishment of presbytery. Upon that event, he retired to a private situation, and died aged 76, in the city of Edinburgh, and in the year 1708.

CHAP.

CHAP. III.

The Civil History of Glasgow—Foundation of the Cathedral—Erection of the Town into a Royal Burgh by William the Lyon—Engagement at Glasgow—The Old Bridge founded by Bishop Rae—Erection of the University by Pope Nicholas V.—Battles of Glasgow, Langside, &c.

IN this department we propose to follow the same plan which has been adopted in treating of the succession of the bishops and ecclesiastical history of the city, narrating the facts as concisely as possible, and in the order of time in which they severally happened.

To fix the period of the origin of the city, as has been already mentioned, is what cannot now be done. The first notice of it is in

560,

When St. Mungo or Kentigern, was appointed superintendent or bishop. From this time, and for the space of betwixt five and six hundred years, no-

F 2   thing

thing farther is to be found in our historians, relative to its history.

1136*.

The cathedral‡ was rebuilt this year, and consecrated by John Achaius, who then held possession of the see, in presence of the king (David I.)

1174.

A charter erecting Glasgow into a royal burgh, was this year procured by Joceline, bishop of Glasgow, in favour of him and his successors in office, with a weekly market upon Thursday, " fully and freely, with all freedoms, liberties and customs, which any burghs throughout the kingdom enjoy§."

1176.

---

* Chronicon Sancte crucis Edinburgen.

‡ Before this period, it would appear a more ancient fabric, dedicated to the purposes of religion, existed here as the mother church of the diocese. It was most likely, however, a mean building, constructed of timber, stone edifices being then but very rare.

§ A copy of this charter, extracted from the Chartulary, vol. i. pag. 79, is here subjoined.

Willelmus Dei Gratia Rex Scotorum, episcopis, abbatibus, comitibus, baronibus, justitiariis vice comitibus ministris, et omnibus probis hominibus totius terræ suæ, clericis et laicis modernis et posteris, salutem. Sciant præsentes et posteri me concessisse, et, hac carta mea, confirmasse, Deo et Sancto Kentigerno, et Jocelino epo. Glasg. et singulis ejus successoribus in perpetuum, ut burgum habeant apud Glasgu, cum foro diei Jovis, bene et honorifice, quiete et plenarie, cum omnibus libertatibus et consuetudinibus quas aliquis burgorum meorum, in tota ter-

ra

1176.

Another charter was this year granted of free access to the markets of Glasgow, " in coming there,
standing there, and returning thence *;" and in

1190,

William the Lyon, by a third charter†, granted
in favour of Joceline, bishop of Glasgow, and his
successors, a fair to be kept at Glasgow, and to be
held every year, " for ever, from the eighth of the
apostles, Peter and Paul, for the space of eight days
complete."

1268.

From an old deed ‡ still extant, the town appears
to have been governed by a provost and bailies, and
to have been in all respects an organized incorporation, having persons in official situations, for the investing and transferring of property, with courts of
justice

---

ra mea, melius, plenius, quietius, et honorificentius habet. Quare volo, et firmiter præcipio, ut omnes burgenses, qui in supra
dicto burgo manentes erunt, meam firmam pacem juste habeant,
per totam terram meam, in eundo et redeundo; et prohibeo
firmiter ne quis eos, aut eorum catalla, injuste disturbet, aut
vexet, aut aliquis eis injuriam aut contumeliam inferat, super
meam plenariam forisfacturam.   Testibus D. D. fratre meo;
Walto Bed. cancel. mo; Comes Dunce. Com. Gilleb. Com.
Gillcest de Meneth, Ric. de Mervill. Constab. Rob. de Quinci.
Ric. Cum. Walto de Berkel, Comes, W. de Veteriponto. Phil-
lip. de Walt. Rob. de Berkel, Ad. de Stanford. Apud Tra-
quer.

* Cart. vol. i. p. 73.   † Cart. vol. i. pag. 80.   ‡ Cart.
vol. i. p. 244.

justice for determining disputes amongst the inhabi-
tants§.

1300.

Glasgow was this year the scene of one of these
bloody contests that in these days often happened
betwixt the rival kingdoms of Britain.

Edward III. of England, in supporting Baliol's pretensions

§ Although the city of Glasgow is of the antiquity mentioned in the text, yet it is a fact, and which is evident from
the copy of the charter subjoined, that in these early ages,
it had not in a civil view, arrived at any great degree of
eminence, for in the ancient charters granted to the burgh of
Rutherglen, it appears to have been placed within the jurisdiction of that town, and by being in such a situation, the community of that place, levied a fee or custom within the city,
for all articles that were brought there for sale. As Glasgow,
however, began to rise in importance, this was found to be a
grievance, application was made to the throne, about the year
1226, and the following act was in consequence procured.

CARTA ALEXANDRI, R. II.
De Tolneo non capiendo in Burgo de Glasgu.

Alexander Dei Gratia Rex Scottorum, omnibus probis hominibus totius terræ suæ Clericis et Laicis salutem. Sciant
præsentes et futuri, nos concessissi, et hac carta, confirmasse
Domino et Ecclæ. St. Kentigerni de Glasgu, et Waltero Epo.
ejusdem loci, et successoribus suis Epis. Ne præpositi, vel
Balivi, vel servientes nostri de Rutherglen, Tolneum aut consuetudinem capiant in villa de Glasgu. Sed illa capiant ad
crucem de Schedeniston†, sicut illa antiquitus capi solebant.
Quare prohibemus firmiter ne præpositi, vel Balivi, vel servientes nostri de Rutherglen, tolneum aut consuetudinem capiant

† Where this place was cannot now be ascertained.—Ure's History.

tensions to the throne, and of his own to the superiority of Scotland, invaded the kingdom with a
powerful army, by which means he got possession
of the chief towns, castles, and fortresses. The
spirit of the people was nevertheless unbroken, a
chosen few, headed by the noted William Wallace,
stood forth in behalf of their country, and by continually harassing the enemy, rendered their possession of Scotland at once hazardous and disagreeable.

In a battle fought near the town of Biggar between these parties, the forces of the English being
defeated, a truce was agreed to for one year, and
signed in the church of Rutherglen.—This with
the English, was rather a matter of necessity than
choice, as they found their forces utterly broken and
disconcerted. Indeed, so regardless was Edward
of the treaty, that in the following month of April,
long before the truce had expired, he, by a most un-
justifiable act, endeavoured to effectuate that purpose, which it was found so difficult to accomplish
by the valour of his arms.

With

---

piant in villa de Glasgu. Testi. Thoma de Strivelin. Cancel-
lario. Henr. de Raitt, Camerario. Rog. de Quince. John de
Maccuswelli. Davide Marscalli. Waltero Bisset. Apud Jedd.
29 die Octobris. Anno Regni Nostri 12.

By this act, the inhabitants of Rutherglen were prohibited
from collecting the tax within the city, but allowed still to do
so at the cross of Shedeniston. This right of enaction, was
most likely, thereafter, by some other deed, done away: at a-
ny rate, it fell at no great distance of time thereafter, into
dissuetude.

With this view it was resolved to call a court of
Justice, apparently for the reformation of abuses,
consisting of the barons who opposed his interest
in Scotland, in two separate places, viz. Ayr and
Glasgow, so that when thus convened he might the
more easily accomplish their destruction.   Accordingly the English force was divided, one party was
ordered for Ayr, while the other, under Percy of
Northumberland, directed their course towards Glasgow.

On the day appointed for holding the court at
Ayr, a great number fell a sacrifice to stratagem.
Wallace, who was lurking in the neighbourhood,
repaid them for their treacherous cruelty; but in
such a manner as could only be justified by the nature of the attack.—He next bent his march with
three hundred cavalry towards Glasgow. Having
arrived at nine o'clock in the morning, he drew up
his men at the north end of the Old Bridge, and after reconnoitering the situation and numbers of the
English, he prepared for the meditated assault, by
dividing his force into two columns, the one, under
the command of Boswell, laird of Auchinleck; and
Adam Wallace his uncle, he directed to form a *corps
de reserve*, while he, with the main body, attacked
the enemy in front.—When so engaged, Auchinleck's party were ordered to march by St. Mungo's
lane, or Burnt Barns, towards the south-east quarter of the Drygate-street, near to which the English
to the amount of one thousand men were placed, and
thus fall upon the enemy in flank.

The action having commenced, with great bravery upon both sides, the English from the superiori-

ty

ty of their numbers, seemed for some time to have the best prospect of success.—However, the column under Auchinleck, to the amount of one hundred and forty, having arrived, by marching up the Dry-gate, they unexpectedly attacked the enemy in the flank, and thus turned the scale of victory in favour of the Scots; who, upon the flight of the English, pursued them to the castle of Bothwell, nine miles east of the city, where they obtained shelter; thereafter Wallace and his army returned to Glasgow, having killed in this engagement, Percy the English general, and seven hundred of his men; if we can credit the accounts handed down to us by the Scotch historians.

1345.

The bridge over the Clyde, which had formerly been constructed of timber, was this year begun to be built with stone, by William Rae, bishop of Glasgow.

1350.

The city at this time * was visited by the plague; and again in

1380,

And the succeeding year,

1381,

What numbers perished by this dreadful disease, cannot now be ascertained.

1450.

Upon the application of bishop Turnbull, a bull ‡

G   was

* Cart. of the University, vol. ii. pag. 591.
‡ Cart. vol. i. pag. 587.

was this year obtained from the pope, establishing
the university upon a similar plan with the university of Bononia, in Italy: of this excellent institution, the bishop was declared chancellor. Immediately thereafter, the same prelate procured from
James II. a charter in favour of himself, and his
successors in office, erecting the city and barony of
Glasgow, and the lands called Bishop's Forest, into
a regality, with full power to them, to constitute
and appoint provost, bailies, sergeants, and other officers for the management and government of the
city, as often as it should seem good to them; and
of putting in, and removing from these offices, whatever persons they should think proper.

1524.

About this period, a council consisting of a great
part of the nobility of the kingdom was held at Glasgow, whither they were called to convene by the
earl of Angus.—That nobleman, the head of the potent family of Douglas, in order to strengthen his
overgrown power, had married the queen dowager
of James IV. after she had been appointed regent
during the infancy of her son.

The duke of Albany then in France, and pre-
sumptive heir to the crown of Scotland, hearing of
this circumstance, and jealous of his right, determined if possible to curb the power of Angus.—Accordingly, being assisted by the king of France, in a short
time he landed in Scotland with a considerable force.
Angus called a meeting of his friends at Glasgow
—but so intimidated were they, with the account of
the strong force ready to act against them, that they

declined

declined their assistance, and he, in disgust, retired
from the country.

1542.

From the erection of the university, downwards
for near a century, there is little worthy of notice,
respecting the civil history of the town, if we except
the circumstance just now mentioned. About this
period, we find its castle besieged, and its immediate
environs, the scene of an engagement betwixt two
of the most powerful factions that then prevailed in
the country.

It will not be improper, before mentioning these
more particularly, to take a short view of the causes
from which they originated.

Upon the dismissal of cardinal Beaton from the
regency of the kingdom, after the death of James
V. and during the infancy of his daughter, the unfortunate Mary Stewart, the earl of Arran, her near
kinsman, was appointed regent. This situation, he
held not by the unanimous voice of the people. A
faction prevailed in the country against him, insti-
gated partly by family feuds, and partly from the
fear of his grasping, in case of the death of the
young queen, the sovereign power, to which it was
thought his abilities or merit did not entitle him.
This party, at the head of whom were the queen
dowager, and cardinal Beaton, with the view of opposing the will of the regent, and establishing their
own power, craved the aid of France. In that country then resided, Matthew Stewart, earl of Lennox,
head of the powerful family of that name: him they
invited over, under the most specious pretences, as
a balance to the power of the regent, to whom, it

G 2 was

was well known, he stood but ill affected, since the death of his father, who was killed by the Hamiltons at Linlithgow. Allured by these promises, Lennox arrived from France. In the mean time, the regent dreading the power and influence of this chief, entered into an accommodation with the queen dowager and Beaton. By this transaction, his power was rendered merely titular; while the artful priest, in reality, managed the reins of government.

The situation of matters was thereby changed; the cardinal looked now upon Lennox in another light, and all the promises which he formerly made him, were now refused to be fulfilled.

Fired with rage and indignation at this treatment, Lennox vowed revenge, and immediately proceeded to that part of the country where his power and influence chiefly lay. At Dumbarton, where he then was, a supply of thirty thousand crowns arrived from France, to aid the queen dowager's party. This money he was directed to distribute by the advice of the cardinal and queen dowager; the king of France, at that time, being ignorant of the change which had taken place in the management of affairs. He fulfilled part of the request, but divided the remainder amongst his adherents and friends. This latter part of his conduct was by no means agreeable to Beaton, who immediately persuaded the regent to levy an army, and march to Glasgow, where he hoped to surprise Lennox, and great part of the money.

Lennox was apprised of their design; and in his own defence he quickly raised an army of ten thousand men. This force he marched from Glasgow to Leith, where he offered battle to the cardinal.

That

That prelate, however, declined the combat from day to day, while he endeavoured by promises and entreaties, to gain over the followers of Lennox. Many accordingly deserted, and Lennox perceiving that more were likely soon to follow their example, and being unprovided for a siege, or continuing the war, he was obliged to capitulate. For several days thereafter, he transacted matters with the regent, in Edinburgh, and in an amicable manner, as if no dispute had ever taken place.

The reconciliation upon the part of the regent and cardinal was only apparent. This, Lennox, on his return to the west, discovered at Linlithgow, from which he hastened in the dead of night to Glasgow, in a short time fortified and garrisoned the bishop's castle, and thereafter proceeded to Dumbarton.

The information he had received by the way, shortly turned out to be true. The regent having summoned a numerous army to meet at Stirling, with ten days provisions, ordered them when so convened, to march to Glasgow. Upon their arrival, they immediately laid siege to the castle, which they stormed with *brass guns*†. This siege continued for ten days, at the termination of which time, a truce was granted for a day: the guards being, in the mean time, gained over, the castle was surrendered upon condition of quarter, and indemnity given to the garrison soldiers, which compact was, however, most treacherously broken, all of them being put to death, excepting one or two.

From

---

† Buchanan, lib. xv.

From the want of proper assistance, Lennox could not much longer contend with his adversaries; he resolved, however, to strike one stroke, and communicating his intentions to the earl of Glencairn, they agreed to levy a force, consisting of their tenants and adherents, whose rendezvous was appointed to be the city of Glasgow, from which they were to make an eruption into Clydesdale, where the property of the Hamilton's principally lay. This coming to the ears of the regent, he resolved to oppose their design, by seizing upon Glasgow, and thereby prevent the assembling of the army. Glencairn was, however, at the city before him, awaiting the arrival of Lennox, and hearing of the regent's approach, he drew out his men into the adjoining fields, and set them in array. His force amounted to about eight hundred, composed of his own vassals and the citizens of Glasgow,

With this small party he courageously attacked the army of the regent, and fought so valiantly, that he beat the first rank of the enemy back upon the second, and took the brass ordnance they had brought alongst with them. While the battle was thus raging, and the victory uncertain, Robert Boyd, a brave and valiant man, came in with a small party of horse, and thrust himself into the midst of the battle. His arrival immediately determined the fortune of the day, many believing a great force had arrived to the assistance of the regent. In consequence of this circumstance, he gained the victory.

In this engagement, which happened at a place called the Butts, where the barracks are now built, there were about three hundred slain upon both
sides,

sides, but the loss fell most heavily upon the forces of Glencairn. At the termination of the battle, the army of the regent entered the city, which they plundered, even to the carrying away the doors of the houses, shutters, and the iron bars of the windows, besides inflicting upon it every kind of calamity *, except that of burning the town†.

1559‡.

This year, as has been formerly mentioned, the see of Glasgow was abdicated by archbishop Beaton's departure into France. The citizens taking advantage of the circumstance, immediately began
to

* Buchanan.

† After this engagement, Lennox retired into England, where he obtained in marriage Lady Margaret Douglas, niece to Henry VIII. From this union sprung Henry Darnley, husband to Mary queen of Scots.

‡ Amongst the records of the town in the following years, are two or three paragraphs, which shall here be quoted, as they afford a contrast with the prices of provisions in the present day.

1560, 30 Sept. " Statute by magistrates and counsil, yat yair be nayne darrer ale sauld nor iiii pennys ye pynt, under ye pane of aught shilling.

" And ordainit be ye provost, baillies, and hail counsil, yat ye four penny laif wee thretty twa ounces; and ye twa penny laif saxteen ounces; and yat ye samyn be gud and sufficient stuffe.

" And ordainit yat ye stane of tallowne be na darrer sauld nor aught shilling.

" And ordainit yat ye punde of candel be na darrer sauld nor sax pennys ye punde.

" And ordainit yat ye peck of horse corn be na darrer sanld for yis present zeir nor aught pennys ye peck."

to elect their own magistrates; a privilege which belonged solely to the person who held possession of the diocese, or to those whom he should appoint. The duke of Chatleherault, was the person who had engaged to defend the privileges of the archbishop in his absence; this, however, he neglected, and thus a precedent was established, which afforded a bone of contention many times thereafter, betwixt the archbishop and the inhabitants.

1563.

Upon the insurrection which took place upon the marriage of Henry Darnley, and Mary queen of Scots, headed by Hamilton, Argyle, and some other chiefs, whose main force lay at Paisley, the king entered Glasgow with an army of four thousand men. At his approach, the insurgents dispersed, and peace was for a time again restored to this quarter.

The city was this year threatened by a famine, a great dearth having taken place, in consequence of which, every article of provision sold for more than three times their accustomed price‡.

1568.

A few years thereafter, we find the citizens of Glasgow, arranged under the banners of the regent Murray, at the field of Langside, against the adherents of Mary. That unhappy princess, whose misfortunes

---

‡ The bow of quheit gave sax punds, ye bow of beir 6 merks and ane half, ye bow of meill 4 merks, ye bow of aits 50 shillings; an ox to draw in the pleuche 20 merks, and a wodder 30 shillings.

fortunes were only equalled by the fortitude with
which she endured them, having escaped from her
confinement in the castle of Loch-leven, came to
Hamilton. In that place, she was quickly joined
by a great number of her friends†, zealous to support the cause of their sovereign, as well as to humble, if possible, the overgrown power of Murray.

The regent at this time was at Glasgow, holding
a court of justice—no sooner did he hear of the situation of the queen, than he used every effort to
draw his forces around him; while, in the mean
time, he amused her by pretending to hearken to
some overtures that had been made him for an accommodation. These, however, he broke off as soon
as he found himself in a situation to take the field.

Accordingly, upon hearing that Mary was determined in a few days to leave Hamilton and pass to
Dumbarton, where it had been agreed to place her
for security, he resolved to intercept her flight and
give her battle. With this view, he drew up his
army to the amount of four thousand men, many
of whom were citizens of Glasgow, upon the burgh
muir, to the east of the town, a road which the
queen's army must have necessarily passed, had they
gone by the north side of the Clyde.

The queen, however, took a different route, by
passing westward on the south of the river. This,
the regent observing, he ordered his cavalry to ford
the Clyde, and his foot to pass the bridge of Glasgow,
in order to take possession of the hill of Langside,

H   before

† To the amount of six thousand.

before the queen's army could arrive.—This situation he had the good luck to seize, and posted his troops in a small village, and among some gardens and inclosures adjacent.—There he waited the approach of the queen's army, whose superiority in cavalry could be of no benefit to them on such broken ground. The Hamiltons who composed the vanguard of the queen's forces, ran so eagerly to the attack, that they put themselves out of breath, and left the main battle far behind. The encounter of the spearmen was fierce and desperate, but as the forces of the Hamiltons were exposed on the one flank to a continued fire from a body of musqueteers, attacked on the other by the regent's best troops, and not supported by the queen's army, they were soon obliged to give ground, and the rout immediately became universal. Three hundred fell on the field, and betwixt that and four hundred were taken prisoners by the regent, who marched back to Glasgow, where he returned public thanks to God for this great, and on his side almost bloodless victory; and, in testimony of the regard which he had for the services of the incorporation of Bakers there, he bestowed upon them the lands of Partick, where their mills are now built.

During this engagement, Mary stood on a hill * at no great distance, and beheld all that passed in the field with such emotions of mind as are not easily described.—When she saw that fortune had declared

---

* The situation where the queen stood is now distinguished by a thorn tree.

clared against her, she immediately took flight upon horseback into Galloway with a few friends, and without ever closing her eyes, till she arrived at the abbey of Drundenan, sixty Scots miles from the place of battle†.

1570.

The castle of Glasgow, this year, was again be-sieged by the Hamiltons, and the others of that party, in the queen's interest, enemies to the earl of Lennox, who had returned from England after the murder of the earl of Murray, and in whose place he was appointed regent. They knew that it was garrisoned but by a few soldiers, that the governor was absent, and that it was unprovided with neces-saries, they therefore thought to surprise it by their sudden approach; for they came into the town in such haste, (says Buchanan,) that they shut out a good part of the garrison soldiers from entering; but being disappointed of their hopes, they began to batter and storm it with the utmost violence. They were, however, so warmly received by the besieged for several days, though only twenty-four in num-ber, that they were obliged to retire with some con-siderable loss. About two days after, Sir William Drury arrived in Glasgow with an English army, from whence he proceeded to Hamilton, the castle of which place he besieged, and having taken it, demolished it in return for the oppressions of its proprietors.

H 2

From

† Keith, 481.

1579.

From the period of the Reformation, in the year
1560, a great humber of stately edifices, dedicated
to the purposes of religion, had been defaced, and
many levelled to the ground, through the enthusias-
tic zeal of the Reformers. The cathedral of Glasgow was often threatened, but by the intercession
of many of the citizens, these threatenings were
not put into execution.   At length, the magistrates after being long solicited by the principal
of the university*, and the ministers of the city
gave them liberty to demolish this venerable pile,
which was considered as a monument of idola-
try, and whose materials, it was said, might be applied to better purposes, in erecting some churches
upon a smaller scale. A great number of workmen
were accordingly engaged, and the time appointed
for beginning the demolition. The day being arrived, and the workmen assembled by beat of drum,
the design was defeated by the incorporations of the
city, who ran to arms, threatening that the person
who pulled down the first stone, should immediately be buried under it; the design was therefore
given up.

In consequence of being thus stopped, the ministers presented a complaint to government, and the
leaders of the insurrection were summoned before
the council. Upon enquiring into the matter, they
were dismissed with an approbation of their conduct; the king saying, " that too many churches
had

* Mr. Andrew Melvile.

had been already destroyed, and that he would not tolerate any more abuses of that kind."

1604.

Some years before this period, many disputes had taken place in the city, betwixt the merchants and the members of the different incorporations or trades, relative to the management of public affairs, and as to the precedence which one class claimed of the other. To settle these matters, both parties, by their submissions, dated the 8th and 10th days of November this year, referred the determination of the disputed points to Sir George Elphinstone of Blythswood, provost, and the ministers of the city, and they accordingly, " after great pains, *long travelling*, and mature deliberation," pronounced their decreet*, Feb. 6th,

1605.

Contained in fifty-four articles, which is the Letter of Guildry. By this decreet, the offices of Dean of Guild and Deacon Convener were established; the one the head of the Merchants, and the other the Trades' House, and a number of other regulations

---

* The merchant rank ordained one or two of their number to *travel* to Edinburgh, for the purpose of bringing home a copy of the Letter of Guildry of that city.

It would appear that at this time neither the Deacons or other members of the Incorporations could write, and only a few of the Merchants; the submissions, at their request, being signed by a notary.

gulations made respecting the election of the town council, and other matters.

1612.

This Letter of Guildry was confirmed at Edinburgh by the king and estates of parliament; and in

1633,

Upon the 16th of October, the city of Glasgow was declared by parliament to be a Royal Free Burgh.

1645.

In an engagement which took place this year at Kilsyth, within a few miles of the city, betwixt the royalists and covenanters, the army of the latter, to the amount of seven thousand, was almost completely cut off † by the king's forces, under the command of the marquis of Montrose. This gallant general, after the battle, marched into the city, where he levied a contribution upon the inhabitants for the disaffection they entertained for the royal cause. Here, however, he remained only one night, owing to the plague, which at that time raged with fury in Glasgow, as well as in most towns in Scotland.

1648.

Shortly after that period, when Charles I. was delivered up to the English government, the Scotch, partly from remorse, and partly from the improper manner in which he was used, and the duty which they

---

† Six thousand it is said perished by the sword, the remainder, to the amount nearly of one thousand, were drowned in the Dollator-bog adjacent.

they owed him as their sovereign, agreed to arm themselves in his favour, and prepared for an invasion of England.

In these preparations they were disturbed by discontents and animosities amongst themselves. Forces were ordered to be levied, and each district being required to furnish a particular quota, the clergy, whose aversion to Charles was extreme, took an active part in opposing the levy. Excited by their discourses, several of the burghs and shires were extremely backward, and even refractory, in providing their contingent of troops. The town of Glasgow being amongst the number of these contumacious burghs, the magistrates and council were summoned to attend parliament to answer for their conduct, and although the fault was common to them with the greater part of the kingdom, they were imprisoned and detained for several days. Having professed scruples of conscience with regard to promoting the levy, they were also deprived of their offices by an act of parliament, dated 11th June, 1648, and a commission was sent to the old council, authorising them to elect new magistrates, which they did accordingly †.

The magistrates thus elected, did not, however, long

† But this was not all the misery (says Principal Baillie in his letters) that came upon the city: for, "before this change, some regiments of horse and foot were sent to our town, with orders to quarter on no others but the magistrates, council, session and their lovers. These orders were executed with rigour.

long enjoy the situation, for by an act of the committee of the estates, the old magistrates were replaced, as having been unjustly ejected.

1649.

To the miseries of civil war, were added this year the plague, and a grievous famine‡, and in three years thereafter, a fourth calamity of another kind befel the city, viz. in

1652.

Upon the 17th day of July, a dreadful fire took place, which threatened Glasgow with universal ruin.

It broke out in a narrow alley upon the east side of the High-street, and within a short space, burnt up six allies of houses, with several very considerable buildings. While the inhabitants of the neighbourhood were assembled for the removal of the goods, and hindering as much as in their power the spreading of the flame, the wind blowing from the north-east, carried such sparks of the fire in the opposite direction, as kindled some houses on the west side of the Saltmarket, insomuch, that both sides of that

gour. On the most religious people of our town, huge burdens did fall, on some ten, on some twenty, on others thirty soldiers did quarter, who, besides meat and drink, wine, and good cheer, and whatever they called for, did exact, cruelly, their daily pay, and much more. In ten days they cost a few honest, but mean people, L.40,000 Scots, besides plundering of those whom necessity forced to flee from their houses. Our loss and danger was not so great by James Graham," marquis of Montrose.

‡ Meal sold during this time at 1s. 9d. per peck.

that street were totally consumed, and in it the best and most considerable buildings of the town.

From the Saltmarket, the fire was carried by contiguous buildings to the Trongate, Gallowgate, and Bridgegate streets, where a great many houses, with the furniture of the inhabitants, fell a sacrifice to its fury. This calamity continued near eighteen hours, before the great violence of the fire began to abate. In this space of time, many were reduced to poverty, and the dwellings of near one thousand families utterly consumed.

The greatest part of these unfortunate sufferers were obliged to betake themselves to the shelter of huts erected in the fields, till more comfortable accommodation could be got ready. By Saturday in the evening, numbers had returned to the city, and it was hoped that the calamity was completely over. However, unluckily, this was not the case, for betwixt the hours of seven and eight on Sunday morning, the fire broke out afresh on the north side of the Trongate, and continued burning violently till near twelve at noon. This new stroke upon the back of the other, not only destroyed a great number of dwelling houses, and occasioned the pulling down of many more, but it so terrified the whole of the inhabitants, that they carried from their houses what moveables they had, and betook themselves for several nights to the open fields, where they continued till the fire was completely extinguished.

This event, whereby one third part of the city was destroyed, is attested in a letter from Colonels Overton and Blackmore to Oliver Cromwell, wherein they reckon the damage at no less than

I
one

one hundred thousand pounds sterling. Cromwell, upon the receipt of this letter, and of a representation
by the magistrates, with whom he had formerly been
acquainted, (by residing for some time in the city
two years before) generously set on foot a *subscription* for their relief. To this cause, however afflicting at the time, is the city of Glasgow partly indebted for that regularity and elegance, which has
hitherto been its distinguished characteristic.

1656†.

In that gloomy period, during the reign of
Charles II. whose ministers exerted every nerve,
without regard to justice or humanity, to establish
the episcopal form of church government, though
contrary to the inclinations of a great part of the
nation—sacrifices of the lives and properties of those
who opposed the scheme, were every where common.

In particular, the citizens of Glasgow were mostly covenanters, and many of these, through the influence of archbishop Burnet, as it is said, were
persecuted with unremitting fury.

1666.

Numbers were hanged in the streets, while others,
under the threatening of the like punishment, were
forbid attending the presbyterian preachers.

1674.

At one time the community of the city was fined

in

---

† This year the citizens were alarmed by the shock of an
earthquake, which luckily did no other damage than the panic
it occasioned.

in L. 100 sterling, for allowing a presbyterian minister to preach within its limits.

And at another time, guards were set at the city gates to prevent the inhabitants on Sunday, from attending field preachings in the country.

1677.

Glasgow was a second time almost destroyed by a dreadful fire, a thousand families being thereby left without a habitation, and one hundred and thirty shops and houses consumed. As it threatened the prison, in which were a great number of people, confined principally for their religious opinions, the citizens broke open the doors and set them at liberty.

These measures, which were used against the covenanters, however severe, were not found to answer the intended purpose, and others, more rigorous if possible, were thought necessary. A bond was made out by order of government, which the inhabitants of Glasgow and the western shires, were ordered to subscribe.—As this deed contained a complete renunciation of presbytery, and an abhorrence of all their former proceedings, it was easy to foresee that few would relish it. To enforce the subscription, an army of highlanders, to the amount of eight thousand, were assembled at Stirling, from whence they issued out against this district. On the 26th of January, 1678, they arrived at Glasgow, where, after exercising for the space of five days, the most wanton acts of cruelty and oppression upon such as would not willingly comply with the bond, they proceeded towards Ayrshire. There, as in Glasgow, they made a prey of whatever came

within

within the reach of their hands, and if they suspected any concealment, compelled by torture the unfortunate objects of their suspicion to discover their
hidden wealth.   Such acts of violence excited a general indignation through the kingdom; the highlanders were recalled, and the west was at once
stripped of her effects, and liberated from her oppres-
sors.

The presbyterians could not but be exasperated
in the greatest degree at this manifold oppression,
and misled by the zeal of their leaders, they proceeded to such lengths in revenging themselves, as
cannot be justified, even though we consider the
acts of cruelty that had been used against them.

1679.

On the anniversary of the Restoration, about
eighty covenanters having assembled at Rutherglen,
they, after extinguishing the bonfires that had been
lighted for solemnization of the birth-day, published
a declaration and testimony expressive of their motives, and burned at the cross the several acts of
parliament, and of the privy-council, that had passed
against them.

Notice of these proceedings having come to Edinburgh, Lord Dundee was dispatched with a party
to quell the insurgents, and at the same time with
orders to give them battle, in case any resistance
should be offered.   He accordingly fell in with the
presbyterians, assembled near Loudon-hill, and having to no purpose desired them to disperse and deliver up the ringleaders, he began an attack.   From
the superiority of the numbers of the covenanters,
Dundee and his party were defeated with a considerable

derable loss; they immediately retreated to Glasgow, where, as they expected to be assaulted by the country people, the streets were barricaded, and other measures taken for their better defence.

These expectations were not ill grounded; the covenanters, flushed with their success, after a night's stay at Hamilton, marched to Glasgow. When near the city, they divided their force into two battalions, the one marching into the town by the Gallowgate-street, and the other by the College Vennal. Immediately thereafter, an engagement took place, which was supported for a considerable time, with great bravery on both sides. At last the covenanters were obliged to retreat, from the superior skill of the soldiery, as well as from the fire kept up against them from the windows and closes adjacent to the street. They accordingly † left the city in good order, after having eight men killed in the engagement, and several wounded. To this in a few days succeeded the battle of Bothwell Bridge, of which the following lines present a slight sketch.

Lord Dundee immediately after this skirmish left the city, and retired to Edinburgh, with the

idea

† So inhuman was Dundee, that he gave orders that the dead bodies of these unfortunate people should not be buried, but left upon the streets to be devoured by the dogs. Some women having attempted to carry them to the grave, were attacked and maltreated by the soldiers, who compelled them to set down the coffins in the alms-house, where they continued till the forces of Dundee left Glasgow, and thereafter were interred.

idea of having completely broken the forces of his adversaries. In this, however, he was mistaken; the covenanters again rallied, and having encamped on Hamilton muir, great numbers joined them, insomuch, that in a few days after their defeat at Glasgow, their numbers amounted to about eight thousand men.

To oppose this force, and if possible to put an end to the rebellion, government displayed great alacrity and judgment. The militia in the well-affected counties were called out, as also the landed gentlemen, whose attendance upon horseback, with as many followers as they could muster, was required. An express was also sent to London for a body of English forces. The passages on the Forth were secured, military stores were seized for the use of government, and great diligence was exerted in supplying and fortifying Edinburgh and Stirling castles. The king by the advice of his English council, named his natural son, James Duke of Buccleugh and Monmouth, commander in chief. In consequence of this appointment, he left London on the 15th of June, and arrived at Edinburgh on the 18th. On the 19th he joined the army, which immediately began to move towards the west, by the way of Livingstone and Bathgate.

Upon the 21st, they came up with the rebels, who were about three times their number, and were drawn up on the opposite banks of the Clyde. The general officers were all of opinion that the army should march directly through the river, which was there fordable, and attack the enemy. But the duke commanded that the army should pass by Bothwell Bridge,

Bridge, which lay about a mile to the right, and
was strongly barricaded and guarded by three thousand of the rebels; and for this purpose, a troop of
dragoons, with eighty musqueteers, and four field
pieces, were dispatched to beat off the party from
the bridge. As the duke approached the rebel army, they beat a parley. They sent one of their
number, accompanied by a minister, to express their
demands, which were, " that they should be allowed the free exercise of their religion, and that a new
parliament and general assembly, unfettered by any
oaths, should be called for settling the affairs of
both church and state." The duke received them
with civility, but told them that he could listen to
no terms till they should lay down their arms, upon which the conference broke up. During the parley, the duke had, unobserved by the rebels, planted
four field pieces opposite to the bridge, which now
began to play. Some hundreds of the rebels were
killed, and the rest being ill supplied with ammuni-
tion, retreated to the main body of the army. In removing the rubbish, passing the bridge, and forming upon the opposite banks, the royal army were
taken up a space of five hours. The artillery were
carried in the centre of the foot guards. At the
first discharge, the enemy's horse fell into confusion instantly, a total rout ensued, seven hundred
were killed in the pursuit, and about twelve
hundred taken prisoners, these were conveyed
to Edinburgh, where they arrived on the 24th
of June. Such of them as would engage to live
peaceably under the government, were dismissed.
Those who were so obstinate as to refuse this

mark

mark of compliance, to the number of about two hundred and fifty, were banished, but unfortunately perished by shipwreck in the voyage, as to the rest an act of indemnity was passed*.

The spirit of the covenanters was, nevertheless, unsubdued; on the contrary, the many cruelties that were exercised against them, in this and the succeeding reign, only served to inflame their zeal, and confirm their attachment to the presbyterian form of church government.—The city of Glasgow, which was mostly composed of presbyterians, beheld these arbitrary acts of power with concern. But the time was near at hand, when their grievances were to be redressed, and an end put

* Immediately after this engagement, it is said, Lord Dundee requested permission to burn Glasgow, and the other towns in the west, on account of their containing a great number who were affected to the cause of the covenanters. This was refused. It is, however said, that to shelter the town from plunder, the community were obliged to quit to the town of Edinburgh, a debt of thirty thousand merks, which they held upon the Canon-mills.

1694.

This year, in consequence of a dispute betwixt a citizen and a soldier, the town clerk of Glasgow, Robert Park, was stabbed in the chamber, by Major James Menzies, in the heat of passion. He immediately fled, was pursued, and in consequence of resistance, shot in Renfield garden. The dispute betwixt the citizen and the soldier was referred to the sitting magistrate. The town clerk embraced the cause of the citizen, while the major supported the soldier: high words ensued; and thus the quarrel terminated.

put to that reign of tyranny and oppression, which had so long prevailed in the country. To that time then, did the lovers of peace look forward, while they hailed the dawn of its approach, upon the flight of the unfortunate James. That event had no sooner taken place, than the city of Glasgow, to testify their regard to the protestant persuasion, levied and armed five hundred men, whom they sent to Edinburgh, commanded by the earl of Argyle and Lord Newbottle, to assist in guarding the convention of estates convened for making a tender of the crown to William and Mary.

That convention, regardful of the general voice of the people of Scotland, which had ever been averse to episcopacy, having constituted themselves into a parliament, abolished that form of church government, and in its stead established presbytery, for which her sons had so firmly contended, during the two preceding reigns. In consequence of this act, John Paterson, who then held possession of the see of Glasgow, resigned his charge, and retired to Edinburgh, where, in ten years afterwards, he died at the age of seventy-six.

Shortly after William and Mary had been raised to the vacant throne, they granted in favour of the community of Glasgow, and in consideration of their loyalty, a new charter of confirmation, whereby they " enact and ordàin, that the city of " Glasgow and town council thereof, shall have " power and privilege to chuse their own magis- " trates, provosts, bailies, and other officers within " the burgh, as fully and freely, in all respects, as

K   " the

" the city of Edinburgh, or any other royal burgh
" within the kingdom." By this charter, their right
of election, which had been again challenged and
infringed upon since the last charter in the year
1633, was established and confirmed, and this right
they have ever since uninterruptedly made use of.

William, though he favoured the citizens by thus
confirming their liberties, yet he, or his ministers,
in another respect, hurt them much, as well as
many others, by discouraging the infant colony,
then lately established at the isthmus of Darien. In
this scheme, Glasgow was deeply engaged, and the
most sanguine hopes were entertained of its success
for a considerable time; till enemies too powerful
to be suppressed, arose and accomplished its destruction, to the unspeakable chagrin of the nation
in general, as well as of many individuals, who were
thereby involved in ruin.

CHAP.

C H A P. III.

Rebellion in 1715—Riot at the extension of the Malt Tax—Contributions levied by the Pretender—Cutting of the Great Canal—Mob at the moving of the Popish Bill—Great Inundation of the Clyde—Scarcity and Dearth—New Town begun—Weaver's Riot—Volunteer Corps, &c.

1707.

FEW towns in Britain derived greater advantages from the union of the crowns, than the city of Glasgow; for although previous to this event, from its inland commerce, and the industry of its inhabitants in other branches of business, it had arrived at a great degree of importance; yet its merchants were fettered in their speculations by the restriction, or rather prohibition, which was issued against their commercial intercourse with America and the West Indies. At the union * these bars were re-

K 2   moved,

---

* As a contrast to that eager desire which is often manifested, and the immense sums which are expended, to obtain

a seat

moved, the merchants of Glasgow took advantage of the circumstance, and thus laid the foundation of its future wealth and prosperity.

But however fortunate such an event has been for the city and the kingdom at large, it was not carried without the most violent opposition from a great part of the people. This spirit of discontent broke out into open resistance with many in the year 1715, when the pretender's claim to the crown was endeavoured to be established by the sword.

On this occasion, Glasgow exerted itself in favour of the protestant succession in the House of Hanover, and with a praise-worthy loyalty, raised a battalion of six hundred men, which immediately thereafter, marched to Stirling to join the king's troops, under the duke of Argyle. The city was also, at the same time, begun to be fortified, by drawing a ditch round it, twelve feet wide, and six feet deep. By the general adoption of such measures as these, and the vigorous manner in which they

---

a seat in parliament in the present day, it will not be improper to present an account of the sums *paid* by the city of Glasgow, from October 1707, to October 1715, to its representatives, viz.

To provost Montgomery for his attendance in parliament, from Oct. 1707, to Aug. 1708,   L.2160

To provost Rodger, from Oct. 1708, to April 1710, being two sessions,   4800

To Dean of Guild Smith, from Oct. 1710, to Oct. 1715, being five sessions,   12224

Scots, L.19184

they were carried into execution, rebellion languished and expired, and tranquillity was again restored
to the country.

1722.

This year, the magistrates, in order to pay the
debts of the community, and to enable them to carry on improvements within the town, obtained from
parliament the continuance of an act, which was
first granted 15th June, 1693, for imposing two
pennies Scots, upon each Scots pint of ale and beer
brewed, inbrought, and sold within the city of Glasgow. This act was continued for sixteen years,
from November 1st, 1722; and has been farther
continued from time to time to the present day: it
extends over the village of Gorbals, and town of
Port-Glasgow.

1725.

At the extension of the malt tax to Scotland,
great murmurs took place throughout the kingdom, and no where were they louder than in
Glasgow, particularly amongst the lower class of
inhabitants. They saw the consequences that
would arise from the act, viz. the raising of the
price of ale, their favourite beverage; and they determined to shew their detestation of it by revenging themselves against its abettors. Accordingly,
they attacked the house of their representative in
parliament, Daniel Campbell, Esq. of Shawfield,
who then resided in the town, and after breaking
the windows, destroyed every article of furniture
they could find within the apartments. While they
were so engaged, a party of the military under the
command of captain Bushel arrived, with a view of
quelling

quelling the disturbance. That officer, after using every lenient means for that purpose, and while pelted by a shower of stones, ordered his men to fire amongst the rioters; by which above twenty, at the first discharge, were killed and wounded. Instead of dispersing, the mob, upon this increased to an immense multitude, arms were procured, and Bushel and his party were obliged to save themselves by flying towards the castle of Dumbarton; whither, for several miles, they were pursued by the enraged multitude.

This coming to the knowledge of the commander in chief, general Wade, he immediately raised a body of forces, and proceeded, accompanied by the lord advocate of Scotland, Duncan Forbes, to Glasgow. He took possession of the town, and from an idea of the magistrates having improperly discharged their duty, in not lending their authority to quell the tumult, they were taken into custody, that they might be brought to trial before the court of Justiciary. They were accordingly conveyed prisoners to Edinburgh, underwent a trial, and were honourably acquitted. The legislature, however, to punish the corporation of the city, upon the application of Mr. Campbell, passed an act granting him as a compensation, the sum of six thousand and eighty pounds sterling, to be paid forth of the funds of the community. This sum was accordingly uplifted, and together with the damages and expences incurred, the funds of the city lost about nine thousand pounds sterling from this unlucky mob.

1745.

1745.

This year, from another cause, the public peace also suffered severely, from the exactions of the agents of Charles Edward Stewart, the pretender. Sensible of the wealth of Glasgow, he sent a demand to the magistrates for fifteen thousand pounds sterling, together with the arrears of their taxes, and all their arms. It was not, however, immediately complied with, upon the idea that the king's forces would speedily arrive, and free them from the contribution. In consequence of this delay in not forwarding the exaction, John Hay, writer to the signet, came with a party of horse to Glasgow, threatened the city with military execution, and even to hang up the chief magistrate, in case of non-compliance with the demand. Inability being pled, Hay accepted of five thousand pounds in money, and five hundred in goods. This was not all. Upon the retreat of the rebels from England, towards the north, they again visited the town, and made and obtained a demand of twelve thousand linen shirts, six thousand cloth coats, six thousand pairs of shoes, six thousand pairs of hose, and six thousand bonnets, which were accordingly provided.

These exactions Charles, no doubt, made with the greater severity, from the steady loyalty and attachment which the city shewed to the established government under the house of Hanover At this time, the community raised two battalions of four hundred and fifty men each, for the service of government, which were engaged at the battle of

Falkirk,

Falkirk, under the command of the earl of Home. During the pretender's stay at Glasgow, from the 25th of December to the 3d of January, 1746, the most sullen sorrow prevailed amongst the inhabitants, and though he often appeared in public, he was not so much as attended by the common retinue of a mob, whose curiosity at this time, seems to have been repressed by that spirit of loyalty which pervaded every class. The temper of the highlanders could not brook this neglect, for no sooner were the contributions levied, than a resolution was agreed to, to plunder and burn the town; which would doubtless have taken place, had not one of their own chiefs, Cameron of Lochiel, interposed, and by threatening to withdraw his clan, forced them to lay their design aside.

The exactions that were at this time made, and the expence of quartering the pretender's army for ten days, and of raising their battalions, cost the city of Glasgow fourteen thousand pounds sterling.

1749.

Of that sum, they recovered by an application to parliament, ten thousand pounds; which, though it did not fully indemnify them, yet seems to have been equivalent to their expectations, and as much as government could then well spare, from the more pressing exigencies of the times.

These commotions were productive of no other inconvenience to Glasgow than what has been also mentioned;—her commerce sustained no shock, nor were the number of her inhabitants lessened; on the contrary, both were rapidly increasing, and new
schemes

schemes were adopted to carry the prosperity of the city to a still greater pitch.

1755.

Accordingly, the merchants of Glasgow with a view of opening a more ready communication with the continent of Europe, at this period projected a canal betwixt the rivers Forth and Clyde, and had nearly obtained an act for this purpose, when they were solicited by a number of gentlemen belonging to Edinburgh, to join issue with them, and enlarge the original plan†, which was found to be projected on too small a scale. The first design was accordingly given up, and a canal of larger dimensions agreed to, which obtained the sanction of parliament. The operations accordingly commenced, under the direction of Mr. John Smeaton, an able engineer, whose numerous public works in this and the neighbouring kingdom, pointed him out as a proper person to engage in this great undertaking.

1771.

To open the communication still farther betwixt Glasgow and other places by means of water conveyance, an act of parliament was obtained this year, for the purpose of deepening the river Clyde, from Dumbuck ford to Glasgow. The magistrates to carry that act into execution, entered into an agreement

L   ment

---

† The original plan was four feet deep, and twenty-four in breadth; the canal on the enlarged scale is eight feet deep, and fifty-six feet broad.

ment with Mr. John Golbourne of the city of Chester, who engaged to deepen the channel of the river seven feet at the quay of the Broomielaw, even in neap tides†. His contract he accordingly executed, to the great improvement of the navigation of the river, which before would scarcely admit vessels of thirty tons, whereas lighters of seventy tons now approach the quay with ease.

Great inconvenience having been found to arise about this time, to the several manufactures in the city, as well as to the inhabitants at large, from the high price of coals, a scheme was set on foot and adopted, for cutting a navigable canal, from the high grounds at the back of the cathedral church, to the parish of Monkland, with a view of lessening the price of that article, by bringing it at once to the town in larger quantities, and at a cheaper rate than formerly.

1775.

These public works of themselves sufficiently demonstrate the wealth and prosperity of Glasgow about this period.—Indeed, as has been before remarked, the union was the era from which this city
must

---

† Before this time the water was shallow, the channel much too wide for the usual quantity of water that flowed down, and the navigation interrupted by twelve remarkable shoals.— The second inconvenience continually increased by the wearing away of the banks, caused by the prevalency of the southwest winds: thus, what was got in breadth, was lost in depth. —*Pennant.*

must date the extension of her commerce.—From that time, in spite of some temporary checks, it was on the increase, and in this year Glasgow employed upwards of sixty thousand tons of shipping; having, in the single article of tobacco, imported from America, the amazing quantity of fifty-seven thousand one hundred and forty-three hogsheads. Unluckily, an event now took place, which gave such a shock to the prosperity of the city, as a length of years, aided by industry turned into another channel, has only been able to overcome.—This was the breaking out of the American war, which effectually cut off that commercial intercourse that had so long subsisted betwixt Glasgow and that country.

1778.

When that contest began, the most vigorous efforts were made throughout the kingdom, to quell the spirit of insurrection that had broke out in the colonies. Glasgow made an offer to his Majesty to raise a regiment of one thousand men for the service of government, which the king accepted. Subscriptions for this purpose were accordingly set on foot in the city, and by the liberal encouragement of the body corporate of Glasgow, of lord Frederick Campbell, the city's representative in parliament, who alone gave five hundred pounds, and of the several incorporations, as well as individuals, a sum was raised in a few days to the amount of nine thousand six hundred pounds, which, aided by the general zeal then manifested in support of govern-

L 2   ment,

ment, completed this corps in the course of the ensuing summer†.

At the same time, the merchants of the city fitted out in the Clyde fourteen privateers, mounting
from twelve to twenty-two guns, and carrying in
whole about one thousand men. These were in
the course of the war of very considerable service,
by driving the privateers of the enemy from the
coast, and protecting the trade of the country.

Shortly thereafter, a numerous body of the citizens of Glasgow, as zealous to defend their religious as civil rights, were cast into a ferment, by a
bill having been moved for, to be brought into parliament for the repeal of the penal statutes against
the Roman catholics. In this city alone, eighty-five
different societies, consisting of upwards of twelve
thousand persons, were formed with a view of opposing

† This regiment having been ordered to embark at Leith,
for Guernsey, on the 20th April, 1779, they willingly expressed their inclination to obey the order; but about fifty of Fra-
ser's highlanders, who had been ordered to incorporate themselves with the Glasgow regiment, and embark, on pretence
of arrears being due them, refused. In order to compel them,
the duke of Buccleugh's regiment was sent for from Edinburgh, but notwithstanding of their arrival, the highlanders
persisted in their resolution, and with their backs to a wall on
the shore of Leith, braved every opposition. A fray was
therefore the consequence of their obstinacy, wherein twenty
of the mutineers were killed, and the remainder taken prisoners, and lodged in the castle of Edinburgh. An officer and two
or three of the fencibles were likewise mortally wounded.

posing the bill by petition: these again corresponded with others in the country, whose business was to form new associations, and thus in a short time, the greatest part of Scotland inveighed against the measure, which was at the time prudently dropt. The minds of the lower class on this occasion, were so inflamed against the catholics, who were represented as conspiring against their liberties, that outrages against the property and effects of persons of that persuasion, were the unavoidable consequence.

1779.

At Glasgow, a mob having collected on Sunday, during the time of divine service, they proceeded to a popish chapel in the High-street, and after forcing their way into the house, they dismissed the congregation, by pelting them with stones, while they destroyed a number of pictures representing the different saints, hung around the altar. The magistrates having arrived after service with a party, the mob dispersed, and no further outrage took place at the time.

On the evening of the 10th of February thereafter, the populace again assembled around the shop of a potter in King-street, of the Roman catholic persuasion, which they effectually gutted, but on the arrival of the magistrates with a party of the military, the mob there seemingly dispersed. They however, went immediately to his dwelling house, at the east end of the town, which having set on fire, it was, with the furniture entirely consumed, before any means could be used to extinguish it; notice being given to the magistrates, upon their arrival the mob was entirely quelled. So faithful

were

were the instigators of this riot to each other, that notwithstanding the magistrates next day, by proclamation, offered a reward of one hundred guineas for the apprehension of any one of the ringleaders, they all resisted the temptation, and none were ever secured. Bagnal, the proprietor of the shop and dwelling house, thereafter commenced an action for damages a gainst the city, and recovered to the amount of his loss.

This was not, however, the only bill brought in this session of parliament, which excited discontent in this quarter.—Another, though of a more local nature, was moved, for taking off the duties formerly imposed upon French cambrics: as the manufacture of cambric was now carried on to a considerable extent in this city, such a bill, which threatened the starvation of many families, could not fail of meeting with a powerful opposition*. However, the minister, before the bill had gone through the customary stages, being convinced of the impropriety

ty

* When the news first arrived at Glasgow, that such a bill was introduced, a mob of weavers belonging to the city and adjacent villages having assembled, they paraded through the streets with an effigy on horseback of the minister who brought in the bill, holding in one hand a piece of French cambric, and in the other the bill for importing that commodity. Having finished their procession, the effigy was conducted to the common place of execution, where it was first hung, and afterwards blown to pieces by the firing of some combustible matter lodged in its inside.—The mob thereafter retired peaceably to their homes.

ty of the measure, consented to withdraw it, upon substituting another tax, of a less hurtful tendency†.

1782.

During the spring of this year, there happened a most remarkable inundation of the Clyde. This took place on Tuesday the 12th of March, and, for its magnitude, was unequalled in the annals of the city.

For some few days before, there had been an almost uninterrupted fall of snow and rain, but more particularly heavy in that part of the country where the Clyde takes its rise, than about the city of Glasgow. The river, however, till the Monday preceding the inundation, did not seem to carry any very threatening appearance, otherwise than what it shews in bad or stormy weather. But, on the afternoon of that day, it began suddenly to swell, and before ten in the evening, the waters had extended over the Green, stopped the communication with the country by the bridges, and laid the Bridgegate in flood to the depth of some feet. As the inhabitants of that street had been frequently used to inundations of the river, they quietly allowed themselves to be surrounded by the water, thinking, that during

---

† So great was the cold this winter, 1780, that upon Friday, January 14th, the thermometer of Farenheit placed at the observatory, stood at forty-six degrees below the freezing point, being twelve degrees lower than what it was in the great cold in January 1768, and twenty-three degrees below where it stood in this city at the great frost in 1740.

during the night it would subside as usual, and in this opinion, many of them went to bed. Instead of decreasing, the flood increased, and the fears of the suffering inhabitants were at last seriously roused, when they perceived the waters getting higher than they had ever witnessed them, by flooding their ground apartments several feet deep, extinguishing their fires, and at last entering these very beds, where, a few hours before, many had lain down to rest. By day, their situation would even have been thought to be particularly afflicting, but how much more so was it now, in a dark and gloomy night, when they found themselves partly immersed, and surrounded on all sides by water, and in these very places where they had promised themselves security.

To fly at this time, from the presence of the calamity was impossible, as the water in the street, from its depth and current, would have frustrated the attempt, by at once sacrificing those lives, which in another situation it so dreadfully threatened. Nothing was now to be heard, but the cries of despair, and the most pitiful exclamations for help, uttered by the old as well as the young. Day at length approached, and hoped-for relief was at hand, from the exertions of their fellow-citizens.

By seven o'clock in the morning of Tuesday, the flood began to abate, to the infinite satisfaction of the sufferers, as well as the other inhabitants, who had it now in their power to administer that relief which before was impracticable. Boats were accordingly sent up and down the streets, loaded with provisions, to furnish such as stood in need, and for

the

the purpose of bringing off others, whose fears cautioned them against staying longer in their houses.

Independent of this scene of misery, which pressed so hard upon the inhabitants of this particular quarter, the river when viewed from another point of view, exhibited a most terrific and threatening appearance, for not only was the whole of the Bridgegate overflowed, but also the lower part of the Saltmarket, Stockwell, and Jamaica streets, as well as the village of Gorbals, which appeared as an island in the midst of an estuary. The current of the river was besides so exceedingly rapid and strong, that not only were the greatest trees borne along like straws upon its stream, but had it continued in such a situation to increase, a few hours longer, the two bridges must have fallen a sacrifice to its fury. Luckily, this did not take place, as the Clyde, after having attained fully the height of *twenty feet above its ordinary level*‡, began to fall, and by Wednesday immediately following, it was again confined to its ordinary channel.

The damage sustained by this unprecedented inundation was very great, from the quantities of tobacco, sugar, and other merchandise, that were either carried away, or destroyed by the stream. With a view of alleviating in some degree the loss sustained,

M

‡ Only one person lost her life by this flood, a young woman in the Gorbals; though a great many cows and horses that could not be removed from their stables were drowned. The exact height of the flood is marked on the walls of a house at the foot of the Saltmarket, upon the east side of that street.

sustained, a subscription was set on foot, and in the course of a few days, to the honour of the citizens of Glasgow, upwards of five hundred pounds sterling, was contributed for this generous purpose.

In the course of the same year, (1782) a calamity of a different kind, though of a more lasting and generally afflicting nature, befel not only the poor in this city, but also those throughout the kingdom, through the failure of the crop, caused by an early and severe frost. The consequence was a dearth, by which many were. reduced to the greatest distress, and had it not been for the humane exertions of the magistrates†, and of some other gentlemen in the city, there is little doubt but several would have fallen before the famine, as was unfortunately the case in the north of Scotland with many, who were situated at a distance from what seldom unites, wealth and a philanthropic heart. By degrees, however, this evil wore off, through the reaping of an abundant harvest, and the great quantity of grain that flowed into the kingdom, so that the price of provisions shortly fell to their ordinary rate.

The

† The magistrates at this time, by several successive proclamations, offered such farmers as brought meal to the market a bounty at the rate of sixpence per boll.—Mr. David Dale also claims notice from his exertions to relieve the poor,—he not only imported into the country great quantities of grain, but sold it again even below the price it cost him.—The meal at this time sold at L.1 1s. 4d. per boll.

1783.

The unlucky contest with America having this year terminated, new exertions were made by the citizens to extend their commerce and manufactures:—and with a view to the general interest, a society of merchants united themselves under the name of the CHAMBER OF COMMERCE AND MANUFACTURES, whose sole aim, as a body, was to employ their influence and funds for the benefit and protection of the trade of the city. Of this society, which was incorporated into a body politic, by his Majesty's charter, we will fall to speak more largely in another place, when treating of the establishment of other associations, not noticed here from the more private nature of their institutions *.

M 2　　　　　　　Nothing

---

* The meteor which so greatly alarmed the whole country, on the evening of Monday the 18th August this year, at nine o'clock at night, was also seen here.—Its appearance was a fiery ball, with a conical tail, and moving from the north-west to the south-east with an inconceivable degree of velocity.—The light was so strong that the smallest pin might have been easily picked from the street. What is remarkable, it was seen through all Britain nearly at the same instant, so that its height must have been very great.—The facts mentioned below are likewise worthy of notice.

1785.

The end of the preceding and beginning of this year, were remarkable for a long continued frost: it lasted four months, till the ice upon Clyde broke, 14th March. At London its continuance was still longer, being no less than five months and twenty-four days, in all one hundred and seventy six days, the longest continuance of frost upon record. The great frost

in

1787.

Nothing very interesting appears to have taken place, from the last mentioned date to this time, if we except the improvements in the town, (which will be taken notice of in another place,) and the facts mentioned in the note, when the peace of the city was disturbed by a tumultuous mob, raised with the view of increasing the wages of the journeymen weavers. A spirit of discontent had, for a considerable time, prevailed amongst that body of men, though no serious consequences were for some time apprehended, as their employers had made every concession consistent with their interest. The operatives, however, were not satisfied, combinations were formed amongst them, and threatening letters sent to several of the manufacturers.

At

in 1739 and 1740, lasted only one hundred and three days. In the latter end of the same year, the inhabitants of Glasgow were first amused by observing the ascent of an air balloon. The æronaut was Lunardi, who ascended from St. Andrew's Square, at twenty minutes before 2, P. M. and according to his account, descended at fifty-five minutes past 3 o'clock, the same afternoon, within two miles of Hawick, a distance of nearly seventy miles. He ascended again a second time, and was carried northwards to the neighbourhood of the Campsie hills, where his aerial voyage terminated.

In the following year a great fire took place in the Gorbals, nine families were burnt out, and one woman perished in the flames. On the 11th of August, a slight shock of an earthquake was felt in the city, and other places of Scotland. And upon the 21st December, the cold was so intense, that the thermometer shewed 20 degrees below the freezing point.

At last, these combinations proceeded to acts of violence. Webs were cut from the looms of such as agreed to work at the former rate; warehouses were rifled, and bonfires kindled with their contents. Insults such as these were to the public peace, could not be borne with, and measures were accordingly taken to suppress them. With this view, (Sept. 3.) the magistrates after having received information that a mob was assembled in the Calton, proceeded, attended by the peace-officers, to that quarter, in order to disperse them, and secure the ringleaders. They were no sooner arrived, than they were attacked by the populace, and forced to retreat into the city, whither they were pursued by the mob. An additional force to quell the rioters became therefore necessary; and this having been obtained by the arrival of a detachment of the 39th regiment, under the command of lieutenant-colonel Kellet, the magistrates again proceeded to the execution of their duty. They accordingly fell in with the mob near the Parkhouse, on the east side of the city, betwixt which place and the Drygate, a very serious conflict ensued. No sooner were the magistrates and military arrived, than the populace attacked them furiously with stones, brick-bats, and other missile weapons, whereby their lives were not only endangered, but many amongst them much hurt. To defend themselves, they were at last under the disagreeable necessity, after reading the riot act, of ordering the military to fire, by which three persons were killed outright, three mortally, and the same number slightly wounded. However disagreeable the adoption of such a measure

measure must have been, yet it had the desired effect. The mob immediately fled and dispersed, and the magistrates and military returned to the cross. An alarm was given in the afternoon, that the populace were again in force in their former situation, upon which a party immediately went in quest of them, but upon their arrival the rioters instantly took to flight.

On the following day they assembled in the village of Calton, to the amount of several thousands; there, as formerly, they wrecked their vengeance upon their peaceable brethren, by cutting their webs from the looms and burning them, while they walked through the streets. Intelligence having come to the sheriff, he immediately with a party of soldiers, proceeded to that village, in order to quell the disturbance. The mob, however, aware of the fatal effects of opposition on the preceding day, no sooner got a glimpse of the military, than they quickly retired and separated.

1790.

From this riot forward to the year 1790, nothing remarkable occurs that has a connection with the city. In that year the great canal, which we formerly mentioned to have been begun in 1768, was finished, and on the 29th day of July the communication was opened between the FRITHS OF FORTH AND CLYDE*. That great work having stopped in
the

* This important event was evidenced by the sailing of a track-barge from the bason at Hamilton-Hill, near Glasgow, to

the year 1775, through a deficiency of funds, it was not again resumed till the year 1784, when government gave L.50,000 from the forfeited estates towards its completion†. In this interval, the city of Glasgow began and carried through a collateral cut

to the river Clyde at Bowling Bay, a space of twelve miles. The committee of management, accompanied by the magistrates of Glasgow, were the first voyagers of this new navigation. On the arrival of the vessel at Bowling Bay, and after descending from the last lock into the Clyde, the ceremony of the junction of the Forth and Clyde was performed in presence of a great crowd of spectators by Archibald Speirs, Esq. of Elderslie, chairman of the committee of management, who with the assistance of the chief engineer, launched a hogshead of the water of the river Forth into the Clyde, as a symbol of joining the eastern and western seas.—This event, so important to the trade of Great Britain and Ireland, is now manifested in a striking degree, by the opening of a navigation which not only shortens the nautical distance from 800 to 1000 miles, but also affords a more safe and speedy passage particularly in the time of war, or at the end of the season, when vessels are detained long in the Baltic.—The extreme length of the navigation from the Forth to the Clyde is exactly 35 miles, sixteen of which is upon the summit of the country, 156 feet above the level of the sea.—To this height the voyager is raised by means of twenty locks from the eastern sea, and nineteen from the west; each lock is exactly twenty feet wide, and seventy-four feet long within the gates. The depth of the canal is eight feet throughout, and the medium width of about fifty-six feet on the surface of the water, and twenty-eight feet at the bottom.

† The dividends arising from this money are appointed to be applied towards repairing of the high roads in the highlands of Scotland.

cut to Hamilton Hill, within a mile northward of the town, and thereafter to another situation, now called Port Dundas, little more than half the distance; by which means, they opened a more ready communication than formerly, with the continent of Europe, and the eastern coast of the kingdom, which has been productive of the happiest effects to the commerce and prosperity of the city. And now, that the original design is finished, these advantages have proportionably increased.

1793.

This year, on the 8th of February, an accident occurred in this city, which, from its singularity, is not undeserving of attention; this was the destruction by fire of the Laigh Church; a fabric originally founded by the citizens, and dedicated to the Virgin Mary in the year 1484.—Between the hours of four and five in the morning, the flames were first discovered issuing through the roof of the session-house, in the west end of the church. Assistance was immediately procured, but as the fire had communicated from the session-house to the church, from which it was only separated by a thin deal partition, and had got to a great head, assistance was of no avail; and in the course of two hours, that pile which had baffled the storms of ages, fell before the all-devouring flame*. Unluckily, the damage

---

* The cause of the fire is not known, though it is supposed to have arisen from the carelessness of some of the persons then

damage did not terminate only in the destruction of the church, the records of the General Session lodged here were entirely consumed, and the register of the proceedings of the presbytery greatly hurt.

1794.

In the following year, a scheme was formed for feuing out on the south bank of Clyde, opposite the city, the lands belonging to Hutcheson's hospital, for the purpose of building; and a regular plan of this new village, to be called Hutcheson Town, was accordingly made out. In order to give a more direct communication to these proposed buildings, a new bridge was determined upon, and the foundation-stone accordingly laid on the 18th June, by the lord provost and magistrates, in presence of a great concourse of spectators.

This was not the most notable incident that took place in the course of the year 1794, relative to Glasgow; an institution was now opened, of a more extensive and benevolent nature, which, by tending to alleviate the miseries incident to the human race, will long remain a monument of the philanthropy of its founders; this was the opening of

N   the

then on guard; the session-house at that time having been used by the citizens as a guard-room.——On the following Saturday, the 13th of February, two porpoises of about ten feet in length each, appeared in the river at the Broomielaw. Numbers of shots were fired at them while swimming, and one having been caught by a net, was exhibited as a shew,——the other got clear off.

the GLASGOW ROYAL INFIRMARY, which had been begun to be built two years preceding. Of the nature of that institution, and of the building itself, we, in another place, will speak at more length; suffice it here only to mention, that it has proved to many of the utmost service, by dispensing that relief, which, without it, probably would never have been procured.

About the middle of December this year, the peace of the city was again threatened by another riot, proceeding, however, from a different cause than that which occasioned the last in the year 1793.—In the beginning of that month, a deserter having escaped from the guard-house, through the negligence of the sentinel, a court martial adjudged him to be punished for this breach of duty.—His fellow soldiers were, however, determined to hinder the sentence from being put into execution, and for several days from this resolution the punishment did not take place. As this combination was contrary to all order, and as it might have been productive of the worst effects, the troops in the neighbourhood were called into the city to assist in quelling the insurgents.—Before their arrival, however, the ringleaders surrendered themselves to the earl of Breadalbane, colonel of the regiment. No sooner had this taken place, than they were ordered to march for Edinburgh, under a strong guard, there to take their trial†. The honourable major Leslie
and

† The ringleaders of this mutiny, after their arrival at Edinburgh,

and an officer of the Breadalbane regiment, having
accompanied the party a short way on their march,
were, upon their return to town, attacked by a mob,
who, after upbraiding them for sending off the mutineers to be punished, assaulted them with stones
and other missile weapons, whereby the honourable major Leslie was wounded, and he and the other
officer obliged to take shelter, by retreating into a
neighbouring house, which could not have long
withstood the assaults of the mob by whom it was
threatened.—Luckily, however, the lord provost
and magistrates, attended by the peace officers, and
a party of the military now arrived, and by a judicious conduct obliged the populace to disperse without bloodshed, and before any damage was done.—
Parties of dragoons having come to town in the e-
vening, no further disturbance upon this occasion
took place, and tranquillity was again restored to
the inhabitants*.

We have had occasion to remark, in the course
of this narrative, that the city of Glasgow has ever
been distinguished for its *loyalty*, and determined re-

N 2   solution,

---

dinburgh, were tried by a general court martial, and four of
them sentenced to be shot.—Only one, however, suffered the
punishment.

* The greatest praise is due to lord Adam Gordon, commander in chief for Scotland, for his exertions in this affair, as
well as to the lord provost and magistrates of the city, who,
by a prudent course of conduct restored peace and good order.

solution, to support that *glorious fabric* the BRITISH CONSTITUTION.

Since the era of the revolution, more particularly, has it exerted itself by raising and embodying, from its own funds, several successive regiments, for the service of government.—Now again, that every Briton was called upon, to exert himself in the cause of his country, against both foreign and domestic foes, did the *loyal citizens of Glasgow* offer their services, as a regiment of volunteers. This very respectable corps had its first existence in April, 1794, when a considerable number of the citizens subscribed a writing, expressing their willingness to form themselves into a Volunteer Corps, for the local defence of the city, as soon as the bill then in contemplation for enabling them, and similar bodies to do so, should receive the sanction of parliament. This having been accordingly obtained, and the corps still increasing in numbers, in the month of August thereafter they divided themselves into two companies, and recommended several gentlemen to be their officers, which recommendation his majesty was pleased to sanction†. In the month of January, 1795, a chaplain, surgeon, and assistant-surgeon, were also chosen, and in like manner approved of; and in the April following, the corps received their colours, after previous consecration by the chaplain.

1795.

---

† Major, now colonel Corbet was appointed to the command, which he retained till the dissolution of the corps.

1795.

On the 18th of November, the Clyde again rose
to a great height, and inundated the lower parts of
the city nearly as much as it had done in that memorable flood on the 12th day of March, 1782; like
to that then, the swelling of the river now, was occasioned by a very severe storm of wind, rain, and
snow, which commenced upon Tuesday the 17th,
and continued almost without intermission, till the
following Wednesday in the afternoon. About the
middle of that day, the current was so strong as to
shake the piers of the newly erected bridge, opposite the foot of the Saltmarket-street, and in consequence, two of the arches immediately gave way,
and with a tremendous crash fell into the river.
The concussion of the water, occasioned by this
cause, was almost irresistible; the doors of the
washing-house, though situated at a considerable
distance, were burst open, and a great quantity of
clothes and utensils carried off by the impetuous
stream. In the afternoon, the three remaining
arches of the bridge shared the same fate with the
others; and thus in the compass of a few hours,
that edifice, which had been nearly a year and a half
in erecting, was completely destroyed. At this
time, the Bridgegate, the lower parts of the Saltmarket, Stockwell, Jamaica-street, and the village
of Gorbals were all under water to the depth of
several feet, while boats were plying up and down
these streets, administering relief to such as were in
danger. On Friday morning, the river was again
confined to its ordinary channel, and till Saturday,
hopes were entertained that the violence of the
storm

storm was over; however, on that day it began to snow and rain afresh, and with such violence, that the Clyde quickly rose, and twice, in the compass of one week, overflowed the lower part of the city. On Sunday the waters appeared to be retiring, and by Monday afternoon the inundation was completely over, to the great satisfaction of the inhabitants *.

1797.

This year, the corps of Royal Glasgow Volunteers was augmented to ten companies†; a second battalion was also unanimously voted by the citizens, and accepted of by his majesty, to the amount of five hundred men, commanded by officers recommended by the lord-lieutenant of the county‡; a third regiment, or armed association, composed principally of gentlemen of the city more advanced in years than those who composed the first regiment, was also embodied; and to add still more to the defence of the

* During this flood, one boy was drowned in attempting to go home, near the foot of the New Wynd.

† The number of this corps amounted to between six and seven hundred.

‡ James M'Dowall, Esq. then lord provost, was appointed colonel. They had their arms, clothes and accoutrements furnished by government, besides a weekly pay of two shillings each man.—Towards defraying the expences of this corps, a subscription was begun, and in the course of a few hours thereafter, upwards of seven hundred and fifty pounds, was subscribed at the tontine coffee-room.

the city, a troop of volunteer cavalry §, composed of the citizens, were raised, so that in respect to internal defence of the city, nothing was to be apprehended from the designs of any enemies to the peace and good order of society.

1799-1800.

From a general failure of the crop throughout the kingdom, every article of provision sold at an exorbitant price, some nearly three times their accustomed rate. Though this was felt by all in some degree, it still pressed with greater severity upon the poor, many of whom might have fallen victims to want, had they not been relieved by the generous and humane.

To alleviate the evil as much as possible, the magistrates and town council of Glasgow set on foot a subscription in each of these years, for the purpose of bringing in grain to supply the inhabitants, to be sold at a rate somewhat reduced from the ordinary price of the country around. By these subscriptions a sum was raised, on the credit of which the managing committee speedily purchased a supply to the value of no less than L.117,000 sterling, from Galloway, Ayrshire and America, and this

contributed

---

§ The cavalry were commanded by John Orr, Esq. of Barrowfield. They, like the first regiment of Royal Glasgow Volunteers, provided every requisite article towards their equipment, (arms excepted) and received no pay.

contributed, in a considerable degree, towards the relief of the poor class of inhabitants *.

From the great quantity of grain of all kinds which the committee managing for the subscribers had on hand at the return of plenty, and fall of prices in autumn 1801, and from damage unfortunately sustained by several cargoes of corn, which could not be recovered from the underwriters, on account of the constant limitation in policies regarding grain, a considerable loss was occasioned to the subscribers. This loss amounted to L.15,000, which exceeded by above L.4000, the amount of the subscriptions; and the city having engaged to guarantee the acting committee from any such surplus loss, this L.4000 came upon the corporation funds in addition to their original subscription of L.500. That payment of this sum might be equalized among the citizens, it was proposed to apply for an act of parliament for a general tax upon house rents for a limited time. In consequence, however, of opposition, the design has not been proceeded in.

In a city such as Glasgow, the want of a proper system of police had long been complained of; a bill some years before had been framed for this purpose, which, however, it would appear, was never passed into a law. Another, at this time was

drawn

---

* Oat-meal sold for some time at 3s. 6d. and 3s 9d. per peck. Its ordinary rate is 1s 3d.

drawn out, received the approbation of parliament, and in consequence, in September 1800, a system of police was established which has since been productive of the best effects, in securing the peace of the city, and the comfort and convenience of its inhabitants. Of this system we will fall to speak more at length in another place.

1801.

The war with France, in which Britain had been engaged for nearly ten years, having concluded in the latter end of this year, a reduction of the army, militia and volunteer corps shortly thereafter happened. Amongst others, that of the first and second regiment of Royal Glasgow Volunteers.

The first regiment was disembodied on the 6th of May 1802, and shortly thereafter the reduction of the second corps took place.

At this time, the first regiment were in possession of funds to a considerable amount; government was likewise due them considerable sums: These together, amounted to betwixt L.1000 and L.1200 sterling. This sum*, with a liberality which does

O   them

---

* As this respectable body served without pay, these funds arose from certain allowances which all volunteer corps had from government, for paying the public expences of the regiment. From their being managed with strict economy, the balance mentioned in the text, remained. Of this, L.700 was in the hands of the committee of finance, the remainder, from the accounts not having passed the Treasury, is, at the time of writing this article (June 1803) still owing them.

The corps also voted, as a mark of esteem for their commanding

them the highest honour, they unanimously voted
as a donation to the Royal Glasgow Infirmary, and
of this, L.700 has been already paid into that charitable institution.

1803.

From the restless spirit of the French government,
their oppression of the nations around, their utter
want of faith, and from the unbridled ambition of
their first consul Buonaparte, Britain was again called upon this year, to assert her privileges and defend her honour and her rights. The war having
commenced in the end of the month of April, the
greatest exertions were made to prosecute it with
that vigour which its justice demands.

The city of Glasgow again came forward in offering to raise a regiment of volunteer yeomanry in
support of government. This offer his majesty has
been pleased to accept of, and during the writing
of this article, many have already enrolled themselves for the laudable purpose of defending all that
is dear to us as men and as Christians.

manding officers, colonel Corbet and major Buchanan, a sum
of money, to be appropriated in purchasing a sabre and piece
of plate for each of these gentlemen.

CHAP.

CHAP. V.

Of the progress and present state of the City.

IN the two former editions of this work, when treating of the historical department, we took a short view of the progress of the city in point of extent, previous to the Union. It is now, however, thought more advisable to draw that sketch upon the conclusion of the history of the town, and previous to the descriptive part of the treatise.

Our opinion respecting the origin of Glasgow, has been already advanced, viz. that the cathedral, or some place of acknowledged sanctity in the early ages of our history, was the cause which brought together inhabitants and habitations. These would naturally increase, till such time as a village was formed, which still advancing, attracted the attention of the sovereign, by whom, viz. William the Lyon, it was erected into a burgh royal.

At this period, the houses that composed the town, appear to have been situated in the immediate

O 2   vicinity

vicinity of the cathedral, or High church, and even to have been almost clustered around it*. These houses were mostly inhabited by the clergy, who officiated in the cathedral, or their dependents. What doubtless, about this time, contributed considerably to its increase, was a bull issued by pope Alexander, enjoining the whole inhabitants of the diocese to visit the cathedral, " their mother church," at least once a year. As these commands in that age, from the respect for the high authority from which they proceeded, would be strictly obeyed, an additional increase of houses as well as inhabitants, would consequently follow.

Still, however, and even in the middle of the fourteenth century, it had not attained that note in the country, which from its privileges and the date of its erection into a royal burgh, we might naturally enough have supposed: for we find that it was reckoned so inconsiderable, even in the year 1357, as not to be admitted into the number of the cautionary towns assigned to Edward of England, for payment of the ransom of David II‡.

Upon the building of the bridge over the Clyde, by bishop Rae, about the period last mentioned, the town seems gradually to have extended itself in that direction, from the high grounds near the cathedral,

* A street called Vicar's Alley, formerly stood to the north of the cathedral, now so entirely erased, that no vestige of it remains.—M'Ure.

‡ Anderson's Dict. Commerce, I.

thedral, where the most ancient part of the city stood. On the accession of bishop Cameron, the town increased rapidly in size. He obliged, as has been already stated, the whole prebendaries of the diocese to erect houses, and to live in the city, while their cures in the country were served by vicars. He also laid out the town upon a new plan*, by forming the High-street, (or rather probably improving its direction) the Drygate, and Rottenrow; and the intersection of these streets was at that period considered as the cross of Glasgow.

From the death of bishop Cameron, to the erection of the university, the town seems to have increased but slowly. Such an institution, however, contributed very considerably to the extension of the city, by the influx of students; and the consequent demand for accommodation, as to houses, provisions and other necessaries. The buildings now went on with alacrity, insomuch, that about the latter end of the reign of James V. the High-street was filled up the length of the cross. The Saltmarket, Gallowgate and Trongate streets were formed, and many houses built in each of them, particularly in the Saltmarket, which continued to be the thoroughfare towards the bridge, from the most ancient part of the city To these streets may be added the Bridgegate, most likely of an equal antiquity with the founding of the bridge. It appears to have been in these times inhabited principally
by

* Brown.

by fishermen, who subsisted themselves, and sup-plied the community with the fish caught in the river, in their immediate vicinity.

Glasgow, nevertheless, appears at the Reforma-tion to have possessed only the eleventh place in point of population and wealth amongst the towns of Scotland§. That event contributed for a consi-derable time to stop the increase of the town. Pre-vious to it, the inhabitants, unacquainted with com-merce, had principally subsisted upon its clergy and the university. But when this took place, the cler-gy were dispersed, and the university almost ne-glected; so that some time elapsed before other means were found out equally to be depended up-on. They appear then to have directed their atten-tion to commerce, and with some degree of success, if we may judge from the increased size of the town, and its population betwixt the years 1611 and 1617, when they amounted to seven thousand six hundred and forty-four†.

Forty years thereafter, that number was nearly doubled‡. Nay, if we credit the account given of the number of families that were burnt out by the first great fire in 1652, and the proportion they held to the rest of the city, we shall find, that they then amounted to considerably more than 15,000, allowing only about five souls to each family.

In

§ Taxation Table in the reign of Mary, dated 1556.
† Parochial Register for these years.
‡ Ibid.

In the year 1695, Glasgow is ranked as the second city in the kingdom, and as such assessed accordingly. We, however, observe with astonishment, that at this period the number of inhabitants were considerably under what they amounted to forty years preceding. Whether this is to be accounted for from any defect in the parochial records, or from some other cause, which took place about the Restoration, cannot now be ascertained.

If we take a view of the mode of architecture that prevailed here during the early stages of the history of the town, we will find that it was in general mean, gloomy and inconvenient. The houses of the greatest antiquity, were built like those in the country around of stone and turf, covered with thatch, or perhaps of still less durable materials. One storey was then most likely the greatest height to which they were carried. In process of time, wooden fronts† to the houses became frequent; they were then constructed of two or more stories, each projecting a little way farther upon the street than the one immediately under it. The greatest part of these, however, appear to have been still covered with thatch, and it was not till the fire in 1652, when many of them fell a prey to the violence of the flames, that stone buildings, covered with slate, became more frequent. These, from being

† A great number of these wooden houses are still in existence, particularly in the Saltmarket and Bridgegate.

being gloomy, incommodious, and constructed without taste, or regard to true ornament or beauty, have, in process of time, become rivals to the city buildings in any town of Britain, with regard to whatever is convenient, healthful, or agreeable in a human habitation.

From the period of the Union are we to date the prosperity of Glasgow—it rapidly increased in extent. In the year 1722, an additional church was found necessary (the North West) and a new street opened from the Trongate towards the situation in which it was erected. About the same time, and from the same cause, an increase in population, the New-street, or King's street, was begun to be built, and shortly carried on for a considerable distance towards the Bridgegate.

Prince's street, or Gibson's wynd, leading from the Saltmarket to King's street, was also opened, and buildings begun to be erected in it about the same period. These streets gradually filled up, while, at the same time, the Trongate, or St. Enoch's gate, appears to have been rapidly extending towards the west. The number of houses, from the year 1677, when the last remarkable fire took place, to 1737, in these different streets, are calculated at two hundred†, each of these of at least two stories in height, and most of them more, besides houses of inferior rank in more retired situations.

It

† M'Ure's History.

It does not appear that Glasgow was ever fortified with a wall. A deep ditch, as has been already mentioned, was begun to be carried round it, twelve feet wide and six feet deep, during the rebellion in the year 1715, which was never completed. The city had, however, eight gates or ports at its different avenues. At the northern extremity of the city stood the Stable-green port, built betwixt the wall surrounding the castle garden and the west side of the street; and upon the opposite side of the archbishop's palace, across the avenue or street leading to the cathedral, and not far from the entrance into the High-church yard, was a gate called the Castle-gate.—A part of the wall of this gate was visible till within these two or three years, when it was removed, with an old tower that bounded it on the south, to make room for the new Barony church. At the western extremity of the Rottenrow there appears also to have been a port, as also at the eastern termination of the Drygate, the space between these two was anciently reckoned the breadth of the city from east to west, and measures 1118 ells.

The avenue to the town alongst the Gallowgate-street was guarded by the Gallowgate port, which was placed immediately to the west of the entry of St. Mungo's lane or Burnt Barns, extending across the street to the house formerly called the Saracen's Head Inn.

The next port upon the opposite side of the city, and at the termination of the Trongate, was the West port, which extended from that house at the head of the Stockwell, upon the west side to the

P   house

house upon the north side of the street. These two gates were, in more modern times, reckoned the limits of Glasgow as to its extent from east to west, there being only a few thatched houses without. They were both taken down in the year 1749. At the foot of the Stockwell was another port called the Water port, the vestiges of which still are to be seen adjoining to the wall of a house at the western extremity of the Bridgegate-street.

Another gate stood at the junction of Bell's wynd with the Candleriggs street, which in point of architectural beauty, much surpassed the others. Whether there were any more of these barriers it is not now easy to say, though it is probable some others, upon a lesser scale, might have been erected at the openings of the different lanes.

When we think of these boundaries to the city formerly, and which were by no means completely filled up with houses, we are naturally led to contrast its situation then, with its present size, and to admire that enterprising spirit which has in these latter times been the distinguishing characteristic of its inhabitants, and the cause of its present extent and prosperity.

Before the year 1756 the Flesh-market stood upon the north side of the Trongate, betwixt the street of the Candleriggs and Glassford-street. At this period they were removed, and new buildings erected in King-street. The Guardhouse, which stood upon the street, which it much incommoded, was, about the same time taken down, and rebuilt at the foot of the Candleriggs, in the situation occupied by the Flesh market. This edifice has also

been

been taken down, and removed to the west side of the same street in 1789. At the period when these changes took place, St. Andrew's church was built, and Virginia-street opened.

The city still increasing in population, in 1762-3, Jamaica-street, Queen-street, formerly called the Cow-lone *, and Havannah-street were laid out and begun to be built.

Previous to the year 1775, and indeed from the beginning of the century, the grounds to the north of the Trongate, called the Ramshorn crofts†, were let out by the patrons of Hutcheson's hospital for sale gardens. In this situation they continued to the year 1775, when the magistrates purchased them for the purpose of building upon. They drew a regular plan to the line of streets in

P 2   which

---

* These lands, now called Bell's and Blythswood's parks, were formerly a large common belonging to the city, where the cows of the inhabitants pastured, under the care of the Town's herd. They were taken in the morning, out by the West-port, milked at Cowcaddens in the evening, and hence Cowcaddens and Cow-lone.

† The Ramshorn grounds, upon which the greatest part of the New Town stands, were bounded on the north by the Rottenrow road; on the south by the Trongate; on the east by the garden wall of the Deanside brae; and on the west by that road called the Cow-lone now Queen street. It was upon these lands, that Douglas earl of Angus encamped with an army of 12000 men, when in rebellion against John duke of Albany, regent of Scotland, in the minority of James V. From this circumstance they were likewise called Pavilion croft, or the croft of the Pavilions.

which every purchaser was bound to keep. The lots they sold at that period, at near the purchase money. Many years, however, elapsed before any considerable number of houses were erected. George's square was begun to be built in the year 1782, and till the year 1786, one house, built for two families, stood alone in the field. Shortly thereafter, the building of this square and these streets called the New Town were carried on with alacrity. The inducement to build on this situation was much heightened by the opening from the Trongate, first, of Hutcheson-street ‡, and secondly, of Glassford-street ‖; which were direct communications

‡ At the end of this street, fronting the Trongate, formerly stood the old building of Hutcheson's hospital, extending a longst that street 73 feet. It would appear it was originally intended to have formed a court. Only two sides of which were finished, the south and the west. The entrance from the Trongate was by a gate decorated with rustics, a few steps above the level of the street. Above this gate was the large hall or academy where the children were educated. This building was ornamented with a spire 100 feet high, having a clock and dial. On the north front, facing the gardens (for the grounds upon which Hutcheson-street is erected were then in that situation) were two niches, in which were placed the statues of the founders, with this inscription,

Adspicis Hutchisonos fratres his nulla propago
Cum foret et numero vix caperentur opes
Hæc monumenta pii votum immortale decorant
Dulcia quæ miseris semper asyla forent
O bene testatos hæredis scripsit uterque
Infantes inopes invalidosque senes.

¶ At the foot of this street stood that house belonging to Mr. Campbell of Shawfield, which in the year 1725, was attacked

munications from the main street to the new buildings.

Since then, and within these twelvemonths bypast, that level track of ground to the westward of George's square, called the Meadowflat has also been laid out for building, by the magistrates and council, streets projected, and some of the houses at present erecting. These streets, and other buildings, and improvements within the royalty will be mentioned more particularly in another place, as well as the other streets projected by individuals, many of which are at present completed, particularly to the south of the river.

CHAP.

by a mob, and his furniture destroyed, as has been already mentioned. It was built within the line of the main street, betwixt and which there was an area fenced with a wall of hewn stone, decorated with busts, looking directly down the Stockwell; in coming up which street, from the beauty of the building and its accompaniments, a fine effect was produced upon the mind of a stranger. This house was acquired thereafter by William M'Dowal, Esq. of Castlesemple, and by him sold to Mr. Glassford of Dougalstone for seventeen hundred guineas. It was thereafter purchased by the last proprietor Mr. Horne, who demolished the structure, and opened a street, 60 feet in breadth, leading towards the north, and one of the finest in the city.

CHAP. III.

*Situation and Description of Glasgow—The Villages of
Tradestown, Hutcheson Town, Calton and Anderston, &c. in its vicinity.*

THIS GREAT COMMERCIAL CITY lies upon the
north bank of the river Clyde, in the county of Lanark, and in the latitude of 55 deg. 50 min. north;
longitude, 4 deg. 30 min. west from the meridian of
London*.

Before proceeding with a particular description,
it will not be improper to give some idea of the situation of the ground on which it stands.

The Clyde in this neighbourhood runs nearly in
a direction from east to west, through a level tract
of country, which extends towards the south for a
considerable distance from its banks.—To the
north of the river and parallel to its direction, at
about

---

* The city of Glasgow is distant 402 miles N. N. W. from
London, 101 miles from Carlisle, 44 W. of Edinburgh, and
24 miles N. W. of the county town.

A PLAN
of the
City of Glasgow
from a Survey in
1804

about the distance of a thousand yards, lies a ridge
of high ground. This is intersected near the eastern
quarter of the town by a rivulet, running from
north to south towards the Clyde, called the Molendinar, or, from the street which it crosses, the Gallowgate burn. Another stream, nearly of the same
size, and running in the same direction, issues from
the high ground, and bounds the royalty towards the
west. The banks of the Molendinar burn, where it
cuts the ridge above mentioned, are steep and precipitous, especially the bank on the east, which rises
considerably higher than the ground on the other
side, whereby there is a dell or glen formed, that
gradually loses itself, as you descend by the course of
the rivulet into the plain. Towards the other stream,
commonly called St. Enoch's burn, the high ground
gradually slopes on each side, thereby forming an
open passage, easy of ascent, from the city to the
country northwards. To the east and west of these
rivulets, that high ground, which we before remarked, lay parallel to the river, by degrees loses itself
in the plain country, nearly opposite to the village of
Camlachie on one hand, and Anderston on the
other.

The most ancient part of the town stands upon
the summit of the ridge, where it slopes to the Molendinar burn, though the modern, and now by far
the greatest part of the city, occupies the plain,
betwixt the bottom of that ridge and the Clyde,
extending in its greatest length from east to west.—
In this direction, lies the main street of Glasgow,
which

runs the whole length of the town; at particular
places, it acquires the different names of the Gallowgate, Trongate, and Argyle-street or Wester-
gate. This great street is again intersected at right
angles by a number of others, which run either
southward to the river, or in the opposite direction.

We shall, in the next place, attempt a description
of the town in a more particular manner, beginning
at its eastern extremity, the Gallowgate toll-bar.

GALLOWGATE-STREET.

From this point the street extends towards the
west, as far as the Cross, though not always in a
rectilinear direction *. After proceeding some way,
and leaving the barracks on the right, the first street
of any consequence that branches off on the other
side, is the main entry to the village of Calton, now
connected by a chain of buildings with the city.
Next, on the opposite side is,

CAMPBELL-

---

* Immediately after leaving the situation at the Toll-bar,
upon the left is Tureen-street, running south to the Calton,
and upon the north Sidney-street, connecting the Gallowgate,
with a large area intended to be built upon according to a regular plan. Nearer to the barracks upon the right hand is
Barrack-street, which connects the eastern termination of
Duke-street with the Gallowgate. Opposite to Barrack-street
is another small street, likewise branching from the main trunk,
called Claythorn-street, and farther on, on the same side is
Gibson-street.

CAMPBELL-STREET,

containing some good houses. Nearly opposite to Campbell-street is

KENT-STREET,

lately opened. Such of the houses as are built, yield to none in the city for the grandeur of their appearance. This street, and another called

SUFFOLK-STREET,

which cuts the former at right angles, are built upon the property of Mr. Struthers. Farther down, (for we are descending gradually to the Gallowgate burn,) and on the left hand is

CHARLOTTE-STREET,

containing many handsome and elegant houses, built within these last thirty years†. Proceeding westward, at a bend in the Gallowgate towards the right, we pass a bridge of one arch, thrown over the rivulet of the same name ‡.

From this situation, strangers cannot fail to be struck with the grandeur of the view towards the

Q ....west,

---

† About 50 years ago, the ground on which Charlotte-street stands was occupied as a sale garden, at the rent of 365 merks Scots per annum. Hence the street obtained the name of Merk-daily street, which, with many, it still retains.

‡ Immediately to the right of this bridge, and directly above the line of the Gallowgate burn, preparations are just now making for opening a street to the north.

west, caused by the appearance of an elegant spire, towering to a great height, and terminating in an imperial crown; while, immediately adjoining, appears the east side of the lofty prison, flanked with square turrets, and pyramidal roofs. After passing the bridge, a street or passage strikes off on the left, towards St. Andrew's square. Leaving this, and still proceeding in the original line of the Gallowgate, you arrive at the Cross, where is discernible all that hurry and bustle amongst the inhabitants, which is the characteristic of a great and industrious city.

From this point indeed, the prospect has an air of great magnificence. To the west, far as the eye can reach, appear the broad and elegant streets of the Trongate * and Argyle-street, adorned throughout with handsome houses, and for a certain length on both sides, supported by pillars of the Doric order, covering piazzas† for the shelter of the inhabitants who have occasion to be on the streets during rain. On the fore ground, and to the right is the prison or tolbooth, five stories high, and immediately adjoining the town house and exchange; a building, which from its elegance, as well as the beautiful

---

* From the Cross west to the Stockwell, the main street has the name of the Trongate.

† The areas of many of these piazzas have been lately filled up, by the shops having been brought forward in a line with the pillars. This is allowed upon the proprietors paying an quivalent to the public funds.

ful simplicity of its parts, is an honour to its founder. Opposite to this on the street, is erected an e-
legant equestrian statue of William the Third, which,
together with the spire of the Tron or Laigh church,
on the left or south of the Trongate, fill up the view,
scarcely to be paralleled by any street scene in Britain.

From the cross, and at right angles to the Trongate and Gallowgate, which though of different
names, are a continuation of the same street, strike
off to the north the High-street, and exactly opposite in a line, the Saltmarket. As the former of
these was originally the principal street in the city,
we shall first take a survey of it and its branches,
and then return to the latter.

HIGH-STREET.

For some distance from the Cross, this, like the
Trongate and Gallowgate has the houses built over
arcades, handsomely faced with hewn stone. These
end near to a lane called Bell's street, which runs at
right angles betwixt this street and another named
the Candleriggs on the west. After passing this
lane, the street which before stands upon a level,
now begins gradually to have an ascent, while the
general appearance of the houses are in a more an-
tique stile than those nearer the center of the town.
Here, on the right, stands the stately buildings of
the university, and on the opposite side is situated
a beautiful edifice, likewise the property of the college, with all the graces of the Grecian architecture.
Two smaller streets a little way above, go off to

Q 2   the

the right and left *, betwixt and the intersection of George's street, lately formed in a direction parallel to the Trongate or main street of Glasgow, and consequently cutting the High-street, which we are now describing, perpendicularly.

From this point northwards to the Bell of the Brae, the street becomes very steep and difficult of access, while the houses more and more demonstrate their antiquity, and the rudeness of the age in which they were erected.

Having gained the summit of the high ground, we are now in the center of the old city, and from which two streets of the greatest antiquity, strike off towards the east and west: The one called the Drygate†, running in an irregular direction from this point eastward, along the sloping, and at this place steep declivity, of the banks of the Molendinar burn. This street, before the building of the bridge over the Clyde by bishop Rae, in the 14th century, was the principal one in Glasgow, and by which the inhabitants drove their cattle to the common, to the eastward of the town, and brought in the greatest

part

---

* That to the right is named Havannah-street, and the other to the left Bun's wynd, formerly Grey-friar's wynd, from a monastery of that order that formerly stood at its western extremity.

† At the head of this street stands one of the wings of the projected palace of the Duke of Montrose, which was never completed. The nobleman who was its founder, became lord of regality after the death of the last Scotch Duke of Lennox, when ambassador to the court of Denmark from Charles II.

part of their necessary articles from the country.

In the upper part of this street, and in a lane called the Limmerfield, is the house where the unfortunate Henry Darnley lodged, confined by a dangerous illness, suspected to arise from poison, administered at the instigation of Bothwell. Here the unhappy prince received a visit from Mary Stewart, and took the fatal resolution of removing to Edinburgh. This sudden return of her affection, her blandishments to inveigle him from his father and friends, and his consequential murder, are circumstances unfavourable to the memory of that princess.

Few things can furnish a stronger contrast to each other, than the appearance which this street now exhibits, when compared with the more modern part of the town. It is exceedingly steep, and the houses dark and gloomy, many of the principal ones seemingly more adapted for defence, than convenience, which indeed, in the age when they were built, was thought to be the most essential requisite. Here, on the west side, stood the mint, where Robert III. struck several coins, many whereof are still in existence *. Nearly adjacent to this, and on the same side, stands a house formerly belonging to the prebend of Cambuslang, who, like the rest of his brethren before the Reformation, lived in the
town

---

* On one side of these coins appears the king's crest crowned, and this inscription, *Robertus Dei Gratia Scotorum*, on the other, *Dominus Protector*, and in an inner circle *Villa de Glasgow*.

town, while their several cures in the country were served by vicars.

When that event took place, the clergy were dispersed, and their houses and possessions given to the noblemen in favour at court; accordingly, this fell into the hands of the earl of Glencairn, by whom it was assigned or sold to the community. It thereafter was used as a public correction-house, till the erection of Bridewell in the adjacent street, and is now occupied as weavers' shops and dwelling houses.

The other street which we before hinted at, as proceeding in an opposite direction from the High-street, is called the Rottenrow, seemingly equal in antiquity with the Drygate. This runs exactly west, upon the summit of that ridge of high ground formerly described; and from its situation, is certainly the most healthy and well-aired in Glasgow. Two others branch out from this towards the north, not yet finished, called *Taylor* † and *Weaver* street.

Continuing

---

† In the month of January, 1795, as some workmen were levelling the ground in the south end of this street, where an old ruinous house formerly stood, they dug up an earthen pot containing nearly a Scotch pint, full of gold coins of different sizes. The eagerness of the by-standers, however, prevented their number from being exactly determined, though it is supposed they did not amount to fewer than 8 or 900.—The greatest part being Scotch, and the remainder English and foreign coins.

Of the Scotch coins were those of James III. & IV. known by

Continuing to go north upon the High-street, on the one hand we find the Alms-house and Trades' hall, an old building, adorned with a small turret, containing a passing bell, which, during the day is almost continually reminding those within its melancholy tinkle, of the uncertainty of human existence*.

Beyond this at a short distance, and upon a triangular piece of ground, presenting its vertex to the center of the street, formerly stood the bishop's palace,

by the name of the Unicorn and its half; the legend *Jacobus Dei Gratia Rex Scoto.* and, on the reverse, *Surgat Deus & Dissipent. Inimici Ej.;* also, the Ryder of James IV. with his title, and, on the reverse, *Saluum Fac. Populum. Tuum. Dne.*—Coins of James V. the legend, *Jacobus 5 Dei Gra. Rex Scotorum,* and, on the reverse, *Crucis Arma Sequamur.*—Also, of queen Mary, the legend, *Maria Dei Gratia Regina Scotorum,* and, on the reverse, *Crucis Arma Sequamur,* and on some, *Diligite Justiciam,* 1553. These were the only varieties which appeared of the Scottish coins.

The English coins consisted mostly of the pieces called Angels, of Henry VI. the coinage of his 49th year; the legend, on the reverse, *Per Cruc. Tua. Salve nor Xre. Red.:* one of Henry VIII. the legend, *Rutilans Rosa sine Spina,* and, on the reverse, *Dei Gra. Rex Angl. & Fra.*

Amongst those of foreign origin, were distinguished some of the French, Spanish, Portuguese, German, Imperial, and Popish coins.

As none of these pieces are later than the days of Mary, queen of Scotland, it is not improbable that they had been deposited during the troubles in her reign.

* Upon the approach of every burial which passes to the High Church yard, the bell is rung, and the attendants on the funeral, or relations of the deceased give what they please into the poor's box, affixed in a window near the street.

'palace, surrounded by a high wall, fortified with a bastion at one corner, and a tower at another. This castle was besieged in 1544 by the regent Arran, in the civil disputes at that time, who took it and hanged eighteen of the garrison placed there by Lennox, a favourer of the Reformation. The great tower of this palace was built by bishop Cameron in 1426, and augmented by bishop Beaton in the beginning of the 16th century. This last prelate also built another tower, and inclosed the whole with the wall and bastions already mentioned. The building having gone to ruin, the crown granted the property of its scite to the community of Glasgow, for the purpose of erecting the *Infirmary*, which now ornaments that situation where this ancient edifice stood. To the left of the High-street, and nearly opposite the scite of the castle, stand the ruins of an hospital, called St. Nicholas' hospital, formerly endowed for the maintenance of twelve poor men; but the funds through some mismanagement are now almost entirely lost.

Immediately to the east, and upon the banks of the Molendinar burn, stands the venerable cathedral, with its lofty spires, which for so many ages has defied the mouldering teeth of time. Of this church, we will fall to speak at more length, when treating of the public buildings. In the mean time, being now arrived at the extremity of the High-street northward*, we return to our

first

---

* Called the Stable-green port.

first situation at the Cross, where that street, the Saltmarket opposite, and the Gallowgate and Trongate meet at right angles.

SALTMARKET.

The Saltmarket runs almost upon a level, towards the south, and like the other streets we have already mentioned as branching from the Cross, had its houses for a considerable way supported by arcades, most of which, as in the Trongate, are now built up. About the same distance down this street, as Bell's street is from the corner at the opening of the High-street, a lane† in like manner strikes of towards the west, and thereby joins King's street. Nearly opposite to this, St. Andrew's street ‡ goes off towards the east, leading to St. Andrew's square and church; a set of elegant modern buildings, scarcely to be equalled any where in the city.

Farther down the Saltmarket the Bridgegate branches off towards the right; a very ancient street, originally unconnected with the old part of the town, as the intermediate buildings and streets were not at its foundation erected. The ground whereon it stands was formerly feued from a lady Lochow, in the year 1350. She was daughter of Robert duke of Albany, and

R grandmother

---

† Called Prince's street.

‡ An act of parliament was obtained in the year 1771 for opening this street.—*Gibson.*

grandmother to the first earl of Argyle. From its vicinity to the Clyde, it was in old times inhabited principally by fishermen, and thence called Fishersgate, but after the erection of the bridge, from being a direct passage thither to the town, the name of the street was changed into that of the Bridgegate.

The house in the Saltmarket, opposite to the entry into this street, called Silvercraig's land, is noted for being the residence of Cromwell for one winter after the battle of Dunbar‡. At the foot, or south end of the Saltmarket, we meet with the Gallowgate or Molendinar burn, which after running a little farther to the west, enters the Clyde at the city shambles. Betwixt the bridge over this rivulet and the Clyde, lies the Green, an extensive and beautiful lawn, of the greatest importance to the health and convenience of the inhabitants. Having traced the Saltmarket downward, we return to the Cross, and going westward along the main street of the Trongate, describe shortly the different branches that spring from it on each side.

TRONGATE.

After leaving that station, and passing on the right the tolbooth, the elegant buildings of the town

---

‡ As great part of his army consisted of artizans, many of whom settled here, Glasgow was indebted to them for several improvements they introduced.

PERSPECTIVE VIEW of the TRONGATE of GLASGOW, from the CROSS.

Engraved for A Macgoun's Guide to Glasgow.

and exchange, the equestrian *statue of William* III.*
and on the left, the spire † of the Tron or Laigh
church, projecting its diameter into the street, and
nearly opposite to which

NELSON-STREET

has been opened within these four years, we arrive
at the point of intersection of the Candleriggs-street
on the right or north, and of King's street immediately opposite, which in like manner with the streets
above described, make right angles with the line of
the Trongate.

CANDLERIGGS.

In this street to the left as you go north, are situated the green market and guard house, and still
farther on the right, Bell's street, which we mentioned before enters this street. Nearly opposite,
another opened within these few years, called Wilson-street, composed of elegant buildings, runs from
this westward in a line parallel to the main street of
the Trongate. Proceeding onwards, we are at
length stopped by the Ramshorn or North West
church, built exactly at the termination of the Candleriggs.

R 2

* This statue was given to the city in the year 1734 by James
M'Crae, esq; governor of Madras in the East Indies, and erected upon a neat ashler pedestal, encompassed with an iron rail,
in the year 1738.

† At the bottom of the steeple there was formerly a tron or
place for weighing goods upon the market days, hence the
name of the street where it is situated.

dleriggs. When viewed from the Trongate, this
church and spire, from their relative situation to the
other objects around, has a very fine appearance.
When thus at the northward extremity of the Candleriggs we find two other streets strike off to the
right and left: That to the right * is narrow, indifferently built, and connects itself with the High-
street by the Grammar School wynd, and Shuttle-
street opposite to the university. In passing along
Canon-street, two others, called

NORTH AND SOUTH ALBION STREETS,

have been lately opened, communicating with Bell's
street and George's street. The street again to
the left exhibits a strong contrast to the other. It
runs straight for a great way west, parallel to the
main street of the Trongate, and at its farthest extremity is terminated by a very handsome building,
with an open court and wings, adorned with all the
ornaments that the Grecian architecture can bestow.
This street, which is called Ingram-street, is of modern date, and as far as it is built, of polished stone.

Returning to the Trongate, at the south end of
the Candleriggs, we find

KING'S STREET

exactly opposite.—This also runs perfectly straight
like the others, and like them very well built. On
the

---

* The name of this street is Canon-street, so called from
the scite of a seminary of canons regular, that formerly stood
immediately to the north.

Engraved for Denholm's HISTORY of Glasgow.

THE TRADES HALL, GLASGOW.

the east side a little way down, Prince's street, a narrow lane, strikes off to the Saltmarket. Proceeding downwards, (for the street has a gentle declivity,) we find on the right the Wynd church, the mutton and fish markets, and on the left the flesh market, the most *elegant* of their kind in Britain *. After passing a little farther, we fall in with the Bridgegate, already described.

Leaving the point in the Trongate where the Candleriggs and the street last mentioned strike off, and going still westward, we find on the north a new street called in honour of the duke of Brunswick, which intersects Wilson-street already mentioned. Shortly after we meet with another on the same side, branching from the Trongate, called

HUTCHESON-STREET,

which in like manner cuts Wilson and Ingram streets at right angles. At the northern termination of this street is at present erecting Hutcheson's Hospital, adorned with a fine spire. After passing a short way farther to the west, the Stockwell and Great Glassford-street branch from the Trongate, the former on the left, and the latter on the right, handsomely built with modern houses. The

STOCKWELL

is terminated on the south by the old bridge, which connects it with the village of Gorbals.—At the

bridge

* Pennant.

bridge strikes off to the west Clyde-street, so called
from its vicinity to the river, and to which it is parallel. In this street, which connects itself with the
south end of Jamaica-street and the Bromielaw, are
situated the Town's Hospital and glass works *.

GREAT GLASSFORD-STREET

which also cuts Wilson and Ingram streets, has for
its termination the Star Inn, an elegant building.
Here also stands the *Trades' Hall*, afterwards to be
described.

The main street, which from the Cross to the intersection of the Stockwell and Great Glassford
street has the name of the Trongate, after passing
these two last mentioned streets assumes the appellation of

ARGYLE-STREET.

The first branching to the north from this is

VIRGINIA-STREET,

adorned with fine buildings, and by one of which it
is terminated. To this street, and near its northern
extremity, Wilson-street, which we formerly took
notice of as proceeding from the Candlerigge, unite
and terminates. Proceeding on Argyle-street, we
meet with another termed

MILLER

---

* It has been proposed to carry this street quite through to
the Green, from the foot of the Stockwell, by removing the
shambles and some old houses.

VIEW of the TRADES HALL and ADJOINING BUILDINGS

Engraved for a Merchant's Guide to Glasgow.

MILLER'S STREET,

which connects and cuts at right angles Ingram-street.—The houses here as in Virginia and Charlotte streets, as well as in Queen-street, St. Enoch's square, and Buchanan-street after mentioned, are occupied by one family from top to bottom as in London; they are besides elegant in the extreme, and flanked with wings, which add considerably to their light and villa-like appearance; unfortunately, however, it is rather narrow.—Nearly opposite to this

DUNLOP-STREET

strikes off towards the left, where is situated the Old Theatre. Afterwards, a little way farther,

QUEEN'S STREET

branches from Argyle-street in a straight line northwards.—This is also of modern date, handsomely built, broad and airy. Near its northern extremity, where it joins George's square, and on the west side is situated that house which we before mentioned as the western termination of Ingram-street. Immediately adjacent, is erecting the New Theatre, the largest, except the London Theatres, in Britain. A little higher up there is also an area to be built upon, called

CAMPERDOWN PLACE,

at the north-western extremity of George's square.

INGRAM-STREET,

which from the above mentioned point, runs east to
the

the Candleriggs, is adorned with beautiful buildings, amongst others the *New Assembly Rooms*, the *Star Inn*, and *Hutchisons Hospital*, which fronts or looks down the street of that name.—Beyond, lies

GEORGE's SQUARE,

having its west boundary on a line with Queen-street. The buildings here are very elegant, particularly those upon the north; which, from the beauty of the design, and taste displayed in the execution, surpass by far any other either in this city or in Scotland. From George's square branch northward

HANOVER AND FREDERIC STREETS,

which rise gradually from the plain up the high ground formerly mentioned. At the north-east corner of this square terminates the finest street in the new town, called

GEORGE'S STREET,

which from thence runs due east, along the side of the hill parallel to the Trongate. And at the south-east corner of George's square,

COCHRAN-STREET,

in which are some fine houses, runs east to Montrose-street. On the north side of George's street is situated the city Grammar School, and after passing two others, viz.

JOHN's STREET,

in which is the *Hall of Anderson's Institution*, and
MONTROSE-

Engraved for I.Denholms Guide to Glasgow

VIEW of SAINT ENOCK'S CHURCH, the SURGEONS HALL, and SQUARE.

MONTROSE-STREET,

it cuts the High-street a little above the University. Here it takes the name of

DUKE-STREET,

and from thence it proceeds in the same direct line, gradually sloping towards the banks of the Molendinar burn, over which there is cast a bridge, and ends not far from the foot of the Drygate.

Returning to the foot of Queen-street, where it branches from the main stem or Argyle-street, and tracing farther west, we meet with

MAXWELL-STREET

on the left; then on the same side,

ST. ENOCH'S SQUARE,

composed of very fine houses, inhabited by their respective families from top to bottom, and having on the south side the church and spire of that name, and on the east the Surgeons' Hall.

Opposite to St. Enoch's square,

BUCHANAN-STREET

goes off from the main stem northwards, to the road leading from George's square to Port-Dundas. The houses in this street are built in so elegant a manner, as cannot fail to arrest the attention of every person of taste.

Opposite to one of the latest built of these edifices, the property of Mr. Gordon, is

S   GORDON-

GORDON-STREET,

running directly west. The houses which compose this street are as yet unfinished. Farther west, upon the line of Argyle-street, and to the left, is

JAMAICA-STREET,

containing some fine houses. Through this street is the principal road to the new bridge, Broomielaw, Paisley, Greenock, &c. On the right side is a building formerly used as a Circus; it is now, however, devoted to the solemn rites of religious worship, under the name of the *Tabernacle.* At the Broomielaw, which lies at the foot of this street, there are a considerable number of buildings, in the same line with Clyde-street, which, from their situation at the quay of a navigable river, where a great number of vessels are daily loading and unloading, are very pleasantly and healthfully situated. At the head of Jamaica-street, and running north from Argyle-street, a new street or line of houses is laid out and erecting under the name of

UNION PLACE,

or Union-street. The buildings that are finished are lofty and elegant, with sunk stories and pallisades, similar to those in the new town of Edinburgh. This street is intended to meet Gordon-street, already mentioned as branching from Buchanan-street.

To the west of Jamaica-street and Union place some other streets of lesser note branch out to the north and south, as

ALSTON-

ALSTON-STREET.

Farther on, and on the left,

MADEIRA AND YORK STREETS,

In this last is the Riding School.

Having thus taken a view, which by some, perhaps, may be thought too minute, of the position of the principal streets with respect to each other, and which may be farther elucidated by the map annexed, we shall, in the next place, proceed to the description of the different suburbs around, and which indeed compose one continued town with the royalty. Before doing this, however, it may not be improper to notice, at more length than we have done before, one of the most delightful appendages to Glasgow:

THE GREEN,

which lies to the south of the city, and forms a continuation of the plain upon which it is built. This lawn extends upwards of three quarters of a mile upon the north bank of the Clyde, though from thence, if its breadth be taken at the most advantageous part, it certainly does not measure more than a quarter of that distance.—The whole of this extent is completely inclosed and surrounded with trees, where, during the summer, the company of the city take the air, or enjoy, while in the Green, the beautiful prospect that presents itself.

The view from this situation is indeed fine, almost on whatever hand. Towards the south the river presents itself in the foreground; beyond this,

follow

follow in long succession fertile fields, completely
inclosed and studded here and there with elegant
villas, trees and humble cottages, while behind,
appears the hill of Langside, distinguished by a
tuft of firs, where the unfortunate Mary Stewart
lost the glory of the day, by the victorious arms of
Murray. Farther still, appear the hills of Cathkin,
and in the extreme distance the towering summit
of Eaglesham closes the view.

More to the right another scene presents itself.
—The broad bosom of the Clyde detains the eye,
while lingering slow and still, it exhibits in inverted
order the numerous images by which its banks
are surrounded. The bridges which cross the river, the continual throng passing and repassing a-
longst them, and the numerous spires of the city,
tinted with a deeper azure the more remote, aided
by the lively objects on the foreground, conspire
to render this a most delightful scene.

To the purposes of pleasure, the Green also adds
those of convenience and utility; here is situated
a public washing-house † for the clothes of the citizens, where, upon paying a small trifle, they have
the use of every requisite utensil, as well as the
benefit of water and of bleaching their linen.—In the
Green also, the regimental corps that reside in the
city

† The washing house pays to the city betwixt L. 300 and
L. 400 sterling of rent. This sum is entirely made up from
the small moieties paid by each inhabitant, for the use of the
house and green, in washing and bleaching their linens.

city exercise; and here a great many cattle graze ‡ for the use of the inhabitants.

In the upper part of the Green, and immediately upon the banks of the Clyde, issues out a spring, called Arns well*, from whence a great number, from the particular excellence of the water, carry it daily into the city. Near to this place, there is also lately erected by the Humane Society, a small, but neat building, for the accommodation and recovery of such as are apparently drowned; accidents of which kind too frequently happen in this neighbourhood, from the daring spirit of the youth that bathe in the Clyde, which here has a marshy and unsafe channel for the free exercise of that amusement †.

Glasgow, like London, is surrounded, as has been just now mentioned, by several villages, which, from the

‡ The revenue arising from the pasturage of the cows fluctuates according to their number; the proprietor of each paying 40s. for five months' grazing.

* So named from a number of arn or alder trees growing in its vicinity.

† This lawn, just now mentioned, was formerly called the 'new Green, to distinguish it from another space of ground which lay upon the south-west side of the city, betwixt the bridges, called, the old Green. This Green was formerly surrounded by trees no less than 140 in number. In it is the rope-work, and at its western extremity the glass-house, with a cone 100 feet high. It is the third erection upon the scite of the oldest bottle-house in Scotland. The first was built here about the year 1730.

the increased size of the town, are become a part of itself. The most ancient of these is the

GORBALS,

situated immediately at the south end of the old bridge, which separates it from the city. The ground whereon this village is erected, was originally acquired by George Elphinston, merchant in Glasgow, from archbishop Porterfield, in the year 1571, though it appears, that for a long period prior to this, there had existed several buildings on the scite of the present village; particularly, here stood a house for the reception of lepers, founded as early as the year 1350, by a lady of the name of Campbell *; the same that feued out the ground upon which the Bridgegate-street now stands.—About the middle of the Gorbals, and on the east side of the street, stands an old building, called the chapel, dedicated to St. Ninian. From the initials of S. G. E. being found inscribed upon several parts of the wall, it would appear, that this building was erected by Sir George Elphinston, who also got the Gorbals erected into a burgh of barony and regality. His house stands at a little distance with projecting turrets. The lower part of this house is occupied as the parish school, the two upper stories as a prison.

A large common belonged to this suburb, bounded

* Lady Lochow.

ed on the north by Clyde, on the east by the Blind burn, and so on to the foot of Langside-hill, its southern boundary. Upon the west, its limits were the Kinninghouse burn. These lands were free of sucken to any mill, but as they were not possessed of any waterfall, a windmill was built for grinding the corn of the tenants. It is, however, now no longer in existence.

These lands and village afterwards came into the possession of Sir Robert Douglas of Blackerstone. He built the great tower on the north side of the chapel, where his arms are to be seen. The property was thereafter sold, some time previous to the Restoration, when it was purchased by the city of Glasgow, the Trades' House, and the Patrons of Hutcheson's Hospital, who joined their funds together for that purpose.

From that period to the year 1790, the lordship and the lands continued under one common management. The city gave out of the council a Baillie of the merchant rank for one year, and for the next year from the trades' rank, out of the same body, a tradesman to succeed him. The Baillie appointed by the city is joined by an inhabitant of the Gorbals as his substitute, and these two choose another townsman as a deputy; these three elect four men as assessors, called Birleymen: their use and powers are similar to that of the members of the Dean of Guild court. In the year 1790, the corporate bodies who had so long presided over this lordship as a mixed body, came to an agreement to divide it into lots, in conformity to the sums advanced. The village

village as one, and the grounds were divided into four parts. The provost drew for the whole. The jurisdiction over the village, came to the city. St. Ninian's croft on the east, was drawn for Hutcheson's Hospital, the lands on the west, to a certain measured line, fell to the Trades' House, and the city received that lot farthest west, bounded by the Kinninghouse burn.

The lands of Gorbals formerly belonged to the parish of Govan. They were disjoined in 1771, and erected into a separate parochial district, of which the magistrates of Glasgow are patrons.

Adjoining immediately to the village, and on the east, lies

HUTCHESON TOWN,

upon a level tract of ground *, belonging to the hospital of that name, from which it was feued. This village was begun in the year 1794, upon a regular plan, and laid out into a number of right lined streets; some of these are already completed with houses from two to three or four stories in height, well built and covered with slate. Betwixt Hutcheson Town and that part of the Green of Glasgow, opposite the foot of the Saltmarket, a bridge was begun to be erected over the Clyde in that year, and nearly finished, when a great flood, as we have mentioned in the historical department, completely

* Formerly called St. Ninian's croft,

pletely ruined the design by overturning the fabric; since then, no farther attempts have been made to rebuild it with stone. It is intended, however, immediately to erect a bridge of cast iron, 10 feet broad within the railing, for foot passengers, and nearly in the same situation, from a most ingenious design, drawn by Mr. P. Nicholson, architect.

On the same side of the river, and betwixt the village of Gorbals and the south end of the new bridge, a space of ground has been feued for building upon, and laid out in streets. It is called

LAURIESTON,

from the name of the gentleman by whom it was feued. One of the streets, and part of another are building. The first of these, called

CARLTON PLACE,

is composed of houses of the first rank, in point of architectural beauty. This street lies exactly parallel to the river, upon a terrace raised to such a height, that no flood can completely inundate it. The second,

PORTLAND-STREET,

cuts the former at right angles, and, at an equal distance, betwixt the eastern and western limits of Carlton place, running towards the south.

Farther down the banks of the river, and upon the same side, is

TRADESTOWN.

The scite of this village was feued in the year 1790,

T   from

encouragement, and the introduction of manufac-
from the Trades' House and Incorporations of Glasgow.

The principal streets extend westward from the
bridge, and parallel with the river. Several of these
are already built in a handsome style *, with small
courts or areas behind; and when completed, we
have no scruple in saying, that it certainly will be
the finest village in Scotland, whether we regard
the position of its streets, its buildings, or the very
healthful and pleasant situation on which it stands.

The villages next in order, are

ANDERSTON, FINNIESTON, &c.

—These lie about a mile and a half west from the
center of the city, and on the same side of the
Clyde, and although they are of older date than the
two former villages, and not built in such a regular
manner, yet they contain several very handsome and
well finished houses. Anderston was so named
from the proprietor of the ground on which it was
built, Anderson of Stobcross; who, as early as the
year 1725, formed the plan of erecting a village.
The estate of Stobcross was sold in the year 1735,
and purchased by John Orr, Esq. of Barrowfield,
who found this projected village in a state of infancy, consisting of a few thatched houses. By proper
encouragement,

* The finest of these streets faces the Clyde, betwixt and
which is a beautiful sloping lawn. It is named Clyde Buildings.

tures, it quickly rose. to be a large and populous place. About the year 1769, the inhabitants built their first church, lying on the north side of the main street, the congregation of which are in communion with the relief. Since then, two others have been erected; one as a chapel of ease of the Barony parish, the other belongs to the Antiburghers. In the year 1793 or thereabout, was erected by subscription, the flesh market and shambles.

Finnieston lies to the west, in it is situated a large manufactory of chrystal glass, called the Verreville chrystal work.

Betwixt Anderston and Glasgow lie the villages of *Grahamston* and *Brownfield* *, now connected with the city.—On the north, the ground is mostly occupied by gardens, running in a direction perpendicular to the river, alongst the banks of which, in this neighbourhood, are situated many elegant and agreeable villas, the property of the manufacturer or opulent merchant.

To the south-east of the royalty lies the old village of

CALTON,

at the beginning of the last century called Blackfauld, from the ground upon which it is built, having been formerly occupied as a fold for the cattle which

T 2   pastured

---

* The ground upon which Brownfield is erected, was part of the Broomielaw croft, consisting of no more than 10 acres. It was feued off in 1791, at a ground-annual, amounting to upwards of L.300 sterling.

pastured upon the Gallowmoor and Boroughroods of the city adjacent. About that period it was laid out in garden grounds, and is described as bounded on the east, by a place still known by the name of the Witch-lone; on the west, by St. Mungo's lane, or Burnt-barns. On the north, by the high road leading to Edinburgh; and on the south by the new Green of Glasgow. This property was purchased in 1705 by Walkinshaw of Barrowfield, from the community of Glasgow. He first projected the village. Its progress for 30 years was, however, very slow†. At the termination of that period, it, with the estate of Barrowfield, was purchased by John Orr, Esq. under whom it appears to have increased in size and population with considerable rapidity.

It was early in the century erected into a burgh of barony, having a prison and a baron baillie. The prison is, however, no longer occupied as such, though the office of baron baillie still continues.

This

†This may be proved from the following facts. In 1706 there were only three feuers; in 1711, one; in 1714, one; in 1715, two; in 1722, ten; 1723, one; in 1724, one. About this date, the estate became the property of the city of Glasgow, and so continued till 1731, when it was acquired by Mr. Orr. In that year he feued off one lot; in 1732, ten lots; 1747, one; 1748, three; 1749, fifteen; 1750, three; 1752, one; 1755, five; 1759, one. The entry of the old feuers, was for the fall of 36 ells, L. 1 : 3 : 4, and five shillings Scots of yearly feu duty, or for 4 falls in a rood, L. 66 : 13 : 4, of entry money, and ten pounds Scots of annual feu duty; and in the same proportion, L. 266 : 13 : 4, Scots, per acre; and forty pounds Scots of annual feu duty; or L. 22 : 4 : 5, sterling as entry, and L. 3 : 6 : 8, sterling, of feu duty.

This village contains a great number of streets, neatly built of brick, and is principally inhabited by artizans of different denominations. In it is a large chapel, depending upon the Barony parish, built in 1792, by a subscription of the feuers, and a meeting-house for that sect called the Cameronians.

Betwixt the Calton and the Clyde, in a southeast direction, lies the village of

BRIDGETOWN,

nearly half a mile in length; so called, from its vicinity to the bridge over the river, leading to the brgh of Rutherglen.

To the east of the city, and on the great road leading to Edinburgh, Hamilton, &c. lies

CAMLACHIE,

inhabited mostly by coaliers, employed in the mines in the neighbourhood.

To the north of the town lies the *Cowcaddens, Parkhouse,* and the thriving and beautiful village of

PORT-DUNDAS,

at the extremity of the Canal. Here the houses are well built, being mostly three and four stories high, and from their elevated situation, enjoy a most delightful prospect of the country around.

CHAP,

C H A P. VI.

OF THE PUBLIC BUILDINGS.

The Cathedral, containing the Inner High Church, the Outer Church, Choir, &c.—The College Church—The Tron or Laigh Church—The Wynd Church—The North West, or Ramshorn Church—St. Andrew's Church—St. Enoch's Church—The English Chapel—Buildings of the University—The Town House and Assembly Rooms—The Tontine Coffee Room and Hotel—The Tolbooth, or Prison—The Merchants' Hall—The Royal Infirmary—Trades' Hall—The New Assembly and Concert Rooms—Hutcheson's Hospital—The Grammar School—The Surgeons' Hall—The Theatre—The Barracks, &c.

AMONGST the Public Buildings, that which deservedly takes the lead, is the

CATHEDRAL, or HIGH CHURCH.

This edifice, the most *complete* specimen of Gothic architecture now in the kingdom, was founded in the year 1123, by John Achaius, bishop of Glasgow, during the reign of David the I. in whose presence it

was

was consecrated, in the year 1136. In the time of Joceline, who continued to carry on the building, it appears to have been dedicated, as we are informed from an inscription * upon a stone, immediately above the door of the choir, in the year 1197, though at that time, the building was not far advanced.—Indeed it was a work of such magnitude, that the wealth of the see of Glasgow, was alone unable to accomplish it, they had therefore recourse to a general contribution throughout Scotland †, which was levied and applied to this purpose.

DESCRIPTION.

* *Dedicata fuit hæc Ecclesia Glasguensis, anno Domini millesimo centesimo nonogesimo septimo pridie, Calendas Junii.*

† This we learn from the 48th canon of the provincial councils of the church of Scotland, held at Perth in 1243 and 1269, of the following tenor: " Moreover, we strictly enact, " that the business of the building of the church of Glasgow, " be, upon all Lord's days and festivals, faithfully and dili- " gently explained in all churches, after saying of the mass, " from the beginning of Lent to the 8th day after Easter, and " that the indulgencies granted to those assisting at the build- " ing, which we have ordered to be written in every church, " may be distinctly explained in the vulgar language to the " parishioners; and that their alms, the effects of persons dy- " ing intestate, and pious legacies, may be faithfully collected " according to usage hitherto approved, and delivered to the " deacons of places, in the nearest chapter, without any de- " duction; and that during the said space of time, no sermon " for any other business be admitted in the parochial churches."

Although the name of the architect by whom the church was designed, does not now appear from any inscription about the

DESCRIPTION.

The cathedral stands at the upper or north end
of the High-street, upon the summit of that ridge,
formerly mentioned, and where it declines to the
Molendinar or Gallowgate burn. Its form, like
most other edifices of the kind, erected during the
reign of superstition in this country, is that of a
cross, whose greatest length lies east and west, and
consequently the transverse parts north and south.—
From the middle of the building springs the great
tower, which, for at least 30 feet above the roof, is
of a square form, and terminates in a battlement and
ballustrade.—Within this rises an octangular spire
to a great height, that is again ornamented by two
smaller ballustrades, at equal distances from each
other and the top of the spire—The octagon betwixt
these is beautified with several Gothic windows, and
four small pyramidal spires, which rise from within
the first battlement at the bottom of the octagon.
Upon the west end of the cathedral, rises another
and

the building, yet from one upon the Abbey church of Melros,
in 1146, we are informed with regard to this particular, in the
following uncouth rhyme:

"John Murdo some time callit was I,
"And born in Parysse certainly,
"And had in kepying all mason werk
"Of Sanctandroys, the hye kyrk
"Of Glasgu, Melros, and Paslay,
"Of Nyddysdayl, and of Galway.
"Pray to God, and Mari baith,
"And sweet St. John, keep this haly kyrk frae skaith.

square tower, till it is upon a level with the battlement of the great steeple. Here it terminates in a pyramidal leaden roof, adorned with a fane.—In this steeple is placed the clock, and a very large bell, no less than 12 feet 1 inch in circumference, which acts as the curfew to the inhabitants at the hour of ten each night; and from its grave and deeply sonorous note is excellently adapted to the purpose *.

U   From

---

* In the winter of 1789 this bell having been accidentally cracked by some persons who had got admission to the steeple, it was taken down and sent to London, where, in the following year it was refounded by *Mears*.—On the outside is the following inscription:

In the year of Grace,
1594,
MARCUS KNOX,
A Merchant in Glasgow,
Zealous for the interest of the Reformed Religion,
Caused me to be fabricated in Holland
For the use of his fellow-citizens of Glasgow,
And placed me with solemnity
In the Tower of their Cathedral.
My function
Was announced by the impress on my bosom,
Me audito venias Doctrinam Sanctam ut Discas †.
And
I was taught to proclaim the hours of unheeded time.
195 years had I sounded these awful warnings,
When I was broken
By the hands of inconsiderate and unskilful men.

In

---

† Come, that ye may learn holy doctrine.

From east to west the cathedral is externally divided on both sides into compartments, by butresses
of equal dimensions, between which are placed
Gothic windows of several different patterns. This
succession of windows is interrupted in the middle
of the building by the transverse section of the cross,
as well as by two very large windows on opposite
sides of the cathedral, each 40 feet high and 22 feet
wide at the base, which are directly under the great
tower in the center of the church. Above this first
range of windows the wall terminates in a battlement, within which springs the lowest roof, till it
meets the second or inner wall, which rises from
thence for a number of feet, and in like manner
with the fore or lower wall, is divided into compartments by small square projections, between each
of which are placed three narrow Gothic windows,
directly above each of those in the first storey; it then
terminates in the same manner with the lower wall,
caped with a leaden roof.

Owing to the declivity of the ground upon which
the cathedral is placed, a great difference of height
appears in favour of the east side, where the ground
is lowest, insomuch, that although on the west side

of

In the year 1790,
I was cast into the furnace,
Refounded at London,
And returned to my sacred vocation.
Reader,
Thou also shalt know a resurrection,
May it be unto eternal life.
Thomas Mears, fecit, London, 1790.

of the church, the bottom of the first range of win- dows are within a few feet of the ground, yet by be- ing carried horizontal, when the succession arrives at the other end they are very considerably elevated, and betwixt them and the ground a lower tier of small windows extend from the east of the cathe- dral to the transverse section, where they terminate. —These give light to what was formerly called the *Barony Church.*

From the south-west corner of the cathedral, the consistorial house projects, adorned on each side with abutments similar to those between the win- dows in the church. In this house the bishop's courts were formerly held for taking cognizance of ecclesiastical disputes, within a certain district called the Commissariot.

The principal entry into the cathedral was from the west, betwixt the consistorial house and the tower, which both project a considerable way from the gable of the church. This gate, which is very large and magnificent, is now shut up, and the com- mon entries are by the south, leading directly into the cathedral, which is divided into the *Outer Church, Choir, Inner High,* and *Barony Churches.*

The most westerly of these divisions is the

OUTER CHURCH,

formerly a part of the choir, and from which it is now separated by a stone partition. Here, two rows of Gothic columns of great height and thick- ness, run from west to east parallel to the walls, from which they are distant several feet. These

U 2

pillars

pillars are connected with each other by arches which spring from the capitals, and at the top unite in a common center.

Upon these arches are built the great inner walls formerly mentioned, which contract the breadth of the buiding in the upper part as much as their supports are distant from the outer wall. Between each pillar is placed through the whole range Gothic windows which illuminate the area of the church on the ground floor. Another tier of smaller windows placed along the upper wall enlighten the vacant space. This church has lately undergone a complete repair, by which it has been rendered much more comfortable, beautiful and convenient.

CHOIR.

Here the grandeur of the architecture manifests itself more strikingly than in the division we have last left. In this place the same range of pillars and windows are continued which were before described. The four most easterly of these columns support the great tower or steeple in the center of the church, and according to the weight they bear, are proportionally strong *. Between the two on each side are the large opposite windows †, which appear, when

---

* Each of these pillars is 30 feet in circumference, and 88 feet high.

† The front window, or that towards the south, is divided longitudinally by four pillars or bars, which in the middle are crossed

when viewed from the outside, in the center of the church. Betwixt these great pillars also, from the floor of the choir, a flight of steps on each side descend into the large burying vault lately occupied as the Barony church, and immediately above or in the partition wall at the east end, is a projecting gallery called the organ-loft, ornamented with rude carvings, representing the twelve apostles. Here is now erected, in a niche designed by Mr. Stark, the organ belonging to the Sacred Music Institution. From the floor of the choir a flight of steps lead up to the nave or main body of the cathedral, called the

INNER HIGH CHURCH.

In this place, as in the choir, two ranges of columns run parallel to the walls, and support in like manner, though by a double tier of arches, the upper row of windows.—The pillars here, are consequently not so lofty as in the last mentioned place, but are evidently of finer workmanship, and have their capitals richly adorned with flowers and fruit. From these capitals spring the arches, which, together with those arising from the corresponding columns

on

crossed thereby, forming 12 parallel windows.—Over these is a large circular one, 10 feet diameter, with two smaller windows to fill up the vacuity which a circle inscribed in a Gothic arch necessarily occasions. The window to the north is perfectly similar, except that it has five bars which run from top to bottom without being crossed.

on the walls, intersect each other at the key-stone, which is in every instance finely carved.

In this manner alongst the church, a gallery on both sides is formed with an arched roof, through which the light strikes from the windows into the body of the church. Above this range of columns is another succession which support the highest tier of windows that enlighten the upper part of the cathedral. From the top of the inner-walls, immediately above these windows, an arched roof springs to a vast height, finely ornamented, and on the east, or in the gable of the church, is a great window divided by parallel bars in the form of columns; immediately below which, and receding from the body of the church, is the space formerly occupied by the altar. The roof here is supported by five pillars, over which was a terrace-walk. On the north side of the altar is the vestry, the roof arched, and supported by one pillar in the center of the house: arched pillars from every angle terminate in the grand pillar, which is 19 feet high.

This church is now undergoing a complete repair from designs of Mr. Stark, architect, and indeed, is at the time of writing this description nearly finished. In making this alteration, every attention has been paid to convenience and utility, as well as elegance of design, and beauty of execution. The great arch which was formerly built up betwixt this church and the choir, has again been opened and glazed, at least for a considerable distance downwards; the remainder of the space is filled with another arch which incloses the organ, facing the

choir,

choir, as well as several beautiful ornaments, corresponding to the style of architecture in the building. New galleries have likewise been constructed, the fronts of which are ornamented with much taste. The pulpit, which formerly stood on the south-side of the church fronting the king's seat upon the north, has now been removed nearly to the east end, so as to look directly west; that part of the gallery opposite, sweeping in a curve, in the middle of which is the seat appointed for his Majesty, with proper emblematic devices. *

The area at the back of the pulpit, formerly the situation of the altar, as just now mentioned, has again been brought into view by the removal of the partition which filled the arches. These arches are now filled with glass richly ornamented, by its surface having been cut into a variety of fanciful figures. By these improvements the area of the church appears considerably enlarged from the prospect that is obtained of the roof of the choir and the altar place, the effect of the whole, of consequence, is thereby rendered much more grand, striking and beautiful.

THE

* The seat appropriated to royalty before the present reparations took place, projected about three feet from the main body of the loft. Upon the breast of the seat were the royal arms, on one side a thistle, and on the other a rose, both crowned, and cut in cedar. Pillars of the Corinthian order arose from the level of the loft, and supported the canopy, ornamented with carvings.

THE BARONY CHURCH[†],

which was formerly used as a burying vault, is situated immediately under the nave or Inner High church, to the east of the cross. The pillars here in like manner, with those in the other divisions of the cathedral, run parallel to the walls; they are exceedingly strong and massive, and from their position and the smallness of the windows, which are no more than narrow apertures, the area is rendered dark and gloomy, which, combined with the grave and solemn air, peculiar to the Gothic architecture, cannot fail to cast a temporary damp on the most volatile spirit.

The principal entries to this church, as we have before remarked, were situated betwixt the great pillars in the choir which support the middle tower: these are now shut up, and the passages lie in the north and south walls. To the east of this place, and immediately below the altar, is situated the place of interment for the heritors of the Barony parish, where is still shewn the monument of St. Mungo or Kentigern, as well as the reservoir, wherein the priests formerly kept their holy water [‡].

A still more dismal gloom here prevails:—the
walls

† It was first opened as a place of worship for the Barony parish 1575. It is supported by no less than 65 pillars, some of them 18 feet in circumference.

‡ In this place, in times of popery, were likewise kept the relics.

walls are black, and hung around with shreds of
escutcheons, these shadowy emblems of human
grandeur, while on every side, lie " skulls and coffins, epitaphs and worms †."

In the north cross of the cathedral was the chapter house, which had a communication with the nave
by a vaulted entry.　The south cross immediately
opposite has never been completed.　It is now used
as a burying-place for the clergy of the city, and is
reckoned a very fine piece of architecture, and superior to any other part of the building.　The roof
which is arched, is supported by a middle range of
pillars running north and south, having their capitals very highly ornamented with the figures of
fruit, flowers, &c.　Corresponding to these, are columns adjoining to the walls, which as they rise,
spring into semi-arches, and are every where met at
acute angles by their opposites, ornamented with
carvings at the crossing and closing of the lines.
The outside, like the main body of the cathedral is
also adorned with abutments and windows, over
which the figures of different animals are cut in
stone; and above the roof, which rises to no great

X height

† Around the cathedral is situated a cemetery called the High
Church Yard, inclosed with a wall, against which are built many sepulchral monuments.—For many ages, this spot has continued to be the principal burying ground of the city, and at
present upwards of 800 are interred upon an average annually.
—Of late, a new piece of ground, immediately adjoining the
church yard upon the north, has been taken in for the purpose
of making an addition to the burying ground.

height from the ground, is now a small garden, ornamented with shrubbery, the life-rent property of.
the magistrate to whose care the disposing of the
burying-ground in the church yard is committed.
This south cross is of a much more recent date than
the other parts of the cathedral, having been founded and built to its present height by bishop Blacadder
about the year 1500.

Though we have endeavoured in the above description to be as clear and explicit as possible, with
a view of conveying some idea of this venerable
structure, yet we are sensible, that after all, no
notion can be formed from that description any
thing adequate to what it merits, as it is one of
these objects, which, to be fully understood, must
be seen *.

From

* The cathedral is enlightened with 157 windows, including
the Barony church; is supported with 147 pillars, high and
low; and is in circumference round the walls, without following the line of measure of the aisles 325 ells, or 975 feet.
—Its length within the walls is 339 feet, and in width 72
feet.—The height of the choir from the floor to the roof is 90
feet, that of the nave or Inner High church five feet less; the
roof of the Barony church 18 feet. The altitude of the great
tower or middle steeple 223 feet from the floor of the choir,
which is 100 feet higher than the level of the Clyde at the
old bridge of Glasgow.

This stately edifice, as we have before mentioned in the
historical narrative, was preserved from destruction by the
townsmen at the Reformation, who, though zealous reformers, listened to the judicious remonstrance of their chief magistrate—" I am for pulling down the High church," said the
provost, " but not till we have first built a *new one*."—*Newte.*

From the elevated situation of the cathedral, its steeples command a most extensive prospect, well worthy of attention either to the stranger or citizen, from its almost unrivalled variety. To the east, the whole vale of Clyde, rich in towns, villages and seats, presents itself to view. In this direction, for a considerable way, long lawns, intermixt with trees and villas, gratify the eye. Beyond, appear the lofty towers of Bothwell, and princely seat of the Hamiltons; and farther on, as the banks begin to grow more steep, a long succession of splendid houses, towering from amongst the woods, tinged with azure, the farther they recede, attract the attention. Still more remote, appears the county town, crowned as it were with the lofty mountain of Tinto, which fills up the back ground of this beautiful scene.—If you turn to the west, the populous manufacturing town of Paisley, the castles of Mearns and Cruickstone, noted for the residence of the unfortunate Mary Stewart, and the noble fortress of Dumbarton, perched upon a rock, appear in full view; the hills of Renfrewshire and the snow-capt mountains of Argyll still farther off, terminate the prospect. To the north, the Campsie hills at the distance of ten, and in the opposite direction, those of Cathkin, distant five miles, close a beautiful landscape.

THE COLLEGE CHURCH.

Upon the scite of the present edifice, which stands on the east side of the High-street, was formerly

X 2   placed

placed the church of the Black friars, a fine Gothic pile, of great antiquity *. Unfortunately, this
building was destroyed by a severe storm of thunder and lightning in the year 1666; and in its
stead, the College church (so called from its vicinity
to the university) was erected at the expence of near
L. 2000 in the year 1699. For either the exterior
or internal appearance of this edifice we can say little; neither indeed could much be expected as to
the display of taste, in such places of worship as
were erected during an age, that considered elegance and ornament still in a worse light than simply superfluous. Upon the west front, which is
separated from the street by an open area, is erected a tower of no great height, in which hangs the
bell for assembling the congregation.

THE

* This church belonged to the college, by the gift of the
crown after the Reformation, and was disposed of by the
Faculty, under several reservations to the community. Mr.
M‘Ure, in his history, published in 1736, says, that it was first
built in the 7th century, and consequently was of an older date
by 500 years than the cathedral. The only reason, but which
to the present writer is inconclusive, Mr. M‘Ure gives in these
words, " For Mr. Miln, architect to King Charles I. perceiv-
" ed by the capitals upon the top of the columns of the steeple,
" which stood near the Black friars church, was after the Goth-
" ic order, which testified its antiquity."

At the razing of the foundations of this old church, there
were found a great many cells, appropriated to such of the religious, as, in times of popery, had secluded themselves from
the world.

THE TRON, OR LAIGH CHURCH.

The Tron or Laigh Church was first founded and endowed by the community in the year 1484. It was dedicated to the Virgin Mary and St. Michael. Its establishment consisted of a provost and eight or nine prebends. This church contained, before the Reformation, a number of altars and chaplainries, founded by wealthy citizens, and towards the support of which, annuities were paid out of several tenements within the city.

In the reign of Queen Mary, the church appears to have fallen almost to ruin, and it was not before the year 1592, that it was again repaired. Several aisles were thereafter added, and in this state it continued, with partial reparations, till the 8th day of February, 1793, when it was destroyed by fire, as mentioned in the historical narrative. The present building stands in the same situation, on the south side of the Trongate, (anciently called St. Enoch's Gate) betwixt the Saltmarket and King's street, and directly at the back of the tower or steeple that projects into the street. It is a fine modern building, erected in 1794.

From being surrounded on all sides by houses, it might naturally enough be concluded that it is but indifferently lighted; this, however, is not the case, for besides a great many windows upon all sides, some of them very large, particularly on the south, the church is crowned by a handsome glass dome, which fully illuminates the whole area. The inside
of

of the church is besides well executed in the workmanship, and during the winter is heated by stoves.

The steeple or spire, which is 126 feet high, and
from its situation, forms one of the most striking features in the Trongate-street, was built in the year
1637†.   It is for at least the half of its height from
the ground, of a square form, terminated by a ballustrade.   Within this rises an octagon spire, ornamented with windows in the Gothic style, projecting perpendicularly as in the cathedral steeple.   A-
bove these another ballustrade encircles it, and then
a second succession of small windows of the same
form with the others,

THE WYND CHURCH,

like the Tron Church, is situated very disadvantage-
ously, by being inclosed with buildings.—It is placed to the west of King's street, with which it has a
free communication, and betwixt the Back and New
Wynds, about half way down towards the Bridgegate.—This church was originally built by a party
of Presbyterians in the year 1687, in consequence
of an indulgence at that time allowed them by government to hear their own preachers, in place of
the curates, then in possession of the established
churches.—It has since then been rebuilt at the expence of the community, and neatly finished within,
Here

---

† The ground flat of the steeple was, within these 50 years,
occupied as a place for weighing butter, cheese and tallow;
hence Tron church and Tron steeple.

Engraved for A Macgoun's Guide to Glasgow.

VIEW of St ANDREWS CHURCH and ADJACENT BUILDINGS, from the WEST.

Here is no tower, clock or bell, so that externally, it has the appearance more of a dissenting meeting-house than one of the established churches.

The NORTH-WEST, or RAMSHORN CHURCH

is situated at the northern extremity of the Candle-riggs-street, to which with its lofty steeple it is a fine termination. This edifice was erected by the town in the year 1724, in consequence of the increasing population of the city. Its form is that of a parallelogram, lying east and west, if we except a transverse part or aisle, that runs from the center of the building a short way towards the north. It is well lighted by several very large windows that run from near the level of the ground to the pediment, circular at the top, and divided perpendicularly by stone pillars. This church is also ornamented with lustres, and a clock in the front of the gallery opposite the pulpit. From the front towards the south, rises a square tower, with a ballustrade, and four dial plates. Above this the steeple contracts its square, and one storey from the ballustrade, terminates in a handsome ogèe roof, covered with lead, and a gilt fane or weather-cock placed at the height of 140 feet from the ground.—The next in order is

ST. ANDREW'S CHURCH,

situated in the square of that name, to the east of
the

the Saltmarket, and south of the Gallowgate, with both of which streets it has an easy and open communication. This church was founded in the year 1739, but not finished till the year 1756. It is a most elegant building, and does great credit to the taste of the architect, as well as those by whom the work was executed *.

The front, towards the west, is graced by a portico, with six columns of the Corinthian order, towards which you ascend by a magnificent flight of steps. Around the building, the same order is continued in the form of pilasters, betwixt each of which are placed arched windows, that enlighten the inside. Above the columns in the front, is placed a triangular pediment inclosing the arms of the city, cut in bas relief, and at each angle of the pediment, as well as around the ballustrade which capes the north and south sides, stand a number of vases cut in stone. Though the church is thus elegant, yet the steeple is by no means corresponding; it is a heavy looking tower, which at some distance appears of a greater diameter near the top than farther down, contrary to all rule or taste. Its summit is crowned with a dome, which, in respect to the rest of the tower, has not unaptly been compared by a late celebrated tourist † to a pepper box.

The

---

* Many of the stones in this edifice having decayed, from their bad quality, in the course of the last year they were removed, and others more durable were put in their place.

† Pennant.

The inside of the church by no means disgraces its exterior appearance, being finished in a very beautiful manner. A double row of elegant Corinthian columns extend from east to west, parallel to the walls, and from which they are distant several feet, thereby forming, as it were, a kind of open gallery on each side. These columns have corresponding pilasters in the walls, with which above the capitals, they join by an arched roof, finely ornamented with stucco work. In the same manner, above the main body of the church, these columns support a similar roof, adorned with the like taste. In the east end of the church, and immediately above where the altar stands in the English churches (from one of which the model of this was taken) is a very large Venetian window. To the north and south of this, the corners are filled up by small apartments, so as to form a recess for the altar in the middle. A little to the west, stands an elegant pulpit, supported by one pillar with a canopy; opposite to this runs down the main entry, and parallel at the sides the other passages. Opposite also to the pulpit, in the west gable, is placed a clock, surrounded with a representation of groupes of fruits and flowers in bas relief. The front of the galleries here, as well as the pulpit, are pannelled or wrought in mahogany; and in the winter season, several stoves, by their heat, contribute to render this church still more agreeable.

ST. ENOCH's CHURCH.

This is also placed in a square of the same name,

on

on the situation of an old church or chapel, so called. The foundation-stone of this church was laid on the 12th day of April, 1780. Its form, like that of St. Andrew's, is a parallelogram or oblong square, running north and south, having a portico above the main entry in the north gable, supported by columns of the Doric order.—At each corner of the church, as well as at the points of the triangular pediments at the termination of the north and south fronts, are placed vases, finely cut in stone. From the north gable rises the spire, adorned in successive stories with pilasters of the different orders, and beautifully tapering, till it terminates in a cone and fane. The inside is suitable to the exterior appearance of this elegant place of worship, being well lighted, particularly by a large Venetian window to the south, as well as having the seats regularly placed and well finished.

NEW BARONY CHURCH.

The old place of worship for the Barony parish in one of the areas of the cathedral, having been found too small for the congregation, as well as inconvenient and disagreeable, the heritors lately resolved to erect a new church upon a modern plan. A beautiful design was accordingly procured from Mr. Adams, and the building begun. Its situation is immediately to the south of the burying-ground belonging to the cathedral, and fronting the open area at the head of Kirk-street, nearly opposite St. Nicholas' hospital. The architecture of this building

ing cannot properly be denominated either Grecian or Gothic; it is of the mixed kind, a species which in general characterises the productions of that architect in this country, and which, from being managed with taste, often, as in the present instance, produces a very good effect. The design has, however, not got sufficient justice, in being constructed with rubble instead of ashler work. The area of the church is well laid out, and if not in a very elegant, yet a very convenient manner. It is divided amongst the different heritors, according to their respective rights.

This church has no spire, and was finished within these two years by-past.

These nine churches are the whole that at present belong to the establishment in Glasgow. Several chapels of ease are, however, here excepted, besides a numerous list of meeting-houses afterwards to be mentioned, belonging to the people of different persuasions. We shall only at present take notice of

THE ENGLISH CHAPEL,

situated at the the south end of the Saltmarket, a little to the east. It was erected in the year 1751, when it met with no little opposition, from the fanatical spirit prevailing amongst the lower orders. The spirit of these times is, now luckily changed, by giving place to more enlarged and generous ideas, insomuch, that any sect, without opposition, may now worship the Deity according to their tenets,

Y 2   provided

provided these are not tending to destroy the public peace, or the civil and ecclesiastical establishments of the country. This church contains an organ upon the west, is handsomely laid out, having the fronts of the lofts finely pannelled, and the seats laid with cushions stuffed and covered with green cloth.—On the east stands the altar, above which is a large Venetian window, with festoon hangings. At a little distance, and looking towards the west, is placed the pulpit, adorned with a canopy hanging from the roof; from whence also hang several beautiful lustres, gilt, that add very considerably to the appearance of the chapel. Unfortunately, however, its situation has been very ill chosen, as it stands in a low and damp situation, upon the immediate banks of the Molendinar burn, whose waters at this place, after receiving the common sewers of the city, cannot be complimented on their transparency or agreeable appearance. Besides, it has been frequently inundated by the overflowings of the river, and that sometimes to the height of several feet, by which it has more than once sustained considerable damage.

Before proceeding with the description of the Public Buildings, which are applied to civil purposes, it will not be improper to take notice of such religious houses and charitable institutions, as are now

now fallen or falling into decay, in the city or its vicinity.

MONASTERY OF BLACK FRIARS.

This religious order * was first established about the year 1220. Several of the friars were shortly thereafter brought over to Scotland by William Malvoisin, bishop of Glasgow. The convent was founded

ed

---

* This order, for a considerable time after settling here, subsisted upon the bounty of the bishop and chapter, and benevolence of the people. Robert I. granted them their first annuity out of the crown lands of Cadzow or Hamilton. Thereafter, a number of pious people bestowed donations to the Black friars, payable from their lands. Amongst these we find Mathew Stuart of Castlemilk, who granted them an annuity of ten merks out of his estate, upon condition of their saying " a mass *for ever* for the soul of the said Matthew, and for his mother and bairns in our place, progenitors and successors, and all Christian souls perpetually." It is thereafter added, " and if it please the heirs of the said Matthew, the foresaid mass shall be changed to a sung mass at night."

By the rules of this order, they were obliged to abstain from the eating of flesh for seven months, viz. from September to Easter. Neither were they allowed to lie in feather beds nor in sheets, but on a mattress. They were obliged to say, every Saturday, the office of the Virgin Mary. They had, notwithstanding these restrictions, the right of preaching every where, without the permission of the bishops, and had the right of confessing all noblemen and their ladies, without the consent of their curates, and were further exempted from all censures of the church.

Their habit was a white gown and scapular, which they pretend was prescribed to them by the Virgin Mary.

ed by the bishop and chapter, in the year 1270. It stood in the neighbourhood of the College church, something farther to the south, and upon the east side of the High-street, betwixt and that wynd, called, from its vicinity to the convent, the Black friars wynd. No vestiges of this fabric are, however, now to be seen; the ground upon which it stood having long since been appropriated to other buildings. The right to the property, and superiority of the tenements so erected, were given by the crown, at the dissolution of the religious houses, to the university, and they, in right of the Black friars, have the uplifting of the feu duties, the property being long since transferred.

MONASTERY, OR CONVENT OF GREY FRIARS.

The Grey friars * were established here by John Laing, bishop of Glasgow, in 1476. Their convent stood at the foot of the wynd, called, from this order, Grey friars wynd, now more commonly, Buns wynd, leading from the High-street to Shuttle-street, and in a place called Craignaught. No traces of this building are now visible, it having almost been

---

* These friars possessed no heritable property, the ground upon which their houses stood, only excepted. They were allowed to go constantly about, with wallets on their shoulders, to beg their subsistence, from whence they were called mendicants, and from the colour of their clothes, Grey friars; their habit being a grey gown, with a cowl, and a rope about their middle; neither did they wear any shirt, and always went barefooted.

been completely demolished by the duke of Chattle-
rault and the earl of Argyle in 1560. It was at the
special request of a prior of this order, that the fair
which is held here from the second Monday of July,
was established. In consequence of his procuring
the community this favour, the magistrates and principal inhabitants, upon the last day of the fair, annually went and paid their respects to the prior of
the order at the convent. And indeed, for many
years, the fair was fenced within the inclosure or garden where the convent stood.

CHURCH OF ST. ENOCH,

without the West-port. A church whose founder
is now unknown, stood with a cemetery around it,
nearly in the situation of the present church of that
name in Argyle-street. Its ruins have been seen,
as well as the tomb stones, by some now living.

ST. JOHN THE BAPTIST'S CHAPEL.

This religious structure was dedicated to St. John
the Baptist, but at what time, or by whom founded,
we cannot tell. It stood at the head of the Drygate,
at the back of that large house, sometime belonging
to the heirs of Sir George Elphinstone.

CHAPEL OF ST. ROQUE.

This chapel stood a little way without the Stable-
green-port, near the head of that street now called
Castle-street. No vestiges of it have been visible
for these 70 years, or perhaps more, though the
wall that inclosed the burying-ground remained to
a much later period. In the cemetery were buried

a

a number of persons of distinction, who died of the plague in the city, during the years 1645 and 1646. This church belonged to the Black friars, one of whom officiated in it weekly.

ST. MUNGO'S CHAPEL

was situated in the Dovehill; like the others, no remains of it are now to be seen.

ST. THANEW'S CHAPEL.

St. Thanew or Thametes was daughter of Loth, king of the Picts, and mother, as is alledged, to St. Mungo or Kentigern. From this circumstance, a chapel was founded and dedicated to her. Its situation was in the High-street, upon the right hand, at no great distance above the opening of the street from the Trongate.

ST. NINIAN'S CHAPEL

stood in the Gorbals, not far from the end of the old bridge, it was founded by lady Lochow, about the year 1350. This lady was daughter of Robert duke of Albany, and grandmother to John first earl of Argyle.

ST. NICHOLAS' HOSPITAL.

This charitable institution was founded and endowed by bishop Muirhead, about the year 1450, for the maintenance of 12 poor men and a chaplain. The funds of this charity were, however, almost entirely dilapidated at the Reformation, and notwithstanding donations by archbishop Leighton, after that

event,

event, they at present afford but a scanty subsistence to four old men, presented by the magistrates and council, who are the patrons. The receipt of each pauper amounts to little more than L. 2 sterling. The building, which was a neat Gothic edifice of ashler, is now in ruins; it stands at the head of the Kirk-street, upon the left hand, and nearly opposite to the new Barony church. On the front and above the door are the founder's arms.

TRADES' HOSPITAL.

This hospital was founded and endowed by the Incorporations, but at what particular time is now uncertain, though most likely about the period of the Reformation. They having, near to that time, acquired for this purpose, the parsonage-house of the rector of Morebattle, archdeacon of Teviotdale. This hospital stands in the Kirk-street, upon the left hand, betwixt the entry of the Rottenrow and St. Nicholas' hospital. It has a small projection towards the street, with a turret and bell, called the Alms-house. The bell tolls at the passing of every funeral, and most commonly a small sum is left or put into a box * appropriated for the purpose, in a window of the house. In this hospital, which is now in a state of decay, is a hall, where the Incorporations used to convene at their elec-

Z   tions

* Above this box is the following inscription cut in stone, " Give to the pvir and thou sal have treasur in Heavin. Mat. xix cha.

tions and upon other public business, prior to the building of the Trades' Hall in Glassford-street. This room, which is only betwixt twenty and thirty feet in length, contains paintings emblematic of the fourteen professions, and six portraits of the most distinguished donors in favour of the charity, besides inscriptions, mentioning many others of its benefactors.

HOSPITAL AT POLMADIE.

Though this hospital was not situated within the city, yet, as it appears to have been connected, in some respects, with it, and under the superintendence of the bishop and clergy, it is thought proper to mention it. It appears to have been a considerable institution, intended for paupers of either sex. The time of its foundation is now unknown; we are, however, certain of its having existed before the year 1391, as we find from the Chartulary, No. 14, that bishop Glendening, that year, preferred a person of the name of Gillian Waugh to its benefits.

ST. NINIAN'S HOSPITAL

was founded by lady Lochow, already mentioned as founder of St. Ninian's chapel, which indeed belonged to the hospital. This lady acquired the whole lands upon which the Bridgegate-street now stands; these she feued out, and the feus were, for many years after, vested in the family of Argyle, who came in her right. She also obtained the property of a tract of land, which she named St.

Ninian's

Ninian's Croft, lying betwixt the main street of the
Gorbals, and the rivulet called the Blind burn. Upon this ground she founded and endowed, from the
feu duties of the Bridgegate, St. Ninian's Hospital,
for the use of such persons as were afflicted with
that loathsome disease, the leprosy; a disease with
which our ancestors were much afflicted. It equally visited the cottage and the palace. King Robert
Bruce, who was said himself to have been a leper,
founded, near Ayr, an hospital for patients labouring
under that distemper.

In the reign of James I. it was so general, as to
be the object of parliamentary regulation. The severity of the regulations which were appointed to
be observed by those admitted into the hospital, se-
gregating them from the rest of mankind, and commanding them to remain within its walls night and
day, demonstrates the loathsome and infectious * nature of the distemper. In some places, they were

Z 2   discharged

---

* This distemper has been inconceivably dreadful among
the Jews, it infected not only persons, but houses also, " And
" he shall look on the plague," of the leprosy, " and behold,
" if the plague be in the walls of the house with hollow strakes,
" greenish, or reddish, which in sight are lower than the wall;
" then the priest shall go out of the house, to the door of the
" house, and shut up the house seven days. And the Priest
" shall come again the seventh day, and shall look: and be-
" hold, if the plague be spread in the walls of the house; then
" the Priest shall command that they take away the stones in
" which the plague is, and they shall cast them into an un-
" clean place without the city. And he shall cause the house
" to

discharged to go out of the building, or to have its door open after sunset, under the penalty of death, and that this might not be deemed an empty threatening, a gibbet was erected at the gable of the hospital, for the immediate execution of offenders.

No remains of St. Ninian's hospital can now be traced, the feu-duties belonging to it were uplifted by the community of Glasgow so late as the year 1664, they having come in right of the family of Argyle.

There appears to have been, as far as the writer of these sheets can learn, no other hospital or religious foundation existing in the city, at least since the Reformation, than what has been already taken notice of. Mr. Gibson indeed mentions, that there was an hospital in Glasgow, *for some waiting-maids to attend the sick,* and another at the Stable-green-port, endowed by Rolland Blacadder in 1491. That these may have existed may be possible enough, though it is likely, that the last mentioned may have been the chapel of St. Roque, already taken notice of.

PUBLIC

" to be scraped within round about, and they shall pour out
" the dust that they scraped off without the city into an un-
" clean place. And they shall take other stones, and put
" them in the place of those stones; and he shall take other
" morter, and shall plaster the house. And if the plague
" come again, and break out in the house, after that he hath
" taken away the stones, and after he hath scraped the house,
" and after it is plastered; then the Priest shall come and
" look, and behold, if the plague be spread in the house, it is a
" fretting leprosy in the house: it is unclean. And he shall
" break down the house." Levit. chap. xiv. 37—45.

Engraved for J. Denholms Guide to Glasgow

VIEW of the INNER COURT of the UNIVERSITY of GLASGOW.

—◆◆◆◆●◆◆◆◆◆◆—

PUBLIC EDIFICES

APPLIED TO CIVIL PURPOSES.

—→◆◆←—

BUILDINGS OF THE UNIVERSITY.

These were deservedly, before the erection of the new college at Edinburgh, esteemed the first in Scotland.—And though they are now, with regard to elegance, excelled by that latter edifice, yet as to situation, in point of air or healthfulness, when we take into consideration the extensive garden opening into the country, the university here has certainly the advantage of that in the metropolis, which is altogether confined, by being situated in the center of a large populous city, and walled, as it were, around with lofty edifices of five and six stories in height.

The college buildings lie about half way up the High-street of Glasgow, on the east side, to which they present a front of about three hundred and thirty feet in length. This consists of three stories, built of polished ashler, and as many tier of windows. The main gate is situated in the center of the front towards the street, and is elegantly ornamented with rustic work; immediately over this is placed the royal arms, cut in bas relief and gilt,

and

and at each side, a ballustrade projecting four or five feet from the wall.—Two other lofty arched gates, at a considerable way north and south of the main passage, enter from the street, the one into an elegant court, where the professors reside, paved with stone at the sides, and in the middle laid with gravel.—In the center is a well, built in a pyramidal form, of polished stone, for the accommodation of the families in the court. The other gate leads into a garden and area, belonging to the principal of the university.

Directly behind the front, and entering by the main gate, are two other areas or courts, one behind the other. The first is 88 feet long and 44 broad. On the south side is a handsome stair-case, consisting of two flights, leading up to the faculty hall, and inclosed by a ballustrade on each side, cut in stone, as are also the figures of a lion and unicorn placed at the middle of the ascent.

In this hall, which is well finished, are two historical paintings after Rubens; the one representing the martyrdom of St. Katharine, the other, the disciples bearing our Saviour, after the crucifixion, to the place of burial. In the charter room, which is immediately adjoining, and where the records of the university are kept, are three very fine portraits, particularly that of the celebrated Dr. William Hunter of London, in a studious attitude, and as if just about to write. Before him, on a table, lie some anatomical preparations, and in the back ground, a view of part of his library. This portrait, which is most admirably finished, was, it is said, the last work that

proceeded

proceeded from the pencil of that English Apelles, Sir Joshua Reynolds.—Another of these paintings represents the late Mr. Orr of Barrowfield, formerly lord rector of the university. This has the date 1730 marked upon it. The last portrait is that of the present earl of Buchan, whose love of literature and attachment to the fine arts is well known.

In this first court is also situated the divinity hall, ornamented with a number of good portraits, some of them very fine. Amongst the number are William III. his Queen and her sister Anne; George Buchanan the Scottish poet and historian; John Knox and Martin Luther, the celebrated adversaries of the church of Rome; archbishop Boyd; Mr. Zacharias Boyd *, formerly minister of the barony church, and a benefactor to the university; a very excellent portrait of professor Simson, the mathematician; and of Dr. Leechman, the late principal of the college, &c.

The second court is much more spacious than the first, being 103 feet long by 79 in breadth, and of which an exact representation is given in the annexed plate.—It is paved, as the other, with hewn stone, and consists of buildings, with circular staircases, terminated by conical roofs. On the west side of this court, and directly above the passage from the outer area, is the university tower or steeple, built of a square form, with a ballustrade, as in the

* There is also a statue of this clergyman over the entry to the inner court.

the steeple of the North-West church, and, like it, terminating in a fane, with an ogèe roof. On the north side of the roof projects a thunder rod, which is carried downwards the whole length of the steeple (135 feet) to the earth. In this spire is placed a good clock, with dial plates fronting the cardinal points. To the east of this court is another area, surrounded on three sides by buildings, but open eastward towards the garden, from which it is separated by a painted rail of iron, with a handsome gateway. This area, like the great side court, with which it has a communication on the north, is laid with gravel.

The garden, which is very spacious, lies immediately beyond. It gently slopes towards the Molendinar burn, and is every where completely inclosed and subdivded by fine trees, grass plots, and gravel walks. In length from north to south, it extends along the back of the College and High-street, from the Old to the New Vennel, with which it has a communication, though in breadth it is considerably less. Within its area are included seven acres of ground, kept always in grass, except at the borders, which are planted with a variety of plants and shrubs. From the garden, a bridge of one arch is cast over the Molendinar burn to the opposite bank, which is steep and finely wooded. A walk leads from thence, in a serpentine direction, to the observatory, placed in an elevated situation.—This building was erected at the expence of the university, to answer the purposes of the professor of astronomy and natural philosophy, and is well furnished with telescopes, qua-
drants,

drants, and other astronomical instruments †. A-
mongst others, a very fine reflecting telescope, constructed by the ingenious Dr. Herschel, ten feet in
length, and as many inches in diameter, the only
one, it is believed, at this time in Scotland.

Upon the south of the area, which we described
before entering the garden, is situated, in a handsome and well lighted building, the library of the u-
niversity. Towards building this apartment, which
contains a gallery supported upon pillars, that bene-
cent nobleman, the first duke of Chandos, when he
visited the college, gave L. 500. Here are kept no
less than twenty thousand volumes for the use of
the professors and students, many of them exceedingly scarce, and some no where else to be found;
amongst this last class are several valuable manuscripts, particularly a very singular version of the
bible, wrote about four hundred years ago, upon
parchment, curiously illuminated, with small emblematical paintings at the beginning of each chapter.

Here are also preserved in cases, numbers of monumental and other stones, taken out of the Roman
wall, or Graham's dyke, in this part of the kingdom;
some are well cut and ornamented: most of them
were done to perpetuate the memory of the party
who performed such or such works, others in me-

A a   mory

---

† It is in contemplation to erect an observatory in a more
favourable situation, but the exact place has not yet been determined upon.

mory of officers who died in the country. The greatest part of these have been engraven, at the expence of the university, in a series of plates. Here, however, it would be too tedious, and probably uninteresting, were we to particularise and describe the several figures that appear upon each.— One or two, however, cannot certainly be improper.

The I. plate exhibits Victory reclined on a globe, with a palm in one hand, a garland in the other, and a pediment above, supported by two fluted pilasters, with Corinthian capitals; beneath, is a boar, a common animal in sculptures found in Britain, probably because they were in plenty in our forests. Both these are in honour of the emperor Antoninus Pius.

None is more instructive than that engraven on plate III. on which appears a Victory about to crown a Roman horseman, armed with a spear and shield. Beneath him are two Caledonian captives, naked and bound, with their little daggers (like the modern durks) by them. On another compartment of the stone, is an eagle and sea-goat, to denote some victory, gained, in the course of their work, near the sea, for it was devoted, by a party of the *Legio Secunda Augusta*, on building a certain portion of the wall.

The XVI. plate is monumental. The figure is very elegant, representing one gracefully recumbent, dressed in a loose robe; beneath, is a wheel, denoting, according to the conjecture of an eminent antiquary, that at the time of his death he was engaged with a party on the road, and by him is an animal resembling the *musimar*, or Siberian goat.

THE

The TOWN HOUSE

is situated at the Cross, immediately west of, and adjoining to the prison, (both of which edifices were built in 1636, during the time Sir Patrick Bell held the office of chief magistrate.) The front is supported by strong rusticated pillars of a square form, which connect with each other by arches, having for their key, sculptured heads, cut in stone. Immediately above these, a range of Ionic pilasters, fluted, support a rich entablature. Over the entablature is a ballustrade, with vases above each pilaster. Under the arches which connect the range of rusticated columns in the ground storey, is a spacious piazza, where the merchants retire, when hindered by the weather from walking on the Exchange *, directly before the front of this building.

The Town Hall is a handsome and large room. In length, it measures 52 feet,—in breadth 27,—and in height 24. Here are full length portraits of all our monarchs since James I. of England, and an excellent one by Ramsay, of Archibald, duke of Argyle, in his robes, as lord Justice-General. It is impossible to view this picture, without being struck with its beauty: The figure almost starts from the canvas, from the able distribution and management of the light and shade; and in viewing the face, you

A a 2 can

---

* The Exchange is well paved with hewn stone, and properly fenced from the street.

can hardly persuade yourself but you see real life. The robes are no less skilfully painted; the several folds, the ermine, and the reflected light which the scarlet produces upon its snowy whiteness in particular situations, are productive of the happiest effect.

Formerly the Assembly Room occupied the west part of the first flat of this building; from its having, however, been found too small in its dimensions, another was built on a larger scale, and this is now converted into parlours for the use of the Tontine inn.

THE TONTINE COFFEE ROOM
AND HOTEL.

In the year 1781, a number of the most respectable citizens opened a subscription, by way of tontine, for erecting these buidings, the produce or rent whereof was to be distributed amongst the subscribers, according to the endurance of any life they should propose at the time of subscription; and thus annually, till such time as only one of the original nominees was in existence; when, upon such an event taking place, the whole buildings became the property of the original subscriber or his heirs, and which he or they could sell or dispose of at pleasure *.—The subscription upon these terms, was in

a

* This Tontine was divided into 105 shares at 50l. each.— Twenty-one of these shares now belong to the common fund,
from

a short time filled up; and a proper place being fixed upon for the buildings, they were accordingly e-
rected in an area immediately adjoining the Town
House, upon the north.

The Coffee Room is 72 feet in length, and of a
proportional breadth, and is universally allowed to
be the most elegant in Britain, and most probably in
Europe. Its main entry is from under the piazza of
the Town House or Exchange. Upon each side of
the door are placed two very large windows, from
the floor to the roof, which communicate the light
to the room from the street. About half way down
the Coffee Room, is a very large Venetian window
upon the east, and upon the other side, exactly opposite, is another, looking into the bar, upon the
north side of which, is a door communicating with
the Hôtel. The extremity of the room northward,
is in the form of a bow, divided by pillars, making
one complete magnificent window from side to side.
Near to the main entry, the roof, which is very high,
is supported by columns of the Doric order, with
correspondent pilasters upon the walls, and in this
place, a dome of glass enlightens, with the other
end

---

from the death of an equal number of the persons nominated at
the time of subscription.—It is impossible to say exactly how
these shares sell at present, as that depends entirely upon the
age, constitution, and mode of life of the nominee.

The Tontine Coffee Room and Hotel draw at present of
rent to the proprietors about L.912 · 10s. per annum.

end windows, the south side of the room. From the roof also, are hung several magnificent lustres, finely gilt, which, when lighted, give an air of grandeur to the place, pleasantly demonstrative of the riches and taste of the city of Glasgow.

Around the inside of the bow, as well as the four fire places, are placed the seats for the subscribers. Betwixt the door and the large windows upon each side, is a space upon the wall for advertisements, and immediately below, a small desk with a book, wherein the arrivals and departures of the several vessels, connected with the city, are daily marked down. Subscribers * of L. 1 : 5s. per annum, are entitled to the use of the room, newspapers and magazines; of which no Coffee Room in Britain can boast a greater variety. For here are not only the whole Scotch papers, but also the greatest part of those published in London, as well as some from Ireland, France, &c. besides reviews, magazines, and other periodical publications. At the daily arrival of the mail, a more stirring, lively, and anxious scene can hardly be imagined. Indeed, no part of the day passes without some concourse of subscribers, or of strangers, at the Hôtel, whom their liberality permits freely to partake the benefit of the room. At those hours when the news of the morning may be said to have grown cold, the monthly publications

claim

* The subscribers, this year, are from 900 to a 1000. In 1797, when the first edition of this work was printed, the number was 803.

claim attention in their turn, or people meet for the sake of looking out their acquaintance, or of engaging in casual parties of conversation.

Here you are not offended as in London, and several other towns, upon entering places of this description, with clouds of smoke and fumes of tobacco, or with that brutal noise, proceeding from the too free use of liquor; neither of which are allowed to be used in the room.

THE HOTEL

consists of a suite of apartments handsomely fitted up, immediately adjoining the Coffee Room and Exchange, and to which the main entry leads from the south, by a fine hanging stair. Under the piazzas of the Exchange are placed several other distinct rooms, occupied by under-writers, insurance-brokers, &c.

THE TOLBOOTH, OR PRISON

is a very handsome, lofty building of five stories, situated immediately to the east of the Town House and Exchange. At each corner towards the top, it is flanked with square turrets, ornamented with o-gèe roofs and balls. Above the windows are circular or triangular pediments, caped with the rose and thistle alternately, which add very considerably to the appearance of this edifice †. The main gate to the

---

† Upon the front is placed his Majesty's arms finely cut, and a little below, this apt inscription:—

Hæc

the south is covered by a square portico, projecting
the breadth of a stair-case from the wall, which
rises on each side towards the door. Upon the east
of the prison is situated a square spire, 126 feet in
height, having its roof something in the form of an
imperial crown, with open arches. Here is placed
a fine clock, which regulates the others in the town,
also a bell, and a well toned set of musical chimes,
that have been long admired. These play an air at
the end of every two hours, by means of machinery
connected with the clock; and on every particular
day of the week the series of tunes is altered.
They are besides played upon by a musician for an
hour, betwixt too and three every day, excepting
Saturday and Sunday.

Within the principal door of the prison is a large
square lobby, with massy columns supporting the
roof. From this lobby upon the left, strikes off the
entry into the Town House, before mentioned as a
separate building. Directly opposite, another door
leads into the apartments of the prison, which are
divided into two different kinds, appropriated for
debtors and criminals, well ventilated and healthy *.
On the right of the lobby is the door that leads into

a

Hæc domus odit, amat, punit, conservat, honorat, nequi-
tiam pacem, crimina jura probos.

* The members of the town council visit the prison in rotation, once a-week, in order to report to the magistrates whatever appears to them proper either to be rectified or altered,
with regard to the state of the jail.

VIEW of the MERCHANTS HOUSE, Bridgegate GLASGOW.

a new fitted up and elegant room, where the Circuit Court of Justiciary is held. Within a niche on the north of this apartment, is the royal arms; and below, the figure of Justice, holding in the left hand a balance, and in the right a sword.

Immediately before this is the bench for the judges, covered with scarlet; below, and railed from the body of the room, is the inside of the bar for the lawyers and clerks. On the right of the bench sits the jury, and in the front, beyond the clerks' table, and without the bar, is a row of seats, rising gradually upwards, in the first of which is placed the pannel, and in the others the auditors. Here are also two handsome galleries with iron rails, entering by a turnpike-stair from the lowest or first flat; and on the east of the room is a very large circular Venetian window, which looks into the High-street. Immediately below the principal stair-case that leads into the prison, and in the first storey, is another door, entering from the street, which opens a communication by the turnpike-stair, just now mentioned, with not only the galleries in the circuit room, but also with the prisoners' apartments, and a handsome suite of rooms appropriated for the town clerks' office, record rooms, &c. These have been only lately laid out and finished, as before they made no part of the prison, but of an adjoining land, situated upon the High-street, which, for this purpose, was purchased by the community.

THE MERCHANTS' HALL

stands in the Bridgegate, upon the south side of that
B b   street,

street, and near to its west extremity. It was rebuilt in the year 1659, by Sir Patrick Bell, then dean
of guild, and consists of two stories of ashler work.
—The lowest, or ground flat, on each side of the
main gate, is occupied by shops, and in the second
storey, a range of large windows, with triangular
pediments, give light to the Hall. On each side
of the principal entry from the street, are two Doric pillars, with an ornamented entablature—and
immediately above, two columns of the Ionic order inclose a sculpture in bas relief, representing a
vessel, and in another compartment, three old men
in the habit of pilgrims *. After passing through
the lobby, and ascending the stair-case, you enter
into the Hall, one of the largest in the city, being about 80 feet in length, and near 30 wide.
In it is hung a list of all the deans of guild of this
city, from the erection of the guildry in the year
1605, to the present time. Also the portraits of
several of the most eminent benefactors to the
poor of the Merchants' house, and a long roll of o-
thers, who have, by their generosity, befriended
the institution †.

This

* Immediately under is the following inscription:
    " Glasguanæ Mercatorum pia liberalitate & impensis fun-
" datum Æræ, vulg (1) denuo ejusdem reditibus, ordinis, ac
" munificentia reædificatum, auctum, et ornatum est, CIC.IC
" ILIX. 1659."
        " Mutuat Jehovæ qui largitur pauperi,
        " Et retributionem illius reddet ei."

    † Here also formerly hung a board with an inscription in
golden

This hall is exceedingly well lighted, especially from the north, and contains two fire places upon the opposite sides of the room. In the center is hung from the roof, a large and beautiful model of a ship, with her whole tackling. Immediately adjoining this building upon the south, is a handsome and lofty spire, one of the finest, if it is not absolutely so in the city.

After rising somewhat more than half its height from the ground, in the form of a square, it is surrounded by a ballustrade, within which the steeple again rises in the same form, but of a more contracted diameter, till it meets with another, from which it springs as formerly. A third ballustrade embraces it, and from this issues a pyramidal spire, terminated by the figure of a ship in full sail, gilt. This steeple, if we except that of the cathedral, is the highest in Glasgow, being no less than 164 feet from the ground to the top of the fane.

THE TOWN'S HOSPITAL.

This building, which was opened for the reception of the poor in 1733, is situated near the east end of that street, called Clyde-street, running from the bottom or lower end of the Stockwell, westward to the Broomielaw. It is three stories in height,

B b 2   and

golden letters, containing directions from scripture, how to buy and sell.—It is now, however, removed.

and consists of a front and wings, which project till they are upon a line with the street. The lower part of the house is occupied by the mess-room and other culinary apartments, such as bake-house, brew-house, hall, &c. Here is also the apartment where the committee of management meet, adorned with the portraits of several of the benefactors to the house. Above stairs are the several rooms appropriated for the reception of the poor, which are always kept clean and well-aired. To the north of the hospital, and from which it is separated by a broad area, is another building, in the first storey of which, called the Cells, are confined lunatics and disorderly persons; and on the second is an infirmary for the sick, belonging to the hospital.

THE ROYAL INFIRMARY

is a most beautiful building, from a design of the celebrated Adams *. It stands at the north or upper

* The foundation-stone of this elegant edifice was laid on the 18th day of May, 1792, in presence of the lord provost, magistrates, principal and professors of the university, &c. and a vast concourse of spectators.

Two crystal bottles, cast on purpose at the Glasgow glass-house, were deposited in the foundation-stone. In one of them, were put different coins of the present reign; in the other, several specimens of the Glasgow muslin manufactures, in their present state of improvement, a printed copy of the charter of the Glasgow Royal Infirmary, a copy of the Glasgow

FRONT VIEW of the ROYAL INFIRMARY, GLASGOW.

Engraved for Denholm's History of Glasgow.

per end of the High-street, on the scite of the bishop's palace, and immediately west of the cathedral.

gow news-papers, and a writing containing the names of the magistrates and council, and the principal and professors of the university, &c. There was deposited, also, a tin plate, properly prepared for the purpose, with the following Latin inscription upon the upper side,

Annuente Deo Opt. Max.

Regnante Georgio III. Principe Munificentissimo,

Ædium,

Ad Morbos Pauperum Sanandos,

A Civibus hujusce Urbis,

Aliisque piis Scotiæ incolis,

Pecuniis sponte collatis,

Extruendatum,

Primum hunc lapidem

Posuit.

JACOBUS M‘DOWAL, Armiger,

Urbis Glasguensis

Præfectus,

Administratorumque operis perficiendi

Præses:

XV Kal. Junii,

Anno Æræ Christianæ M.DCC.XCII.

Architectis ROBERTO et JACOBO ADAM,

Q. F. F. Q. S.

TRANSLATION.

By the favour of God, All-good and All-mighty, in the reign of our most beneficent sovereign George the third, James M‘Dowal, esq; provost of the city of Glasgow, and preses of the managers for carrying on the work, laid this first stone of a building to be erected, by money voluntarily contributed by the inhabitants of this city, and other benevolent persons in Scotland, on the 18th day of May, in the year of our Lord, 1792. The architects, Robert and James Adams, esquires.

dral. The general form is that of a parallelogram, running east and west. On the front, and at each side, are two square projections of about three feet deep, and in the center, another still more considerable.

This building consists of four stories; the ground or lower rusticated, the upper ones of polished ashler; each storey being lighted by a range of windows. At the beginning of the second storey, and on the center projection, rise four beautiful Corinthian columns, with corresponding pilasters in the wall, from which they are separated by the depth of the projection; these support a triangular pediment, above which is a ballustrade, with the royal arms cut in *alto relievo*. Immediately over this, and in the center of the building, is a large and lofty dome covered with glass.

On the east and west wings or projections, and in the second storey, are two very large Venetian windows; and also, correspondent to these, another upon the same level, under the pediment, formed by the middle columns. These windows and the columns, reach the height of two range of square windows. A little above, a very deep and elegant cornice runs alongst the building, exactly upon the level with the entablature over the central pillars. Another tier of windows succeed, though of lesser dimensions as to height, than those in the two last stories; and after these, another cornice, though not so deep as the last, terminates or capes the head of the wall. The gables of this edifice, as well as the north front, are also handsomely finished, and

well

well lighted, by successive tiers of windows, correspondent, or on the same lines with those before-
mentioned.

The principal entry, which leads into a hall or
lobby, is in the middle of the center projection, supported on each side by two columns of the Doric
order, fluted. To the right and left of the hall
strike off doors, which lead into the wards No. 1
and 2, on the ground flat *. These occupy the
whole breadth of the building, and are well lighted.

In every ward, a succession of beds, having their
frames constructed of cast iron, run down the sides
of the room, leaving an open area or passage betwixt each row, which conducts to the fire-place at
the farthest end. On each side of the fire-place, a
door leads into four small apartments, destined for
the nurses and such patients as are either under an
infectious disease, or who have undergone an operation.

Leaving these wards on the ground flat, and passing the house-keeper's room on the left, and another
apartment to the right of the lobby, an elegant hanging stair conducts to the second storey. Here, directly opposite, is a handsome apartment, enlightened by the large center Venetian window, where the
committee of management meet to transact the business of the house. Two other wards, No. 3 and
4,

* The wards are divided into what are called the physicians
and surgeons' wards; the first occupies the lower stories, the
second the higher.

4, as well as two small apartments, called the clerk's or accountant's rooms, lie at each side of the committee room. These wards are fitted up in the same manner, and have the same conveniencies with those in the ground or first flat. Ascending the stair-case another storey, you find opposite you the consultation-room, and at each side the wards No. 5 and 6. In the third flat is the operation-room, a most beautiful circular apartment, very large, and fitted up in the form of an amphitheatre. This is enlightened by the glass dome already mentioned, which rises to a considerable height above the roof of the building.

In the center of the operation-room is a circular area or space, appropriated for the operator and patients, and in the successive rows of seats, sit the students attending the house. Two other wards go off from the operation-room, No. 7 and 8, the first of which is set aside for the reception of sick or disabled soldiers, that may be brought into the Infirmary.

A flight of stairs also lead from the lobby, on the ground flat, to another set of apartments below. A long gallery, running the length of the building, opens a communication with each of these rooms. These to the north of the gallery are very small, and built in the form of cells, for such patients as are subject to temporary fits of lunacy. The rooms on the other side are large and well lighted. Here is, in separate apartments, a warm and cold bath. The room or laboratory where the medicines are kept and compounded, as well as several bed-chambers,

lie

lie in this department of the building; and to the west of the gallery is situated the kitchen, where the whole provisions made use of in the hospital are prepared.

Two other stair-cases, besides that already mentioned, lie at each end of the house, and connect the different wards. By these stairs, such patients as it is thought fit to allow the benefit of the open air, walk into the garden, immediately to the north of the Infirmary.

Every ward, as well as most of the other apartments of the house, has the benefit of a supply of water, by means of leaden pipes and stopcocks, which convey it from a reservoir near the Monkland canal, in a more elevated situation than any part of this hospital. The greatest attention is paid to the airing of the apartments, to white-washing the walls, and to the removing of such patients as are afflicted with infectious disorders, into separate rooms by themselves. In short, every requisite attention is paid, and convenience here provided, that can tend either to restoring the patients' health, or to the keeping of them clean and comfortable, while in the hospital.

Of the institution of this truly charitable foundation, we will afterwards fall to speak at more length.

TRADES' HALL.

Before the erecting of the present building, the incorporations of the city used to convene in an old hall of the same name, situated in the High-street,

now generally known by the name of the Alms-
house, already taken notice of. This having been
found incommodious, and no way suitable, either
to the respectability of the incorporations, or the
taste of the times, a new hall was projected and a-
greed to, and the foundation-stone accordingly laid
upon the 9th day of September, 1791 *.

'This building is situated on the west side of
Glassford-street, nearly in the middle betwixt the
intersection of Wilson and Ingram streets. It consists of three separate flats or stories, the first of
which is rusticated and ornamented by doors, in the
                                             Venetian

---

* Under the stone was laid a plate, with the inscription following:

By the blessing of GOD,
The Foundation-Stone of this Fabric
(A HALL for the TRADES' HOUSE
And INCORPORATIONS of GLASGOW)
Was laid by JOHN M'ASLAN, Esquire,
Convener of the Trades,
On the ninth day of September,
In the year of our Lord M.DCC.XCI.
And
The 31st year of the reign of George the III.
And of the æra of Masonry 5791,
In presence of
James M'Dowal, Esq; Lord Provost,
Richard Marshall, Esq; } Merchant Bailies,
John Hamilton, Esq;
Robert Mann, Esq; Trades Bailie,
Gilbert Hamilton, Esq; Dean of Guild,
John Gardner, Collector of the House.
Then follow the names of the deacons of the fourteen incor-
porated trades, and of Robert Adam, Esq; the architect.

Venetian style. The center or main door is placed in a projection, which, on the level or base of the second storey, supports four Doric columns, with a triangular pediment. Immediately under this pediment is a large Venetian window, which enlightens the middle of the Hall. Similar windows upon the same level, are in each wing or side of the building, betwixt which and the great center window, are two square ones, ornamented at the top with cornices, and the figures of griffins cut in bas relief. Corresponding windows enlighten the third storey, which is terminated by a handsome ballustrade rail of stone, upon which rest the city arms, cut in *alto relievo*, supported by two female figures, as large as life, in a recumbent posture. From the roof rises a dome or canopy covered with lead, and ending in a fane.

Upon entering the main door and passing the lobby, a hanging stair, which at the end of the first flight, divides to the right and left, conducts into the Hall, a very fine room, 70 feet long by 35 broad, and, excepting the Assembly Rooms, the most spacious in the city. The roof is decorated with stucco work, in a light and elegant style; and above the door is an inscription in gold letters, of the date of opening the Hall, and of the names of the gentlemen who held the government of the house at the time. The other apartments in this building are likewise well finished and ornamented.

THE

THE NEW ASSEMBLY AND CONCERT ROOMS

were built by way of tontine, and are situate[d]
the north side, and near to the west end of Ing[ram]
street.—The foundation-stone of this beau[tiful]
building, from a design of the late Mr. Adam[s,]
laid upon the 11th day of March, 1796.

Like to the Trades' Hall, which we last de[scrib]
ed, this consists of three different stories; only [two]
of these, however, appear when viewed from [the]
front, as the height of the Assembly Room oc[cu]
pies, on this side, the whole space towards [the]
roof.

The basement storey, which is rusticated, h[as a]
very deep square projection from the middle of [the]
front, which supports four Ionic columns, [with]
their correspondent pilasters and entablature. [Be]
tween these columns is placed the large center [Ve]
netian window, which, with the two others on e[ach]
side of the projection, give light to the hall. [Four]
similar pilasters, with those immediately behind [the]
central columns, ornament the building at the c[or]
ners, and rise to a like height; so that the same [cor]
nice, which is very deep, runs along the top o[f the]
whole. The front rises a few feet above this [cor]
nice, and terminates in stone ballusters.

Upon entering the main door there is a h[and]
some lobby, supported by Doric pillars; to the [right]
and left of which are situated apartments, or [dress]
ing rooms, for the ladies and gentlemen, the house-
keeper's

PERSPECTIVE VIEW of the NEW ASSEMBLY ROOMS GLASGOW.

Engraved for Denholm's History of Glasgow.

keeper's room, store room, and kitchen, &c. At the farther end of the lobby, is a hanging stair, which leads to the first flat above the basement storey. After passing another lobby, you enter the Assembly Room, extending the whole length of the building *. On each end of the room are placed the musicians' galleries, and on the north side, or opposite the large Venetian side windows, are two marble chimney pieces, above each of which is a very large mirror.

Betwixt the windows are placed columns, and a number of fine emblematical figures, in the attitude of dancing. The ceiling is also ornamented with fancy work in the angles, which a large ellipse, drawn longitudinally occasions. On this flat, and in that immediately above, there are several other rooms, to be used as retiring apartments, to which two smaller stair-cases lead, from the first flight of the great stair-case, as well as from the flat below.

Upon the whole, this building is certainly very deserving of encomium, whether we consider it simply as a piece of architecture, or relatively, with regard to its possessing every convenience, that the nature of the design requires.

The GRAMMAR SCHOOL

is situated upon the north side of George's street,
New

* Viz. 80 feet,—In breadth it measures 35, and in height 27 feet.

New Town.—It was erected in the year 1790, the
old school-house having been found incommodious.
The main body of the front consists of two stories
in height, though the projections or wings at each
end are three; these wings, towards George's street,
reach only two or three feet outwards, from the line
of the front, but to the north they project a great
deal farther from the main body of the building, so
as to inclose partly an area or court. In the basement storey of the wings which look to the street,
there are two very fine Venetian windows, divided
by small Ionic pillars. In the second storey, the
same kind of window is continued, in a plain style.
Two row of square windows, upon a level with
these, run along the front, above which is a deep
cornice, the whole length of the building. The
wings rise above this another storey, and are terminated by a pavilion roof.

Upon each side of the wings, alongst George's
street, are built handsome gateways, which lead into the area or back court, from whence are the entries that lead into the teaching rooms.

On the basement storey is the large hall, 51 feet
in length by 27, and in the wings two rooms, enlightened by the Venetian windows, each being 30
feet by 19.—The second flat immediately above the
hall, is divided into two apartments, and on each
side, as in the first flat, lie two more. In the third
storey, which applies only to the wings, there are
the remaining rooms of the house, making nine in
whole;

whole; these are all of the same size, excepting the hall, and the rooms in the storey above it †.

Only

† In this school there are four classes, and as many teachers. One of these teachers begins with the boys when they enter, and so continues to carry them through, rising a class every year till the fourth year, which is reckoned the last of the course. Here is no established rector, the presidency going yearly by rotation to the person who teaches for the time the highest or fourth class; when his term is finished, he begins with a new set of pupils, and the teacher of the third class succeeds him in the office, and so on. Every morning, at the calling together of the school, prayers are said in the hall, by the presiding teacher, after which the boys adjourn into the separate apartments allotted to the respective classes.

The magistrates of the city generally visit this seminary seven or eight times every year; at which times, the classes are examined before them separately, and every boy's situation in the class marked. At the end of the year, these boys who have kept, at an average, the highest places, are rewarded with a premium of a book, commonly some good edition of a classic author, elegantly bound, as a premium for their industry, and a stimulus to their fellows to exert themselves.

The hours of teaching in the summer session, (which commences on the first Tuesday immediately after the celebration of the Sacrament in the city in the month of April, and closes after the general examination about the end of September,) is from seven o'clock in the morning to nine,—from ten o'clock in the forenoon to twelve,—and from one afternoon to three. In the winter, the hours are from nine in the morning to twelve, and from one o'clock to three afternoon. During the summer session, however, there is a recess or vacation, which begins the 10th of June, and ends on the Tuesday after the Fair of Glasgow, in the month of July.—The wages paid by each scholar is 6s. per quarter, besides a trifle yearly to the janitor;

2s.

Only four of these apartments and the hall, are at present used for the classes, the remainder of them being appropriated as a place for the teaching of the children belonging to Wilson's charity, and as lecture rooms, for the use of an institution lately established in the city, for promoting a more general knowledge of the science of chemistry and natural philosophy.

THE SURGEONS' HALL.

This building stands on the east side of St. Enoch's square, and consists of two stories in height. The first is of rustic work, the other of polished ashler, caped above the cornice with ballusters. In the middle compartment of the front, and at each end, are Doric pilasters, with their entablature. Between these is a Venetian window, which, with two square ones enlighten the Hall.

Below the center window, and in the basement storey, is the door which conducts into a lobby, hung round with a collection of old portraits, representing Hippocrates, Galen, &c. At each side are

doors

---

as. during the winter season for firing, and a gratuity to the teachers at Candlemas.

The salaries of the masters, independent of their fees, amount yearly to L.25 each, and every fourth year, to L.5 more to the persons under whose care the three junior classes are; and L.10 to the teacher who that year presides, in consideration of his extra trouble.

doors leading into apartments; that to the right is now occupied by an extensive library, bequeathed by the late Mr. Walter Stirling, merchant here, to certain trustees for the public good.

At the extremity of the lobby is a hanging stair that conducts into the hall, which is lofty, large, and well finished. Here the Faculty of Physicians and Surgeons meet, and transact the business of their society.

In this Hall is likewise placed the library of the Faculty, containing a good collection of professional books, besides a very fine painting of Hygeia, the goddess of Health, leaning upon an altar piece, and holding in the right hand a cup, from which, a serpent entwined around a bough, drinks. About the principal object are several other figures emblematic of health.

The BARRACKS

lie at the east end of the Gallowgate, upon the north side of that street, from which they are inclosed by a very strong and lofty wall. These buildings were erected in the year 1795. They consist of three compartments, two whereof are built at right angles to the third, in such a manner as to inclose an area or space upon three sides, that to the south being open.

The front or middle building is very handsome, and consists of four stories in height, with the royal arms under an angular pediment above the middle of the cornice. This within, is divided into well fi-

D d   nished

nished apartments for the officers commanding the troops in the Barracks, according to their rank; here is also the mess-room, public parlours, &c.

The wings are of coarser workmanship, but of the same height with the principal or front building. These are destined for the accommodation of the soldiery, who are here well lodged in large and airy apartments *. Immediately behind the wall, which bounds the limits of the Barracks from the street, is situated a guardhouse.—The gates are shut every night at nine o'clock, by which time, every soldier belonging to the garrison must be within, excepting those who are out upon duty. This regulation is productive of the best effects, not only to the men themselves, but to the public in general, from its obvious tendency to discourage that dissipation and vice, the too frequent companions of late hours.

The GUARDHOUSE and POLICE OFFICE.

The Gaurdhouse, which was erected in the year 1789, is situated upon the west side of the Candleriggs-street, and consists of a piazza, supported by

four

---

* The two wings are divided into 72 different apartments, each of which contains 14 men; here they sleep and mess, though their victuals are dressed in the kitchens upon the ground storey; there being one for the use of every three rooms, or 42 men. At this rate, the number which the barracks will contain amounts to 1008.

four Ionic columns, with their entablature, and the guard-room immediately behind.—In the attic storey are apartments for the officer on guard, store-room, &c.

The Police office also occupies part of the upper flat. Its entry is, however, more to the south upon the street, than that to the Guardhouse. To the use of this very useful establishment there has been lately built another set of apartments, immediately behind, where some of the officers of Police are always stationed, and where stores, &c. are kept.

The NEW BRIDEWELL.

The magistrates, in the year 1789, in order to try the effects of a plan of solitary confinement and labour with delinquents, fitted up in separate cells, some buildings belonging to the city, formerly used as granaries. From the great addition of inhabitants, within these few years, the old Bridewell was found insufficient, on account of the narrowness of the scale; and a new one was projected upon a more enlarged plan, which has been accordingly erected.

This building stands upon the north side of George's street, where it approaches to, and runs nearly parallel with the Drygate. It consists of a front of six stories, extending 106 feet in length by 30 in breadth, with two projecting wings.—A gallery or passage in each flat runs the whole length of the house, having at each end two large windows.

D d 2   From

From this gallery branch off the cells *; the entry
to each being directly opposite to that of the other.
These passages are again connected by a large stair-
case in the center of the house, which leads to the
door in the front.

The wings, which are only three stories in height,
are occupied by the keepers, and as warehouses for
lodging the cotton, &c. at which the persons confined
are employed.

The prisoners here are kept separate from one another, and employed in such labour as they can perform, under the direction of the keeper, who is
likewise under the inspection of a committee of
council that enquire into his management, &c.
The members of the town council in rotation, are
appointed to visit and report upon the state of the
Bridewell.

The keeper has a record of sentences upon which
each prisoner is confined: he also keeps an exact account of the wages of their labour, and after defraying the expence of their maintenance, the surplus
is paid to them when the period of their confinement
expires; and some have received from L. 5 to L. 7.
Experience in this and other great towns, where
this institution is established, has demonstrated, that
of all the species of punishment for offenders of a
certain description, solitary confinement and labour
is not only the most humane, but the best calculated
to answer one great end of punishment, the amend-
ment of the offender.

* On each flat there are 21 cells, 8 feet by 7; consequently
in whole they amount to 126.

The WEIGH HOUSE

is situated on the east end of Ingram-street, immediately adjacent to the Ramshorn or North West church. It is of a square form, with a pavilion roof, and adorned at each angle and both sides of the doors with Ionic pilasters.

The MARKETS IN KING'S-STREET.

These stand upon both sides of the street. That upon the east, which is appropriated entirely for butcher meat, is in length 112 feet by 67 in breadth.—In the center of the front line, is the main gate, on each side of which are two Ionic columns, supporting an angular pediment.—Upon the north end of the Market is the hall, where the incorporation of butchers convene to transact their public business. The Markets upon the other side of the street, are in three divisions, viz. fish, mutton and cheese market. The front of these towards King-street, extends 173 feet by 46 in breadth. The mutton market, which is in the center, has a gate adorned as on the opposite side. The entries to the other two are arched at the top, and faced with rustics.

The whole are paved with freestone, and covered over for shelter by roofs standing upon stone piers, under which the different commodities are exposed to sale. By means of wells in the areas, they are likewise kept always perfectly agreeable and clean.

THE GREEN MARKET

is placed upon the west side of the Candleriggs, to which there is a front of 130 feet. The entry here is decorated in the same manner with the markets in King-street, and laid out nearly on a similar plan.

THE OLD MEAL MARKET

stands in the High-street, upon the west side, nearly opposite to the University.

THE NEW MEAL, BUTTER AND CHEESE MARKET.

Markets for retailing these different articles have been lately erected upon the east side of Montrose-street, and adjoining the Weigh-house upon the north. They are neat, spacious and cleanly. Before their erection, the usual place for retailing the articles of cheese, butter, &c. was the Cross and Salt-market-street, which were much crowded, so as to render the passage difficult and disagreeable. By the erection of these buildings, this inconvenience is now removed.

THE THEATRE.

The first building appropriated for theatrical purposes, and which stood in a narrow alley, to the west

of

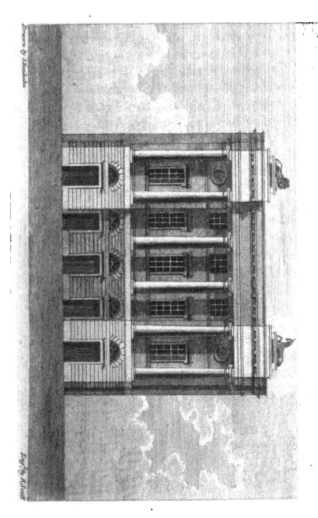

Engraved for Denholm's History of Glasgow.

of that new street called Union place, having been destroyed by fire†, another edifice was erected, upon the east side of Dunlop-street, which continued for many years to be used as a play-house. The town having, however, increased much in size, it was found, at some times at least, too small in its dimensions, to contain the numbers who requested admission; an enlargement of the house was therefore thought upon, and accordingly the manager, Mr. Jackson, in the course of last year, began to execute the design, by building a wall, considerably distant from the old wall, and which should extend farther to the west, and thereby, when roofed, embrace a much larger area. The work was considerably advanced, when the idea struck some gentlemen of the city, that at best, the alteration would make but a patched piece of work, and that it would be more becoming the wealth and respectability of the town, to have a theatre built, according to an elegant plan, and upon such a scale, as would, at all times, accommodate the citizens. A subscription was accordingly proposed, and set on foot, divided into shares of L. 25, each person being restricted to ten shares, and to prevent improper influence, the person that held that number was restricted to four votes. The subscription having met with success, a committee of the subscribers was appointed, to take in plans and estimates of the proposed building, which, it was thought, would not exceed L. 7000 sterling. Several plans were accordingly lodged, and the preference given to that

drawn

† This accident happened 5th May, 1780.

* These shares are transferable, and descend like heritage.

drawn out by Mr. David Hamilton, architect. Accordingly, a piece of ground having been purchased, the building was immediately begun, and at the time of writing this article, is considerably advanced.

This elegant edifice stands at the head of Queen-street, upon the west side, alongst which it extends in front, 70 feet, its depth towards the west is 158 feet. The front is of polished ashler, adorned with columns of the Ionic order, and a corresponding entablature, each near 30 feet in height, and rising from the upper part of the first storey. Betwixt the columns which project from the wall, their whole diameter are two ranges of windows, and immediately above the entablature, and at the north and south ends of the building, the figures of the lion and unicorn *couchant*. The principal doors, it is almost unnecessary to add, are on this side of the building. The other sides are of rubble work, but strong, massive, and well constructed.

With respect to area or size, it is of nearly the same dimensions as that of Covent-garden, and is esteemed the largest provincial theatre in Europe. The greatest attention is bestowed by the managers, towards the proper execution of the work, to the procuring of able and skilful workmen and artists, to execute the many various departments which are requisite; so that, when completed, it promises, in point of size, convenience, scenery, and other decorations, to yield to none but the winter theatres of the metropolis.

HUTCHESON'S

HUTCHESON'S HOSPITAL.

The old building which stood upon the north side of the Trongate, having been taken down, as formerly mentioned, in order that a communication, now called Hutcheson-street, might be opened to the north. A new house was proposed thereafter to be erected. Several years, however, elapsed, before this took place. At length, the managers having fixed upon a proper situation, and having adopted a plan given in by the same architect who designed the theatre, Mr. Hamilton, they in the autumn of last year, proceeded to the execution of the work.

This Hospital is situated at the head of Hutcheson-street, to which it is an elegant termination. It extends in front 58 feet, and in depth 55. Its front, as well as its side, which looks into John-street, is of polished ashler. It is adorned with columns and an entablature of the Corinthian order, and an handsome octagan spire, with a clock and dial plate. Its height is 150 feet. The largest room, which is very spacious, and fitted up with a gallery, is to be appropriated to the reception of Stirling's library; the other apartments, which are numerous, will be occupied as lodgings and teaching rooms for the masters, children, housekeeper, and servants upon the foundation.

The OLD BRIDGE,

Which extends across the river Clyde, from the
E e   south

south end of the Stockwell to the village of the Gorbals, and Hutcheson-town, was erected in the year
1350, being constructed of timber. Its founder was
William Rae, then bishop of Glasgow. This
structure formerly consisted of eight arches, two
of these are, however, now built up. It was also
crossed by a gateway or porch, on that side nearest to the village of Gorbals, which has been taken
down, in order to open or widen the communication.

The old bridge continued without repair till
the year 1671, when the arch situated farthest to
the south, fell *. This was again built up. Many
partial reparations thereafter took place, betwixt
and the year 1777, when an addition of several
feet was made to its eastern side, by which, not only was the fabric much strengthened, but the passage rendered free and convenient for carriages.

THE NEW BRIDGE.

In consequence of the extension of the city towards

* This accident took place on the 7th. July that year, "the
very day of Glasgow fair," says M'Ure, "and about 12
of the clock, and though hundreds, yea, I may venture to
say thousands, had passed and repassed of horse and foot, yet
not a single person got the least harm." The middle arch
was built at the expence of Lady Lochow, formerly mentioned, she having asked it *as a favour* from the bishop, that he
would allow her to assist in this public spirited undertaking.
Above this formerly was placed her bust, it is, however, now
removed.

wards the west, it was proposed to build another bridge across the river, to open a more ready communication from that quarter, with the country on the south and west.—It was accordingly begun to be built (in consequence of an act of parliament having been procured for that purpose,) in the year 1768, and was finished at the expence of little less than L. 9000 sterling.— It consists of seven arches, rising upon peirs, with angular points, and extends in length 500 feet, by 32 n breath, having a paved foot-path on each side, for foot passengers.

Between every arch, and directly over the center of each peir, is a small circular arch, which contributes to break the force of the water, when the river rises to a flood; they also add considerably to the light appearance of the bridge. Immediately above, there is a strong and deep cornice, with a parapet wall, in the Chinese stile.

Upon the bridge are placed, as on the old bridge, a number of lamps, which in the night, when lighted, have a beautiful effect, appearing in the form of an immense bow, extending betwixt the banks, and reflecting their images in the water; this is particularly observable from the west.

THE RIDING SCHOOL.

A house for teaching this useful accomplishment, was built about three years ago, upon the west side of York-street. Its front is of ashler work, in a plain and unaffected style.—Here such pupils, as wish to acquire a proper knowledge of horsemanship, are instructed by a person appointed for the purpose.

E e 2   CHAP.

CHAP. VIII.

Of the Population of Glasgow, its supply and Consumption of Provisions, Revenue, &c.

In order to ascertain the number of inhabitants in any given place, without having recourse to a particular enumeration, political writers have had recourse to several methods. These are mostly deduced from the lists of births, funerals, or the number of families in the city or district; various objections are, however, obvious to each of these modes, particular the two former, and principally for this reason, that the inhabitants in any particular place, are by no means stationary; numbers who are born in the country, live and die in the city,† while others

born

---

† For the same reason, it also appears unfair to argue against the unhealthfulness of a city, because the lists of funerals surpass in proportion the register of births which we find in country districts.

born in the city, increase the funeral register of a country district, or die in foreign parts. Many again, who are neither born nor die in the city, have resided in it for the greatest part of their lives, and consequently tend to increase the population, beyond what any calculation, founded upon the number of births or funerals, will give.

The third method mentioned, is certainly less liable to objection, though even by it, from the great disproportion betwixt the numbers in different families, even although what may be reckoned a fair medium is struck, very great errors will take place.

Before proceeding to detail the statement of the population of Glasgow and its suburbs, from the most exact of all methods, the particular enumeration of its inhabitants, it may not be amiss to present the reader with a statement of their number at different periods, drawn from the modes of calculation just now mentioned, being the only methods left us to determine the point, but which may give some idea at least, of the population in each of these years.

In the year 1609, a register of baptisms was begun in this city, which has since been carried down to the present day. In taking a view of that register for the first seven years, the medium number of children registered is 294, which multiplied by 26, the number usually allowed, as that which comes nearest the truth, in ascertaining the population of a place, makes the number of souls in Glasgow, 7,644. If we examine that record several years afterwards, viz. for four years preceding the Restoration, in 1660, the average number of births appears to be $564\frac{1}{3}$, which, by the same rule, gives 14,670;

yet

yet we are surprised to find the medium, in the next four years after, to be only 473, which multiplied in the same manner, gives 12, 298.

Whether this decrease in the population arose from some cause about the time of the Restoration, or whether, as is most likely, from some defect in the register of baptisms, cannot now be determined with precision; but if the register is accurate, and to be reckoned a rule for calculation, the city does not appear to have recovered the same population it had the year preceding the Restoration, till about the year 1720. As this register includes only the number born within the royalty, the inhabitants of the suburbs are therefore excluded, besides it is unfair, to place too much reliance upon this mode, as many, particularly the members of the secession, neglect to register their childrens, names in the general record.

To give somewhat of a more just idea of the population, it will be necessary to present a detail of the number of burials, from the register kept for that purpose, and which includes both royalty and suburbs. This we have done in the following table, from the beginning of the last century to the year 1791, for every ten years, striking the average for every year in the same manner, proceeding from 1791 to 1796. From the year 1796, to the end of the last year 1802, the annual amount of each year is marked, and in that last mentioned in the note, the diseases of which they died, and the numbers interred in each church-yard are particularly expressed.

Average

Burials.

Average from 1701 to 1711 inclusive,			493
——————— 1711—1720	-	-	639
——————— 1721—1730	-	-	711
——————— 1731—1740	-	-	728
——————— 1741—1750	-	-	823
——————— 1751—1760	-	-	1003
——————— 1761—1770	-	-	1159
——————— 1771—1780	-	-	1484
——————— 1781—1790	-	-	1924
——————— 1791—1796	-	-	2008
——————— 1796	-	-	1813
——————— 1797	-	-	2064
——————— 1798	-	-	2181
——————— 1799	-	-	2499
——————— 1800	-	-	2096
——————— 1801	-	-	1928
——————— 1802	-	-	2325

In the last year, of this number of 2,325,
there were interred in the different church-yards;
in the respective months after-mentioned, viz. in

	Males.	Fem.	Total.		Whereof have died,	
					Age.	Number.
January,	60	74	134		Under 2 years.	372
February,	47	48	95		Between 2 & 5	171
March,	46	71	117		——— 5 & 10	48
April,	38	30	68		——— 10 & 20	41
May,	36	37	73		——— 20 & 30	51
June,	30	29	59		——— 30 & 40	72

July

	Males.	Fem.	Total.	Whereof have died, Age.	Number.
July,	31	32	63	40 & 50	79
August,	33	36	59	50 & 60	73
September,	38	50	88	60 & 70	91
October,	56	61	117	70 & 80	72
November,	47	51	98	80 & 90	35
December,	69	68	137	90 & 100	2
				At 103	1
	531	577	1108		

1108

Of these there were interred in the High church-
yard, - - - - - - 520
    In do. from the Infirmary, - - 30

550

In the Black Friars and North-West yards, 588
In the Towns Hospital, do. 53
In the English Chapel, do. 37

1227

In the Calton burying-ground, 508
In the Gorbals, do. 358
In Anderston relief, do. 152
In do. Antiburgher, do. 80
Excess above 1801—397.

2325

Of this number the 1108 who belonged to the city, died of
the following diseases, viz:

Abortive and still-born,	67	Child-bed	12
Accidental,	6	Chincough,	48
Aged,	193	Colic,	3

In deducing the population of a place, for any particular year, from lists of this kind, political writers endeavour to ascertain what proportion die within the district annually, and having this number fixed, the average population is estimated, by simply multiplying the number of burials by the quantity thus found.

In ascertaining the proportion of those who die annually within the city of Glasgow, we are

F f   furnished

Apoplexy,	-	-	4	Iliac passion,	-	2
Asthma,	-	-	5	Inflammation,	-	8
Bowelhive,	-	-	68	Jaundice,	-	1
Cancer,	-	-	1	Measles,	-	117
Cramp,	-	-	3	Palsy,	-	2
Consumption,	-	202	Rheumatism,	-	1
Croup,	-	-	36	Vomiting,	-	1
Dropsy,	-	-	6	Stopping,	-	10
Dysentery,	-	-	2	Sore throat,	-	3
Drowned,	-	-	2	Small-pox,	-	104
Fever,	-	-	142	Suddenly,	-	21
Fistula,	-	-	1	Teething,	-	19
Flux,	-	-	1	Water in the chest -	1
Gravel,	-	-	1	Water in the head -	13
Hysterics,	-	-	2			

1108

From this list, as well as others in some preceding years, it appears that the most fatal diseases here are consumption, fever, and the small-pox. This last disease is, however, not nearly so fatal as it appears to have been some years ago, in this city. At an average, betwixt 3 and 400 were annually cut off by it. This is owing partly to the almost general adoption of inoculation, and still more lately, to the introduction of the vaccine inoculation, the invention of Dr. Jenner, which bids fair, if universally adopted, to annihilate this scourge of the human race.

furnished with very ample information, from lists that have been taken up in an official manner, at different periods, by which it appears, that the average of deaths is about 1 to 32 annually *. Proceeding according to the rule just now mentioned, the average number in the city and suburbs for any year preceding, may be estimated.

In order to assist any calculations of this kind, and to give a comparative view of the population of the royalty of the city at different periods, we have subjoined the result of the principal enumerations. In the year 1712, the number of inhabited houses were, 3,405, which, at four to a family, makes the number of inhabitants, 13,620. In the year 1753, when Dr. Webster made his calculations for the widows' fund, the number supposed then in Glasgow was 18,336. In the year 1765, when a new division of the parishes was made, the number was reckoned 28,100. In 1780, from a survey then made, the number of families in the eight parishes was found to be 8,144, which at four to a family, makes the number of inhabitants, 32,576. In the year 1785, a very accurate survey was made by Mr.

* According to Mr. Gibson, in his history, the number of inhabitants in the year 1775 were 43,000, as taken up by the ministers and elders. Of this number there died that year, 1,333, being nearly in the proportion of one in thirty-two; for several succeeding years, this proportion was considerably above the truth; it has, however, since the year 1791, been as much below, there having, from the last enumeration, only 1 in 37 died per annum. Thirty-two, however, may be taken as the average. And from this it will appear, that the city of Glasgow is

Mr. Smellie, by which it was found that the number of inhabited houses were 9,102; number of males, 16,363; females, 19,776; total, 36,139. The next enumeration took place in 1791, from which it appeared, that the number of houses were 10,291, and inhabitants, 41,777.

From the want of proper date, previous to this last mentioned period, we are unable to give the exact enumeration of the suburbs, which, in every city, bear such a great proportion to the size of the town itself. But in this year, they were likewise numbered, from which the population at that time, is deduced as follows, viz.

Number within the city as stated above,	41,777
In the Calton, - - - -	6,695
Anderston, - - - - -	3,895
Grahamston, - - - - -	896
Gorbals, - - - - -	6,448
Cowcaddens, Parkhouse, &c. - -	1,257
Camlachie, - - - - -	977

Total, 61,945

From this last mentioned period, downwards to the year 1801, the city seems to have increased in
F f 2   population,

---

is as healthful as any town in Britain, if not in Europe; the proportion of persons dying, according to the number of inhabitants, being much more in almost every other city. Thus in Edinburgh, noted for its air and healthy situation, one in thirty is the proportion; nay, according to one of its historians, (Maitland) it is one in twenty-eight. In London, one in twenty, three-fourths. Manchester, one in twenty-eight, and Liverpool one in twenty-seven, seven-tenths.

population, in an almost unprecedented manner. This principally arose from the flourishing state of its commerce and manufactures.

Government having ordered an exact account of the population of the kingdom to be taken that year, the greatest activity and accuracy was used in the execution of the command. The result, with respect to Glasgow, was as follows.

In Ward No.	Number of Families.	Number of Males.	Number of Females.	Total.
1	239	423	553	976
2	456	766	956	1722
3	509	852	1111	1963
4	416	705	936	1641
5	344	730	1001	1731
6	155	332	537	869
7	427	793	1156	1949
8	215	503	674	1177
9	184	377	458	835
10	552	855	1187	2042
11	667	1045	1485	2530
12	481	667	942	1609
13	760	1189	1555	2744
14	331	687	954	1641
15	797	1514	1924	3438
16	299	512	620	1132
17	369	655	880	1535
18	410	698	1012	1710
19	572	1009	1283	2292
20	597	1000	1214	2214
21	1048	1804	2281	4085
22	602	1066	1318	2384

In Ward No.	Number of Families.	Number of Males.	Number of Females.	Total.
23 - -	532 -	996 -	1216 -	2212
24 - -	818 -	1735 -	2090 -	3825
	11780 -	20913 -	27343 , -	48256
Towns' Hospital,		137 -	252 -	389
Bridewell asylum, .		-	2 -	2
Infirmary,		38 -	46 -	84
Jail,		30 -	8 -	38
Bridewell,		2 -	58 -	60
Barracks, including wo-men and children, }		615 -	196 -	811
		21735 -	27905 -	49640

SUBURBS.

		Males.	Females.	Total.
Brought down,	-	21735 -	27905 -	49640
Gorbals, -	-	1844 -	2052 -	3896
Tradestown, -	-	922 -	940 -	1862
Hutcheson-Town, -	-	443 -	447 -	890
Muirhouses, &c. -	-	441 -	470 -	911
Calton, -	-	4732 -	5322 -	10,054
Bridgetown,	-	1850 -	1946 -	3796
Camlachie, -	-	465 -	470 -	935
Lady-well and Parkhouse, }	-	126 -	117 -	243
Anderston, - -	-	2090 -	2372 -	4462
Cowcaddens, - -		65 -	61 -	126
Remaining inhabitants in the other suburbs and Barony, around the royalty,			.	9815
Total number of inhabitants* in 1802.				86630

From

* It may not be improper in this place likewise, to state the

From the statement of the population in 1791, with respect to Dr. Webster's, it appears, that the city had gained an increase from the year 1755 to that time, of 38,399 inhabitants. But how much more rapidly has it advanced since the year 1791 to the period of the last enumeration, a space of only 11 years, when we find an increase of no less than 24,685, a fact almost incredible, was it not vouched by the best authority. This increase has been at the rate of upwards of 2000 per annum.

It also appears from this survey, and the others, throughout the empire, made at the same time, that Glasgow, by containing 86,630 inhabitants, is the most populous town in Britain, next to London; the third being Manchester, whose population it exceeds by 2,610. Edinburgh stands in the fourth place, the number there being 82,000, including Leith, the port of the city.

From this enumeration, the number of females exceeds the number of males in Glasgow, by 7,389, which is to be accounted for from the great number
of

population of the County of Lanark, in which Glasgow is situated, as lately ascertained by order of government; it is as follows.

COMPLETE POPULATION of LANARKSHIRE.

From the return made to the Justices of peace, in consequence of the late act of Parliament.

Upper Ward.

Biggar, - -	1216	Crawfordjohn,	712	Lesmahagow,	3070
Carluke, - -	1756	Coulter, - -	369	Libberton, -	706
Carmichael, -	832	Dolphington,	231	Pettinean, -	430
Carnwath, -	2680	Douglas, -	1730	Symington,	307
Carstairs, -	899	Dunsyre, -	352	Walston, -	383
Covington, -	456	Lamington, -	375	Wiston and }	
Crawford, -	1671	Lanark, -	4692	Roberton, }	757

of the latter that continually recruit the army and navy;
from their going abroad, and from the many accidents to
which they are exposed. Whereas, women are generally stationary in the place where they were born, and are
commonly not engaged in any employment that is hazardous or unhealthy. This survey, compared with
the bills of mortality, shows, that out of this number
about 178 die, at an average, every month; $44\frac{1}{2}$ every
week; and every day, $6\frac{1}{4}$; a serious but useful lesson.

There are, perhaps, no articles so essential to the
convenience of a large town, as the supplies of fuel
and water. With respect to the first of these articles,
no city in Europe, it is believed, is better supplied.
Coal is found in great abundance in the ground
towards the east of the city, and likewise upon
the south of the river. In the ground upon the
east * there are five different strata or seams,

from

Middle Ward.			Lower Ward.	
Blantyre, -	1751	Kilbride (East,) } 2330	Barony, -	26710
Bothwell, -	3017		Calder, -	2130
Cumbuslang,	1558	Monkland (East,) } 4613	Carmunnock,	700
Cambus- } - nethan, }	1972	Monkland (West,) } 4006	Glasgow rovalty, }	49640
Dalserf, - -	1100		Gorbals, -	3896
Dalziel, - -	611	Shotts, - 2127	Govan, -	6701
Glassford, -	953	Stonehouse, 1259	Rutherglen,	2437
Hamilton, -	5908	Strathaven, 3623		

Total in Lanarkshire, - - - - - 150,666

Increase since 1791, when the Statistical } account of Scotland was published, } 25,133

* At one of these coal-pits in this situation, and belonging
to James M‘Nair, Esq. of Shettleston, the first steam engine
for drawing off the water from the coal-pits was erected in the year 1764. Since that time, a great number of
others

from 3 to 4½ feet thick, all of which are wrought to a great extent, so as not only to supply the demand of the town, which consumes about 160,000, tons per annum, but likewise to afford great quantities for exportation. The price of these coals differs at different pits; in general, however, at the present time, they are sold and delivered in the town, at the rate of 6s. per cart, of 12 cwt.

As to the quality or quantity of the water with which the city is supplied, we can say less. It is in general, not of the best kind, as most of the springs contain selenite, in greater or lesser proportion and some of them contain iron, which is, for the most

part

others have been set up in the neighbourhood of the city. At these pits, as has been mentioned, there are several strata or seams of coal, of different thicknesses, and at different distances from one another. These all lie nearly parallel to each other, but not parallel to the surface of the earth; having the *dip*, as it is termed by the colliers, or their declination towards the river Clyde, and rising as you retire from the river, nearly to the surface of the earth, till they *crop* out. And what is very remarkable, the seams of coal on the other side of Clyde also, have their dip towards its bed, so that the strata of the different sides of the river, instead of lying in the same plane, are inclined to each other, at a certain angle. In some pits, the strata of coal are of the following thicknesses. First, the upper coal from 4 to 4½ feet thick; 2d ell coal, from 2½ to 3 feet; and 3d main coal, from 4½ to 5½ feet. These are the only seams that have as yet been wrought. Above the coal there lies a thin but very rich stratum of iron-stone, which, till the erection of the Clyde-iron-works in the neighbourhood, was regarded as an incumbrance; now it is a source of wealth, and gives employment to many. The value of the coal mines in the Barony Parish, is estimated at upwards of £.40,000 sterling, per annum.

part, suspended by the carbonic acid *. Towards
the west † quarter of the city, the water is much
purer than towards the east, and there is, in the
Green belonging to the town, a spring of water, called Arns well, of the very best quality in the country. The quantity of it, however, is not sufficient
to afford a supply to the whole inhabitants, and it
lies so much below the level of the greater part of
the city, that it has prevented its being conducted into it. Many proposals have been given in for
supplying Glasgow with water, from different sources, and surveys have been made, by order of the
magistrates, in order to ascertain where a proper
quantity can be procured, in a situation sufficiently
elevated, to serve the purpose. As yet, however, nothing has been concluded upon, though it is evident, that there are many considerable springs, in

G g   proper

* One spring, not far from the city, contains calcareous earth,
which it deposites, in its course, on the vegetables, &c. forming
many singular incrustations.

† In this quarter is a well called the West-port well, which
is noted for the purity of its water, when compared with the o-
thers. It is so much frequented, and so excellent is the spring,
that according to repeated observations of the writer, who resides in its neighbourhood, there are drawn from it 5,850
gallons per day, at an average. There are several chalybeate
springs around the town, particularly on the side of the Clyde, a-
bove Rutherglen bridge. At Anderston there is a spring, which
contains one grain of mineral alkali or soda, in the pint of water. And at north Wood-side, there is a sulphureous spring
upon the side of the river Kelvin, which formerly was often
used, it is said, with success, for scorbutic disorders.

proper situations, which, if added together, would answer the proposed end. Two of these shall only be mentioned. The first, or that nearest to the town, is in the lands of Burnhead, in the parish of East Monkland, about one half mile east of Airdrie, and eleven from Glasgow. This spring, which is called the Wand-spring, affords a plentiful supply, at all seasons, of the most excellent soft water, and sufficient to fill a pipe of 2½ or 3 inches calibre. The second spring lies two miles farther, in the lands of Braco, and parish of Shotts, belonging to Robert Carrick, Esq; its quality is similar to the Wand-spring; its produce is at least equally abundant. Its name is Tipper-davy well. These two united, or one of them, with some others in the neighbourhood, would, at all times, furnish the city, by means of a cistern and pipes, with a proper quantity of water; in the same manner is Edinburgh supplied, from the cistern at Comiston. This cistern, which is about 7 miles from that city, receives five distinct streams, from as many pipes, collecting the water from different and distant fountains. These, when at the fullest, discharge into the cistern from 800 to 900 Scots pints, or almost 7 hogsheads a minute; when at the lowest, from 150 to 170 pints. From Comiston, the water is brought, in a leaden pipe, of 4¼ inches calibre, to the reservoir upon the Castlehill of Edinburgh, the highest part of the city; yet, at the same time, 44 feet beneath the level of the water at Comiston.

But if still there should be good objections against
bringing

bringing water thus into Glasgow, why not take advantage of the Clyde, which would always afford an abundant supply.

Indeed it is surprising, that a scheme for this purpose has never hitherto been put into execution. It can only be accounted for, from a prejudice which is entertained by many against river-water, which, they alledge, is inferior to that direct from the spring. Unless the quality of the spring, however, be excellent, which is not often the case in this neighbourhood, the waters of the Clyde, in point of intrinsic goodness, if properly managed, are, much superior; a fact that is known to every chemist, or other person acquainted with the nature and qualities of water. That river-water is considered in a different light, in most other great cities, is a fact well known. London is supplied from the Thames and New river, and Paris from the Seine; cities, whose inhabitants are as nice and distinguishing, as those in any other quarter.

The expence of conducting the waters of the Clyde into a proper reservoir, and of the several erections, filters, and pipes, which would be necessary, no doubt would be very considerable. This, however, could easily be defrayed, by an assessment, which, it is believed, the inhabitants would willingly agree to, in compensation for an article, which is every where so universally in use.

Its waters might be conducted into a reservoir, properly placed, in an elevated situation, by either of those two methods.— 1st, By a channel or pipes, brought from a point up the Clyde, which should be found to be higher than the situation of the greatest part of the city; or, 2dly, raising the waters of the river, by means of machines.

With respect to the first plan, some objections may be made, as to the distance from which it must be brought, in order to accommodate the principal part of the town, for as the river has no great fall for a number of miles upwards, it is evident, that that point must be at a considerable distance. If this is reckoned, however, no good objection, a reservoir of proper dimensions could be constructed at the east end, in such a situation, that at the time of the greatest drought, it might still be full of water; from this reservoir, a channel might be cut, or pipes laid, winding alongst the banks of the river, till they have passed any high grounds, whose height is greater than the level of the water in the reservoir; after this, the direction might be varied, so as to lead to a water-house, placed as high as possible in the vicinity of the city, towards the east. This plan, however, no doubt, could not be effected, but at a great expence; it would likewise, most likely, meet with much opposition from some of the landholders.

The second method of bringing the water into the city by means of machinery, appears not so liable to objection. It is most likely to be effected by means of steam engines,* which would force the

water

* An engine of a four horse power, on Bolton and Watt's patent plan, will raise to the height of 80 feet, 3,333 gallons of water per hour. The neat calculation, however, is 5,074, but as there is always a loss in opening and shutting the valves, there cannot be allowed less than a fifth of the whole for that deficiency.

water into a reservoir, from which pipes might branch into the town. As to purifying the water from all extraneous substances, filtration might be adopted, through beds of sand or gravel.

In speaking thus upon the different plans for supplying Glasgow with water, the canals might likewise be mentioned, which would afford it in great abundance, it might be brought, likewise, to the upper stories of every house; the bason of the Monkland canal being exactly upon a level with the top of the spire of the Tolbooth steeple, whose height is 126 feet from its base. This water would be of the greatest use in extinguishing fires.

As to the quantity of water which the city requires daily, it is evident, no exact calculation can be made, though considering the consumption, and taking in public works, &c. it is believed, it cannot be less than 80,000 gallons every 24 hours, as already stated in the note.

In such a city as Glasgow, the consumption of provisions must necessarily be very great, these are not

---

ciency. Such an engine as this, would therefore, most likely, answer the demands of the greatest part of the town, as it would raise into the reservoir, placed 80 feet above the level of the river, about 80,000 gallons every 24 hours, a quantity, perhaps, fully sufficient. Neither would its annual expence for fuel be very considerable. It would require 12 cwt. of good coal per 24 hours, which, at the present rate of 6s. amounts yearly to L.109. 10s. If coal culm was used, the expence would be less, but the engine would require double the quantity.

not only brought from the country immediately surrounding it, which would be unable to supply the demand, but from other places at a much greater distance. Oats, meal, and butter, have long been brought from Ireland, to a very great amount annually; meal is likewise brought from Galloway, Stirling, and Ayrshire, as well as different other articles of provision, for the use of the city. It, however, cannot be said, that these articles are retailed here, at the cheapest rate; or even nearly so cheap as in the city of Edinburgh, the reason of which, it is believed, is not so easily to be accounted for.

To ascertain the quantity of provisions of all kinds, used annually, in Glasgow, is what cannot be done; we shall, however, state some particulars, which may, at least, give some idea of the consumption.

The quantity of wheat manufactured from May 1802, to May last, 1803, at the mills of Partick and Clayslap, was 69,000 bolls. And it is supposed, by a person well acquainted in the business, that there may have been manufactured, at the different mills of Garscube, Scots-town, Woodside, &c. around the city, from 20 to 25,000 bolls, during the same space. Besides a great deal of flour is imported here from Leith and America; though indeed, it cannot, be said, that the whole of this is used in Glasgow, considerable quantities being sold to Paisley, Port-Glasgow, Greenock, Dumbarton, Kilmarnock, &c.; upon the whole, however, it is probable, the city may use betwext 60 and 70,000 bolls per year.

The

The quantity of oatmeal, pease, and barley meals, used here, is not nearly so considerable as formerly, from the more frequent use of tea and wheaten bread; they may, however, amount to 20,000 bolls per annum.

Quantity of Butcher-meat used in Glasgow, in the respective years under mentioned, viz.

In the year 1771	-	1772	-	1793	-	1802
Oxen, -	5827	-	6411	-	6608	- 5632
Calves, -	11597	-	9204	-	9597	- 8120
Sheep, -	27955	-	23110	-	27401	- 29657
Lambs, -	14723	-	10790	-	44107	- 27886
Swine, -	116	-	89	-	12	- 84
Goats, -	438	-	443	-		- 1

John-street Market,

Oxen,	-	-	-	-	-	160
Calves,	-	-	-	-	-	190
Sheep,	-	-	-	-	-	270

A considerable number of cattle are likewise killed in the Calton and Anderston markets, but their number we have not had it in our power to ascertain.

It will be observed, that the number of cattle slaughtered in these different years, is not in proportion to the population; with respect to the two last mentioned years, 1793 and 1802; this is accounted for from the encreased weight of the cattle, which, from an improved management, are at least one fourth heavier than they were 20 years ago. The great supply of herrings of late years, may also be taken into the account, as another cause tending to diminish the consumption

consumption of butcher-meat, particularly amongst the labouring classes of the community; neither should a fall of wages, which took place last year, from a temporary cause, it is hoped, and an increase in the price of provisions, be neglected in accounting for this circumstance.

It is impossible to estimate the quantity of poultry or game used in Glasgow, as no particular account is kept by the people who deal in them. Their prices are, within these few years, greatly raised, from the increased demand, and increased riches of the inhabitants; vast numbers are brought to the city, particularly in the winter season, from the adjoining counties, and even from the Highlands, from whence, likewise, are brought, or rather imported, in great abundance, dried ling and cod, of a very good quality. Of the larger fowls, the goose and the turkey do not seem to be so plentiful here as in the Edinburgh market, neither are game so easily procured as in that city. The other kinds are equally plentiful and good.

Glasgow has been hitherto but indifferently supplied with white fish, though the demand is great, and though the Firth of Clyde, at no great distance, would yield an abundant supply. A new fishing company have, however, been lately established, who promise to provide the markets more plentifully, and with a greater variety. Instead of bringing them, when caught, up the Clyde, they are carried over-land from the coast of Ayrshire, where the fish are reckoned to be of a better quality, and in greater quantity, than nearer the mouth of the river. Salmon are, in the proper
season,

season, in plenty, and are here a rich and well tast-
ed fish; their price, however, is very high, though
caught almost at the door. This arises from the
high rents the fishers pay for a particular tract of
the river, upon which they are allowed to exercise
their profession. Of the finer fish, such as the tur-
bot, sturgeon and mackerel, they are almost
never to be obtained. As a recompence, we have a
much more useful species, the herring, often in
great abundance, and of a much better quality than
those caught upon the east coast. So plentiful are
they some years, that it has been reckoned, two
millions are brought to the Broomielaw, fresh,
from July to November. Great quantities are
annually sent salted, from the mouth of the river,
to America and the West Indies. Indeed, at one
time, they were the staple trade of the Clyde.

The shell-fish, such as oysters, lobsters, crabs,
mussels, and shrimps, are here sold at a very high
price. Neither are the four last kinds plentiful,
they are mostly brought from the east coast, and
consequently are not so fresh or good as those exposed in the Edinburgh market. The oysters sell
here at 4s. and 4s. 6d. per hundred. During
the season, a considerable quantity are brought
from Loch Ryan and the Western Isles, to the
Broomielaw; they are, very small, and consequently sell at a reduced price, comparatively
with those brought from the Forth. The markets
at Glasgow are well supplied with butter of an excellent quality, its price, however, is higher than at
Edinburgh, it sells at 1s. 7d. per pound; a few years

ago, the best sold at 1od. Cheese is also in plenty, both Scotch and English; the Dunlop cheese, which is made not many miles from the city, is deservedly esteemed; it sells from 8d. to 1od. per pound, of 22 ounces.

Vegetables are to be had in abundance, and mostly very low, speaking comparatively, potatoes, the most useful root with which we are acquainted, are sold during the greatest part of the year, at 1od. the peck. Green pease, at the first of the season, are sold for about 8s. per peck, towards the end, at 1s. 6d.

Asparagus and cucumbers are in plenty, and moderate, melons are not in such abundance, neither are peaches, apricots and nectarines, to be met with, but in the fruiterers shops, where grapes are likewise, in their season, to be procured, at the *moderate* price of 2s. 6d. per pound. A few pine apples are likewise to be had in the shops, mostly reared in the green-houses of gentlemen in the country.

The markets are well supplied with the more common fruits. Apples and pears are brought here in abundance from the orchards on the Clyde, between Hamilton and Lanark, in great variety and of a superior quality, to those to be met with any where else in the kingdom. Great quantities of apples are likewise imported here from America and England. The price per sleek, this year, is from 10 to 12s. Plumbs are likewise brought from the same quarter. The smaller fruits are also plentiful, of these the strawberry takes the preference. The cultivation of this rich fruit was almost neglected

glected here, till within these few years. They
are now in abundance, and in the throng of the
of the season, if the expression may be allowed, sell
from 8d. to 10d. per pint.

It is not easy to say what is the quantity of wine
consumed in Glasgow, but it must be considerable.
The port is excellent of its kind, not resembling the
adulterated trash sold under that name in England.
Rum is also to be obtained here of the best quality.
Good brandy and whisky are, however, more rare. *
With respect to the produce of the brewery, Glasgow manufactures excellent porter, acknowledged
inferior to that brewed no where but in London,
which it very nearly resembles, at least, when compared with the produce of the Edinburgh brewery. In ales, however, we are much behind Edinburgh, Newcastle, or Burton.

To give an idea of the present prices of the principal articles of provision, we have affixed the following table, in which every article stands higher charged than in the preceeding years, except
1801; and as a contrast, the rate of the same arti-

H h 2   cles

* Though good spirits of the last mentioned kind are not
easily procured at a moderate rate, yet we cannot complain
of a scarcity of inferior spirit. It is indeed too plentiful, and
notwithstanding the late duties, still too cheap. Its use a-
mongst the lower classes, is almost universal. Ale, which was
formerly their common beverage, being now seldom used, it
having given way to this pernicious spirit, whose use is equally destructive to health and morals. Yet the demand for it is
increasing amongst this order of people, of all ages, with a
rapidity which threatens the most important effects upon society.

cles 26 years ago, viz. in 1777, as far as we have been able to collect them.

Prices of butcher-meat, poultry, wild fowl, fish, &c. in Glasgow, Anno 1803.

	1803.	1777.
Beef per pound, 22½ ounces,	from 10d. to 1s. -	from 4d. to 7d.
Mutton, per pound, - -	9d. to 1s. - - -	3d. to 7d.
Lamb, - - - - - -	6d.	- - 2½ to 7d.
Veal, - - - - -	8d. to 1s.	4d. to 7d.
Pork, - - - - - -	8d. to 1s.	3d. to 6d.
Fowls, per pair, - - -	4s. 6d. to 6s. - -	1s. 8d. to 4s.
Ducks, per pair, - - -	3s. 6d. to 4s. - -	2s. to 3s.
Chickens, - - - -	1s. 6d, to 2s. - -	8d. to 1s. 8d.
Goose, per piece, - -	3s. to 3s. 6d. - -	2s. to 3s.
Partridges and Muirfowl, very rare,		
Turkey, per piece, - -	8s. to 10s.	
Salmon beginning of the season this year, in Oct. 1st,	2s. 6d. to 4s. - - English pound,	1d. to 3
Haddocks, per pound, - -	4d. to 6d.	
Cod, per pound, - -	2d. to 4d.	
Whitings, per pound, - -	4d. to 6d.	6d. to 1s. per doz.
Lobster, per piece, - - -	10d. to 1s. -	6d. to 2s. 6d.
Crab, per piece,	10d. to 1s.	
Herrings, per 100, fresh,	5s. - - - -	2s. to 8s. 4d.
Oysters, per 100, - - -	4s. -	8d. to 1s. 8d.
Butter, - - - - - -	1s. 6d. 1s. 7d. - -	6d. to 9d.
Potatoes, per peck, of 7 English gallons, heaped,	10d - -	9d.
English cheese, - - - -	16s. per stone,	
Dunlop, do.	10s. to 12s. - -	
Meal, per peck, of 8 pounds Dutch weight,	1s. 5d.	11d.
Barley, per stone, - - -	-	2s. 8d.
Common, Do. - - -	-	2s.
Eggs, per doz.	10d. to 1s. 3d.	3d. to 7d.

REVENUE of GLASGOW.

The revenue of this city, arises from the rents

of

of lands and houses, belonging to the community; from a duty upon all grain and meal brought into the town which is called the ladles; from an impost of two pennies Scots, upon every Scots pint of ale or beer, brewed or sold within Glasgow; from the rents of the seats in the churches; from dues payable out of the markets; from the dues of cranage at the quay, at the Weigh-house, &c. and from the other customs peculiar to, or customary in royal burghs.

This revenue has been long upon the increase, upon an average of years, though it is still very inadequate to answer all the ends to which the public spirit of the magistracy could apply it, for the benefit of the city. At the time Mr. Gibson wrote his history of the town, it appears to have been about L. 6000 sterling. From that time, which was the year 1777, it increased gradually to the year 1797, when the first edition of this treatise was published; at that period it amounted nearly to the sum of L. 8000 sterling. In the last year, the revenue was L. 9975 : 1 : 6¼d. sterling, and the expenditure 10093 : 18 : 4. Of the sources from which this is derived, and of the expenditure, a better idea will be formed from the following tables, which contain an account of both revenue and expenditure for last year, with which the writer has been favoured, through the politeness of James Spreul, Esq. city chamberlain.

REVENUE OF THE CITY OF GLASGOW, 1802.

Ladle-dues, - - - L. 1050 0 0

Beef

Beef and mutton market dues,	L. 410 - 13 - 4
Wash-house dues, - -	571
Pontage and cranage dues, - -	296
Tron and Weigh-house dues, -	360
Multure dues, - - -	60
Fish and potatoe market dues, -	120
Butter milk, and egg market dues,	20
North-west burial ground, - -	216 - 13 - 4
Burgess and freedom fines, - -	148 - 6 - 10
Royal Closs, Greenock, - -	290
Feu-duty Gorbals, and ground annuals,	27 - 12 - 0$\frac{5}{8}$
Feu duty, Port-Glasgow, - -	51 - 5 - 6
Dry-dock, Port-Glasgow, - -	230 - 12
Forth and Clyde Navigation, -	105 - 13 - 4
Entry money lands, Port-Glasgow,	12
Rents, greens, yards, parks, and steadings,	53 - 12 - 6
Rents, powder Magazine -	8 - 11
Rents, mills and their lands, -	253 - 11
Rents, houses, shops, and warehouses, -	478 - 4
Rents, Gorbal Barony lands, -	309 - 4 - 8
Rents, green market, - -	70
Rents, church seats, - -	1366 - 11 - 4
Green of Glasgow, - -	202 - 10
Gorbal Barony coal, - -	25
Quarries, - - - -	22 - 3 - 2
Impost dues, beer and ale, -	2404 - 3 - 1
Shore dues, Port-Glasgow, -	20
Feus, Ramshorn, Deanside, &c.	209 - 19 3$\frac{4}{12}$
Fues of land and ground annuals,	536 - 15 - 1

Entry

Entry money, Gorbal Barony lands, L.45   -   -

L.9975 - 1 - 6¼

EXPENDITURE OF THE CITY OF GLASGOW, 1802.

Bridewell,	224 - 4 - 3
Interest accompts,	L. 1539 - 14 - 4
Criminal prosecutions,	243 - 9 - 10
Mortifications,	178 - 16 - 10
Feus, tiend, stent, cess, &c..	303 - 11 - 1
Council warrants,	3522 - 10 - 3
Appointments, Ministers stipend, &c.	2549 - 18 - 3
General charges,	1281 - 5 - 10
Outer high-church,	24
Church vacancies,	121 - 7
Barony glebe,	20 - 7 - 1
Buchanan street,	85

L. 10093 - 18 - 4

From these tables, an idea will be formed, of the income and expenditure of the city of Glasgow. It is not however, to be supposed, that every year the expenditure exceeds the revenue, as that depends mostly upon accidental circumstances, such as new erections, repairing churches, &c; which may happen to bear heavier upon the funds one year than another. Neither is it proper to conclude this article, without mentioning, that the revenues of the city of Glasgow have been, these many years, managed with an economy that does the greatest honour to those gentlemen with whom they have been intrusted, so that, in this city, that grumbling

bling at the expenditure of the public money, which is in many places so prevalent, is never heard.*

* Having thus, in the text, stated what appeared to us most material, with respect to the population, consumption of provisions and revenue, it will not be uninteresting to note down some other facts which could not, with propriety, be taken notice of in any other place.

According to the statement in the books of the collector of the Cess, it appears, that the assessed taxes levied on the city at present, amounts to £.13,317 : 1s. : 5½d. And from a report by Mr. Bald, surveyor of the Police, it appears that the valued rent of dwelling houses within the royalty, independent of shops or warehouses, is £.57,735. The number of inhabited houses, and their respective rents, are as follows, viz.

2888 houses from £5 and under £.20 valued rent, £ 28,444
774   do. from £.20 and under £.40 do. do. 20,139
171   do. from £.40 and upwards   do. do. 9,152
                                                   ─────
                                              £.57,735

To this amount of the valued rent we may safely add one fifth more, or £.11,547, which will give at least some idea of the real rent—Its amount will therefore be, if we are right, £.69,282 sterling.

As to the number of shops and warehouses, they are certainly not under 2000. Many of these rent at 100 yearly, and very few below £.15. Taking £.20 as an average, they will yield £ 40,000, which, added to the rent of the inhabited houses, makes the real rent of the city of Glasgow, £.109,282 sterling. This calculation is, however, offered with much diffidence; it may amount to much more, but certainly is not less.

The number of houses licensed in Glasgow, for retailing spirituous liquors last year, amounted to no fewer than 1280. Besides 110 who take out a licence for dealing in wines. There were fined by the justices for retailing liquors without a licence, 200, during the same period.

CHAP.

CHAP. IX.

THE Political Constitution of Glasgow—The Town Council—The Merchants' House—The Trades' House—The Fourteen Incorporations—Of the Courts of Law which sit in the city—The Circuit Court —The Sheriff and Commissary Courts—The Town, Dean of Guild, and Justice of Peace Court, &c.

THE city of Glasgow, as we have already no- ticed, was first erected by William the Lyon into a royal burgh, in favour of Joceline, bishop of Glasgow, in the year 1172. This erection was afterwards confirmed by several succeeding monarchs. Upon the application of bishop Turnbull, in 1450, king James the II. † erected the city and barony into a burgh of regality, in favour of that prelate and his successors in office, and they, the more effectually to secure the obedience of their vassals, tenants, and other inhabitants of the barony, appointed powerful nobles as bailies of the regality. This office continued long in the family of Lennox; and in the year 1621, they

I i

they

† In King James's charter, the bishop held the city as a burgh of regality, by paying yearly, upon St. John's day, a red rose, if the same should be asked.

they acquired from the archbishop, an absolute and irredeemable right thereto.—The duke of Lennox at length resigned it to the crown, who, after the Revolution, until 1748, appointed Baillies of the regality.

In the year 1611, James the VI. granted to the city, a very ample charter, erecting it into a royal burgh; and in 1636, his immediate successor, Charles the I, granted another, containing many important privileges, and confirming its power of electing a Baillie on the river Clyde, whose district extends from the bridge to the Cloch, (about four miles below Greenock) within which he exercises a maritime, civil and criminal jurisdiction. This charter was in the year 1661, ratified by Parliament, as were the whole, passed in favour of the city, by another act, in 1690.

Although, from the period in which Glasgow was first erected into a royal burgh, it held its commercial and political privileges by successive grants from the crown; yet as these grants were in favour of the bishop, he, afterwards the archbishop, and then the lord of regality (who, upon the abolition of episcopacy, came in place of the archbishop) had the privilege of electing the magistracy. In times, however, of violence and disorder, this right was sometimes interrupted, and occasionally exercised by the king, by the convention of estates, by parliament, or by the citizens themselves; but according to the legal constitution of the burgh, the archbishops, and the lord of regality,

regality, on his coming in their place, did, previous to the year 1641, elect the provost and bailies annually, from lists for the latter, sent them by the town council; and as the new council were nominated by the provost and bailies, the archbishop or lord of regality had, in fact, the nomination of the whole. This ample power was considerably abridged by an act of parliament in the year 1641, which gave to the city the liberty of electing their own magistrates, with this exception, that a list should be made out yearly, and presented to the duke of Lennox (then in the right of the archbishop, as lord of regality) of three persons, from which he should, either by himself or his commissioners, nominate the provost, and in case of their absence, or failing to do so, the election of the provost was vested in the magistrates and council.

This constitution continued only till the restitution of episcopacy in the year 1662, when the archbishop was restored to the full privileges of nomination, and which he or his successors enjoyed till the Revolution. At that period, William and Mary, by their charter, authorised a free election, and empowered the magistrates and council to elect the provost. This charter was afterwards confirmed by an act of parliament in 1690, wherein it is inserted, that the Town Council shall have power and privilege of chusing the magistrates, and other officers of the burgh, as fully and freely in all respects as the city of Edinburgh, or any other royal burgh within the kingdom.

The form and manner of this election by the

I i 2   Town

Town Council, has since varied according to the different sets or constitutions adopted at different periods. In 1711 the former set underwent some alterations. In 1748 another set was adopted, and afterwards confirmed by the convention of royal burghs, which is at present adhered to with this alteration, that instead of two merchant bailies, three are now elected, and instead of one from the Trades, two are chosen. This alteration was allowed upon a petition of the Magistrates and Council to the convention of royal burghs in 1801.

By the original constitution and set of the city, as well as by that which is at present in use. The civil establishment of Glasgow consists of three different bodies, viz. 1st, The Magistrates with the Town Council.—2d, The Merchants' House.—And 3d, The Trade's House;—the two last being in fact the constituents of the first.

THE TOWN COUNCIL

consists of the Lord Provost, five Bailies, a Dean of Guild, a Deacon Convener, a Treasurer, a Master of Work, and twenty three Councilmen, twelve of whom are merchants, and the remaining eleven tradesmen. These compose what is called the ordinary Council of the city; but in case of the Dean of Guild, Deacon Convener, Treasurer, or Master of Work, who are, *en officio*, Counsellors, be elected from persons not in Council at the time, they become upon such election, extraordinary Counsellors.

In the Council is vested the care of the public interest, and in the Magistracy in particular, the executive government of the city.

The.

The gentlemen who at present compose this very respectable body are,

Laurence Craigie, Esq; Lord Provost.

Archibald Campbell, Esq.

James Robertson, Esq

William Cuthbertson, Esq. } Baillies.

David Scott, Esq.

William Aird, Esq.

Robert Carrick, Esq. Dean of Guild.

George Lyon, Esq. Deacon Convener.

John Laurie, Treasurer. } Counsellors

Richd. Smellie, Master of Work. } ex officiis.

John M'Caul, Baillie of Clyde.

James Cleland, Baillie of Gorbals.

Kirkman Finlay, Baillie of Provan.

Archibald Falconer, Baillie of Port-Glasgow.

Alexander Struthers, Visitor of Maltmen.

John Orr, senior Town Clerk.

Richd. Henderson, junior do.

Robert Thomson, depute do.

John Bennet, Procurator Fiscal.

MERCHANT COUNSELLORS.

James Black,	William Muir,
John Hamilton,	William Smith,
Archibald Smith,	Alexander Stewart,
James M'Dowall,	Kirkman Finlay,
James M'Kenzie,	Gilbert Hamilton,
Robert Dunlop,	John M'Caul,

TRADES' COUNSELLORS.

John Morison,	Archd. Newbigging,
	Andrew

Andrew Patton,	John M'Ilwham,
John Tennant,	James Cleland,
Thomas Smith,	John Strang,
Basil Ronald,	Charles Household.

Every year, in October, a new election takes place in the following order, viz: Upon the first Tuesday after Michaelmas, the Magistrates and Council convene, in order to elect a Provost and three Baillies, two of the merchant and the other of the trades rank, for the ensuing year. The Provost being elected from the merchant rank, it is divided by the Magistrates for the time into four lists (or leets as they are called) from each of which one is chosen; these four are again divided into two leets, from each whereof one is chosen; and these two being put in one leet, a vote of the Council determines by a plurality of voices which of the two shall be Provost or Chief Magistrate for the ensuing year.

The Provost being thus elected, the nomination of the Baillies is next proceeded in, by dividing the Merchant Counsellors for the election of the two eldest Merchant Baillies into the same number of leets, as was done in the election of the Provost; and from the last division two are chosen, as Baillies. The Trades' Counsellors are then divided into three leets, from which three are chosen, who being put into one leet, a plurality of votes determine who is to be Trades first Baillie.

The Baillies of the immediate preceding year, are leeted in this election of the two oldest Merchant Baillies and eldest Trades Baillies. The three Baillies authorised by the old constitution being thus chosen, the

the election of the two new Magistrates, then proceeds in this manner, first, by dividing and putting into leets, the whole Merchant Counsellors who by the old set were eligible as Baillies, (except the persons just chosen first and second Merchant Baillies, and the Baillies of the preceding year who shall not have been re-elected;) one person is then chosen from each of these two leets, in the same manner as was done in the election of Merchant Baillies by the former set, and then these two persons are put upon one short leet, and he that is chosen from that leet, is the youngest or third Merchant Baillie for the subsequent year. The whole Trades' Counsellors, (except the person just chosen first or eldest Trades' Baillie, and the Baillie or Baillies of the preceding year who shall not have been re-elected,) are next put into two leets, and one person is chosen from each of these two leets, in the same manner as was done in the election of Trades' Baillies by the former set. These two are then voted upon, and the person chosen, is the second or youngest Trades' Baillie for the following yeaa.

The election of the Town Council follows, upon the first Friday after the choosing of the Provost and Baillies. The Magistrates for the three preceding years are constituted by the set of the burgh, the electors, and in default of any of them by absence or death, the requisite number of eighteen is filled up according as the absentees are of the Merchant or Trades' rank. After the number of electors is completed, they proceed to choose twelve Merchant Counsellors, and eleven of the Trades' rank, in the following manner,
viz.

viz. by retaining the Provost for last year (when not re-elected), the Merchant Baillies, and the Dean of Guild, who in case he has, by virtue of his office, been an extraordinary member of Council in the former year, is now to supply and fill up the room of a new Merchant Counsellor; but in case he has been of the ordinary Council, when so elected Dean of Guild, then the eighteen electors chuse a member of the Merchant rank in his room, who, with another of the same rank, are elected new Counsellors for the ensuing year, in place of the two senior Merchant counsellors, who, by the set of the burgh, are yearly disqualified†. The remainder of the Counsellors of this rank for the ensuing year, to make up the proper number of twelve, are composed of the twelve junior members of the last year's Council.

The election of the Merchant rank being finished, the nomination of the Trades' counsellors fol'   , in which the same rules are observed, viz. by retaining the preceding years Trades' Baillies, the last elected Convener nominating a new Counsellor and disqualifying the two oldest in that rank †.

The Dean of Guild, Deacon Convener, Treasurer, &c. are chosen upon the first Wednesday after the election of the Council; at which time there are present the Provost, Baillies, and Counsellors, both of the Merchant and Trades' rank, together with the Deacons of the incorporated trades; and because

---

† Such Counsellors as are disqualified, cannot be again elected into Council for the space of three years.

cause the number of the latter exceed that of the
Magistrates and Merchant Counsellors, as many of
this last rank are added, as makes the number of
both equal. A leet of three merchants is then produced from the Merchants' House, one of whom
is chosen by the Magistrates, Town Council, and
others aforesaid, as Dean of Guild. There is also
produced a leet of three persons from the Trades'
House, one whereof is in like manner elected Deacon Convener for the year ensuing. Upon these
offices being filled, the election of Treasurer takes
place, by the Magistrates and Council, who put two
or three persons upon the leet, from whom one is
chosen. The leet out of which the Treasurer is
elected, is made up of the merchant and trades'
ranks, *per vices*, or year about.

In electing the Baillie of Gorbals †, the Magistrates put two or three upon the leet, from which
one is chosen, who is also alternately a merchant
or tradesman. The Water Baillie and Master of
Work are also elected by the Council, from a leet,
composed either of Counsellors or of others, as they
think fit.—The leet from which the Water Baillie
is chosen is composed of the merchant or trades'
rank year about. The Magistrates and Council likewise elect annually a Baillie of Provan, and the Visi-
K k   tors

† The barony of Gorbals was purchased by the town in
the year 1647, from Sir Robert Douglas of Blackerstoun.
Since then a Baillie has been yearly appointed for its Government, by the Magistrates and Town Council of Glasgow.
He generally nominates a substitute, who resides in the suburb.

258

tors of the Gardeners and Maltmen, from leets produced by these incorporations, besides a Procurator Fiscal of Court, from a leet of two, made up by themselves [*].

In the event of the death of the Provost, any one of the Baillies, or Treasurer, during the time of their being in office, the first, or eldest Magistrate calls a council within forty-eight hours thereafter; at which diet, after explaining the cause of meeting, and the necessity of supplying the vacant office, another Council is appointed to be held, not under four, or above eight days distance from the former, for the purpose of a new election.—At this second meeting the election proceeds, according to the method already described at the usual annual elections. Upon the death of a Dean of Guild or Deacon Convener, while in office, a similar plan is adopted by the persons who immediately preceded in these offices, by calling together their respective houses, and making out the leets in the common form.

MERCHANTS'

[*] In the set of the burgh, it is provided that every person who shall be elected into any one of the offices of Provost, Baillies, Dean of Guild, Deacon Convener, or Treasurer, shall, on his refusing to accept, at the first meeting of Council after the election of the Dean of Guild, be fined in the sum of eighty pounds sterling; and also that every Counsellor nominated and refusing to accept, shall be fined, within three months after his election, in the sum of forty pounds sterling. Which fines, when so incurred, are to be levied for the behoof of the poor of the Merchants' and Trades' Houses respectively, according to the rank which the refusing office-bearer shall be of.

MERCHANTS' HOUSE.

The first constitution of the Merchants' House a-rose from a dispute between the merchants' and trades' rank, which having subsisted for some time, was at last settled in a submission by the parties to Sir George Elphinstone, then Provost, and two of the Ministers of the city, who, in 1605, pronounced an award, which is called the Letter of Guildry.

By this award, the powers and privileges of both ranks were fixed and ascertained, and having been approved and ratified by the Magistrates and Council the same year, it was afterwards confirmed by act of parliament, 11th September, 1672.

Agreeable to this, the Dean of Guild and his Council or Assistants, thirty-six in number, (elected annually, in manner after-mentioned,) together with the Lord Provost, Merchant Baillies, and the Collector, represent the community of the Merchants' House; the management of which is vested in them, the major number being a quorum.

The Dean of Guild, who must be a merchant, becomes by office a member of the Town Council, and is elected annually, on the second Wednesday after the election of the Magistrates, by the Magistrates and Town Council, together with the Deacons of crafts, and as many of the merchant rank, as are necessary to equalize the merchant and crafts' ranks, from a leet of three persons, presented by the Merchants' House.—This leet is made up as fol-

K k 2   lows:

lows: The Dean of Guild and his Council, with the Lord Provost and Merchant Baillies, and the Collector, meet in the Merchants' Hall, at eleven o'clock of the day of election, when the Dean of Guild divides the thirty-six members of his council into six leets, from each of which, the meeting chuse one, who are again divided, if the Dean of Guild has been two years in office, into three leets, from each of which, the meeting chuse one, to make up the leet of three, to be presented to the Magistrates, and other electors above mentioned; but if he has been only one year in office, then the six persons chosen from the first leets are divided into two, from each of which the meeting chuse one, who, with the Dean of Guild, make up the leet of three to be presented to the Magistrates and other electors, that one of the three may be chosen to bear the office of Dean of Guild for the ensuing year. At the same time, as many of the members of the House are chosen to present this leet to the Magistrates and Council, and to vote at the election of the Dean of Guild and Deacon Convener, as will balance the merchants' and crafts' ranks at said election.

The Dean of Guild may convene the Council or Assistants, and also the whole recorded members of the House, as often as he shall think proper, for ordering the business of the Hospital, or other necessary affairs; but there are certain fixed and stated meetings, which must be regularly called.

The first of these is on the afternoon of the day of election of the Dean of Guild, and is the only regular meeting of the whole recorded members, when
the

the Dean of Guild's Council is chosen, by his nominating in the first place, twelve of the members, either home or foreign traders, and leeting the remaining members into twenty-four leets, whereof twelve are to be foreign, and twelve home traders; and by plurality of voices, one is chosen from each leet, making up twenty-four persons, who, with the twelve nominated by the Dean of Guild, together with the Lord Provost, Merchant Baillies, and Collector for the time, compose the Dean of Guild's Council, and with him represent the community of the Merchants' House, for the ensuing year, to the next usual time of election.

By the regulations made 23d April, 1747, no person can be admitted a member of the Merchants' House, without previously being a burgess.

If a Dean of Guild is chosen that does not accept the office, the Town Council pass an act, authorising the Provost to name a day for electing another in his place.

The second meeting is on the Thursday thereafter, when the Dean of Guild and his Council, with the Merchant Magistrates and Collector, make choice of four of their number, of whom the Dean of Guild for the preceding year is necessarily one, and who with four persons elected by the Trades' House, together with the present Dean of Guild, constitute the Brethren of the Dean of Guild Court for the ensuing year, who meet every Thursday or oftener, and judge in sundry matters as settled by the Letter of Guildry.

At this meeting, there is elected an annual committee,

mittee, which consists of five persons, of which the Dean of Guild, Lord Provost and Collector (when acting without a salary) are three, and the other two are chosen by the House; but when the Collector has a salary, he is not to be one of the Committee*.

At this meeting also, the Collector, Clerk, and Officer, are elected; and the Collector finds security for his intromissions, to such an extent as the House thinks fit.

Twelve of the members are also appointed to be directors of the Town's Hospital for the ensuing year.

The third meeting is on the second Tuesday of December, at which meeting, the apprentices on Mr. Saunders of Auldhouse's mortifications, are presented.

The fourth meeting is on the second Tuesday of March, when the docquet of the annual Committee on the books, and the state of the funds of the House are taken into consideration; and at this meeting, the directors are chosen for Stirling's Library.

The fifth and sixth meetings are on the second Tuesdays of June and September, but no particular business is allotted to these.

All the members are obliged to attend these meetings,

* This committee meet four times a year, viz. on the first Tuesday of December, March, June, and September, for the dispatch of business; the result of their proceedings being examined by the several meetings of the House.

ings, or to pay five shillings for each absent day, unless in case of sickness, or being from home.

The stock and revenue of the House may be reckoned of two kinds; the one, which may be called its fixed revenue, arising from the rents of their lands and houses, the feus and ground-annuals belonging to them, and the interest of their bonded money: and the other, which may be called its casual revenue, arising from matriculation-money, burgess fines, Gold Book* subscriptions, and from new donations and mortifications.

Part of the money mortified to the House, and from which this fixed revenue arises, is left to the free disposal of the members for the time, while in other cases, they are tied down and restricted in the application of the funds, to certain rules and regulations prescribed by the donors.

The stock of this respectable body at present amounts to L.18,000 sterling. And the expenditure last year amongst the poor of the hospital and contingent charity, amounted to the sum of L.1000.

Every person who settles in this city as a merchant or trader, must immediately enter with the Dean of Guild, by paying according to his situation, if a stranger or otherwise, one of the following sums, for which he is admitted a burgess and guild-brother.

If

---

*In this book the new admitted members are enrolled, upon paying the customary fees after-mentioned.

If he is a stranger, - - -	L 8	7	10½

If he is the eldest son of a burgess, his } father alive,   1   9   1¼

If he is the eldest son of a burgess, his } father dead,   1   0   9¼

If he is the younger son of a burgess,   1   11   11

If he marries the daughter of a burgess,   1   14   7½

If he serves an apprenticeship, -   1   15   10

After his having paid one of these sums, and a customary fee to the Gold Book, not less than one guinea, he is furnished with a burgess ticket, which he produces to the Clerk of the Merchants' House, who, upon his paying L. 10, enrols him a matriculated member.

THE TRADES' HOUSE,

which forms the third member of the political body of the city, is composed of representatives from each of the fourteen incorporated trades, together with a president, who is called the Deacon Convener, a Collector and Clerk, &c.

The different incorporations, according to their sets or seals of cause, send each to the House the deputies* following, viz.

The Hammerman send	6	The Masons, -	3
Taylors, -	6	Fleshers, -	3
		Cordiners,	

---

* One of these deputies is always the deacon of the particular incorporation, and has the power of nominating the others.

Cordiners, -	6	Gardeners,	3
Maltmen, -	6	Barbers, -	3
Weavers, -	4	Dyers and Bon-	
Bakers, -	3	netmakers,	2
Skinners, -	3	Who with the Dea-	
Wrights, -	3	con Convener, &	
Coopers, -	3	Collector, -	2

Make up the ordinary members of the House, —
    amounting to   56

The extraordinary members of the House are the
Trades Baillie while in office, the Deacon Convener
and the Collector, if chosen out of the last nine
trades during the time they are in office, and for
two years after they go off. In this case the total
members are fifty-nine, but if the Convener and
Collector are chosen out of the first five trades,
it makes no alteration in the members of the
House, they being in that case fifty-six in all.

Upon the first Wednesday after the election of
the Town Council, the Deacon Convener is chosen in the following manner:

The House is divided into six leets, No. 1, 2, 3,
4, 5, and 6, from each of which one is chosen. The
gentlemen chosen from leets No. 1 and 4, are classed together, and so on, 2 and 5, and 3 and 6; from
each of which one is chosen. The names of the
three gentlemen so chosen by the House, are transmitted by the deacons of the Hammermen and Taylors to the Magistrates and Council, who, along with
the Dean of Guild, fourteen members of the Merchants' House, and the Deacons of the fourteen incorporated trades vote upon these three gentlemen,

                    and

and the one having the majority of votes, as has been elsewhere noticed, is returned to the House as Convener for the year.

After being in office for one year, the House is divided into four leets, and two of these, along with the Convener, are sent to the Magistrates and Council, and voted upon in the same manner as before stated; although this may be called mere form, as the Convener is always re-elected, and continues in office for two years, as doth a Collector; who is chosen solely by the House.

The revenue of this House, which is considerable, arises partly from heritable property, and from freedom fines paid by those of the trades' rank, and partly from sums mortified to the House, and the following annual payments by each incorporation in this proportion, viz.

	To the House.			For Chaplain.			Town's Hospital.		
	L.	s.	d.	L.	s.	d.	L.	s.	d.
The Hammermen pay,	3	6	8	1	10	0	12	0	0
Taylors,	4	3	4	1	10	0	14	0	0
Cordiners,	3	6	8	1	10	0	14	0	0
Maltmen,	4	3	4	1	10	0	15	0	0
Weavers,	2	10	0	1	5	0	12	0	0
Bakers,	2	10	0	1	5	0	9	0	0
Skinners,	2	10	0	0	15	0	3	0	0
Wrights,	2	10	0	1	5	0	10	0	0
Coopers,	2	0	0	0	12	0	2	0	0
Fleshers,	2	0	0	0	15	0	4	0	0
Masons,	2	0	0	0	10	6	2	15	$6\frac{2}{3}$

Gardeners,

Gardeners,	2	0	0	0	10	6	1	10	0
Barbers,	2	0	0	0	12	0	3	8	0
Dyers, &c.	2	0	0	0	10	6	1	1	0

L.37 0 0   14 0 6   103 6 6¼

From the funds so arising, besides defraying the incidental expences, the House pays annually to † twenty-seven poor brethren, from the fourteen trades on the roll, who are termed the Hospital poor, the sum of L.137:4:5¼ in the following proportions:

To the Hammermen's poor men, L.11 16 1⅓	Wrights', do. 10 12 6
Taylors', do. 11 16 1⅓	Coopers', do. 8 10 1
Cordiners', do. 11 16 1⅓	Fleshers', do. 8 10 1
Maltmen's, do. 11 16 1⅓	Masons', do. 8 10 1
Weavers', do, 10 12 6	Gardeners', do. 8 10 1
Bakers', do. 10 12 6	Barbers', do. 8 10 1
Skinners', do. 10 12 6	Dyers', &c. do. 5 0 0

In all, L. 137 4 5¼

Upon a vacancy happening in the Hospital through the death of any of the paupers, the Deacon, Collector, and Master Court of that incorporation to which the deceased belonged, meet and chuse a leet of two others, whom they present to the House, and out of these two, one is chosen, who is immediately entered as the person in the Hospital, belonging to that particular incorporation.

L l 2

We

† The Incorporation of Dyers present only one poor man.

We have been favoured with the following statement of the revenue and expenditure of the Trades' House, at this time, through the politeness of Mr. B. Mathie, their clerk.

Trades' House, Dr.	L. s. d.	Contra, Cr.	L. s. d.
To interest money in bonds	267 12 0	By 27 decayed brethren	137 4 5
Feu duty of Cowlairs	34 8 10	Mr. Govan's five tradesmen	22 7 11
Rent of a house at the Townhead	23 5 0	Mr. Thomson's six do.	33 6 8
Rent of the Gorbal lands	110 0 0	Messrs. Pettigrews' two do.	280 0
Ground annual of houses	6 0 0	Mr. Howison's bursar in the college	5 0 0
The 14 Trades pay jointly	154 7 0	Mr. M'Gilchrist's do.	5 0 0
To the rent arising from the new Hall	51 13 0	The Town's hospital yearly	170 0 0
Entry of burgesses last year *	34 14 0	The widows and children of house pensioners	31 0 0
		The chaplain	20 0 0
		The clerk	20 0 0
		The officer for salary, house, rent, &c.	14 0 0
			477 19 0
		By balance to increase of stock	213 0 10
	690 19 10		690 19 10

Converting this yearly revenue, at five per cent. the Trades' House hold at present in stock, the sum of

* This arises from a small sum paid to the House, by the Town clerks, at the entry of every tradesman as a burgess, &c. which is included in the general sum paid for the ticket.

of thirteen thousand eight hundred and one pounds sterling, and which, as long as a balance remains against the expenditure, must still accumulate.

OF THE FOURTEEN INCORPORATIONS.

The greatest part of the incorporations of this city, derived their existence as corporate bodies, either from the archbishops of Glasgow, or the Magistrates in their right, betwixt the commencement and end of the 16th century. Some are indeed of a more antient date, while there are others of a more recent origin.

The funds of each, which are set aside for the poor, and other incidental expences, arise from the freedom fines, &c. paid at the admission of each member into the incorporation, who is besides, in every case, obliged first to enroll himself a burgess of the city.

The following is a list of each particular incorporation, according to the order in which they stand in the Convener's books, with the sums at present paid by every individual before admission.

OF THE INCORPORATION OF HAMMERMEN*.

This body includes a number of artizans engaged

---

* This incorporation is of a very old standing.—We have seen

ed in particular branches, such as blacksmiths, copper and tin-smiths, saddlers, silversmiths and jewellers. They are governed by a Deacon, Collector, and twelve Masters, chosen annually, who, in this as well as in the other incorporations after-mentioned, have the disposal of the public money vested in them.

	L.		
The freedom fine paid for admission of a stranger into this corporation, is	12	12	0
If he is a freeman's son, - - -	1	10	0
If a son-in-law, - - -	3	0	0
Upon serving an apprenticeship to a freeman, - - - - -	3	10	0
They distribute to their poor per annum, about	200	0	0

THE TAYLORS

are under the government of a Deacon, Collector, and twelve Masters.

	L.		
A stranger pays of freedom fine,	12	0	0
Upon serving an apprenticeship, -	3	10	0
If he is a freeman's son, -	1	0	0
If a son in-law, - -	1	0	0
They pay yearly to their poor, about	270	0	0

CORDINERS,

seen a charter or seal of cause from the Magistrates of the city, in favour of the Hammermen, dated the 11th October, 1536, during the time of Archbishop Dunbar; and that even proceeds upon a narration, that the craft had been in a corporate capacity before, but that their privileges were not prior to this charter sufficiently ascertained.

GORDINERS, OR SHOEMAKERS

are governed by a Deacon, Collector, and twelve Masters.

A stranger pays at admisson, -	L.12	0	0
Upon serving an apprenticeship, -	3	12	0
If a freeman's son or son-in-law, -	2	0	6
They give yearly to their poor, about	200	0	0

THE MALTMEN‡

are governed by a Visitor, Collector, and eight Masters.

A stranger pays of freedom fine, -	L.15	15	0
Upon serving an appenticeship, -	1	15	4
If a freeman's son or son-in-law, -	2	2	0
They pay to their poor per annum, about	250	0	0

THE

‡ The making of malt at one period, appears to have been the employment of a very considerable part of the citizens. Many regulations were enacted for the management of the business and the conduct of the members. Amongst others, in the letter of Guildry, 1605, it is ordained—" That the Visitor shall take special notice of those of his calling, who profane the Sabbath day, by cleaning, receiving, or delivering meal, bear, corn, or malt; carrying of steep water, kindling of fire in kilns, or such like;" and such transgressors being convicted, shall forfeit ten shillings, and *be delivered over to the Kirk Session.* It is afterwards ordered, " that the Visitor shall have power to visit all malt in the markets, or in kilns, barns, &c. and when he finds *insufficient stuff, as bot, rotten, frostie* stuff, either mixt amongst good stuff, or by itself, and likewise where they find good stuff spoiled in the making, he shall report the same to the Baillies, &c.

THE WEAVERS*

are governed by a Deacon, Collector, and fourteen Masters.

A stranger upon admission pays   -   L.5   7   0

An apprentice serving five years' apprenticeship, and two years a journeyman with a freeman, is entitled to the freedom, upon payment of   L.2   7 · 0

If a freeman's son or son-in-law,   1   7   0

They destribute to their poor annually from L.250 to 280 sterling.

THE BAKERS†

are governed by a Deacon, Collector, and eight Masters.

No stranger can now be admitted.

Upon serving an apprenticeship,   -   L.6   0   0

A

*We have been able to ascertain exactly the date of the set or seal of cause of this incorporation.—Their first charter was granted them on the 4th June, 1528, by the Provost, Magistrates, and Council of the city.—This was afterwards in the year 1581, ratified by the archbishop of Glasgow. Another charter or seal of cause was granted by the town in 1605; this was likewise ratified by Parliament in 1681.—At present there are upwards of 700 freeman belonging to this incorporation.

†This incorporation is upwards of 300 years standing. In the year 1568, the Regent Murray, as we have already noticed, bestowed on it the lands of Partick, in consideration of their services while he resided with his army in the town, previous to the battle of Langside.—Upon these grounds, excellent flour mills are erected, capable of grinding per annum, 50,000 bolls.

A freeman's son pays at admission,   L.3   0   0

A son-in-law who enters by that right,   20   0   0

They give to their poor yearly, about   170   0   0

THE SKINNERS*

are governed by a Deacon, Collector, and nine Masters.

Freedom fine for a stranger,   -   L.10 10   0

Upon serving an apprenticeship,   -   3   0   0

If he is a freeman's son or son-in-law,   1   10   0

They give to their poor yearly, from 45 to 50

THE WRIGHTS

are governed by a Deacon, Collector, and thirteen Masters.

Freedom fine for a stranger,   -   L.17 11 10

Upon serving an apprenticeship,   -   3   6   0

If a freeman's son or son-in-law,   -   2   2   3

They give annually to their poor about 200   0   0

THE COOPERS

are governed by a Deacon, Collector, and twelve Masters.

Freedom fine for stranger,   -   L.80   0   0

Upon serving an apprenticeship,   -   7   7   0

If he is a freeman's son,   -   -   4   4   0

If he is a freeman's son-in-law,   -   7   7   0

M m   They

*This incorporation obtained their seal of cause in the year 1516, during the time of archbishop Beaton.

They give to their poor per annum, about 45 0 0

THE MASONS

are governed by a Deacon, Collector, and nine Masters.

Freedom fine for a stranger,	L.21	0	0
Upon serving an apprenticeship,	2	2	0
If he is a freeman's son,	3	3	0
If he is a freeman's son-in-law,	5	0	0
They give annually to their poor, about	50	0	0

THE FLESHERS‡

are governed by a Deacon, Collector and nine Masters.

A stranger pays,	L.8	9	5
If the person wishing admittance is a freeman's son,	3	9	5
A son-in-law pays,	4	11	7½
They give yearly to their poor, about	70	0	0

THE GARDENERS

are governed by a Deacon, Collector, and ten Masters.

A stranger upon entry pays,	L.10	0	0
Upon serving an apprenticeship,	2	0	0
If a freeman's son,	1	10	0
If a freeman's son-in-law,	2	0	0

They

‡ This incorporation got their charter or seal of cause in the year 1580, in the time of archbishop Boyd.

They give at an average yearly to their
poor, -   -   -   -   L.30   0   0

THE BARBERS

are governed by a Deacon, Collector, and nine Masters.

A stranger pays at entry,	-	L.12	0 0
Upon serving an apprenticeship,	-	3	0 0
If he is a freeman's son or son-in-law,		2	0 0
They give yearly to their poor, about		100	0 0

THE DYERS AND BONNET MAKERS

are governed by a Deacon, Collector, and four Masters.

The freedom fine payable by a stranger,	L.4	4	0
Upon serving an apprenticeship,	-	1 14	0
If a freeman's son,	- -	1 14	0
They give to their poor yearly, about		20	0 0

Besides these particular sums which each tradesman pays at entering with his trade, he must, prior to such payment, enter with the town as a burgess and guild brother, by paying, if a stranger, the sum of L.5 : 7 : 10½. If he is in any other situation, as being a freeman's son, &c. he pays the same sums, before obtaining his burgess ticket, as are paid by those of the merchant rank, which have been before specified.

These fourteen incorporations, with the Merchants' House, are the only chartered societies that have a share in the government of the city, and from whom the Counsellors, and consequently the Magistrates are elected. The other citizens, however, individually, are not debarred from having a voice in, or share of, the government, because each of them may, by becoming a member of the one rank or the other, acquire every privilege which either enjoy. The set of the city of Glasgow is therefore upon as liberal a plan as any in the kingdom, and as well calculated to promote the interests and equalize the rights of government, amongst the citizens.

OF THE COURTS OF JUSTICE.

The highest of these, which sit in the city, is the Circuit Court, anciently called the Justice Ayre, which meets twice in the year, in the months of April and September. The judges are the Lords of Justiciary, two of these most commonly sit during the assize, though one is empowered, in case of the absence of his colleague, to do the business. Before this Court are tried all criminal cases, which are competent to the Court of Justiciary at Edinburgh, excepting the crime of high treason.

The council for the prisoner here is entitled to sum up the evidence on his behalf, and to be the last speaker before the jury withdraw. The Court, which generally continues sitting for two or three days at a time, is attended by the Sheriffs of Lanark, Renfrew, and Dumbarton, the three counties, within its particular district, by the Lord Provost and Magistrates of the city, and by the macers and other proper officers, attendant upon the high Court of Justiciary at Edinburgh.

THE

THE SHERIFF COURT.

The Sheriff of each county was anciently the King's Lieutenant, within his particular district, and enjoyed an extensive jurisdiction, civil and criminal. Of old, the Sheriff reviewed the decrees of the Baron Courts, within his territories. He mustered those military companies or bodies of militia, whose exercises were known by the name of *weapon shawings*. He received, and still continues to receive, from the collectors within his district, the royal Revenues, which he pays into the exchequer. He summons a jury of 45 persons, out of whom the Court of Justiciary, or Lords of the Circuit select 15, to sit upon trials held before them. He returns as member of Parliament for the county, the person having a majority of suffrages upon the roll of freeholders, and establishes, by the assistance of a jury, the *fiars* or rates which must be paid for grain, that ought to be delivered when no precise price is stipulated. Many of these powers are vested in the Sheriff substitutes, of whom, in the county of Lanark, there are three; one to each division or ward, and in each of which a Court is held.

The Court, which sits in Glasgow, the capital of the last division, has two sessions in the year; the first beginning on the 12th of May, and rising on the 12th of July; the second sitting down on the 12th of November, and rising on the same day of the month of March, during which two terms it meets once a week, upon Wednesday. In the time

time of the vacation, which includes the space betwixt the sessions, a Court is also held every third week, for the determining causes betwixt the inhabitants of the city.

All civil actions, are here competent to be tried, excepting a few peculiar to the Court of Session. The Sheriff also exercises a criminal jurisdiction in matters of theft, and other crimes of a lesser moment: His sentences are, however, subject to review of the Courts of Session and Justiciary.

THE COMMISSARY COURTS OF GLASGOW, HAMILTON, AND CAMPSIE

are held in this city. Their jurisdiction is very extensive, not only in the county of Lanark, but also over great part of the shires of Renfrew, Stirling, Dumbarton and Ayr †.

This

---

† We have been favoured with the following list of the parishes over which the Commissaries of Glasgow, and of Hamilton and Campsie, exercise their jurisdiction, viz.

COMMISSARIOT OF GLASGOW.

Lanarkshire.——Glasgow and Barony parish——*Edicts served at the market cross of Glasgow.*——Rutherglen; Cambusnethan; Carmunnock; Bothwell; Glassford; Bartonshotts; Strathaven; Cambuslang; Blantyre—*Edicts served at Rutherglen, head burgh of the nether ward of Clydesdale.*

Dumbartonshire.——Roseneath; Bonhill; Dumbarton; Luss; Lenzies; Easter and Wester; Kilpatrick; Easter and Wester; Kirkintilloch; Kilmaronnock; Cumbernauld; and Row, except the lands afterwards to be mentioned as under the Commissariot of Hamilton and Campsie. The following Lands in Cardross parish belong to the Commissariot of Glasgow—Dal-

This court was constituted here about the reign of James I. probably by Bishop Cameron, or his successor Bishop Turnbull, as we find an Official (as he was called) or Commissary acting here in the year 1451, before which period we have no accounts of any such judge. It was anciently called Bishop's Court, being under his particular cognizance, and was formerly confined solely to the decision

qahurn; Whitehill of Keppoch; Ballimenoch; Kilmahue ten pound land; Ardardan; Keppoch; Lyleston; Hill of Ardmore, Buntine of Gielston; Drumhead; Farms hail Lands; Colgrain —*Edicts served at Dumbarton.*

Renfrewshire.—Innerkip; Killellan; Kilbarchan; Greenock; Houstoun; Eaglesham; Lochwinnoch; Inchinnan; Mearns; Kilmacolm; Paisley; Neilston; Port-Glasgow; Erskine; East-wood; and the following lands over the bridge of Cathcart, the rest of the parish belongs to Hamilton and Campsie; Williamwood; Bogtown place thereof; two merk land of Merrylee, twenty shilling land of Merrylee—*Edicts served at Renfrew.*

Stirlingshire—Town of Kilsyth and east barony thereof, the west barony belongs to Hamilton and Campsie; Drymen; Fintry; Balfron; Strathblane; Killearn; and Baldernock, excepting the lands after mentioned, under Hamilton and Campsie—*Edicts served at Stirling.*

Ayrshire.——*Bailliary of Cunningham*—Loudon; Dalry; Ardrossan; Kilmarnock; Stewarton; Kilbride, Wester; Finwick; Beith; Largs; Kilmaurs; Irvine; Kilbirnie; Dreghorn; Kilwinning; Dunlop; Preston; Stevenson.——*Bailliary of Carrick*—Maybole; Girvan; Kirkoswald; Colmonnel; Kirkmicheal; Ballantrae; Straiton; Barr; Daillie.——*Bailliary of Kyle*—Galston; Tarbolton; Auchinleck, Dalquain; Riccarton; Muirkirk; Cumnock, Old and New; St. Quivox; Craigie; Monkton; Prestick; Dundonald; Ochiltree; Barnwall; Coylton; Mauch-

cision of ecclesiastic matters, or what the Clergy
presumed to be so, such as confirming testaments,
ascertaining debts, contracted by persons deceased,
and giving decree for payment of them, especially
if the debts relate to the illness of the deceased, his
funeral charges or obligations, arising either from
testaments or from the ties of nature, supported by
law, requiring alimony out of the effects of the
deceased, and in deciding in all actions of scandal,
&c. Now, however, besides these, civil actions are
likewise here tried to the amount of forty pound
Scots, or L.3 : 6 : 8d. sterling; nay, they may e-
ven be prorogated to a greater extent. These
Courts meet during the time of session, which
is here the same with the Sheriff Courts, before mentioned, upon Thursday weekly, and
during the time of vacation, in matters purely
consistorial,

ine; Dalmellington; Crosby; Dalrymple; Symington—*Edicts
all served at Ayr.*

COMMISSARIOT OF HAMILTON AND CAMPSIE.

The Commissary of Hamilton and Campsie has jurisdiction
over the following lands and parishes:

Dumbartonshire.——Cardross, except the lands above men,
tioned, under the Commissariot of Glasgow; the following
lands in the parish of Row belong to the Commissariot of Hamilton and Campsie, the remainder belong to Glasgow;
two Banachrains; two Drumphads; three Kilbrides; two Blair
Carns; Durling; Balevouling; Ballinoch; Auchinvennelmore;
Auchinguichty; Faslain; Strone of Glenfron; two Ballernicks.
—*Edicts served at Dumbarton.*

Stirlingshire.——Campsie; and the following lands in

consistorial, such as serving edicts, &c. also once a-week.

This Court was formerly held in the consistory house, adjoining the Cathedral. It is now removed to the ordinary Court-hall. The Commissary, like the Sheriff Depute, is appointed by the crown, as come in the place of the archbishops.

THE BAILLIE, OR TOWN COURT.

This Court appears to have been instituted as early as the erection of the town into a Royal Burgh. It is afterwards mentioned, as existing, in the year 1268, as has been noticed elsewhere, and from that period has been continued downwards to the present time.

Its chief judge is the Provost *, in whose name proceeds its summonses, decrees, &c. Its

N n   has

Baldernock parish belong to the Commissariot of Hamilton and Campsie, the remainder belong to Glasgow: Balmore, Kilhead, Bankierlings, Orchard, Barreston, Holl of Bankier, Easter and Wester Blairskaiths, Balgrochan, West Barony of Kilsyth—*Edicts served at Stirling.*

Lanarkshire.——Cadder, Gorbals, Govan, Cathcart, except the lands above mentioned, under the Commissariot of Glasgow—*Edicts served at Glasgow.*——New Monkland, Old Monkland, Hamilton, Dalziel, Dalserf, Easter Kilbride—*Edicts served at Hamilton.*

Renfrewshire.——Renfrew—*Edicts served at Renfrew.*

* The Provost is, from courtesy and custom, styled Lord Provost; he is properly Lord of the Police of the city, president

has for its bounds the royalty of the city, within which its judges, the Magistrates, exercise both a civil and criminal jurisdiction. In civil cases, all actions for performance of obligations, or for payment of debts above thirty shillings, are competent; and in those of a criminal nature, the Magistrates are authorised to decide, and to order punishment according to the nature of offence, by imprisonment, stripes, pillory, or bansihment from the liberties of the burgh; they can, however, judge in

dent of the community, and *ex officio* a Justice of the Peace for the Burgh and County.

We have no account of the persons who filled this office excepting Richard De Dunidovis, Alexander Palmes and William Gley, till the time of Bishop Cameron, who appointed John Stewart of Minto, in 1472. This family held the office mostly in their possession, till their decline—the last of this name was Sir Mathew Stewart of Minto, Provost in 1586. The tomb of this once repectable family, is still to be seen in the choir of the Cathedral upon the left of the main entrance. The family of Bell, also, continued long in the chief Magistracy, the last of this name was Sir John Bell, in 1680. In latter times, this office was long in the possession, though not in continued succession, of gentlemen of the name of Anderson, then in that of Murdoch. The last was George Murdoch, in 1766. Since then, this office has not been continued so uniformly in one or two particular families, but has in general been filled without partiality, by such citizens as are best entitled to it by their worth, respectability, and the estimation, in which they are held by their fellow-citizens.

Annexed is a list of the Provosts of Glasgow from the earliest account down to the present time.

A

in no capital causes, or such as may infer demem-
bration.

This

A list of the Lord Provosts of Glasgow, and principal buildings, &c.
founded or completed when they were in office.

1268, Richard de Dunidovis.
Cathedral building.
Alexander Palmes.
William Gley.
1424, *Steeple founded.*
1452, *University founded.*
1472, John Stewart of Minto.
1480, Sir Thomas Stewart of
Minto.
1513, Sir John Stewart of do.
1528, Sir Robert Stewart of
Minto.
1538, Archibald Dunbar of
Baldoon.
1541, Lord Belhaven.
1543, Johny Stewart of Minto.
1545, Andrew Hamilton of
Middop.
1553, Andrew Hamilton of
Cochnay.
1560, Robert Lindsay of Dun-
rod.
1566, *Laigh Kirk built.*
1569. Sir John Stewart of
Minto.
1574. Lord Boyd.
1577, Thomas Crawford of Jor-
danhill.
1578, Earl of Lennox.
1580, Sir Mathew Stewart of
Minto.

1583, Earl of Montrose.
1584, Lord Kilsyth.
1586, Sir Mathew Stewart of
Minto.
1600. Sir George Elphinston
of Blythswood.
1607, Sir John Houston of
Houston.
1609, James Inglis.
1613, James Stewart.
1614, James Hamilton.
1617. James Stewart.
1619, James Inglis.
1621, James Hamilton.
1623. Gabriel Cunningham.
1625, James Inglis.
1627, James Hamilton.
1629, Gabriel Cunningham.
1633, William Stewart.
1634. Patrick Bell.
Prison and Townhouse.
1636, Colin Campbel.
1637, James Stewart.
Laigh Kirk Steeple buil
1638, Patrick Bell.
1639, Gabriel Cunningham.
1640, James Stewart.
1642, William Stewart.
1643, James Bell.
1645, George Porterfield.

1647,

This Court also sits weekly, upon Friday, and hath no vacation.

1647, James Stewart.
1648, George Porterfield.
1650, John Graham.
1651, George Porterfield.
1652, Daniel Wallace.
1655, John Anderson.
1658, John Bell.
Merchant's Hall.
1660. Colin Campbel.
1662, John Bell.
1664, William Anderson.
1667, John Anderson.
1668, William Anderson.
1669, James Campbel.
1670, William Anderson.
1674, John Bell.
1676, James Campbell.
1678, John Bell.
1680, Sir John Bell.
1682, John Barns.
1684, John Johnston.
1686, John Barns.
Wynd Church.
1688, Walter Gibson.
1689, John Anderson.
1691, James Peadie.
1693, William Napier.
1695, John Anderson.
1697, James Peadie.
1699, John Anderson.
College Church.
1701, Hugh Montgomerie.
1703, John Anderson.
1705, John Aird.

1707, Robert Rodger.
1709, John Aird.
1711. Robert Rodger.
1713, John Aird.
1715, John Bowman.
1717, John Aird.
1719, John Bowman.
1721, John Aird.
North-West Church.
1723, Charles Millar.
1725, John Stark.
1727, James Peadie,
1728, John Stirling.
1730, Peter Murdoch.
1732, Hugh Rodger.
Towns Hospital.
1734, Andrew Ramsay.
1736, John Coulter.
1738, Andrew Aiton.
St. Andrew's Church.
1740, Andrew Buchanan.
1742, Lawrence Dinwiddie.
1744, Andrew Cochran.
1746, John Murdoch.
1748, Andrew Cochran.
1750, John Murdoch.
1752, John Brown.
1754, George Murdoch.
1756, Robert Christie.
St. Andrew's Church finished.
1758, John Murdoch.
1760, Andrew Cochran.
1762, Archibald Ingram.
1764, John Bowman.

772,

THE DEAN OF GUILD COURT.

This is of great utility, especially in such a city as Glasgow, where property is very valuable, and, consequently, where disputes concerning it are not unfrequent. The Dean of Guild, assisted by a Council of eight, half being of the merchant rank, and the remainder tradesmen, are the proper judges of this Court. Their business is to determine disputes betwixt conterminous proprietors; to adjust and regulate the weights and measures; to take care that buildings within the city be carried on according

ing

1766, George Murdoch.
1768, James Buchanan.
1770, Colin Dunlop.
    Bridge, foot of Jamaica Street.
1772, Arthur Connel.
1774, James Buchanan.
    Rutherglen Bridge.
1776, Robert Donald.
1778, William French
    St. Enoch's Church founded.
1780, Hugh Wylie.
1782, Patrick Colquhoun.
    Tontine Coffee-Room and Buildings begun.
    Instituted the Chamber of Commerce.
1784, John Coates Campbell.
1786, John Riddel.
    Grammar School, George's Square, and St. Andrew's Square begun.

1788, John Campbell, jun.
1790, James M'Dowall.
    Physician's Hall, and Trades' Hall, founded 1791.
    Infirmary, 1792.
1792, Gilbert Hamilton.
    Laigh Church.
    New Bridge, now swept away, at the foot of the Saltmarket, over the Clyde.
1794, John Dunlop.
    The Assembly and Concert Rooms.
1796, James M'Dowal.
1798, Laurence Craigie.
    Barony Church and Police.
1800, John Hamilton.
    Hutcheson's Hospital.
1801, Laurence Craigie
    New Theatre.

ing to law; that encroachments be not made upon the public streets; to consider the state of buildings, whether they be in such a condition as to threaten damage to those dwelling in them, or to the neighbourhood; and to grant warrant for repairing, pulling down, or rebuilding them, according to the circumstances of the case. They also admit burgesses, and fine all unqualified persons, who usurp the privileges of freemen, &c.

This court is held every week during the year, upon Thursday.

THE JUSTICE OF PEACE COURT.

The proper judges here, are the gentlemen who hold the office of Justice of Peace for the nether ward of Lanarkshire, within which their jurisdiction is confined.

Agreeable to a late act of Parliament, this Court meets upon the first Monday of every month, for the discussion of business, two Justices forming a quorum.—All actions for debt to the amount of forty pound Scots, or L.3 : 6 : 8d. sterling, are here competent; also, all such as have for their conclusion, the fines or penalties to any amount, that may have been incurred by illegal traffic; breaking of the game laws; cutting of wood without permission; killing salmon in forbidden time; selling or manufacturing such goods as are prohibited to be vended without a licence; in determining disputes betwixt masters and servants; or such causes as are brought for aliment in particular cases, &c.

THE

THE COURT OF CONSCIENCE,

in which the Magistrates of the city are judges, meets every Monday, for the determination of small causes, brought for payment of sums not above 40s. Procurators, neither here nor in the Justice Court, are admitted to plead, the parties themselves stating their own case.

Besides these stated Courts, a Magistrate attends daily at the Council Chamber, for the purpose of discussing such causes as require dispatch, without awaiting the ordinary forms of Court. Another Magistrate also attends daily at the Police Office, for enquiring into and punishing offences, committed against the Police laws, lately established.

Corps of VOLUNTEER INFANTRY and CAVALRY, raised for the defence of the Country, by the City of Glasgow.

Since printing the historical department, besides the corps of Volunteers noticed, there as raising, which are now embodied to the number of 800, several other corps have been formed, through that spirit of loyalty and patriotism, which pervades all ranks. These, including that just now mentioned, are contained in the following list.

I. The FIRST REGIMENT of Glasgow Volunteers, commanded by the Lord Provost for the time. They receive pay when on duty, and have their arms and accoutrements furnished by government.

II.

II. The CORPS OF SHARP-SHOOTERS. This corps amount to 500 in number. They furnish their own arms and accoutrements, and receive no pay.

III. The ARMED ASSOCIATION. They furnish every thing requisite to fit them for the field, and receive no pay. The corps, when com⸍lete, will also amount to 300.

IV. The TRADES' BATTALION, raised by the incorporations. This regiment, which, when completed, will muster 600 men, receive no pay, have arms and accoutrements from government, and provide their own cloaths. Two field-pieces have been lately gifted for the service of this regiment, by three gentlemen of the city.

V. The GROCERS' CORPS, like the Armed Association and Sharp-Shooters, serve without pay, and provide their own arms and accoutrements. Their number, when complete, will be 300.

VI. The HIGHLAND CORPS, composed mostly of such inhabitants as are natives of the Highlands. Their number is 600. They receive pay, arms, &c. from government. To this regiment is attached a corps of Sharp-Shooters, who furnish themselves with every thing requisite, and are upon the same establishment with the corps, No. II.

VII. The ANDERSTON REGIMENT of Volunteers. This regiment has been raised by the public-spirited exertions of some gentlemen in that suburb.

suburb. In number they are 300. They furnish their cloaths, receive no pay, and have their arms, &c. provided by government.

VIII. A Troop of Volunteer Cavalry. The gentlemen who compose the Corps, serve without pay, and provide horses, arms, and accoutrements.

The city of Glasgow, in conjunction with Rutherglen, Renfrew, and Dumbarton, sends one member to the British House of Commons. This situation is at present filled by Boyd Alexander, Esq. of Southbar.

The armorial bearing of the city is on a field parti. p. fess, argent and gules, an oak tree, surmounted with a bird in chief, a salmon with a gold stoned ring in its mouth * in base, and on a branch in the sinister side, a bell langued *or*, all proper.——

O o   The

* Archbifhop Spottiswood, in his history of the Church of Scotland, narrates the following story, to which our readers may give what credit they please, as accounting for the salmon and the ring having a place in the Glasgow arms. In the days of St. Kentigern, a lady having lost her wedding ring, it stirred up her husband's jealousy, to allay which, she applied to St. Kentigern, imploring his help for the safety of her honour. Not long after, as St. Kentigern walked by the river, he desired a person that was fishing, to bring him the first fish he could catch, which was accordingly done, and from its mouth was taken the lady's ring; the recovering whereof, in this manner, effectually took away her husband's suspicion.

The motto, LET GLASGOW FLOURISH. Before the Reformation, St. Mungo's or Kentigern's head, mitred, appeared in the dexter side of the shield, which had two salmon for supporters.

RELIGIOUS ESTABLISHMENT.

We have already mentioned that Glasgow became, at a very early period, the seat of a religious establishment. From the time of Kentigern to the Reformation, an almost uninterrupted succession of bishops, and latterly of archbishops, continued to preside in this see. When that event took place, one minister who was superintendent of the west of Scotland, officiated in Glasgow, and had the pastoral charge of the inhabitants. The session of Glasgow was regularly constituted of one minister, thirty-five elders, and twenty-six deacons, on the 7th November, 1583.

At this period, and for a long time subsequent, the session was assisted in judging of matters of scandal, by an inquest summoned from the neighbourhood. In the year 1636, public worship was performed in three different churches, the High Church, the Tron Church, and the Blackfriars or College Church; and the same number continued till after the Revolution. In 1691, a fourth was added, called the Wynd Church.

The city of Glasgow, though originally only one parish, was afterwards divided into seven, and lately

into eight parishes, exclusive of the Barony *, which
are at present held by the following clergymen:
These are the Inner High Church, Principal Wil-
liam Taylor; the Outer High Church, Dr. Robert
Balfour; the Tron Church, Dr. Stevenson MacGill;
the College Church, Dr. John Lockhart; the Wynd
Church, Dr. William Porteous; the North West
Church, Dr. Alexander Ranken; St. Andrew's
Church, Dr. William Ritchie; and St. Enoch's
Church, Dr. William Taylor.

These ecclesiastical charges are all, except the Inner High Church and Barony, under the patronage
of the Town Council. The stipend of each of the
ministers was at first L.90; in 1723 it was augmented to 2000 merks; in 1762 to 2500 merks;
in 1788 to L.165; and in 1795 to the sum of
L.200; last year, by the Magistrates and Council,
it was again augmented to L.250. The Inner and
Barony Churches are under the patronage of the
Crown, the ministers of whom enjoy each of them
glebes, which have been allowed, by act of Parliament, to be feued, greatly to the advantage of the
benefices.

Each of these churches has a session, composed
of its particular minister, and a certain number of
elders, who judge in matters of scandal, and if

O o 2   they

* As the Barony parish includes a tract of country lying a-
round the town, it is not here reckoned as one of the parishes
into which the city is divided. Mr. John Burns is the present
minister.

they see cause, inflict censures upon transgressors
—enquire into the situation of the poor within their
respective districts, to whom they administer such
relief from the funds, as circumstances may require.
The members of these particular sessions also meet
upon the first Thursday of each month, in a general
session, where such business as relates to the administration of the funds, which arise from the collection at the churches, and from other charitable donations, with such other objects as belong to general ecclesiastical order in the city, are discussed.

PRESBYTERY OF GLASGOW.

The ministers of the city, and of the twelve
surrounding parishes, the Barony of Glasgow,
Gorbals, Rutherglen, Cumbernauld, Carmunnock,
Cadder, Campsie, Govan, Kirkintilloch, Kilsyth,
Cathcart, and Eaglesham, also convene in presbytery at Glasgow, every month, to receive reports, and
decide causes from the different sessions, in which
they are the competent judges; to elect deputies to
the general assembly, and to moderate calls to vacant charges within their bounds.

SYNOD OF GLASGOW AND AYR,

is the next higher ecclesiastical court that meets
here.—It is composed of seven presbyteries, these
are the presbyteries of Glasgow, Ayr, Irvine, Paisley, Hamilton, Lanark and Dumbarton.—The Synod convenes twice a year, in spring and autumn,
and sits here twice for once at Ayr, or Irvine.—
To it lie appeals from the presbytery, in the same
manner

manner as they may be made from its decision to the general assembly.

Besides the churches above mentioned, there are also four Chapels of Ease, under the inspection of the presbytery of Glasgow, one in the city, the other three belong to the Barony parish; and the College Chapel, in which divine service is ordinarily performed by preachers or licentiates in divinity. There are also two Gaelic Meeting Houses, in which the service is performed partly in Gaelic, partly in English. The Clergymen belonging to the Chapel within the city, are Messrs. John McLeod and Archibald Williamson; the ministers of the other Chapels in the barony, are Messrs. Muschet, Love and Graham, and of the Gaelic Meeting Houses, Messrs. McLaren and McKenzie.

Besides these houses and establishments for the exercise of the public ordinances of religion, agreeable to the institution of the Church of Scotland, there are various other places of worship occupied by Dissenters. There are two Burgher, and two Antiburgher Meeting Houses; an English Chapel, with two officiating clergymen; a place of worship belonging to a congregation of Independents; one for Anabaptists; one for Glassites; a large Methodist Meeting House; three others belonging to the Relief communion; and two new houses of worship, under the name of the Tabernacle, and Albion Street Chapel; also three Churches in Anderston; one in the Calton, belonging to the covenanted Presbyterians; and a Popish meeting, which is conducted with such discretion, that it does not give the slightest cause of offence.

CHAP.

CHAP. X.

Of the System of Police.

FROM the state of society, it becomes necessary, in every large city, or particular district, that a set of regulations, in unison to the public law of the land, should be enacted, for its internal government, and for promoting the convenience and comfort of its inhabitants, as well as the more effectually to aid and assist the executive power in putting the national laws into force.

In the principal cities of Europe, regulations of this kind, called a system of Police, have been long established, but no where are they upon a better plan, than in the city of London, and, before the Revolution, in Paris; by which the lives, and property, of their inhabitants are rendered infinitely more secure than they would otherwise have been.

So sensible were a great part of the inhabitants of Glasgow of this fact, that several years before the bill, establishing the system of Police, was passed, they took measures for that purpose, but owing to the vigorous opposition of several individuals, the design was, at the time, carried no farther.

The city, however, daily increasing in size and population, and consequently, irregularities of every kind

kind becoming more frequent, it was at length generally seen, that such a set of regulations must be adopted, in order to continue to the inhabitants a proper degree of security and comfort.

A bill was accordingly framed for this purpose, presented to Parliament, and passed into a law in the year 1800, the 40th year of the reign of his present Majesty.

By this act, and the powers which it gave, the management of the Police is vested in the Lord Provost, Baillies, Dean of Guild, Deacon Convenor, and twenty-four Commissioners, one from each ward or district, into which the city, by that act, was divided.

The object of this Bill was more particularly for the purpose of extending the Royalty of the city over certain adjacent lands, for paving, lighting, and cleansing the streets, for regulating the Police, and appointing Officers and Watchmen, dividing the city into wards *, and nominating Commissioners, and for raising funds, and giving certain powers to the Magistrates and Council, Town and Dean of Guild Courts; and other purposes.

The

---

*By the act, the city is divided into the following Wards or Districts, viz.

1. The north side of Trongate Street from the Cross to Candleriggs Street, the east side of that street from Trongate Street to Bell Street, the south side of that Street from Candleriggs Street to High Street, and the west side of that street from the Cross to Bell Street, with all the intermediate streets, lanes, and buildings.

2. The

The substance of the principal clauses in this act, and regulations since made, are contained in the text and notes of the following pages,

1mo. The royalty of the city was extended over the

2. The west side of High Street from Bell Street to Grammar School Wynd, the north side of Bell Street from High Street to Candleriggs Street, the south side of Grammar School Wynd and of Canon Street from High Street to Candleriggs Street, and the east side of that street from Canon Street to Bell Street, with all the intermediate streets, &c.

3. The west side of High Street from Grammar School Wynd to George Street, the north side of Grammar School Wynd and of Canon Street, and of Ingram Street from High Street to John Street, the south side of George Street and of Cochran Street from High Street to John Street, and the east side of that street from George Street to Ingram Street, with all the intermediate streets, &c.

4. The west side of High Street from George Street to Rottenrow Street, the north side of George Street and Cochran street from High Street to John Street, the south side of Rottenrow Street from High Street to John Street, and the east side of that street from Rottenrow Street to George Street, with all the intermediate streets, &c.

5. The north side of Trongate Street from Candleriggs Street to Glassford Street, the west side of Candleriggs Street from Trongate Street to Ingram Street, the south side of that street from Candleriggs Street to Glassford Street, and the east side of that street from Ingram Street to Trongate Street, with all the intermediate streets, &c.

6. The north side of Argyll Street from Glassford Street to Queen Street, the west side of Glassford Street from Argyll Street to Ingram Street, the south side of that street from Glassford Street to Queen Street, and the east side of that street from Ingram Street to Argyll Street, with all the intermediate streets, &c.

7. The

the lands of Ramshorn and Meadowflat, including such parts as were feued by the partners of

P p   the

7. The north side of Ingram Street from John Street to Queen Street, the west side of John Street from Ingram Street to Rottenrow Street or Lane, the south side of that lane from John Street to the road to Cowcaddins, and the east side of Queen Street, and of the said road to Cowcaddins from Ingram Street to the said lane, with all the intermediate streets, &c.

8. The north side of Argyll Street from Queen Street to the boundary of the royalty in that direction, and the west side of Queen Street, and of the road to Cowcaddins from Argyll Street to the bridge on that road over St. Enoch's Burn, with all the streets, &c. within the royalty to the north and west of these lines; and also those parts of the royalty situated to the west of the road from the aforesaid bridge to Port Dundas on the canal, and to the west and south-west of the canal.

9. The south side of Trongate Street from the Cross to King Street, the west side of Saltmarket Street from the Cross to Prince's Street, the north side of that street from Saltmarket Street to King Street, and the east side of that street from Trongate Street to Prince's Street, with all the intermediate lanes, &c.

10. The west side of Saltmarket Street from Prince's Street to the Green Dyke, the south side of Prince's Street from Saltmarket Street to King Street, and the east side of that street and of the Slaughter-house Lane from Prince's Street to the Green Dyke, with all the intermediate lanes, &c.

11. The south side of Trongate Street from King Street to New Wynd, the west side of King Street and of Slaughter-house Lane from Trongate Street to the Green Dyke, and the east side of new Wynd from Trongate Street to Bridgegate Street, with all the intermediate lanes, &c. and also the south side of Bridgegate Street from Slaughter-house

the Inkle factory ; over the ground called Cribb's Croft, and over 28 acres of land, purchased from

house Lane to the old Bridge over the river Clyde, and all the lanes and buildings betwixt that part of the Bridgegate Street and the river.

12. The south side of Trongate Street from New Wynd to Old Wynd, the west side of new Wynd from Trongate Street to Bridgegate Street, the north side of that street from New Wynd to Old Wynd, and the east side of Old Wynd from Trongate Street to Bridgegate Street, with all the intermediate lanes, &c.

13. The south side of Trongate Street from old Wynd to Stockwell street, the west side of Old Wynd from Trongate Street to Bridgegate Street, and the east side of Stockwell Street from Trongate to Bridgegate Street, and the north side of that street from Stockwell Street, to Old Wynd, with all the intermediate lanes, &c.

14. The south side of Argyll Street from Stockwell Street to Maxwell Street, the west side of Stockwell Street from Argyll Street to Clyde Street, the north side of that street from Stockwell Street to the line of Maxwell Street, and the east side of that street from Argyll Street southwards, and of a line continued in the same direction to Clyde Street, with all the intermediate streets, &c.

15. The south side of Argyll Street and of the Anderston Road from Maxwell Street to the boundary of the royalty, the west side of Maxwell Street from Argyll Street southward, and of a line continued in the same direction to Clyde Street, with all the streets, &c. within the royalty, situated to the south and west of these two lines.

16. The east side of Saltmarket Street from the Cross to St. Andrew's Street, the north side of that street to the Burn, and the south side of Gallowgate Street from the Cross to the Burn, with all the lanes, &c. situated betwixt these lines and the Burn.

17.

from Colin Rae, Esq; of Little Govan, lying
contiguous, at the head of the Old Green, likewise

17. All sides of St. Andrew's Square, with the lanes, &c.
betwixt that square and the Green Dyke, the south side of
St. Andrew's Street, and the east side of Saltmarket Street
from St. Andrew's Street to the Green Dyke, with all the
intermediate lanes, &c.

18. The south side of Gallowgate Street from the Burn to
St. Mungo's Lane, both sides of Charlotte Street, and all the
other lanes, &c. betwixt the Burn and the grounds belonging to St. Andrew's Square on the west and St. Mungo's Lane
on the east.

19. The north side of Gallowgate Street from the Cross
to Spoutmouth Lane, the west side of that Lane to the foot
of old Vennel, the east side of High Street from the Cross to
the head of Old Vennel, and the south side of that Vennel
till it join Spoutmouth Lane, with all the intermediate lanes,
&c.

20. The east side of Spoutmouth Lane from Gallowgate
Street to the College Grounds, and the north side of Gallowgate Street from that lane to the new road from Gallowgate
Street to Drygate Bridge, with all the streets, &c. to the
north of that part of Gallowgate Street, and betwixt that
street and the College Grounds.

21. The north side of Old Veunel, the east side of High
Street from that Vennel to Duke Street and the south side of
Duke street from High Street to the Burn, with all the inter-
mediate lanes, &c. and also all the lanes, &c. within the royalty,
to the east of the Burn and to the north of the College
Grounds, including the parts about Drygate Bridge, Lady
Well, and both sides of the road towards Carntyne, east-
ward to the boundary of the royalty.

22. The north side of Duke Street from High Street to
the Burn, the east side of High Street from Duke Street to
Drygate Street, and also the east side of Kirk Street to Castle

wise over the land of Provost Haugh, and the road leading thereto, lately acquired from Mr. Bell of Cowcaddins.

By this act, the Magistrates were authorised to exercise the same jurisdiction, and to levy the same duties and taxes, over the grounds thus annexed, as they exercise over the old royalty, reserving a right to all merchants, being burgesses of the city, to exercise any trade or calling, within the limits of the lands so annexed, although they be not entered with the Corporations of the town. Also, that the Sheriff

tle Street, and of Castle Street, and of Howgate, and the road to Edinburgh by Kirkintilloch to the boundary of the royalty in that direction, and the west side of the Burn from Duke Street northwards, with all the intermediate streets, &c. and whole royalty situated to the north thereof, and to the east of the said road.

23. The west side of Kirk Street, from Rottenrow Street northward, and of Castle Street, and Howgate, and the road to Edinburgh, by Kirkintilloch to the boundary of the royalty in that direction; the north side of Rottenrow Street, and the lane continued from it Westward, to the Cowcaddins Road; and the east side of that Road, northward, and of the Road to Port Dundas on the Canal, to the boundary of the royalty in that direction; with all the intermediate lanes, &c. and the whole royalty to the west of the said Kirkintilloch Road, and the north and east of the said Canal.

24. The east side of Saint Mungo's Lane, the south side of the Gallowgate Street, from that lane to opposite the said road from that street to Drygate Bridge, and both sides of Gallowgate Street, from thence to Camlachie, or the boundary of the royalty in that direction, including Craignestock, and the other streets, &c. adjacent, and within the royalty.

riff and Justices of the Peace should have the same
powers within this extended royalty, as are competent to them in the old royalty; and that the tenure
of the lands so acquired, should remain as before,
without any change thereof into burgage—likewise
that the inhabitants should pay an equal portion of
the cess, trades-stent, poors-rates, and other taxes,
payable by the inhabitants of the city of Glasgow*; but that although they continue still liable
to their proportion of the public burdens, imposed upon the county of Lanark, that the amount
shall be discharged by the community of the
city.

By this act, it was also declared, that the
grounds so annexed, should, from the passing
thereof, be for ever separated from the Barony parish, and annexed to the parishes within the city to
which they lye most contiguous, or to which they
might be annexed by act of Council. That the
tythes of these lands shall still belong to the proprietors, but that the right of patronage of such churches

---

* Reserving to the partners of the Incle factory, or their as-
signs, their claims for any exemption from the city burdens,
(except multures), and to the Magistrates and Town Council,
all defences against the same, the validity whereof, may be discussed in a court of law. But that the prohibition contained in
the feu rights of that said partners of the Incle factory, against
selling, or brewing ale for sale, in their grounds; and all restrictions as to building shall be discharged, they and their
successors being subject to the same regulations, with regard
to building, as the other purchasers of the Ramshorn grounds.

es, as shall be built thereon, and endowed by the community, should belong to the Magistrates and Council. Saving always to his Majesty, and all other persons concerned, all interest other than the extension of the royalty, which they had, or may have in the lands so annexed.

For the more effectually carrying the system of Police into execution, the city was divided into 24 wards, in the manner mentioned in the note, from each of which, a Commissioner is appointed, by such inhabitants as pay a yearly rent of ten pounds or upwards, such Commissioner being head or ruling constable within the ward, and having it in his power to take lists of the persons therein, to prevent necessitous people from gaining a settlement, so as to entitle them to the funds of the city.

The appointment of these Commissioners, their times of meeting, collective powers, and method of exercising them, are now to be taken notice of.

The first Commissioners, by the act, were appointed to be elected on the 1st Monday of August 1800, by a majority of votes of the occupiers of dwelling-houses, warehouses, and other buildings within the respective wards, valued at L. 10 sterling or upwards of yearly rent, out of the number of householders, whose dwelling houses, exclusive of those parts occupied as shops or warehouses, are valued at L.15 or upwards of yearly rent. Provided, that in wards where there are not ten householders so qualified, the Commissioners may be elected out of the number of those whose dwelling houses are valued at L. 10 of yearly rent, and where dwelling houses and shops

contiguous

contiguous, are possessed by the same person, one half of the aggregate rent shall be accounted house, and the other half shop rent.

The votes for such Commissioners, are given separately in each ward by written tickets, subscribed by the voters, specifying their names, designations, and qualifications, and containing the names and qualifications of the person voted for. These votes are put into boxes appointed by the Provost, Magistrates, and other Commissioners, in each ward previous notice of eight days being given where they are placed, and of the election in two or more of the Glasgow newspapers. These votes must be lodged in these boxes upon that day, between the hours of ten o'clock forenoon and four o'clock afternoon, at which last hour the election is closed, and the new Commissioners are declared by the Provost, Magistrates, Dean of Guild, Deacon Convenor, for the first time, and afterwards by them and the other Commissioners for the preceding year; they determining by a majority of votes at their own meeting in all cases of equality of votes for Commissioners. And in the election of Commissioners, it is provided, that no persons shall have more than one vote upon his total possession or qualification, or vote in more than one ward or district.

To guard against the non-freedom of election, it is ordained, that if any person obstruct, hinder or molest any one who is qualified in giving his vote, or putting his ticket into the proper box, he shall forfeit twenty shillings sterling for each offence, *toties quoties*. And that any person not qualified
fied

fied voting, or attempting to vote, shall forfeit in like manner, the sum of L. 5 sterling for each transgression.

In case any Commissioner after election, dies, refuses, or neglects to subscribe an acceptance of the office on being required by the other Commissioners, or ceases to reside within the ward or district for which he was elected, his place is supplied by another, the Lord Provost, or in his absence, the next senior Magistrate, within fourteen days after the vacancy, advertising in the public papers, that such an election in the manner before mentioned is to be made, and this election proceeds at not more than four days after the publication of the advertisement. All disputes relative to the qualifications of the electors or elected which arise, being determined by the same persons, who nominate a Commissioner in case of an equality of votes. And as it may happen, that the electors of some particular ward may refuse or neglect to appoint a Commissioner upon the appointed day, in such case, the vacancy is supplied by the Lord Provost, Magistrates, and other Commissioners, who shall have accepted their offices such person so appointed, enjoying the same privileges as if elected by the qualified voters of the particular district.

In the framing of this system of Police, care has been very wisely taken, that the Commissioners should not enjoy the office for life, or for a long period, unless re-elected, but that every one properly qualified, should have a chance for the situation, and consequently a voice in the management

ment of the funds, the manner in which they are applied, and the regulation and direction of every thing else relative to the institution. This is effected by a clause in the act, ordering, that on the first Monday of November, 1801, eight should go out by ballot; on the first Monday of November, 1802, eight of the sixteen senior Commissioners should also go out by ballot; on the first Monday of November, 1803, the remaining eight senior Commissioners should go out by seniority, and on the first Monday of November, annually, thereafter, the eight senior Commissioners shall be disqualified and go out of office; and their places shall be filled as before-mentioned, by a new election, reserving, however, power to the electors, if they think fit, to re-elect the former Commissioner, in which case, he, or if there are more than one so re-elected, they come in, and are enrolled as the youngest Commissioners *.

By the act, four quarterly meetings of the Magistrates and other Commissioners, are held within

Q q   the

---

* After the Commissioners are by, one or other of their ways appointed and in office, they within a month thereafter, make up exact lists of the persons in their respective wards, qualified to elect or to be elected Commissioners, which are entered in books kept for that purpose, so as to be open to all parties concerned, at all reasonable times; these lists are corrected by the Commissioners from time to time, as the situations may vary of the persons capable of electing or being elected. One of these lists is also delivered, ten days previous to the election, by the Commissioner, to the Lord Provost, or in his absence, to the next senior Magistrate present at the time, in the city.

the Council Chamber, or any other place which the Magistrates think proper to appoint, viz. upon the first Monday of March, June, September, and December, at noon; for putting the act and the powers thereby committed to them, in execution. To which meetings the Lord Provost, or in his absence, the senior Magistrate, issues an order for summoning the whole Commissioners resident at the time within the city, and this at least twenty-four hours before the time of meeting. These meetings the Commissioners may adjourn to the same,; or any other place within the town, if they see cause.

Besides these quarterly meetings, the Lord Provost, or senior Magistrate in his absence, upon the requisition of any four Commissioners, can call other meetings, by summoning the Commissioners within forty-eight hours after being required to do so; he, the Lord Provost, or in his absence, the next senior Magistrate, acting for the time, may also appoint other meetings of the Commissioners, to be held at such times and places, within the town, as he thinks expedient, the whole Commissioners being always summoned in the manner before mentioned.

In ordinary business, seven Commissioners are declared to be a quorum, but when money is to be assessed for or voted, clerks, servants, watchmen, or other officers appointed, or balances fixed, the majority of the Commissioners who have accepted of their offices, must be present. And at these meetings, the Lord Provost, and in his absence, the next senior Magistrate present, or in absence of all the

Magistrates,

Magistrates, a person to be chosen by the meeting, presides, and has a deliberative and casting vote in all matters before them.

In order to carry the act into execution, the Magistrates and Commissioners, at their quarterly meetting, on the first Monday of September, annually, ascertain the assessment to be levied from the inhabitants, and the sums necessary to be expended for the current year; no money can, however, be levied or expended by any person, under the authority of the Commissioners and Magistrates, unless previously assessed and voted by the Commissioners.

The Magistrates and Commissioners may also, whenever they think expedient, cause an enumeration of the inhabitants to be made, such as refuse to comply in delivering up the exact number living in their houses, being liable in payment of 10s. sterling. The Commissioners are further empowered to appoint collectors, treasurers, clerks, or other officers, with suitable salaries, for levying or paying away the monies raised by the assessments, and the other funds provided by virtue of the act, &c.; such collectors finding security for their respective intromissions.

That a distinct account of the funds raised, and money paid away may be kept, books are provided. These are regularly balanced, on the first Monday of September, yearly, and a statement of the payments and disbursements for the preceding year, made out and printed, on or before the first of October.—A copy is delivered to each of the Commissioners, and the members of the Town Council, Merchants and Trades' House, and
for

for the inspection of the burgesses, and such as contribute to the assessment; the book lies open in the
Council Chamber for six weeks, and to which they
have access, without fee or reward.   Another book
is kept, by order of the Commissioners, in which
is written, the minutes of all their transactions, with
the amount of the salaries and emoluments paid tò
their clerks, treasurer, servants, &c. which is likewise open to the inspection of every burgess, or person contributing to the assessment, without fee or
reward.

By the act, it is declared, that it shall be competent to the Town Council, Merchants House, and
Trades' House of the city, or any one of them, to
bring actions against the Commissioners, for the time
being, or a majority of them to bring actions against
their predecessors in office, before the courts of
session or exchequer, in case they shall embezzle,
squander, or misapply any of the funds vested in
them, provided that such actions shall be commenced within twelve calendar months after the offence
prosecuted for, shall be alledged to have been committed.

In order to raise funds for defraying the expence
of the Police establishment, the Lord Provost, Magistrates and Commissioners, upon the first Monday
of September, annually, assess all renters, occupiers,
or possessors of dwelling-houses, cellars, shops,
warehouses, and other buildings and pertinents,
within the city and royalty, subject to the payment
of cess or land tax, in such proportion, according to
the rent of the subjects, as they find necessary to
exact.   In the first year of the establishment, the
assessment

assessment was exacted, according to the following
table:

On the yearly rent of Subjects rented or valued at	An annual assessment, not exceeding
L.4 and under L.6 sterling yearly,	4d. per pound, sterling
At L.6 and under L.10 do.	6d. do.
At L.10 and under L.15 do.	9d. do.
And at L.15 sterling yearly or upwards, 1s.	do.

Since the institution of the Police, however, the
proportion payable per pound of rent has been diminished, so that property paying annually L.15, instead of contributing 1s. now pays only 10d. per
pound *. In addition to the sum raised by assessment, the Magistrates and Council are bound to

pay,

* Such rents as are below L.4, the lowest sum in the table, are assessed in proportion as they stand stated in the
rent roll, according to which the cess or land tax is levied,
or in the rent roll, according to which, the duty on dwelling houses is collected, or partly from each, as to the Magistrates and Commissioners seems expedient, or so much
of these sums as they judge necessary to lay on at the time.
An annual assessment is calculated for the current year,
from Whitsunday to Whitsunday, annually, upon the aggregate rent of each person's possession, and payable in the proportions, and at the times appointed by the Magistrates
and Commissioners, or a quorum of them, and for collecting
of which, a proper allowance is made. For enforcing payment of this assessment, the like exaction is competent, as are
authorized for levying the cess or land tax, and which sums,
when so collected, are paid to the Magistrates or Commissioners, or to such other person, and at such periods as they
shall appoint. By a clause in the act, proprietors and life-
renters are liable in payment of the assessment for the hou-
es,

pay, from the ordinary funds of the community, annually, to the establishment, a sum not less than
L.800 sterling, by half-yearly payments, at Whitsunday and Martinmas, and that the whole money
arising from the assessments, and this addition, shall
be vested in the Magistrates and Commissioners,
and be applied annually in lighting and cleansing
the public streets, lanes, passages, squares, and o-
ther principal places within the city, and defraying
the expence of the establishment of clerks, servants,
watchmen, and other officers, and for the other purposes of the act, and any surplus which shall remain
shall be applied towards the same purposes for the
year following, so that the assessments may thereby be diminished proportionally.

No sooner had the act passed some of the principal clauses, of which we have noticed in the preceding pages, than the gentlemen to whom its execution was intrusted, began to follow out the
purposes of the institution. The more effectually to carry it into effect, they appointed the following office-bearers and assistants, viz.

A

es, cellars, shops, warehouses, and other buildings possessed
by themselves and their servants only, but not for those occupied by their tenants.

It is also thereby declared, that no vintner, tavern-keeper,
or coffee-house-keeper, shall be assessed in a higher sum than
L.10 sterling yearly, for the property possessed by him in the
way of his business, whatever the rent may be. Neither
can any assessment be levied from gardens or arable grounds,
within the royalty, or for waste or empty houses.

A Master of Police †. .   Treasurer of Police.
A Clerk of do.   Surveyor of do.
Collector of do.

besides fifteen officers of Police, and seventy-four watchmen. And in them, under the Managers of the institution, was the executive power more immediately vested. Their duty may be summed up in the following words.

It consists in aiding and assisting the Magistrates, in detecting and bringing to justice persons guilty of street robberies, house-breakings, assaults, theft, reset of theft, shop-lifting, picking pockets, swindling, and other crimes of that nature; by causing the persons accused to be apprehended, imprisoned, and proceeded against, in terms of law; in apprehending, and putting the law into execution against vagabonds, idle and disorderly persons, and public and sturdy beggars, and other persons who follow no lawful employment or occupation; in suppressing disorderly public houses, and other houses frequented by persons of the foregoing description; in suppressing

† The gentlemen who hold the principal offices are at present, Walter Graham, Esq. Master of Police. Mr. Robert Nimmo, in whom the offices of Clerk, Collector, and Treasurer are conjoined, and Mr. Andrew Bald, Surveyor. The Police Office, as mentioned elsewhere, is situated in the Candleriggs, where the principal part of the business is transacted, and to which offenders are brought for examination, before a Magistrate, who attends for the purpose. In this office, the officers of Police, or sergeants and assistants, attend in rotation, day and night.

312

pressing mobs and riots; in assisting to extinguish
fires; in putting the laws into execution, by which
carters, owners and drivers of carts and other carriages are prohibited from leaving the same on the
streets, roads, and passages, and riding on their
carts and carriages, and driving them or horses, or
other cattle, furiously or improperly on the streets;
in seeing that the said streets, squares, lanes, passages, and other places are properly lighted and
cleansed; in keeping in good order the public markets of the city, and the persons dealing therein;
in guarding *, patroling, and watching the streets,
and in general, in assisting the Magistrates in all
matters relative to the police, peace and good order
of the city, and for executing the different purposes
of the act of Parliament, establishing the system of
Police.

This duty, as yet, has been performed in a sa-
tisfactory manner, the streets are kept clean, well
lighted, and guarded. Nuisances are removed, property

* The watchmen have each a particular part of a street allotted to them. They begin their watch from April to September, inclusive, at ten o'clock, at night, and continue until
five in the morning; and in the months of October to March,
inclusive, at nine o'clock at night, and continue until six in
the morning. Every half hour the watchman goes through
his range, and calls the time.

The public fairs in the city are Whit-Monday, the Fair
of Glasgow, St. Mungo's or Twentieth day of Yule and
Skairs Thursday. The public market days are Monday,
Wednesday, and Saturday.

perty protected, and the personal safety of the inhabitants in a manner insured from the attacks of de-
predators or irregular persons, either by night or
day; in short, as has been already mentioned, this
establishment has been, and promises still to be productive of the best effects in promoting the interests
and comfort of the community.

CHAP. XI.

Of other Societies, acting under a charter, act of Par-
liament, or otherwise, viz. The Faculty of Physi-
cians and Surgeons—The Faculty of Procurators—
The Chamber of Commerce—Commissioners upon
the River Clyde—Committee of Management of the
Forth and Clyde Canal Navigation—The Banks—In-
surance Companies—Post Office, &c.——Societies
for Philosophical and Literary Purposes, viz. An-
derston's Institution—The Philosophical Society—The
Philotechnical Society—The Literary Society—Stirling's
Library—Society for promoting Agriculture.——
The Public Amusements, viz. The Stage—The As-
semblies and Concerts—The Sacred Music Institu-
tion—Mason Lodges, &c.

THE Physicians and Surgeons were first erected
into a body corporate, by a charter from James
the VI. in the year 1599, granted upon the application of Peter Low, surgeon in Glasgow, in conjunction with Robert Hamilton, professor of medicine in the university.

This charter, which was confirmed by King
Charles II. in the year 1672, contains very ample
privileges, particularly a right which the Faculty exercise to this day, of examining, and if found qualified, licensing all practitioners of medicine or surgery,
within the boroughs of Glasgow, Renfrew, and
Dumbarton,

Dumbarton, and the sheriffdoms of Renfrew, Lanark, Kyle, Carrick, Ayr and Cunningham; and in
case of non-compliance, the Faculty have a power
of enforcing a penalty or fine of L.3 : 6 : 8d. sterling, from such persons within these bounds, as
have not undergone an examination. Likewise, a
special privilege to all the members of the Faculty
of being exempted from all " weapons showing,
" roads, hosts, bearing of armour, watching, ward-
" ing, stenting, taxations, passing on assize, in-
" quests, justice courts, sheriff, burgh courts, in
" actions civil and criminal, excepting in giving
" their counsel, in matters appertaining to the said
" arts."

This respectable body was for a considerable
time incorporated with the barbers †; about the
year 1722 a separation took place, since which time
they have continued a distinct body, and at present
consist of about forty members.

The freedom fine of admission into the Faculty,
whether a stranger or not, amounts to the sum of
L.84 : 11, including the fees to the library, clerk
and officers. From these fees, and the yearly pay-

R r 2   ment

† It is a curious fact, that formerly in this country, as well
as in England, and several places on the continent, the business of a barber and surgeon were united in the same person.
In the year 1682, we find an act of the town council of Edinburgh, recommending to the incorporation of surgeons to
supply the town with a sufficient number of persons well
qualified *to shave, and to cut hair.*——*Arnot.*

ment of members, the Faculty, in 1792, established a fund, which at present amounts to L.3469 : 14 : 3 sterling, this they have converted into a scheme for behoof of their widows and children, it is divided into three classes, and according to the proportions which each member shall pay annually into the common stock, his wife is enrolled in the one or other.

The widows of the first class, whose husbands have paid annually for a certain term of years, L.2 : 5, have L.34 : 10, during their life, while they continue a widow; if a member of this class dies and leaves no widow, but a child or children, they are entitled to receive the sum of - - - L.215 : 2 : 6.

The widows of those of the second class whose husbands have paid for a certain term of years, L.1 : 2 : 6d. have annually, L.29 : 5. And if no widow, the child or children have paid them the sum of - - - L.182 : 16 : 3.

Members who pay nothing annually, their widows have L.24, of an annuity and if no widow, the child or children have the sum of - - - L.150.

Licentiates pay for a diploma, upon being found qualified, to practise surgery and pharmacy, five guineas.

This Faculty is governed by a president, Visitor, Collector, two Box-keepers, a Seal-keeper, Librarian, and two Inspectors of Drugs.—They
have

have an elegant Hall in St. Enoch's Square, with a Library, containing some thousand volumes, not only of professional books, but of others in various branches of literature, a neat and accurate catalogue of which has been lately printed.

THE FACULTY OF PROCURATORS

have for some centuries past been united into a Society under this denomination, for the purpose of managing their affairs, and for raising a fund for their poor and decayed members, and their widows and children. In order to carry the views of the Society fully into execution, and to enlarge and confirm their privileges, an application was lately made for a royal charter, which his present Majesty granted in the month of June, 1796, erecting them into a corporation and body politic, with full powers to make bye-laws for the good of the whole, to sue and be sued, to hold a seal, and elect office-bearers, &c.

According to this charter, the Society is governed by the following office-bearers: A Dean of Faculty, a council of five Managers, a Treasurer, Fiscal, and Clerk. There are two general meetings of the Faculty annually, upon the third Friday of May, and the third Friday of November. At the first of these, the election of the office-bearers for the ensuing year takes place; at the other the ordinary business of the Society is discussed. Besides these stated half-yearly meetings, prescribed

by

by the charter, there are monthly meetings of the
Council, and the Dean may, upon any urgent occasion, call a meeting of the whole Faculty upon
twenty-four hours' notice being given to the members.

In order to qualify a person for admission into
the Faculty, it is necessary that he have served a
regular apprenticeship of five years with one of the
members, practising before the Courts in this city;
and a further term of at least one year as a clerk,
either with the practitioners here, in the Court of
Session, or any proper Court of Law: And further,
that he must be of twenty-one years of age, and
have attended the Scotch law class in any of the
Universities of Scotland, for at least one session, besides being of a good character and deportment.

The apprentice fee which is due, and must be
paid at the entry of the apprentice to his indenture,
is for the son of a member L.25, and for every
other person the sum of L.50.

THE CHAMBER OF COMMERCE *

was first incorporated by a royal charter of his present Majesty, dated the thirty-first day of July,
1783

---

* The Chamber of Commerce was first projected by that
spirited citizen, Patrick Colquhoun, Esq; then Lord Provost.

1783, granted upon the application of several of the most respectable merchants and manufactur-, ers in the city, who had previously formed themselves into a society, under the above designation.

The Chamber of Commerce and Manufactures, consists not only of members residing in Glasgow, but also of merchants, traders and manufacturers in Paisley, and Greenock. By the charter there are two general half-yearly meetings, upon the first Tuesday of January, and first Tuesday of July; at the first of which there are thirty directors chosen, called the Chamber of Directors *. Within eight days thereafter, the directors again meet, and from their number elect a chairman, deputy chairman, and secretary, from amongst the members of the incorporation.—At the meeting in July, as well as that in January, the business or transactions of the directors is taken into consideration, as well as the subjects of discussion for the ensuing six months.

The great outlines of the business committed to the charge of the directors of the Chamber of Commerce, is,

1. To consider of such plans and systems as shall contribute to the protection and improvement of those

* Four general quarterly meetings of the directors are also held in the year, on the following days, viz. on the second Tuesday of January, the second Tuesday of April, the second Tuesday of July, and the second Tuesday of October.—The fees of admission are L.5 : 5, and L.1 : 1 yearly; or if L.21 is paid at admission, no farther sum is due.

those branches of trade and manufactures which are peculiar to this country, and which may be interesting to the members of the Chamber at large.

2. To regulate all matters respecting any branch of trade or manufacture, which may be submitted to the directors, for the purpose of establishing rules for the convenience and assistance, either of foreign traders, or manufacturers.

3. To read and discuss all public and private memorials and representations of members of the Chamber, requesting the aid of the directors in any matter regarding trade or manufactures.

4. To afford aid to members, whether as individuals or otherwise, who may apply for assistance in negociating any matter of business, whether local, or of a nature which requires the weight and influence of the directors, in making application to the Board of Trustees, to the King's Ministers, or to Parliament.

5. To procure relief or redress in any grievance, hardship, oppression, or inconvenience, affecting any particular branch of trade and manufacture, carried on by the members of this society, by interposing the weight and influence of the directors in any public negotiation that may be thought necessary to effect such relief.

6. To consider all matters affecting the corn-laws of this part of the united kingdom in particular, as being of the utmost consequence to its trade and manufactures.

And, in general, to take cognisance of every matter and thing that shall be in the least degree con-
neated

nected with the interests of commerce—and to assist in pointing out new sources for promoting whatever may be useful and beneficial—and to attend to every application made to parliament, which may be thought injurious to the trade and manufactures of this country—to support an intercourse and friendly correspondence with the Convention of Royal Boroughs, and Board of Trustees for Fisheries and Manufactures, for the purpose of communicating new and useful improvements to their attention.

By a prudent plan of conduct, and keeping these objects in view, the Chamber of Commerce have, since their erection, rendered very essential service to the commerce and manufactures of the kingdom, which cannot fail of entailing upon them the gratitude of every well-wisher to his country.

BOARD of COMMISSIONERS upon the RIVER CLYDE.

Until of late years, the Clyde was only navigable to Glasgow for small vessels, and even these met with many obstructions from shoals and sand-banks. An act of parliament was obtained in 1759, in order to render the river navigable for large vessels, by means of locks. Many difficulties having, however, occurred, this scheme was dropped, and another act was afterwards obtained, for improving the navigation of the river from Dumbuck ford to Glasgow, by deepening the bed of the river, and straitening the channel by means of jetties on the sides of it, for defraying the expence of which, a tonnage duty of 8d. a ton on coals, and 1s. a ton on all goods and merchandize, that should be carried betwixt Dumbuck ford and the city, was allowed to be levied.

In the year 1775, the work was so far finished, that the depth was increased so much as to allow vessels drawing six feet water to navigate to the city. By the strength given to the current of the river by the jetties, and by the operations since that time, vessels drawing about 8 feet are now navigated to Glasgow, and vessels drawing 9 feet to Renfrew ferry. The money expended in these operations, with the interest thereon, amounted to upwards of L.50,000. The first tonnage dues that were levied, (from first July, 1770, to first July, 1771) amounted to L.1,021 : 5 : 1d. since which they continued to increase gradually until July, 1790, when the increase became still more rapid. From that time till July, 1791, they amounted to L.2,144 : 16s. The next year they let for L.2,400. In 1793, for L.3,205. Since then the increase has been more gradual; in the present year, 1804, they amount to L 4,759 : 0 : 4d. The debt upon the river is now very much reduced, and it is hoped it will be soon altogether discharged *.

The

* As it does not appear that there are any rocks or great stones in the river, it is expected that, by a continuation of the operations of dragging and erecting jetties and dykes, the bed of the river may be brought to a level from Dunglas

10

The management of these funds, as well as the direction of all operations relative to deepening and improving the navigation of the river, is committed, by act of parliament†, to thirty-four commissioners, nine of whom are declared to be a quorum. These meet annually on the first Tuesday of July, at the Town clerk's chamber, when they receive from the Magistrates, in whom the more immediate direction is vested, an account of the rates and duties collected the preceding year, and of all cash which has been issued and applied, agreeable to the purposes intended by the act of parliament.

COMMITTEE of MANAGEMENT of THE FORTH and CLYDE CANAL NAVIGATION.

The company of proprietors of this navigation were

first

---

to the quay of Glasgow, and that, in the course of a few years, vessels drawing ten feet water, may be able to navigate to the city. At present vessels of ninety ton often arrive at the quay.

† In this act, a power is also given to the Magistrates, to enlarge the Bromielaw quay. This quay appears first to have been erected about the year 1680. It cost 30,000 merks scots. In 1792, it received an addition of 360 feet at the west end.

The time of high water at the Broomielaw, is three hours, at an average, later than at Greenock; if the wind is easterly, rather more; if in the opposite direction, somewhat less. The tides at a mean, rise seven feet at the quay of the city. The difference betwixt high water at Leith and Greenock, is half an hour.

first incorporated by act of parliament in 1767, for the purpose of carrying the projected design of joining the rivers Forth and Clyde by a navigable canal, into execution.

The affairs of the company were originally under the direction of two general meetings, one held at London, and the other at Edinburgh, each of which met quarterly, and the first of these chose a committee of management annually. The two general meetings having interfered with each other, and their orders to the committee of management being sometimes contradictory, an act of parliament was passed in the year 1787, forming a new constitution, whereby the direction of the company was placed in a governor and council in London, and a committee of management at Glasgow, who meet monthly or oftener, as occasion may require. Both of these are chosen by a general meeting at London, in the month of March, yearly. The committee at Glasgow consist of a chairman, deputy chairman, and ten directors, the Lord Provosts of Edinburgh and Glasgow being, *ex officiis*, two of the number. This committee appoint several officers, such as a superintendant, surveyor, sub-surveyor, and three collectors, these last are severally stationed at Port-Dundas, Bowling Bay, and Grangemouth.

OF THE BANKS.

The first bank opened in Glasgow still continues to transact business. Since its erection, several others

thers have been established, some of whom have been unfortunate, while others, and particularly those which carry on business at present, have succeeded, and obtained what they justly merit, the highest degree of commercial confidence and respectability.

THE OLD OR SHIP BANK *

just now alluded to, was the first established in the city, it having opened in the year 1749.

THE THISTLE BANK †

has also carried on business since the year 1761,

THE ROYAL BANK ‡.

The banking company under this name was erected at Edinburgh by act of parliament, in 1727. The Glasgow branch was established in 1783. The business transacted in this city, it is believed, exceeds considerably that which is done by the mother bank in the metropolis.

THE BANK OF SCOTLAND

has also a branch in Glasgow. Besides these there are branches of the following banks, viz. The British linen company—The Greenock bank—The Falkirk bank—The Paisley bank—The Paisley union bank—The Leith bank—The Stirling merchant bank—The Perth bank—The Renfrewshire bank—The Ayr bank.

INSURANCE

* This office is situated in Argyle-street, foot of Glassford-street.
† The Thistle bank is in Virginia-street.
‡ The office of the Royal bank is in St. Andrew's Square.

INSURANCE OFFICES AGAINST LOSS AND DAMAGE BY FIRE.

The principal insurance companies in Britain, have agents or offices in Glasgow, these are enumerated in the subjoined list. Companies of this kind have likewise been formed by the citizens, amongst the oldest may be reckoned the *Glasgow Friendly Fire Insurance Society*. This society is, however, now about to be dissolved; another has been lately instituted, under the name of

THE GLASGOW FIRE OFFICE.

This company, which consists of a number of the most respectable and wealthy citizens, was formed in 1803, with a capital of L.100,000, divided into 400 shares of L.250 each. It is governed by a council of directors and secretary, who meet every Monday and Thursday, for transacting the business of the society.

This office insures houses, buildings, manufactories, goods, merchandize, ships, vessels, barges, and other craft, and their cargoes in port or used in navigable canals, and all other property within Great Britain, excepting books of accounts, deeds, bills, bonds, written securities, money and gunpowder, upon as moderate terms as any office in the kingdom; it likewise makes good, the loss or damage sustained, when duly proved, to the full amount, without allowance of discount, or any other deduction whatever.

.The

The following offices have also branches or agents established in Glasgow, viz. The sun fire office—The Edinburgh friendly insurance office,—The phœnix fire office—The imperial fire office—The Newcastle fire office—The Dundee fire office.

Besides these offices, there are several others established by Government, such as the

POST OFFICE,

which alone brings a great revenue to the state. At this office, a mail coach first arrived from London, Monday, July 7th, 1788; it departs daily at two o'clock, and arrives in the metropolis in sixty-three hours; another arrives at the post office here, every morning. Two other mail coaches are also dispatched to Greenock* and Ayr, from the city; the mail is conveyed to the former place twice a-day, and to the latter once, the same number of arrivals take place. Till lately, the Edinburgh letters were conveyed from Glasgow, daily, by a post-boy upon horseback; they are now carried in a single horse chaise, by a person properly armed.

A penny post office has also been lately established in the city, for the accommodation of the inhabitants, from whence letters are sent to the different parts of the town, four times a-day.

In the city there are also the offices of excise, customs, stamps, window and house-taxes.

---

* The Greenock mail first began to run, Nov. 12. 1788.

ANDERSON'S INSTITUTION.

Every establishment which has for its leading object the extensive diffusion of knowledge, classical, scientific, or technical, must secure a large portion of the attention and approbation of the liberal and enlightened part of the community, ever ardent in the promotion of measures tending to accelerate the tardy, yet progressive improvement of the human species. That the establishment of the distinguished Mr. John Anderson, late professor of physics in the university of Glasgow, a noble, and we hope it will prove a permanent memorial of his patriotism and philosophical spirit, possesses claims of this description, will be readily granted, we apprehend, without attempting a complete display of the varied advantages which might result from its vigorous prosecutions, when we make known a few of the very important purposes which it comprehends. By the peculiar constitution of this institution, an easy opportunity is afforded to young men, who are prevented by the pursuits in which they are necessarily engaged, from pursuing a regular course of studies at the long established, and highly respectable university in this place, of partaking of the gratifications and benefits which arise from the cultivation of physical science; the different subjects being discussed in the most popular manner, illustrated by every variety

riety of experiment, and often being particularly directed to the elucidation of the most useful arts of life; to those likewise, who are further advanced in years, an opportunity is afforded, without mingling with the youngest pupils, of reviving the knowledge they formerly have possessed, but which, from intervening avocations, they may have allowed to escape; or to those, who not having obtained, in the earlier periods of life, any scientific information, may be anxious to supply in part the deficiency they experience; and what ought, perhaps, to be deemed of the greatest consequence, an opportunity is offered to the *female sex*, of procuring information, valuable to them in the highest degree, yet in every prior establishment most unjustly withheld; although it could not have escaped observation, that the most ample instruction should be imparted, since to females is often committed the important and dignified office of molding the mind, whilst yet in its most plastic state, and of forming a foundation for the future intellectual structure; which, if neglected or injudiciously conducted, vain must be every expectation, of subsequent elevation or stability.

In order that the public may acquire a knowledge of the constitution and regulations of this recently established school of science, we shall introduce the following abstract of the deed of settlement, by which Mr. Anderson disponed and conveyed his property of every kind, to the community at large, for its establishment and support. This institution is directed to be placed under the management of eighty-one trustees, appointed by its founder, and

T t   selected

selected from nine classes of men, viz. Tradesmen or mechanics, agriculturists, artists, manufacturers, physicians and surgeons, lawyers, divines, natural philosophers, and lastly, kinsmen or namesakes. These classes are empowered to fill up by ballot, all vacancies which may happen in any of them, either by resignation or death, within the space of four calendar months from the date of such vacancies; but if they shall allow this time to expire, the vacancies must be filled up by ballot, at the first general meeting of the trustees.

For the superintendance of the conduct of the trustees, and the regulation of the affairs of the institution, nine visitors are likewise appointed, viz. the Lord Provost of Glasgow, the oldest Baillie, the Dean of Guild, the Deacon Convener, the President of the Faculty of Physicians and Surgeons, the Dean of the Procurators, the Moderator of the Synod of Glasgow and Ayr, the Moderator of the Presbytery of Glasgow, and the Moderator of the Presbytery of Dumbarton, any six of whom to be a quorum.

Four general meetings of the trustees or governors, before-mentioned, are appointed to be holden in the course of every year, viz. on the day of the summer and winter solstice, and the day of the vernal and autumnal equinox: At these meetings, every thing which relates to the interest of the institution is considered; a majority, in all cases, deciding the questions which may be agitated.

Nine ordinary Managers are also directed to be chosen by the Trustees annually, from those resident in Glasgow; to these Managers, who are required

quired to meet upon the first Thursday of every month, is committed the regulation of the ordinary business of the institution, of which they are expected to present a report to each of the four general meetings.

This institution, when completed, is intended to consist of four colleges and a school or academy; these are the colleges of arts, medicine, law and theology. Each college to consist of nine professors; the senior professor being president or dean.

The endowment of this institution by the learned professor, its founder, consisting principally of a very extensive and valuable apparatus for illustrating the various branches of natural philosophy and chemistry, together with a large library, composed of the most select scientific works in different languages, and a museum, containing a neat, well arranged collection of fossils, it has been found expedient hitherto, to execute only a small part, although that part is perhaps the most useful, of the original plan. Should the funds experience a considerable increase, either from a more general encouragement of the present undertaking, or from the continued liberality of the friends of science, who have already afforded it very important patronage, it may be hoped that the trustees will hereafter be enabled to establish the institution upon the large and extensive basis delineated by Mr. Anderson.

During the period of three years, succeeding the establishment of this seminary upon its present limited plan in 1796, lectures on natural philoso-

T t 2

phy

phy and chemistry, popular and scientific, were delivered by the late Dr. Thomas Garnett, with great success and approbation. For the two first sessions, the lectures were delivered in the Trades' Hall, and in a part of the Grammar school, but previous to the third session, several public-spirited gentlemen, friends to the institution, purchased and fitted up for its accommodation, a very spacious and convenient hall, with adjoining rooms for containing the library, museum, and apparatus. When Dr. Garnett accepted an appointment in the royal institution of London *, at the latter end of the year 1799 †, Dr. George Birkbeck was elected professor of

* It is agreeable to the local predilections of an inhabitant of this place, and must be flattering to the prepossessions of the friends of professor Anderson, (who, judging from the respect in which his memory is held by those who knew him, appear to have been very numerous,) to observe this very splendid and flourishing establishment in London, and another more recently formed in Newcastle apparently prospering, arising from the institution we have now described; borrowing, if not, the original idea, at least much of the plan of management from it.

† A situation which he had left only a short time before the public were deprived of the important services, medical and philosophical, which he was then conferring, and which might still have been expected to accrue, had his life been prolonged, from unremitted efforts, directed by active zeal for the promotion of science, most persevering industry, great scientific acquirements, and a considerable share of inventive genius, always controuled by a judgment, logically and mathematically correct.

of natural philosophy and chemistry, in this institution; since that period he has continued to deliver lectures upon these subjects, and has occasionally added a course of geography and astronomy. Dr. Birkbeck has likewise endeavoured to give additional effect to the excellent design of diffusing philosophical information, by conducting a course of lectures upon a very familiar and elementary plan, for the instruction of *Operatives*, or that portion of the community engaged in the actual execution of the mechanic and chemic arts: these lectures, (at first delivered gratis, but afterwards for a very trifling payment from each individual,) have been attended by nearly five hundred persons, each season; and from the eager assiduity and active enthusiasm uniformly displayed, we are authorized to hope, that consequences highly advantageous, will result from this branch of the establishment.

THE PHILOSOPHICAL SOCIETY.

It had often been regretted by the friends of science, that no institution of this kind was established in Glasgow, the more particularly as this city owes so much of its prosperity to its various manufactures, whose improvement is so intimately connected with a proper acquaintance with many of the branches of physics.

Impressed with the idea of the utility of such an institution, a number of gentlemen formed themselves into a society, under this title, upon the 9th

of

of November, 1802. Its objects are—that its members, by regular conversations on scientific subjects, in mechanics, chemistry, and other arts, may derive that improvement which is to be obtained from a free communication of their ideas on such topics. For this purpose, they hold meetings every Wednesday evening in winter, and once a fortnight in summer, when an essay is usually read by one of the members, on the subject of which a conversation ensues. Models are often presented at these meetings, illustrative of improvements proposed in mechanical subjects.

A library is forming by the society, and it is intended to procure for its use a collection of apparatus for the different branches of natural philosophy, astronomy, geography, and chemistry.

Its government is vested in a president, vice-president, treasurer, secretary, and twelve directors, chosen by ballot by the whole society. Each member is also admitted by ballot, and pays three guineas as the fees of admission, and half a guinea annually thereafter.

THE PHILOTECHNICAL SOCIETY.

In the latter end of the year 1800, several gentlemen of the city formed themselves into a club or society, for the purpose of conversing upon such subjects as were connected with painting, engraving, architecture, or other branches of the fine arts.

In this society, essays upon any appropriate subject are sometimes read, and such remarks thereafter

ter made, as occur to any of the members; drawings, prints, and paintings are also allowed to be produced, and in such a case they furnish subject of conversation for the evening.

The society is governed by a president and secretary, chosen annually by the members. No gentleman proposed can be admitted without the unanimous consent of the club, a mode of election, which ensures the greatest harmony amongst the members of the society.

THE LITERARY SOCIETY *.

This very respectable society was established in 1755. It consists chiefly of professors and lecturers in the university, and clergymen of the city and its neighbourhood.

The meetings are held every Friday, at six o'clock in the evening, from November to May, in a convenient apartment of the college.

Agreeably to the regulations, each member, in his turn, gives a discourse upon some subject, announced at the preceding meeting, and the president thereafter invites the other members to offer their remarks, which, when finished, the society adjourn.

The president is changed weekly, the gentleman who gave the last discourse filling that situation at the first meeting thereafter. The secretary is elected

* Under the general denomination of literary, are comprehended also theological and philosophical discussions.

ed annually, though the same person is general'y re-elected, as long as he chuses to remain in office. When a gentleman is proposed as a member, his his name must lie on the table till next meeting, when he is admitted or rejected by ballot.

STIRLING'S LIBRARY.

This public-spirited institution had its rise from the generosity of Mr. Walter Stirling, late merchant in Glasgow; who, by his will, dated the third day of February, 1785, mortified, in favour of the then Lord Provost of the city, and his successors in office, the sum of L.1000 sterling, his tenement in Millar's street, and share in the Tontine Society, for the sole purpose of purchasing a library, for the use of the citizens, and supporting a librarian, for taking charge of the books. The management of this library, according to Mr. Stirling's will, is vested in thirteen managers, elected and chosen from the following corporations or societies, viz. from the Town Council of Glasgow, three of their number, (besides the Lord Provost of the city, who is a director *ex officio;*) from the Merchants' House of Glasgow, three; from the Presbytery of Glasgow, three; and from the Faculty of Physicians and Surgeons in Glasgow, three.—The Lord Provost to be preses, whenever he shall be present at the meetings of these directors.

The directors, by a regulation which they made in the year 1791, meet four times per annum, viz. on the second Mondays of February, May, August,

gust, and November, for discussing the business of the institution. At the meeting in August, the accounts for the preceding year are balanced.— The librarian is chosen, and according to the state of the funds, orders are given for the purchase of new books, which are produced at the next meeting of the directors in November.

By the original constitution of this library, no books were lent out except upon an order from two of the directors, and depositing the value of the book required; so that such of the citizens as could not conveniently attend at the library room, were, in a manner, debarred from the benefit of the institution. The managers in a short time saw the impropriety of this scheme, and in its stead they substituted the following, which not only tends to increase the funds, but also to further the intention of the benevolent donor:

Every person subscribing five guineas is entitled to the use of the library during life, and not only may he use the library room for three hours daily, for the purpose of reading, but he is entitled to carry home whatever book or books he chuses, upon a proper receipt, provided they do not amount to more in value than half his subscription; if the value of the books required is greater than that sum, he is bound to deposit the difference of the value of the book, or the difference of double the value of one or more volumes, if the books consist of a greater number of volumes than what are borrowed. These books he must again return to the library in a specified time, according to their size; not exceeding

U u ＇ two

two weeks for an octavo, four for a quarto, and eight weeks for a folio. In case this regulation is not complied with, the subscriber is charged sixpence weekly for each volume he detains beyond the limited time. If not returned within a month, this sum of sixpence is doubled, and one shilling weekly per volume, is thereafter due, till returned to the library, and no person from whom any forfeiture is due, or who has defaced or damaged any book, is permitted to have another book, till satisfaction be made.

Nonsubscribers may also have books, upon an order signed by two directors, provided they give a proper receipt therefore, and agree to comply with the regulations as to returning the books they have borrowed.

In every competition betwixt subscribers for a particular book, the first applicant is preferred, though the case varies betwixt a nonsubscriber and subscriber, the latter being always preferred.

This library, which is at present situated in St. Enoch's Square, is to be removed at Whitsunday, 1804, to a large apartment in Hutcheson's Hospital, finished for the purpose. It is open every lawful day, betwixt the hours of twelve o'clock, noon, and three o'clock, afternoon. Since the commencement of the scheme, very considerable benefactions in books have been made to it, many of them highly valuable and interesting; these, with the regular yearly additions, and other donations which may be expected, will, in a few years, it is hoped, compose a selection, equalled, in point of variety, by few collections in the kingdom *.

THE AGRICULTURAL OR FARMER SOCIETY

was instituted about 17 years ago, and consists of members from above 30 parishes around the city. Its object, at first, was chiefly the improvements in agriculture, but latterly, it is more of the nature of a charitable institution, although a ploughing-match, as it is called, is yearly appointed, and premiums given to three of the competitors, who appear to be best entitled to such a reward.

The funds of this society amount now from L.1200 to L.1500. The management is vested in delegates, sent from the different parishes, each of which send two. And these representatives form the board of directors, which meet in Glasgow quarterly.

Each parish has also its own managers, without whose recommendation no member is entitled to a-

U u 2   ny

---

*At this time, January, 1804, this library contains between seven and eight thousand volumes; the number of subscribers, at the same time, amounting to upwards of 500.

Every donor of L.100 or upwards, is an extraordinary director for life; the contributor of L.20, a director for five years. And in case any person shall bequeath a sum by way of legacy, such donor shall have power, by his deed, containing the bequest, to name an extraordinary director, who shall be continued in the management, for such a number of years as shall correspond to the sum given.

ny benefit from the society. This recommendation is sent to the board of directors at Glasgow, who have no power to reject it, unless there appears to be something very improper, either as to the qualification or situation in life of the applicant.

THE STAGE.

In Scotland the acting of dramatic entertainments can be carried to a much higher degree of antiquity than what is generally imagined. These, in times of popery, were often represented in dumb show, or perhaps with short speeches intermingled, the most interesting scenes in the history of our Saviour, or the lives and miracles of the saints. In the beginning of the sixteenth century, they were very common and popular in Scotland, and the players so numerous as to be complained of as a nuisance*. Theatrical exhibitions came not to be restricted to religious matters, but embraced all subjects which could gratify the passions or taste of the people.

These performances were, for many years, exhibited to the multitude in the open air, almost every town of note having a place for the purpose, called the Playfield.

Shortly after the Reformation, plays, either upon

a

---

* Book of universal kirk history, p. 488.

a religious, or other subject, were prohibited by the church, and for almost a century and a half thereafter, we hear of no such representations. Previous to the middle of the last century, however, itinerant companies appear to have visited the metropolis. By degrees, from the encouragement they met with, actors of more distinguished merit appeared, and at length established a regular theatre in the Canongate of Edinburgh, about the year 1746. For a long time after this took place, we can find no accounts of any such entertainment having been brought forward in Glasgow, the prejudices here against these representations being still greater than in the metropolis.

The first, we are informed, were a set of itinerants, who performed in a room called Barrels Hall, upon the east side of the High-street. The first edifice, however, purposely built for stage representations, was only a wooden booth, placed against the old wall of the Bishop's palace, in an area called the Castle-yard, adjoining to the cathedral. Mr. Lee was the projector, it was consequently since the year 1752. This hovel had the credit of exhibiting to the then audience of Glasgow, Messrs. Digges, Love, Stamper, and Mrs. Ward. It was little relished by the lower order of people, and was attacked by the weavers, who were spirited on to the assault, by Mr. Whitfield, by stones and other missile weapons, but not destroyed. It was erected in the years 1752 and 1753.

In the spring of 1762, Mr. Jackson, one of the present

present managers of the theatre, accompanied Messrs.
Beat and Love to Glasgow, to solicit the building of
a regular theatre within the liberties of the city.
Five gentlemen * undertook to erect a house at their
own expence, which was to be rented by Messrs.
Beat and Love; no one being hardy enough to accommodate them with ground for the purpose, within the royalty, they purchased a plot at the west end
of the town, without its jurisdiction. The proprietor of this ground was Mr. Miller of Westerton;
he sought 5s. the square yard, which was then reckoned a most extravagant price, it was, however, a-
greed to, and a theatre in consequence erected.
These gentlemen entered into an engagement with
the company at Edinburgh, to play in this new theatre. Amongst the performers in that city at the
time, was Mrs. Bellamy.—She opened the theatre
here.

Though the house was thus raised, the ferment
it occasioned could not be laid in the minds of the
people. Before the intended night of opening, the
house was set on fire, and with difficulty saved from
being totally reduced to ashes, in this conflagration
all

* William M‘Dowal of Castle Semple, William Bogle of
Hamilton Farm, John Baird of Craigton, Robert Bogle of
Shettleston, and James Dunlop of Garnkirk, Esquires. Their
shares of the expence amounted to L.100, besides a subscription of L.200; they sold it to the directors of the assembly,
who laid out L.700 or L.800 more, so that the whole building
cost L. 500.

all the paraphernalia and wardrobe was consumed by the flames *.

The fire was, it is said, occasioned by the preaching of a methodist preacher†, who so much inflamed the minds of his hearers against the erection of the theatre, that they hastened away in a mass, to put the design of destruction into execution. The stage was set fire to, but a discovery being very shortly thereafter made, no other part of the building suffered ‡. Such being the case, the company resolved to perform next day; a temporary stage was therefore fitted up in the best manner they could, for the time. They opened with the Citizen, by way of a play, and the Mock Doctor for the farce. Besides Mrs. Bellamy, Mr. Reddesh and Mr. Aiken were the other principal performers at Glasgow that season.

From this time, the Glasgow theatre was occupied at different periods by the Edinburgh company,

till

* In the spring 1764.

† This gentleman told his auditors, that he dreamed the preceding night he was in the infernal regions, at a grand entertainment, where all the devils in hell were present, when Lucifer, their chief, gave for a toast the health of Mr. ——— who had sold his ground to build him a house upon.

‡ Mrs. Bellamy's wardrobe did not, however, escape; it was reckoned by herself, to be worth at least L.900, there being a complete set of garnets and pearls, from cap to stomacher, (Life of Mrs. Bellamy, vol. iv. p. 59.)

till it was taken by one Williams *, an adventuring itinerant manager, who, being active and enterprising, for one season, cleared a considerable sum.

The Edinburgh theatre having been let by Mr. Ross, to Mr. Wilkinson of York, he brought his performers along with him; the greatest part, therefore, of the Edinburgh one forming themselves into an independent company, fitted up a temporary theatre at Dundee; Messrs. Bland and Mills were their managers, the former had procured the lease of the house at Glasgow; the following winter, he prevailed upon Mr. Jackson to become a partner alongst with Mr. Mills and him for the season ‡, only upon certain conditions. The scheme succeeded, and they were induced to embark in it for a permanency; accordingly, before the close of the season, Mr. Jackson purchased one full third of the wardrobe and moveable property. Before even the theatre opened, however, it was burnt to the ground†, how the accident happened, was never known—it had all the appearance of design: there had been no play, and consequently no fires for two days, nor could there have been any at the gallery end of the house, from which the flames first issued, as the

dressing

---

* He possessed it from 1768 and 1769 to the end of 1771. Digges had it in 1772 and 1773.

‡ The season commenced January 12th, 1780.

† May 5th, 1780.

dressing rooms were, and indeed always are contiguous to the stage.

Soon after this unfortunate catastrophe, Mr. Jackson applied to the proprietors, to know whether it was their design to rebuild the theatre; he was informed that they had not the least intention of doing so, and that he was at liberty to erect such a house, if he thought proper. Mr. Jackson accordingly fixed upon a situation which he purchased, on the east side of Dunlop-street, called then St. Enoch's croft. The foundation was dug, and the first stone laid, February 17th, 1781. In this, however, he met with some interruption, from some gentlemen, who imagined their property, situated in the neighbourhood, would thereby be injured. This being got the better of, the building was carried on and finished, at an expence, according to Mr. Jackson's account, of upwards of L.3000 sterling.

The house was opened in January, 1782, and its performances represented through the season, by a detached company, occasionally recruited from Edinburgh, where the theatre was likewise open, under Mr. Jackson's management, at the same time. But afterwards, the seasons of performing were so settled, that one set of performers supplied both houses. The actors' wardrobe and exhibitions were the same, its theatrical arrangements being upon a conjunct plan with that of the metropolis.

Mr. Jackson continued thus in the right of the theatre and its management, till his affairs unfortunately went into disorder. At that period, the ma-

nagement

nagement was, in virtue of a purchase, vested in Mr. Stephen Kemble, who continued to fill the situation for some seasons. It again recurred to Mr. Jackson, as well as the right to the remainder of the lease of the Edinburgh theatre.

From the great increase of Glasgow, the theatre built by Mr. Jackson, was often found incommodious*. It was, besides, unsuitable in its appearance and decorations to the wealth of the city. Mr. Jackson was himself sensible of this, and with a view of remedying the defect, he began to enlarge it. These operations, however, soon ceased, a number of gentlemen in the city, thinking it more adviseable to build a house altogether new, and which would, at all times, accommodate the public†. For this purpose, a subscription was set on foot, at L.25 the share, and in a short time, near L.7000 was subscribed for. A committee was appointed, ground purchased at the head of Queen-street, and the building, as has been formerly mentioned, begun.

Mr. Jackson made overtures for this house, in conjunction with Mr. Aiken of the Liverpool theatre, and shortly thereafter, the committee and these gentlemen entered into a contract of agreement. By this contract, the committee agreed to grant them a lease for the remaining years of the Edinburgh patent,

* It held from L.90 to L.100.

† These gentlemen agreed to pay Mr. Jackson L.100, as an equivalent for keeping possession of the materials he provided for this alteration.

tent, providing that if the patent should not expire till after the lapse of six years, from Whitsunday, 1802, then the tack should terminate at the end of that space. It was also agreed to by the parties, that the lease should cease, upon Messrs. Jackson and Aiken ceasing to be managers of the Edinburgh theatre, but if one of them continued in such management, then the tack stood equally valid, as if both were managers ‡.

In consideration of the agreement entered into, Messrs. Jackson and Aiken became bound to pay to the subscribers, as rent, a clear yearly interest of five per cent. upon the whole money expended by the proprietors in purchasing the ground for the theatre, and in building and completely finishing it, and in general, upon the whole money expended by the proprietors, in relation to the house, including interest at five per cent. calculated upon the money from the respective times of the advance.

By this contract it is also stipulated, that a committee, named by the subscribers, shall have the full management of all matters connected with lighting and cleaning the house, and the sufficiency of the band of music, and in general, of such other matters, as may be proper to secure a regular and respectable amusement to the public. It is also pro-

X x 2   vided,

---

‡ The lease also expires upon the bankruptcy of the said Messrs. Jackson and Aiken, should such take place; and also on the death or bankruptcy of the survivor of them, and that in case of the bankruptcy of one of the partners, the other continuing solvent, the lease shall devolve upon the solvent partner.

348

vided, that the seasons for performing shall commence, for the winter, on or before the 15th day of
November, annually, and continue to the 15th day
of January, thereafter; and shall begin, for the
spring and summer season, on or before the 15th
day of April, and continue as long thereafter, as
may be found agreeable to the managers of the theatre, who are also bound to perform, each winter
season, a play, to be fixed upon, as well as the night
of performing, by the committee, for the benefit of
such a public charity as they shall think proper to
name.

Such are the principal facts in the history of the
Glasgow stage, which it was thought necessary to
take notice of. In addition it may be mentioned, that
an act of parliament and patent has been obtained
since the date of the contract, erecting the theatre, a
Theatre Royal, that the house is not yet nearly finished, (January, 1804) though the greatest exertions are used for that purpose, and that, when
completed, it promises, in point of internal decoration, to do honour to the taste of the gentlemen,
who originally planned, and who at present superintend the execution of the work.

OF THE ASSEMBLIES.

Assemblies have been long held weekly in the
winter season in Glasgow. For a considerable period, they were kept in the old assembly room in
the Tontine buildings; since the building of the
hall for the purpose, they have, however, been removed

moved thither. The management of the funds,
and regulation of the whole, is vested in a number
of directors, and a secretary or clerk; but the economy of dancing, and other business of the night,
is superintended by a woman of fashion, appointed
by the directors.

The assemblies, during the winter season, are
held weekly; the first, however, which is well attended, is generally that kept in honour of her Majesty's birth day, on the 18th of January; upon that
night the tickets sell at 5s. and on every other at
4s.

The present assembly room was first opened on
the Queen's birth day, 1798; Mrs. Kennedy, directress. The company, which was uncommonly
brilliant, consisted of 350 ladies and gentlemen.
The numbers on the same occasion, have since fluc-
tuated, as may have been expected. The greatest
number since, it is believed, attended the assembly
of 1799, when there were 460, including 180 ladies †.

THE

---

† The following is a copy of the regulations or rules to be
observed at the Glasgow assemblies, which may, at least, be
interesting to some of our readers:

1. The company to meet at eight o'clock, and the Tickets
to be drawn precisely at half past eight.

2. Each Set to consist of twelve Couple, and the Ladies to
draw Tickets for their places.

3. No Ladies to stand up in the Country Dances, except in
the place to which their Ticket entitles them, and are requested to keep their Ticket for the evening.

4. Only

THE CARD ASSEMBLY.

Last winter, an assembly of genteel people was held, in rotation with the dancing assembly, once a-fortnight; for this season, however, it is given up.

SACRED MUSIC INSTITUTION.

Music, in all ages, and in every country, has been held in estimation, from the congeniality of its powers to the feelings of the human heart. Sacred music possesses, of all others, the most extensive influence. From the nature of its composition, it is exquisitely adapted to touch the passions, and to inspire

4. Only two Set to be allowed to dance Country Dances at a time.

5. No Ladies to leave their places till the Dance is finished.

6. No Reels to be allowed but with permission of the Directress or Director.

7. No Gentleman to stand before the Ladies, so as to intercept their view.

8. When a Lady has called one Dance, her place in the next is at the bottom of it.

9. No Gentleman to be admitted in Boots or Half Boots, (Officers on duty excepted) and those who have sticks are desired to leave them at the Bar.

10. No servant to be admitted up stairs.

The same Regulations to be observed at the Card Assemblies, only that the Company are to meet at eight o'clock, and the Tickets to be drawn at half past eight; and no Country Dance or Rubber at Cards to be begun after twelve o'clock.

spire that awe and veneration, which is so essential to worship. In listening to its strains, our hopes are enlivened, and our griefs are softened; our joys are refined, and the best affections of the heart called forth.

Impressed with a sense of its consequence, several gentlemen, in the course of the year 1796, formed themselves into a society, for encouraging and promoting a taste amongst the inhabitants of Glasgow, for this noble species of musical composition; with this view, a general subscription was opened, which met with a degree of encouragement, highly flattering to the projectors of the institution.

The society, which consists of the whole subscribers, is governed by twelve directors and a secretary, who is, *ex officio*, a director, chosen annually by ballot. Six public meetings are held in the season, at which each director presides by rotation; and a private rehearsal is held once a-week, at which two directors attend, and any other of the society who chuse *.

The

* A new and elegant organ, built by Mr. Donaldson of York, was purchased by the society, and erected at first in the Trades' Hall, for the use of the institution. Its stops, which are more powerful and smooth than any in Scotland, are as follow, viz. an open diapason in front, from G,G pipes, gilt, stopped diapason, principal, flute, twelfth, fifteenth, tierce, sesquialtra, cornet, trumpet bass, trumpet treble. In the choir organ, with a pedal, an open diapason, stopped diapason, and flute. In the swell, there is a stopped diapason, open diapason, principal, hautbois, and trumpet.

The meetings of the gentlemen composing the institution, were for some time held in the Trades' hall, where the organ was erected; since then they have been kept in the choir of the cathedral, in consequence of an act of council having been obtained for that purpose, in January, 1801. To this place the organ was also removed in August last, by the approbation of the Magistrates, and placed in the organ loft, on the east end of the choir, under a beautiful Gothic arch, designed by Mr. Hamilton, architect *.

The vocal band of the institution is composed of persons, regularly bred to the study of sacred music, who have, by the assistance of Mr. Fergus, organist to the society, acquired an excellency in performing the compositions of Handel, and other eminent masters, hitherto unequalled in this country. From the exertions that have been thus made, the public meetings, to which access is given by tickets, upon payment of a small sum, are, during the season, attended by a great number of people of the first respectability†. Indeed, we can hardly conceive any

* In the description of the choir, page 157, this arch is, by mistake, said to have been designed by Mr. Stark.

† To render this institution as extensively beneficial as possible, part of the money arising from the public meetings, is always appropriated to charitable purposes. On the 9th January, 1798, the secretary paid into the infirmary, L.70 : 6 : 6d. and on the 22d February, 1800, L.23 : 15s. to the several overseers of the public soup kitchens, being the clear produce of two public meetings.

any thing more likely to give pleasure, than a concert of this kind, and in such a place, where the solemn, but highly captivating sounds, and the majestic and grand appearance of the venerable edifice,
and other objects around, are so entirely in unison,
as to excite such sensations and ideas, as must highly gratify every person of feeling and taste.

THE GENTLEMENS' SUBSCRIPTION CON-
CERTS AND OTHERS.

Three years ago, a number of gentlemen, ama-
teurs of the musical art, entered into a subscription
for the purpose of holding regular concerts in Glasgow in the winter season. To these concerts they
brought some of the best vocal and instrumental performers in Britain, and many of the subscribers also
assisted themselves. This concert is now (at least
for this season) discontinued, a number of the subscribers having declined their further patronage. In
its stead, this winter, there are concerts established by
one of the first people in the professional line, Mr.
Corri of Edinburgh, who has engaged a number of
the first rate performers; these concerts are held in
the Assembly Hall.

In Glasgow there are also a great number of concerts given annually, in the winter season, and in
different places, by the different teachers of music.
In some of these, the performances are excellent,
and the company genteel; in others, little, it is believed, can be said, either with respect to the one or
the other.

Y y   On

Of the SOCIETY of BOWLERS.

The pleasing amusement of bowling is practised by many gentlemen of the city. Several of them some years ago, purchased a piece of ground at the back of the alms house, which they converted into a bowling green for the use of the society. The fee of admission of a new member is 10s. 6d ‡.

The golf is another favourite exercise with many of the inhabitants of the city; its use is, however, not nearly so general here as in Edinburgh, or the other parts of the eastern district of Scotland; this is, most likely, owing to the want of a proper place, to which access can be got at all seasons; the exercise of this amusement being confined to the Green, which is only open for a certain period in the year.

Some gentlemen also practise archery, during the summer months; their number, however, though respectable, is not very considerable.

In the winter season, when the Clyde is covered with ice, the most favourite pastime, during the day, appears, amongst the younger part, to be skating. Curling, as it is termed in Scotland, is another amusement resorted to sometimes, during an intense frost; neither is it, like the golf, so much practised
here,

‡ Another bowling green is situated in the Candleriggs street, upon the east side, the property of Robert Crauford, Esq. of Possil. The person who rents it, admits those who wish to amuse themselves in this manner, for payment of a trifle.

here, as in the eastern parts of the country, though no place can be more inviting than the surface of the Clyde, which here in general, when frozen, is smooth as the finest mirror.

Of the MASON LODGES in GLASGOW,

Holding of the Grand Lodge of Scotland, with their number on the roll of the Grand Lodge.

Amongst the many social institutions in the city, it would be unpardonable to neglect mentioning the different associations or lodges of free masons, several of whom are of very considerable antiquity. Each of these lodges, in general, meet monthly; they also have anniversary meetings upon St. John's day, at which time, they commonly walked in procession, with their different insignia. Except at laying the foundation stone of some remarkable building, processions are now, however, very unfrequent, though the same conviviality and harmony still subsists amongst the brethren, which has all along distinguished the members of this ancient institution.

The several lodges existing at present in the city, are the following;

No. on the Roll of the G. Lodge.

1	7	Glasgow Kilwinning.
2	29	Glasgow St. Mungo.
3	70	Glasgow Montrose.
4	76	Glasgow Argyle.
5	77	Glasgow Royal Arch.
6	87	Glasgow Thistle and Rose.

7   111 Glasgow Thistle.
8   128 Glasgow St. Mark.
9   129 Glasgow Union and Crown.
10 144 Glasgow St. David's.
11 145 Glasgow St. Mungo, Royal Arch.
12 169 Glasgow Shewelston St. John.
13 194 Calder Argyle, Glasgow.
14 239 Glasgow St. Patrick's.

CHAP.

CHAP. XII.

BEFORE the Reformation, almost every charitable donation was vested in the church, and its revenues, together with those charities, whose object went no higher than the preservation of life, were dispensed by the clergy. Charities of a higher order, which regard the character and former situation of their objects, were scarcely known, and when the church was overturned by the Reformation, the sacrilegious rapacity which accompanied it, seized on every thing within its reach, leaving very few remains of ancient beneficence.

ST. NICHOLAS' HOSPITAL

was founded by bishop Muirhead, about the middle of the fifteenth century, and endowed for the maintenance of twelve old men and a priest. Archbishop

shop Leighton, in the year 1677, mortified to this charity the sum of L.150 sterling, for the benefit of two poor men, one belonging to the burgh, the other to the barony parish, to be chosen by the Magistrates. The revenue of this Hospital is, however, now almost entirely delapidated; and even after the greatest efforts, yields little more than L.20 a-year, which is divided amongst several poor men, agreeably to the intention of the founder.

MERCHANTS' HOSPITAL.

It is impossible now to ascertain the date of this foundation, though it is evident from the Letter of Guildry, in the year 1605, that it existed before that time. In the year 1659, this Hospital being found to be in a decayed condition, was agreed to be taken down, rebuilt and enlarged, which was accordingly done, and the present edifice, called the Merchants' Hall, erected in its stead. The stock at that time, seems to have been about L.2000, but has now arisen, from entry money and mortifications, to the sum of L.18,000 sterling. Their revenue at present amounts to much above L.1000 per annum, part of which is employed for particular purposes, expressly specified by the mortifiers, and the rest is employed for the relief of decayed members, their widows and descendants. Towards this last mentioned purpose, there was last year expended about L.1000 sterling.

TRADES'

TRADES' HOSPITAL.

We have before, when treating of the Trades' House, specified the stock and revenue that belongs to this Hospital, also the manner and extent of the expenditure yearly, which renders any recapitulation unnecessary. This Hospital also appears to have been founded previous to the year 1605.

HUTCHESON'S HOSPITAL,

the next point of antiquity, was founded and endowed by George Hutcheson of Lambhill, writer in Glasgow, and Thomas Hutcheson of the same profession, his brother, in the years 1639 and 1641, for the support, originally, of 12 old men and 12 boys. The patrons of this Hospital are a Preceptor, the Magistrates and Council, and Ministers of the city. From good management, and various donations which this Hospital has received, the funds have increased very considerably, so that the annual income is now above L.2300. This is employed so as to have the least possible bad influence on the industry of the people, by following out the intentions of the founders in supporting old men, who have been of character and credit in the city, by giving them pensions from L.5 to L.20 per annum. The charity has likewise been extended to women of the same description, in pensions, from L.5 to L.15. A part of it, aided by a mortification of Scot of Scotstarbet, afterwards to be mentioned, has also been allotted to give education and clothing to forty-eight boys for four years, during which time, they

they have an annual pension of L.3 each; and all of them, at leaving the school, are completely clothed, and bound apprentices to different trades.

THE TOWN'S HOSPITAL.

was founded in the year 1730, and opened for the reception of the poor upon the 15th of November, 1733. The reasons that induced the community to build this Hospital, were, that the poor might be better provided for than formerly, with wholesome food, good clothes, clean lodging, and all other necessary accommodations of life, at a less expence than they used to cost the community for their maintenance. And further, to maintain and give good education to orphans, or such as were left destitute; to afford an asylum to the old; and to promote the best interests of all, in the cheapest possible manner.

This Hospital, last year (1803) contained 336 persons; besides 168 children boarded out of the house on full nursing wages, and 147 children on half nursing wages. The revenue arises as follows:

	L.	s.	d.
From the Town Council, - -	220	0	0
From the Merchants' House, -	110	0	0
From the Trades' House, -	120	0	0
From the General Session, -	300	0	0
The annual assessment on the inhabitants, from the 1st of August, 1802, to the 1st of August, 1803.	3663	8	10
Interest, - - -	101	0	0
Money received from boarders, -	418	18	3

Produce

Produce of manufactures,	-	219	15	11½
Received with two infants admitted into the house, - -	}	50	0	0
Contribution by the College, -		25	4	0
Gained by sundry small articles,	-	31	16	8

Making in whole,   L.5260   3   8½

The expenditure for the same year was as follows:

Meal for the poor out of the house, 1150 bolls, at 16s. 10d. }	966	16	1
Shoes, - - -	49	2	0
Coal and candle, - - -	208	15	8
Fish and flesh, - -	222	17	4
Out of the house pensioners, -	213	9	2
Nurses' fees, - - -	965	18	8
Milk, 27,760 pints, - -	99	11	10
Surgeon, apothecary, and drugs, -	136	19	0
Salaries, - - -	117	17	0
Spirits and ale, - - -	111	5	7
Petty houshould charges, - -	270	7	6½
Petty provisions, - -	101	12	4
Premiums, - - -	24	13	6
Clothing charges, - - -	289	6	3
Washing materials, - - -	47	10	2½
Barley, 144½ cwt. beans and groats, 12 bolls, }	116	16	2
Butter, 117 stone, 9½ libs. Cheese, 251 stone, 5 libs. }	186	18	3
Meal, 628 bolls, at 17s.	533	16	0

Total expenditure for 1803,   L.4663   12   7

In

In this Hospital the poor are well lodged, cloth-ed, and fed, the house is kept clean and well aired, the young are instructed in the principles of Christ-ianity, in reading English, writing, and arithmetic; and are employed in such labour as is fit for them, as making thread lace, tambouring muslins, setting card teeth, &c. The old women are employed in spinning, cleaning the house, and as far as they can in doing the work of the family. Some of the old men weave, and others are employed in such busi-ness as they can perform.

Here is also an infirmary, where the sick are ac-commodated with medical assistance, and where o-perations are performed, when necessary. It has al-so a number of cells for the reception of insane per-sons.

This Hospital is under the management of a pre-ceptor, treasurer, and fifty directors, chosen annual-ly by the Town Council, Merchants' House, Trades' House, and General Session. These directors visit the Hospital in rotation, and five days each week, a written report is signed by one of the directors. E-very Tuesday, the preceptor and eight directors sit in the Hospital, for the purpose of admitting pau-pers to the benefit of the charity, and other necessa-ry purposes.

THE GENERAL SESSION

is composed of the ministers and elders of the dif-ferent parishes of the city. They have a revenue of from L. 1,300 to L. 1,400 per annum, arising from the interest of sums mortified to them and their own capital;

capital; from sums given by many at the time of their marriage; from donations at funerals, which are never less than L.5, and seldom exceed ten guineas, (in which case the bells of the city are tolled); and from the collections at public worship.

This is laid out in paying sums, agreeably to the will of the mortifiers; in paying L.300 a year, towards the expence of maintaining the Town's Hospital; and in giving to the particular Sessions, every month, certain sums of money, to be distributed amongst the poor of their respective parishes. What remains, is also divided in the same manner amongst the poor, as an additional supply during the winter season.

THE ROYAL INFIRMARY.

The Royal Infirmary is undoubtedly the most noble of the institutions in Glasgow, reared by the hand of charity. Its purpose is to relieve the diseases of those who are oppressed by poverty.

Although the city of Glasgow, prior to the establishment of this institution, had ever paid the greatest attention to the diseased poor, and the physicians and surgeons not only gave gratuitous advice and assistance, but on many occasions furnished them with medicines, yet as their number was constantly increasing, it was found altogether impossible to give that relief which their cases required; particularly as the objects of that charity lived dispersed in different parts of a large city and its suburbs, and consequently could not be under their regular and daily inspection. In consideration of these circumstances, a number of the friends of humanity, in the year 1790, feeling

Z z 2   for

for the miserable state of many of their fellow mortals, oppressed with poverty and disease, raised a sum of money by voluntary subscription, to be applied to the erecting and supporting an Infirmary, where the sick poor might be collected together, and have all the advantages of lodging, attendance, diet, medicine, and the ablest advice and assistance. In order to render their charitable scheme more beneficial and extensive, they applied for and obtained from his Majesty, a royal charter, dated the 21st of December, 1791, investing them and their successors with corporate powers, and prescribing the rules, regulations, and form of government afterwards to be noticed.

Shortly after obtaining this charter, the managers were enabled, through the generosity of the public, to begin the buildings, and in less than two years, the house was opened for the reception of patients, viz. upon the 8th day of December, 1794.

The stock of the Infirmary at the date of its opening, after paying the expence of the buildings and furnishings previous, amounted to   L.2296 11 6
This fund has yearly, from the generosity of several public bodies, and the donations of individuals, increased; on the 31st December, 1796, it amounted to L.4374 : 14s.   Since then the increase has been still more rapid, from a continuation of the public favour, insomuch, that they now hold in stock, L.7317 : 4 : 4
Amongst the many donations during this last period, it would be improper to neglect mentioning L.700 given by the first regiment of Glasgow Volunteers,

lunteers, at the period when they were disembodied, upon the termination of the late war, a donation that reflects the highest honour to them, either in a corporate or individual capacity.

It also cannot but give great satisfaction to state, that though the number of patients has been annually increasing, and of course, the necessary annual expenditure of the house, the bounty and generosity of the public have increased in the same proportion, so that last year, (1803) not only the ordinary and extraordinary expences of the house were defrayed, but an addition made to their capital. But though it is agreeable thus to mention the prosperous state of this institution, it must still be evident, that it cannot as yet continue its beneficial effects, without the assistance of its friends, for though the capital, as has been already mentioned, has so much increased, yet after all, the interest of it amounts to only L.350, and the expence of the Hospital this last year, amounted to L.1600; it is therefore necessary that the public aid should still be continued, till such time, (and we hope it is not far distant) when it will be no longer required, at least but in an inconsiderable degree *.

That

* Subjoined is a state of the Treasurer's accounts for last year, together with a general state of the funds at this time:

CHARGE.

1803.
Jan. 1. To Stock in Thistle Bank, - L 2544 4 3
Dec. 31. To Dividends on Stock, - - 105 0 0

To

That this institution is deserving of the highest encouragement,

To Interest from the City of Glasgow,	L.150	0	0
To Ditto Thistle Bank, - -	72	18	3
To Collections in the Poors Box, -	20	1	6
To Affidavits before Justices, -	38	18	6
To Rent of a House and Garden, -	16	0	0
To Soldiers admitted as Patients, -	60	14	8
To Students for Tickets, - -	79	16	0
To First Regiment of Royal Glasgow			
Volunteers, - - -	700	0	0
To Annual Subscriptions, 1803, per list,	805	13	0
To Contributions, 1803, per list, -	386	12	11
To Benefits Fines, &c. 1803, per list,	205	3	0
	L.5185	2	1

DISCHARGE.

1803.
Dec. 31. By 3 per cent. Stock purchased, 3000l,

cost, - - - -	L.2159	17	4
By House and Garden paid in part,	320	0	0
By the ordinary Annual Charges,	1152	4	7
By Medicines, &c. per Account, -	246	18	2
By Furniture, Repairs, &c. per do.	195	10	3
By Insurance, Stationery, &c. do.	42	4	9
By Thistle Bank, per Receipt, -	1068	7	0
	L.5185	2	1

GENERAL STATE OF THE FUNDS.

1803.

Dec. 31. City of Glasgow's Bond, -	L.3000	0	0
Three per cent. Stock, 5000l, cost,	3248	17	4
Thistle Bank, per Receipt, -	1068	7	0
	L.7317	4	4

couragement, and that it has already been of the utmost consequence to the country, is a fact well known.
It may, however, be mentioned in support of this position, that since its opening in December, 1794,
no fewer than 3573 patients have been discharged,
completely cured, many hundreds have received relief, above 300 capital operations have been performed, and medical advice has been given at the Infirmary, to above 20,000 out patients. What a blessing then is such an institution to a country, by
means of which many valuable lives have been saved, that otherwise would have been lost to the community, the situation of many of the patients being
such, as to circumstances, as to preclude the possibility of obtaining the proper means of cure, or e-
ven though obtained, of following the directions giv-
en by the prescription of the physician.

Further it may not be improper to present a state
of the number of patients admitted into the Hospital for the two first years after it was established,
and also another statement of a similar nature, for
the last year, which present as conclusive arguments
as can possibly be mentioned in its support.

Patients admitted in the course of the year 1795.

Medical, 145 ⎫ Men, 186 ⎫ In all, 276
Surgical, 131 ⎭ Women, 90 ⎭

Cured, 142   Irregular, 4
Relieved, 28   Dead, 18
Dismissed, 34
Remaining in the Infirmary, ⎫ 50
31st December, 1795, ⎭

Total, 276

Patients

Patients remaining in the Infirmary, ⎫
⎭
31st December, 1795,   -   50

Admitted from that time, till 1st Ja- ⎫
⎭
nuary, 1797,   -   -   352

In all,   402

Medical,   228 ⎱ Men,   253 ⎱ In all, 402
Surgical,   174 ⎰ Women, 149 ⎰

Cured,   -   213   Dismissed by desire, 24
Relieved,   -   59   Irregular,   -   5
Dismissed with advice, 17   Dead,   -   -   20
Remaining 1st January, 1797,   -   -   64

Total, 402

Report of patients admitted and discharged, from
1st January, 1803, till 1st January, 1804.

Patients remaining in the Infirmary, ⎫
⎭
31st December, 1802,   -   91

Admitted from that time, till 1st Ja- ⎫
⎭
nuary, 1804,   -   -   804

In all,   895

Medical,   638 ⎱ Men,   570 ⎱ In all, 895
Surgical,   257 ⎰ Women, 325 ⎰

Cured,   -   561   Desire,   -   88
Relieved,   -   44   Improper,   -   3
Advice,   -   35   Dead,   -   -   48
Irregular,   '-   27
Remaining 31st December, 1803,   -   -   89

Total, 895
Neither

Neither has the benefit of this institution been confined solely to those admitted into the house, as will appear from what has been already mentioned, the physicians and surgeons give medical advice daily, gratis, betwixt the hours of two and three afternoon, in the waiting room to such as attend, and whose situation, and other circumstances, will not allow them to become resident patients in the Hospital.

We have here subjoined the following abstract of the charter, and regulations for the admission of patients, which, to many, cannot fail to be acceptable.

ABSTRACT OF THE CHARTER.

By the charter, the management of the affairs of the Infirmary is vested in twenty-five managers or Directors, of which number, seven, from their office, are managers without election or nomination, viz.—the Lord Provost of Glasgow—the Member of Parliament for the city—the Dean of Guild—the Deacon Convenor—the Professor of Medicine—the Professor of Anatomy—the President of the Faculty of Physicians and Surgeons.

Eighteen Managers annually elected, viz.

One by the Magistrates and Council—one by the

3 A   Merchants'

Merchants' House—one by the Trades' House—
one by the Faculty of the College—one by the Ministers of Glasgow—three by the Faculty of Physicians and Surgeons—ten, by contributors of L.10
or more, and subscribers of L.2 : 2 annually, or
more, and by the preses's or heads of the societies
or bodies of men who have contributed L.50 or more,
or who have subscribed annually L.5 : 5 or more.

The charter appoints—That a general court of
contributors shall be held annually on the first Monday of January, which shall be composed of all
those who have contributed L.10 or more, or subscribed annually L.2 : 2 or more, and of the preses's
of all societies or bodies of men who have contributed L.50 or more, or who have subscribed L.5 : 5
annually, or more. This general court is vested
with the power of chusing ten annual managers,
qualified as above—of making such bye-laws and
regulations as shall be found necessary for the management of the Infirmary—of inspecting the whole
proceedings of the managers—examining accounts,
&c. and of giving such directions on these subjects
as they shall find expedient. To this court also,
an annual report is to be made by the managers, of
the state of the sick or diseased poor admitted into
the Infirmary—their names—the parishes to which
they belong—their diseases, and the number annually received, cured, dismissed or dead.

*Regulations respecting the Admission of Patients, enact-
ed by the General Court held on the first Monday of
January, 1794.*

1. That no patient, except in cases which do not
admit

admit of delay, shall be admitted into the Infirmary, without the consent of a committee to be appointed for that purpose, of which committee the attending physicians and surgeons shall be members, but their number shall not exceed one third of the committee.

2. That patients shall be admitted by the recommendation of contributors, according to the following rules.

3. That all contributors of 10l. or more, or of 1l. 1s. or more of annual subscription, may recommend one patient annually.

4. That all contributors of 20l. or more, or of 2l. 2s. or more, of annual subscription, may recommend two patients annually, but not have more than one patient in the Infirmary at the same time.

5. That all contributors of 50l. or more, or of 3l. 3s. or more, of annual subscription, may recommend four patients annually, but not have more than one patient in the Infirmary at the same time.

6. That all contributors of 100l. or more, or of 5l. 5s. or more, of annual subscription, may recommend six patients annually, but not have more than two patients in the Infirmary at the same time.

7. That incorporations or societies, from which regular and perpetual recommendations may be expected, who have contributed 50l. or more, or 3l. 3s. of annual subscription, may recommend two patients annually, but not have more than one patient in the Infirmary at the same time.

8. That incorporations or societies, who have contributed 100l. or more, or 5l. 5s. or more, of

annual

annual subscription, may recommend four patients annually, but not have more than two patients at the same time in the Infirmary.

9. That societies and persons who are both contributors and annual subscribers, shall be entitled to recommend both as contributors and annual subscribers, according to the above rules.

10. The contributors shall not be qualified to recommend till they shall have paid their contribution; nor annual subscribers till they have paid their annual subscription one year.

11. That in all cases of competition in the recommendation of contributors, or annual subscribers, a preference shall be given to the priority of recommendation.

12. That security shall be given for defraying the expences of burial, in case of death, which expence shall be fixed at a moderate rate; and also, that the patients be removed from the Infirmary, when it is not proper they should continue longer there.

13. That the servants of all contributors or subscribers, shall be admitted into the ward, to be appropriated for sick or diseased servants, in preference to the servants of non-subscribers, and that the expences incurred during their continuance in the Infirmary, shall be fixed at a moderate rate.

14. That a book shall be kept, in which shall be enrolled the names of the patients, and the subscribers by whom they are recommended, the dates of their admission, and other particulars which the observation of the above rules may require.

SCOTSTARBET'S

SCOTSTARBET'S MORTIFICATION.

Sir John Scott of Scotstarbet, one of the Senators of the College of Justice, by a contract between him and the Magistrates and Council of Glasgow, dated 7th and 13th June, 1653, mortified and conveyed to the Magistrates and Council, the lands of Pucky and Pucky Mill, lying in the parish of St. Leonard's and shire of Fife, for putting four boys to apprenticeships within the city, whose apprenticefees, to the extent of 100 merks each, were to be paid out of the rents of the lands; and after their apprenticeships are over, they were to be admitted burgesses by the Magistrates, gratis. Three of these boys are presented by the donor's successors, and the other by the Magistrates and Council.

By an act of Council in 1781, an agreement was made, between David Scott of Scotstarbet, Esq; and the Magistrates and Council, by which it was provided, that when the lands should yield a yearly rent of L.30, Mr. Scott should have a right to present four boys, and the Magistrates two. When the lands should yield L.40, Mr. Scott should present six boys, and the Magistrates and Council two.

MITCHEL'S MORTIFICATION.

In the year 1729, Mr. William Mitchel, merchant in London, a native of Glasgow, left the sum of L.2000 sterling to the Magistrates of the city, as trustees; the interest whereof to be applied to the maintenance of poor burgesses or their children, at the presentation of his executors, and their heirs for ever.

TENNENT'S

374

TENNENT'S MORTIFICATION.

Robert Tennent, merchant in Glasgow, by his latter will, dated in the year 1739, left in favour of the Magistrates and Council, the sum of 5000 merks Scots, the interest arising therefrom, to be applied towards the maintenance of poor children in the charity schools, erected by his brother. Also, the sum of 4000 pounds Scots, the interest whereof was to be applied by the Magistrates annually, to the relief of three widows, relicts of the citizens. He further left the sum of 10,000 merks Scots, to be lent out by the Magistrates, in separate sums, for five years, free of interest, to fifteen merchants and five tradesmen of the city, of a sober and decent character.

This mortification is under the management of nine trustees, who appoint a factor for transacting the business.

COULTER'S MORTIFICATION.

James Coulter, late merchant in Glasgow, by his will, dated 22d November, 1787, left in trust to the Magistrates and Council, the sum of L.200 sterling, as a fund for an annual premium to ingenious persons, who should have invented, or improved, or confirmed in practice, any machine, or method of working a valuable manufacture in Glasgow, or within ten miles of it, if such invention or improvement be deemed prize worthy by the Provost and Dean of Guild of Glasgow for the time, with six assessors most capable of judging in the matter. He

He further mortified the sum of L.1200 sterling, as a charitable fund in perpetuity, in favour of worthy and deserving persons, in narrow or indigent circumstances, the interest whereof to be so divided, as that no pensioner should receive more than L.10, or less than L.4 sterling yearly. The right of presentation of this charity is vested in the brother and sister of the donor, during their life, and thereafter in the Ministers of the city, and an equal number of the members of the Town Council.

WILSON'S MORTIFICATION.

Mr. Wilson of London, who formerly belonged to this city, in the year 1778, mortified in favour of trustees, the sum of L.3000 sterling, for the purpose of educating and clothing boys. This fund has been augmented by sundry donations from other persons, and it now educates and clothes forty-eight boys, who, at the end of four years, are bound apprentices to trades.

BAXTER'S MORTIFICATION.

Daniel Baxter, bookseller in Glasgow, also left a fund for educating a certain number of boys. At present there are upwards of forty boys upon this charity.

MILLER'S MORTIFICATION.

Archibald Miller, merchant in Glasgow, bequeathed, upon his decease, which happened in the year 1790, his whole estate, to the amount of upwards of L.7000 sterling, in favour of trustees, for the purpose

pose of applying the interest of that sum to the clothing and educating girls belonging to the city, the children of indigent, but reputable parents.

These girls continue in the school for the space of five years, during which they are taught reading, writing, arithmetic, needlework, and knitting; and above all, they are instructed in the principles of religion, and formed to the habits of piety and rectitude. A superior class are better clothed, and taught such other useful branches of education, as will qualify them for acting with propriety and comfort in a higher station.

The Ministers of the Established Churches in the city, together with the Principal and Professor of Divinity in the University, and a person chosen annually by each of the Kirk Sessions are appointed governors of the charity.

BUCHANAN'S SOCIETY.

This is the oldest society in Glasgow, for the purpose of giving relief to the poor. It was founded in the year 1725, by several persons of the name of Buchanan, for putting out poor boys of that name to apprenticeships; and also, for giving relief to such poor widows as belonged to the members of the society.

THE GLASGOW HIGHLAND SOCIETY

was first instituted in the year 1727, by several of the citizens of Glasgow, natives of the Highlands, or descended of parents who were such. The object of this association is to raise a fund, the interest whereof

whereof is to be applied towards the clothing, educating, and putting to apprenticeships, the children of such Highland parents, as cannot afford to do it themselves.

This society has a charter or seal of cause from the Magistrates, incorporating it into a body politic, with powers to sue and be sued, &c. is governed by a preses, twelve directors, a treasurer, two box-masters, and clerk, chosen annually. The funds arise from the rent of the Black Bull Inn, which was erected by the society, and yields at present above L.300, and from the admission fees of new members.

THE MARINE SOCIETY

was first begun in the year 1758, and incorporated in the year 1789, by act of Parliament, for the relief of seamen belonging to the river Clyde, and their families; the funds of which arise from a small sum collected from their wages.

GRAHAM'S SOCIETY

was instituted in the year 1759, for the relief of poor people of that name.

SOCIETY FOR THE RELIEF OF THE STRANGER POOR.

If to succour our neighbour in distress, and relieve his wants, be praise-worthy, how much more so is it, to lend that aid and assistance to the diseased, though industrious, stranger; who, at a distance from those whom the ties of blood or of friendship require to shelter him, has no other resource left than the benevolence of the humane.

3 B   Impressed

Impressed with pity for such of their fellow creatures as might come under this description, a number of the citizens, in the year 1790, formed themselves into a society for their relief; and, through
the contributions and subscriptions of the benevolent, they have been enabled, from the commencement of the institution to the present year, (1803)
to administer pecuniary and medical assistance to
about 900 families, consisting of near 2600 persons,
and at the expence of L.820 *.

The management of the society is by a committee
of twelve, with a treasurer. The city and suburbs
is divided by the society into six districts; two of the
committee visit the cases in each district, and report,
in order that pecuniary or medical aid may be given.

THE HUMANE SOCIETY.

The want of an institution in this city, for the recovery of persons apparently drowned, was long regretted; as, from the neighbourhood of the Clyde,
numbers annually were drowned, by bathing, without scarce an instance of one being brought to life;
whereas, in England, where such an establishment
has been for some time, upwards of 1500 (prior to
the year 1790) all of them apparently dead, were
recovered

* All persons are, by this society, considered as strangers,
who have been industriously employed in or about the city, but
have no legal settlement there, or any claim to its charity; and
who, through unavoidable distress, are in want of the necessaries of life, and unable to remove to the parish on which they
have a claim for support.

recovered through the means prescribed by the Humane Society of London.

This laudable institution here, had its rise first from the benevolence of Mr. James Coulter, (the founder of another charitable establishment we have lately mentioned) who left towards its foundation, the sum of L.200 sterling; which was paid at the first meeting of the society, in the year 1790.

In 1795, a house was built on the side of the river, at the upper Green, for lodging the apparatus necessary; where also a boat lies. and fit persons attend to administer assistance, in case of accidents happening by bathing, or otherwise.

The society is governed by a president, treasurer, secretary, and four ordinary directors, chosen annually on the second Tuesday of February.

THE GLASGOW SOCIETY OF THE SONS OF MINISTERS OF THE CHURCH OF SCOTLAND.

This institution, formed for the relief and protection of such children as are descended of ministers of the Church of Scotland, was first established here, in the month of May, 1790, and in the following year incorporated into a body politic, by a charter from the Magistrates.

The society is governed by a president and secretary, who also acts as treasurer; and by nine members, who compose the council of directors, chosen at the general annual meeting, on the last Thursday of March. The council, besides convening occasionally, have three stated meetings in the year, viz. upon the last Thursday of July; the last Thursday

3 B 2   of

of November; and the third on the Thursday immediately preceding the annual meeting. At this last meeting are the applications for relief (which must be lodged on or before the first day of March) deliberated upon, and such persons as appear proper objects of the charity, are relieved, by dividing amongst them a sum, not exceeding a year's interest of their capital. This society, besides affording relief to their own poor, make it their business to assist the children of ministers, by their good offices, in finding employment for them, as opportunities shall offer, and as their qualifications deserve; and this as well during their fathers' lives, as after their death.

New members at admission, pay a sum to the society, not less than five guineas. The capital at present amounts to about L.5000 sterling.

THE COMPANY OF GROCERS.

This company was first instituted in the year 1789, and thereafter incorporated by a charter or seal of cause from the Magistrates.

Like the other societies and corporations we have before mentioned, this has for its object the relief of its poor. The company is governed by a president, treasurer, and ten directors, chosen annually, at the general meeting upon the second Thursday of January.

Each member, upon admission, pays L.5 : 5 of freedom fine.—The stock of the company amounts at present to above L.1600 sterling.

SOCIETY

SOCIETY OF TEACHERS.

The object of this society (which was established in the year 1794) is also meant for the relief of such members, their widows and children, as by bodily infirmity or misfortunes of any kind, may be deprived of the means of supporting themselves in a comfortable manner. The society is composed of ordinary and honorary members, limited to Glasgow and its suburbs. The ordinary members are schoolmasters, engaged in teaching the following branches of education, viz. English, Latin, Writing, Arithmetic, Book-keeping and Mathematics. Honorary members are or may be ladies and gentlemen subscribers of one guinea or upwards. Every candidate for admission as an ordinary member, must be a man of approved worth and abilities, and when admitted, he pays three guineas as entry-money, and 4s. sterling annually thereafter.

The business of this society is entrusted to the management of twelve office-bearers, chosen annually, viz. a president, treasurer, secretary, and six directors, and the president, secretary, and six directors of the year immediately preceding. The society meets four times annually, viz. upon the last Saturdays of May, August, November, and February. At the meeting in May the office-bearers are chosen.

THE SOCIETY FOR MANAGING THE SUNDAY SCHOOLS.

Sunday Schools were first instituted in this city in November, 1787, for the purpose of educating poor

poor children, whose parents could not afford the expence of getting them taught in the ordinary manner. Here they not only acquire a competent knowledge in reading English, but the principles of morality and religion, so essential to their welfare, are inculcated and enforced.

In the year 1788, the number attending twelve schools was 497; and last year, 1803, 460.

The funds for supporting this laudable institution are raised by subscription. The management is vested in a president, treasurer, secretary, and sixteen ordinary directors, chosen in equal numbers from the council, ministers, elders, and subscribers.

THE FEMALE SOCIETY.

A few years ago, a society, under this name, was formed by a number of ladies, the object of which is to assist distressed females, in procuring them employment, clothes, or subsistence, as their situation may require: an institution much to the honour of our fair townswomen, and which has already rendered essential service to the destitute, the widow, and the orphan.

ASYLUM FOR PENITENT FEMALES.

In 1802, a number of gentlemen, feeling for the wretched condition of many unhappy females, who, once seduced from the paths of virtue, cannot, but with difficulty, again regain their character and reputation, (and from which idea, even with unwillingness, perhaps, they persist in the ways of vice)
formed

formed themselves into a society to establish and superintend an asylum for penitent females, and also
to apprentice and take notice of destitute boys, when
dismissed from Bridewell, to which their offences
have sent them.

THE COW-POX DISPENSARY.

Amongst all the discoveries that have hitherto
been made in medical science, or indeed in any o-
ther department, it is believed, that there are none
which, in point of importance to the increase and
welfare of mankind, can vie with that of the vaccine
inoculation, the invention of Dr. Jenner; a discovery which bids fair, after the prejudices of the multitude are entirely subdued, to exterminate a disease
that has long been one of the most fatal scourges of
the human race.

Sensible of the importance of this discovery, and
thoroughly satisfied that the proper inoculation of
the cow-pox *infallibly* prevents *small-pox*, the Faculty
of Physicians and Surgeons in Glasgow, with a liberality worthy of their profession, for two years
past, appointed two of their number to attend in
their hall, St. Enoch's Square, every Monday, to i-
noculate the children of the poor, gratis, by which
humane arrangement, the cow-pox has been already
communicated to upwards of 5000 children.

But as there were many, who though in but ordinary circumstances, were yet unwilling to be classed
in the list of paupers, and consequently were backward in coming forward with their children, two
members of the Faculty, (Messrs William Anderson
and

arfd Archibald Millar) much to their honour, opened
a Dispensary *, May, 1803, where, twice a week,
on Wednesdays and Saturdays, children are inoculated at the small sum of 2s. 6d. each.

By means of this institution, it is hoped, that the
blessings of vaccination will be more widely disse-
minated, by inducing a number of people, in circumstances, although far from wealthy, yet not
willing to be accounted in need of public charity, to
inoculate children at such a trifling expence.

At the Dispensary, tickets are also issued, to be
purchased by masters of public works, or others who
wish to make a present of that value to those of
their workmen, who, from a numerous family or a-
ny other reason, may yet be unable to pay the small
sum above mentioned †.

Another institution of a humane and philanthropic nature, has also lately been opened in this city,
under the superintendence of Dr. James Watt,
M. D. viz:

THE SUBSCRIPTION DISPENSARY,

Its design is to afford the sick poor at their own
houses,

---

* Situated nearly opposite the Exchange.

† It may also be mentioned that, by the Surgeons attending two days in the week at the Dispensary, instead of one at
the Faculty hall, more frequent opportunies of examining the
progress of the inoculated patients are afforded. The dispensary is open from eleven to one o'clock.

houses, medicine, advice, and inoculation to their children, and medical attendance when necessary.

By its means, the humane are furnished with an occasion of exerting their benevolence, and of alle-viating, amongst the poor, the complicated misery of sickness and indigence, without the patients leav-ing their own houses, or being absent a moment from the bosom of their families.

According to the regulations of this Dispensary, a subscriber of one guinea annually, may keep suc-cessively on the books, one patient for advice and medicine, or for attendance to the distance of one mile; for two guineas, two such patients, or one, for attendance to the distance of two miles; and likewise, when several of one family are ill at the same time, the recommendation of one serves for the whole.

In the note prefixed, is the annual report of each year, since the opening of the Dispensary, from which it appears, that the number of patients have been yearly increasing, and that consequently it meets with that encouragement which every useful establishment so highly deserves*.

3 C

We

*ANNUAL REPORT.

	Cured.	Relieved.	Dead.	Irregular.			Total.
1800—	91	18	24	12	-	-	145
1801—	118	17	19	12	-	-	166
1802—	142	31	18	20	-	-	211
1803—	174	28	33	-	9, on the books 4,		248

770

The Dispensary is kept, No. 17, Gallowgate.

We have thus enumerated the principal societies, the public institutions, charitable foundations, &c. as briefly as we thought their nature would admit of. There are, however, several endowments, made at different times, by well disposed persons, in favour of the Magistrates and Council, Merchants' and Trades' House, as trustees, for the education of bursars at the University, which we are sorry our limits will not allow us to detail. There are, likewise, a very great number of associations in the city, known by the name of Friendly Societies, instituted, in like manner, for supporting their members, when in distress. These are, for the most part, not tied down in the admission of their members, to a particular class or set of men, engaged in the same line of life; but such persons as come from the same county, or parish, or live in particular streets, however different their professions may be, are associated together; and, by weekly or monthly payments, create a fund, out of which their wants are supplied, when, through disease or old age, they are disabled from attending to their ordinary occupations.

Neither is an individual, though a member of one society, debarred from becoming a member of any other, so that a person belonging to several of these associations, when in distress, receives the stipulated support from each. These societies seem to be well calculated for the relief of the work people in a manufacturing country, as it makes them look forward in time of health and prosperity, to the calamities and misfortunes so incident to human life; and, by appropriating a part of their earnings, which
they

they can easily spare, affords them the satisfaction of knowing they will be supported, when reduced by sickness or old age, to be unable to work for themselves, without the humiliating idea of supplicating charity, or being a burden on their friends. These benevolent associations arose with the manufactures, and with them have gradually increased. At present they are upwards of one hundred in number, belonging to the city and suburbs. Every one has, therefore, himself alone to blame, if, by refusing to part with a small moiety, at stated times, to this purpose, he entails misery upon himself and family, when his exertions can no longer support them.

3 C 2   CHAP.

CHAP. XIII.

Of the University—The Commerce and Manufactures
—Miscellaneous Observations—Of the Environs of
Glasgow.

THE UNIVERSITY.

THIS celebrated seminary of learning, was founded in the year 1450, by William Turnbull, then Bishop of Glasgow, in virtue of a bull from Pope Nicholas the V. He also endowed it with an ample
revenue, and procured several privileges for its members from James II. The institution, at its establishment, consisted of a Chancellor, Rector, a Dean
of Faculty, a Principal, who taught Theology, and
three Professors of Philosophy.

At the Reformation, the University was almost
ruined, its members, who were ecclesiastics, having
immediately dispersed themselves, to avoid the popular fury; and it was not till the reign of James
VI. that this establishment revived, from the effects
resulting from that event. That monarch granted a
new charter of erection, and bestowed upon it the
tiends of the parish of Govan.

From the many donations made in its favour,
by the bounty of Kings and private persons, since
that time the number of Professors have been greatly

ly increased. At present it is composed of the following office-bearers and Professors, to which is added, the names of the Lecturers under their patronage.

Duke of Montrose, Lord Chancellor.

Right Honourable Lord Chief Baron Dundas, Lord Rector.

Archibald Campbell, Esq. Dean of Faculties. Patron, the University.

Rev. William Taylor, D. D. Principal. Patron, the Crown.

Professors.	Profession.	Patron.
Robert Findlay,	Divinity,	University
Hugh Macleod, William M'Turk,	Church History,	Crown.
Patrick Cumin,	Oriental languages,	University.
William Meikleham,	Natural Philosophy,	Do.
James Millar,	Mathematics,	Do.
James Mylne,	Moral Philosophy,	Do.
G. Jardine,	Logick,	Do.
John Young,	Greek,	Do.
W. Richardson,	Humanity,	Do.
Robert Davidson,	Civil Law,	Crown.
Robert Freer,	Medicine,	Do.
James Jeffray,	Anatomy & Botany,	Do.
James Couper,	Pract. Astronomy,	Do.
Richard Miller,	Lect. Mat. Medica,	University.
Robert Cleghorn,	Lect. Chemistry,	Do.
J. Towers,	Lect. Midwifery,	Do.
Lockhart Muirhead,	Lect. Nat. History.	Do.
James Chapman,	Elocution.	
James Denholm,	Drawing & Painting.	

The

The office of Chancellor was formerly held, *ex officio*, by the Bishop of the diocese; but, since the establishment of Presbytery, it has, most commonly been filled by some nobleman, or other gentleman of rank in the country. He is chosen by the Rector, Dean of Faculty, Principal and Professors. The Chancellor, being the head of the University, presides in all its councils, and in his name are all academical degrees bestowed.

The Rector is chosen annually in the *comitia*, that is, in a court in which all the students, on this particular occasion, are entituled to vote, as well as the other members of the University. He, with the advice of his assessors, whom he nominates, judges in all disputes amongst the students themselves, or between the students and citizens: he also summons and presides in the meetings of the University, called for the election of his successor, or for drawing addresses to the King, electing a member to the general assembly, &c.

The officer next in rank, is the Dean of Faculty, who is chosen annually by the Rector, Principal, and Professors. His office consists in giving directions, with regard to the course of studies; in judging, together with the Rector, Principal and Professors, of the qualifications of those who desire to take academical degrees; and in such meetings as are called for these purposes, the Rector presides.

With respect to its government, the whole property and revenue * is vested in the College, and is
administered

* The revenue arises from the tiends of the parish of Govan,

administered by a meeting of the Principal and Professors, commonly called the College meeting, and very often the Faculty meeting. The record of this meeting is visited and authenticated by the Rector, Dean of Faculty, and minister of the High Church of Glasgow. Other business of the University, besides matters of revenue, and the discipline of the students, is managed in what is called an *University meeting* or *Senate*, in which the Rector and Dean of Faculty sit, along with the Principal and Professors. The Rector and Dean are chosen annually. The Rector always names the Principal and Professors to be his assessors, and with them occasionally forms a court of law, for judging in pecuniary questions, and less atrocious crimes, wherein any member of the University is party. The University has always maintained its exemption from all jurisdiction of the city Magistrates, but not of the Sheriff or Court of Session.

The alterations which the University has under-

gone,

---

van, granted, as we have mentioned in the text, by King James the VI. in 1557; from the tiends of the parishes of Renfrew and Kilbride, granted by that monarch, in 1617, and confirmed by King Charles I. upon the 28th June, 1630; from the tiends of the parishes of Cadder, Old and New Monkland, conveyed to them by a charter from King Charles II. in 1670; from a tack of the Archbishopric; and from several donations, which the University has, at different times, received from private persons.—This revenue is expended in paying the salaries of the different Professors; in repairing the buildings of the University; and in adding new ones when necessary, &c.

gone, since the date of King James's charter, are such as might be expected from the changes of opinion with respect to literary objects, and from other varying circumstances. The progress of knowledge, and the increasing demand for literature, have produced many additional departments of science, to those which were originally thought worthy of a particular teacher. What is called the *curriculum*, or ordinary course of public education, comprehends, at present, five branches, the Latin and Greek languages, Logic, Moral Philosophy, and Natural Philosophy; these branches are understood to require the study of five separate sessions.

During their attendance upon these courses of languages and philosophy, and particularly, before they enter the class of Natural Philosophy, the students are expected to acquire a knowledge of Mathematics and Algebra, for which there is a separate Professor, and which is understood to be subservient to Natural Philosophy, and to many of the practical arts. There is also a Professor of Practical Astronomy, whose business it is to make observations for the improvement of that great branch of physics. After the course of general education above mentioned, a provision is made for what are called the three learned professions, Divinity, Law, and Medicine.

For the peculiar education of churchmen, there are four Professors;—the Principal, who is, *primarius* Professor of Theology, and has, besides, the superintendance of the whole University, and the respective Professors of Theology, of Oriental languages,

guages, and of Church history; this last is also Lecturer in Civil history.

In Law there is one Professor.

There are, by the constitution, no more than two Professors allotted to the Faculty of Medicine, viz. a Professor of the theory and practice of Medicine, and a Professor of Anatomy and Botany. But the University, out of its funds, and with the assistance of private donations, has made an annual provision for three additional Lecturers in Chemistry, in Materia Medica, and in Midwifery. The progress of the medical school was, until the erection of an Infirmary, much retarded; since this was effectuated, the number of students have been annually upon the increase.

In this University, the Principal and Professors of Church history, Law, Medicine, Anatomy, Botany and Astronomy, are nominated by the King. The Professors of Theology, Oriental languages, Humanity, Greek, Logic, Moral Philosophy, Natural Philosophy, and Mathematics, and the Lecturers on Chemistry, Materia Medica, Midwifery, and Natural history, &c. are nominated by the College.

From the state of the University funds, the Professors are allowed very moderate salaries. This, it is believed, has greatly promoted their zeal and their diligence in their several professions. In seminaries of literature, possessed of rich endowments, and where there is access to large ecclesiastical benefices, by seniority, the business of lecturing has generally gone into disuse, or been reduced to a mere matter of form, as few persons are willing to labour,

3 D

who,

who, by doing little, or by following their amusement, find themselves in easy or comfortable circumstances. In the Scottish Universities, on the contrary, and particularly that of Glasgow, where the Professors have no benefices in the church, nor any emolument of any kind, independent of their labour, that radical defect in the conduct of education is altogether removed, they are stimulated to exertion, and gradually acquire that interest and zeal in the discharge of their duty, which are most likely to call forth the activity and industry of their pupils.

With respect to the time of lecturing, the annual session begins in the ordinary *curriculum*, on the 10th of October, and ends, in some of the classes, about the middle of May, and in others, continues to the 10th of June; the lectures in all the other branches, commence on the 1st of November, and end about the beginning of May; the class for Botany begins on the 1st of May.

During this period, the business of the College continues without interruption; the Professors of Humanity or Latin, and of Greek, lecture and examine their students, receive and correct exercises, three hours every day, and four hours for two days every week; the Professors of Logic, Moral Philosophy, and Natural Philosophy, two hours every day, and three hours during a part of the session, excepting on Saturdays, when, on account of a general meeting of the public students, there is only one lecture given. The other Professors lecture, in general, one hour every day; the Professor of Mathematics, two hours every day, except on Saturdays;

days; the Professor of Law, in his public department, two hours; the Professor * of Practical A-
stronomy gives no public lecture.

Every Saturday there is a general meeting of all
the public or *gowned* students †, which is attended
(3 D 2) by

* The number of students considerably exceeds 600. In
order to stimulate their exertion, prizes have been bestowed
for many years past, on the most deserving; these consist either of books or medals.

To accommodate the Professors and students, there is public worship every Sunday in the College; three or four preachers are annually appointed. The Principal and such Professors
as have received licenses occasionally preach during the session.

Besides the salaries bestowed upon Professors, additional encouragement has been often given to Universities, by the mortification of certain funds for the maintenance of students. Of
this description of students, called bursars, there are several.
Such of these bursaries as are in the gift of the College, are bestowed by the Principal and Professors, upon students of superior genius and industry, but who have not the means of prosecuting their studies.

The College have also a right, in virtue of a mortification,
of an estate in Warwickshire, made in 1688, by Mr. Snell, to
present ten students, who have an income of L.70 each, to Baliol College, Oxford, after having studied some years at the
University of Glasgow. Another foundation, of L.20 per annum, at the same College, to each of four Scotch students, is
generally given to the Glasgow exhibitioners, so that four of
them have a stipend of L.90 per annum, for ten years.

† They are so called from their wearing scarlet gowns.—
a privilege of matriculated students.

Formerly a great part of the students were accommodated
with lodgings in the College, and dined at a common table,
under the inspection of their teachers; this practice has, however, been discontinued, and no students now live in the College, but a few of considerable standing, whose regularity of
conduct is perfectly known and ascertained.

by the Principal, and their respective Professors; a Latin oration is delivered by the higher students in their turns, after which, all smaller matters of discipline are discussed. By this weekly meeting, the whole of the students are brought, in a more particular manner, under the inspection of their teachers; and a good opportunity is regularly afforded, of mutual information respecting the studies, and deportment of their scholars.

In conferring degrees, *these passports* of learning, the candidates are, by express regulations, obliged to attend the hours of lecture, and the separate hours of examination in the *curriculum*, or public course already mentioned, and the laws of the church, oblige all students to pass the same *curriculum* before they can be enrolled students of Theology. But no such qualification is requisite for entering upon the study of law or medicine.

The rules for conferring degrees, were formerly much the same in the University of Glasgow, as in the other ancient Universities, the student being obliged to compose and print a thesis, and to defend it in a public syllogistic disputation. By degrees this mode of trial, degenerated into mere matter of form and ceremony. The same subjects of disputation, the same arguments of attack and defence, were preserved and handed down among the students, so that degrees became, not the rewards of abilities and diligence, but merely the marks of standing or residence at the University. These circumstances gave occasion for a material change in the rules for conferring degrees in the University of Glasgow;

Glasgow; the composing and defending a thesis, have now become optional on the part of the candidate. The same standing is still required, and the candidates for degrees in arts, are obliged to undergo a minute examination in the Greek and Roman classics, in the different branches of philosophy, which compose the *curriculum*, and by each of the Professors, in their respective branches.

Degrees in Theology are, without any regard to standing in the University, conferred on clergymen, respectable for their abilities and literature. Degrees in Law, are either bestowed upon eminent men, as marks of respect, or upon students of a certain standing, after a regular examination of the candidate. The University of Glasgow admits students who have passed a part of their academical course in other Universities, *ad eundem*, as it is commonly called; that is, whatever part of their academical course is finished at any other University, upon proper certificates, is admitted as a part of their standing in the University of Glasgow, so that, without again beginning their course, they can pass forward to degrees, and be enrolled students of Theology.

Degrees in Medicine are conferred, after having finished the medical course at the University, or upon proper certificates of having finished it at some eminent school of Physic, but the candidates are obliged to undergo both a private and public examination, on all the different branches of medicine, before they can receive that honour; it is very common also, for them, though not absolutely necessary, to defend a thesis in the common hall.

Since

Since the establishment of this University, it has ushered into the world some of the most learned and eminent characters, that have existed in any age. Here was educated the celebrated poet and historian, *Buchanan*, whose works will remain a monument of his fame, as long as a taste for the chaste and beautiful in style and composition prevails in Britain. *John Spottiswood*, archbishop of Glasgow, afterwards of St. Andrew's, and author of the History of the Church of Scotland, first received here the rudiments of that learning, which afterwards rendered him so conspicuous. To descend to latter times, we cannot with justice pass, *Hutcheson*, whose merits as a moral philosopher are universally known.—*Leechman*, his friend and biographer, was another ornament of this University.—The late *Dr. Adam Smith*, distinguished through Europe for his eminence in commercial philosophy, received his early education at the University of Glasgow, went from thence as an exhibitioner to Oxford, and at his return became Professor of Moral Philosophy here. He was succeeded in the chair of Moral Philosophy, by the late *Dr. Reid*, the great and successful opponent of the ideal philosophy. While in Aberdeen, Dr. Reid had published his Enquiry concerning the Senses, in which the sceptical metaphysics of Hume and Berkeley were refuted, with more of philosophical percision, than by any other of that legion of adversaries whose opposition Hume roused against himself. After continuing long to oppose these dangerous principles from the Professor's chair, Dr. Reid in his old age, gave to the

the world a work upon the *Intellectual and Active Powers of Man*, in which he has certainly proved, that the accountable absurdities and inconsistencies of the ideal philosophy have generally originated in a strangely unthinking ascription, without evidence, and indeed, against all the appearances of the qualities of matter to mind; and from the very connect ap-plication of language and allusions, appropriated to the description of material objects in speaking of mind.—In the other departments of science, names, no less illustrious, have ornamented, by their talents, the University of Glasgow, whether as teachers or as students. *Simpson*, the famed mathematician, here delivered his lectures; and here were taught *Cullen* and *Hunter;* the former, the first physician of his day; the latter, surpassed by none for his knowledge in anatomy *.

Besides

*Amongst the many donations made to this University, we cannot but notice the two following, as particularly calculated for the advancement of science: the first, by Dr. William Hunter of London, whom we have just now taken notice of. He, by his will, bequeathed his museum to the University (reserving the use of it for thirty years to his nephew, and failing him, to his partner) for the purpose of promoting anatomical and natural knowledge. He also left to the University L. 8coo sterling to be paid to them within two years; one half of the interest whereof, to be applied for supporting the museum, while in London; the other half, together with the capital, to be at the immediate disposal of the University, for the purpose of buying ground, and erecting proper buildings for the reception of the museum. The principal articles of the museum are, a most curious and valuable

Besides the University, the city of Glasgow contains seminaries of learning for the initiation of
youth

valuable library of books and manuscripts; his own large
and incomparable anatomical preparations; a choice collection
of natural curiosities, containing among other particulars, the
large collection of shells, corals, insects, and fossils of the late
Dr. Fothergill; and a cabinet of coins and medals, ancient
and modern, of which the different series are confessedly the
most complete and best connected of any in Europe, and are
said (this last article alone) to have cost him upwards of
L.25,000 sterling.

This donation, by the decease of the last assignee, has now
taken effect, the faculty of the University have accordingly fixed
upon a situation in the College garden, where the building, to
be appropriated for the museum, is intended to be erected in the
course of the ensuing summer, after a very beautiful design by
Mr. Stark, architect—a design, which if followed out, will do
much credit' to the taste of the Professors, as well as to that
of the architect—It indeed promises to be one of the finest
buildings in the city.

The other benefactor, Alexander M'Farlane, Esq; of Jamaica, left, by his will, in 1757, to the University, his noble
apparatus of astronomical instruments, which were shortly
after received. In testimony of their gratitude, the University, at laying the foundation stone of the Observatory, destined
for the reception of these instruments, named it the *Macfarlane
Observatory.*

Under each of the four corners of this building, was deposited a medal, having on one side an inscription, viz.

Observatorii Macfarlanei fundamenta jecit,
Alma Mater Glasguensis, XVII. *Aug.* M. DCC. LVII.

And, on the other side, a portion of a convex celestial
sphere, with the constellations; and round it these words:

Felices animae quibus haec cognoscere cura.

In describing the public buildings, we have taken notice
of

youth, in the various branches of literature, as well as every polite accomplishment.

THE COMMERCE OF GLASGOW.

The origin of the extensive commerce for which this city is now so far famed, appears to be of a considerable antiquity; indeed, its situation upon a large river, in the western part of the kingdom, and open to the Atlantic, Ireland, and other parts, must naturally, at an early period, have directed the attention of the inhabitants to this object; and this the more especially, from the vast quantity of fish, particularly herrings, which then abounded in the frith

3 E   and.

of the college library; in addition to what was mentioned there, we may add, that it was founded about two centuries ago, and that is enriched with many early editions; proper attention is also paid from time to time, to supply it with the more elegant and improved productions of the press. The funds which are destined for its support and increase are considerable, and many donations of books have been made to it from time to time. It was lately greatly enriched, in the mathematical department, by the library of the late celebrated Dr. Robert Simson, Professor of Mathematics, and it will soon receive an important addition, by a collection of many rare and splendid editions of books in all the different departments of science, but particularly in the medical department, bequeathed by *Dr. William Hunter*. To this library, the students who are entitled to the privilege, have easy access. The Librarian is Mr. Lockhart Muirhead, Lecturer in Natural History.

and river, and which afforded them an excellent and steady article of export.

Prior to the Reformation, however, it appears that commerce was here but in an in fantine state, for though Glasgow had vessels at sea * before that time, it is most likely they were but few in number, of a small burden, and that their trade was confined to Ireland, or at farthest to France. No sooner, however, had that great event taken place, than many of those who formerly drew their support from the rich revenues of the archi-episcopal see, finding these no longer in existence, naturally turned their attention to the cultivation of trade and commerce; from this period, therefore, the commercial spirit of the people began to be more active, though in comparison with latter times, but feeble and unenergetic.

The staple article of export still continued to be the produce of the river, a produce which then, it appears †, was a source of considerable wealth,

great

* That the merchants of Glasgow had vessels at sea about the middle of the sixteenth century, appears evident from an order of council, dated at Edinburgh in 1546, which discharges all Scotch vessels, and among the rest, those belonging to Glasgow, from capturing or carrying on war against the English traders.

† The most enterprising merchant during this period, in the city, was Walter Gibson. He, about the year 1668, cured and exported in a Dutch vessel, 300 lasts of herrings, each containing six barrels, which he sent to St. Martin's in France, where he got a barrel of brandy and a crown for each; the

ship

great quantities of herrings* and salmon having beeñ
been exported, particularly to France, from whence,
in return, they imported considerable quantities of
brandy, salt, and wine. The fishery continued to
be carried on with advantage the greatest part of the
seventeenth century; towards its conclusion, a number of merchants in the city formed themselves into
a society, in which Charles the II. also took a share,
for the purpose of monopolizing this branch of business, at least for a certain period of the year; that
monarch accordingly suited their views by granting
them a charter, with the exclusive privilege of fishing for themselves alone, in the frith, until the 20th
of September, annually. This company was erected in 1670, and continued to 1684; for the better
carrying on of the business, they fixed upon a situation at Greenock, then consisting of but a few huts,
where they built a range of houses, called the Royal Closs, for the purpose of curing and packing their
3 E 2 fish.

---

ship returning laden with brandy and salt, the cargo was sold
for a great sum. He then launched farther into business,
bought the vessel and two large ships besides, with which he
traded to the different parts of Europe, &c.

---

* The herrings, about that period, it would appear, frequented the mouth of the river, regularly, and in immense
shoals. We are told, that about the beginning of the 17th century, 900 boats have been employed, during the season, within
the Cloch, each boat carrying 4 men and 24 nets.

fish. This company was dissolved in 1684 *, and this trade again became free †. Numbers of new adventurers rushed into the business, and great part met with that success which prudent enterprise deserves. Besides the staple article of export just now mentioned, other natural productions of the country began to be in request, together with such articles of home manufacture, as were in demand at the places to which they traded.

Thus commerce gradually advanced, the merchants of the city sought out new ports where to vend their commodities; they traded to France, Sweden, Denmark, and the other parts of the Baltic, and in return brought home the productions of these different countries. But though it appears that the trade of the city was rapidly upon the advance, about the period of the reign of William the III. ‡, and during the intervening space, betwixt and the Union. Yet

it

* At this period the Royal Closs was bought by the city of Glasgow, who still hold it in possession.

† Another company of adventurers called the whale-fishing company was, about the same time established in Glasgow; they built two ships at Belfast, the first of 7co and the second of 4co tons burden; these ships were victualled and manned for the west Greenland whale-fishing. The company erected a court of warehouses at the head of the Candleriggs, for carrying on the business; it would appear, however, they were unfortunate.

‡ Previous to this period, the community of Glasgow feued
ed

405

it is certain, that had not that event taken place,
Glasgow would never have attained the degree of
consequence which it at present possesses; for though
a free communication was open with these ports, yet
the navigation to them was so circuitous, and they
lay so much the more conveniently for other towns upon the east coast, that a successful competition in trade
might have been carried on, if those places had exerted themselves much to the injury of the commerce
of Glasgow. By the Union, however, new views
were opened up to the merchants of the city, they
thereby obtained the liberty of a free commerce to
America and the West Indies, from which they had
been before shut out; they chartered English vessels
for these voyages, having none at first fit for the purpose, sent out cargoes of goods for the use of the
colonies, and returned home laden with tobacco.
The business doing well, vessels were built belonging
to the city, and in the year 1718, the first ship, the
property of Glasgow, crossed the Atlantic.

The tobacco trade of Glasgow was, shortly thereafter, in such a thriving condition, that it so much
excited the jealousy of the merchants in London,
Bristol, Liverpool, and Whitehaven, that they entered into a combination for the discouragement, if not
the ruin of it. For this purpose, they accused the

3 E 2 merchants

<hr>

ed the lands of Newark, and built a quay, as has been elsewhere
noticed, for the accommodation of their shipping. In more
early times, their vessels lay in the sea-ports of Cunningham, a
district of Ayrshire.

merchants of frauds against the revenue, first before
the Commissioners of Customs of London, afterwards by petitions to the Lords of the Treasury, and
when both these failed, by a direct application to the
House of Commons. Though no fraud against the
revenue could be detected, yet the powerful influence of the English merchants prevailed, and new officers having been appointed at Greenock and Port-
Glasgow, in whose power it was to teaze and harrass
the merchants, their scheme became successful,
the trade languished and declined, and till the year
1735 †, there seemed to be little prospect of its
reviving. About that time, however, some favourable circumstances having occurred, commerce began gradually to advance, though slowly, till about the year 1750, when a new mode of
carrying on the American trade was adopted, by
the merchants sending out factors and disposing
their goods upon credit, instead of the former
method of bartering one commodity for another.
By this, though they increased the extent of their
dealings, yet the risk was thereby infinitely greater
than it had been before, and the trade more speculative
and uncertain. Still, however, it increased till the
commencement of the American war, in the year
1775, when it attained its greatest height. In order to give an idea of its extent at that time, we
have

† The number of vessels, belonging to Clyde, that year,
trading to foreign ports, amounted only to 67, and their
burden about 5100 tons.

have here subjoined a short abstract of the principal imports, in the year 1775 *:

Tobacco, from Virginia, - 40,854 hhds.

From Maryland, - 15,040

From Carolina, - 1,249

Total, 57,143 hhds.

Sugars from Jamaica and the other West India Islands, { 4,621 hhds. 691 tierces. 462 barrels.

Rum, - - - { 1,154 puncheons. 193 barrels.

Cotton, - - - 503 bags.

The American war was a dreadful stroke to Glasgow; all commercial intercourse was put a stop to betwixt and that country, and as the fortunes of many of the merchants were embarked in that trade, and America deeply indebted to them, it proved the ruin of many, who before had reckoned themselves possessed of independent fortunes. Though the commerce of the city was thus interrupted, yet the spirit which had been raised, was not extinguished.

The

* It is a fact, that in the year 1772, out of 90,000 hogsheads of tobacco imported into Britain, Glasgow alone engrossed 49,000 of these. A proof of the extent of this trade.

It is likewise worthy to be noted, that in the French war, immediately preceding the contest with America, one merchant in Glasgow (John Glassford, Esq;) had at one time *twenty-five* ships, with their cargoes, his own property, and is said to have traded for above *half a million* sterling, yearly.

The merchants began to look out for new sources, and accordingly extended their commerce to the West Indies and the Continent of Europe, considerably more than before; and though the shipping, at the time of the greatest extent of the American trade, was more than at present, yet, it now appears to be annually on the increase, for though, at the commencement of the contest with the colonies, many of the merchants who embarked in the American trade were ruined, yet there were others, who, from having a large stock of tobacco on hand, and a fortunate rise, as that time, in the price, were enabled to launch out into other branches of trade, particularly manufactures; these having proved successful, and furnishing such useful articles of export, together with the termination of the war with America, may be reckoned the principal causes of the revival of the commerce of Glasgow, as well as of the ports of Greenock and Port-Glasgow, with which it is so intimately connected.

That the commerce has, since the period above alluded to, been gradually increasing here, will appear from the following states, with the exception of one or two years. In 1783, the number of ships belonging to Clyde were only 386, and their tonnage 22,896, whereas, in 1790, their number was 476, and their tonnage 46,581. In two years thereafter, the registered vessels belonging to Glasgow, Port-Glasgow and Greenock, were 464, and their burden 46,806 tons.

In the year 1796, there were employed the number of vessels in the list subjoined, in the trade of the river, viz.

From

From 5th January, 1796, to 5th January, 1797.
At Greenock.

110 ships, 13,797 tons.

At Port-Glasgow.

45 ships, 5,323 tons.

Total—155 ships, 19,120 tons.

That this number has greatly increased, will be obvious from the following statement.

From 5th January, 1803, to 5th January, 1804.
At Greenock.

Inwards.

Foreign Trade—406 ships, 53,546 tons, 5183 men.

Coast and Fishing—730 vessels, 35,532 tons, 3147 men.

Total—1130 ships and vessels, 87,078 tons, 6330 men.

Outwards.

Foreign Trade—352 ships, 50,366 tons, 3673 men.

Coast and Fishing—1016 vessels, 43,009 tons, 3326 men.

Total—1368 ships and vessels, 93,375 tons, 6999 men.

At Port-Glasgow.

Inwards.

Foreign Trade—113 ships, 18,722 tons, 1081 men.

Coast and Fishing—182 vessels, 7226 tons, 551 men.

Total—295 ships and vessels, 25,948 tons, 1632 men.

Outwards.

Foreign Trade—177 ships, 25,137 tons, 1692 men.

3 F   Coast

Coast and Fishing—119 vessels, 7202 tons, 424 men.

Total—296 ships and vessels, 32,389 tons, 2116 men.

Grand Total—3095 ships and vessels, 238,790 tons, 17,077 men.

The principal articles of exportation from Glasgow and the ports farther down the river, to America and the West Indies, are British manufacture, also coals, fish, &c. To the Continent of Europe, and the ports in the Baltic, besides British manufactures, raw and refined sugar, coffee, cotton, rum, and other productions of the western hemisphere. Glasgow imports, from the West Indies and America, the principal articles of growth or manufacture there, such as coffee, cotton, sugars, rum, wheat, mahogany, and flour, staves; pearl and wood ashes, fruits, &c.; and from Spain and Portugal, wines, and other productions of these countries; from the Baltic, wood, iron, flax, hemp, pitch, tar, Russia linens, and wheat. To Ireland Glasgow sends manufactures, and in return receives hides, grain, salted beef, butter, meal, &c.

Amongst all these articles of import, however, the principal are, sugar, rum, coffee and cotton; the sugar and rum, besides serving the consumpt of the country, is exported again in great quantities, and often even to England, for the use of the navy, the merchants here sometimes entering into government contracts for that purpose. The cotton not only supplies the extensive cotton manufactures in Scotland, but is sent to Manchester, Liverpool, and other

ther towns of England, as well as to the Continent.
The following list contains an account of the cotton
wool imported into Clyde these two last years.

In 1802,   -   51,366 bags and seroons.
In 1803,   -   38,174 do.   do.

Less in 1803, - 13,192 do.   do.

MANUFACTURES.

Like to the commerce of the city, its manufactures
arose from very small beginnings. Indeed for many years after the Reformation, it is likely that such
manufactures as were carried on, were merely for
the use of the inhabitants of the city and its environs. By degrees, such articles were made in greater quantities, and consequently disposed of in commercial intercourse. Amongst the most noted of
these, Glasgow is said to have been celebrated for
its manufacture of plaids; coarse linens and Scotch
cloths were also fabricated, but to no great extent.

In the reign of Charles II. a considerable manufacture of soap was begun, by a society of merchants;
though carried on with a considerable capital, it,
however, did not succeed, and was consequently
given up. Nearly about the same time, the refining
of sugar† appears to have been carried to a consider-

3 F 2   able

† The sugar, in its raw state, at this period, was brought
from Bristol and other English ports.

able extent, no fewer than four sugar houses, called by the names of the easter, wester, south, and King-street sugar-works, having been erected within ten years after the year 1667; at no great distance of time thereafter, we find the rope-work company e-stablished, a branch of business which still conti-nues, and in the same situation where it was o-riginally begun.

It is to the period after the Union, however, that we are to look for the causes which gave rise to the prosperity of the Glasgow manufactures. As it gave new life and energy to the commerce of Glas-gow, so it equally favoured the manufactures.

That event had no sooner taken place, than it was perceived that a wide field opened for the prosecu-tion of manufactures, from the freedom of trade which Scotland then enjoyed to America and the West Indies. The opportunity was accordingly em-braced, and from that time to this, manufactures, of almost every kind known in Britain, have been car-ried on in Glasgow.

The linen manufacture, which began here in the year 1725, was, for a long time, the staple, not on-ly of this city, but of the west of Scotland. This, however, from the predilection for Irish linens, which has all along been entertained, and the rising demand for cotton goods, has not, for this some time by-past, been on the increase, though there is still a very considerable quantity of linens, lawns, cambrics, checks, diapers, &c. made.

About the same period, or rather prior to it, the tanning of leather was carried on to a considerable

extent,

extent, a company of merchants having embarked in
the business; they also manufactured shoes and sad-
lery for the American market; various other branches shortly thereafter began, many of which still continue to prosper, and of some of which we will
fall afterwards to take notice.

After the decline of the linen trade, the cotton
manufacture, and the various arts depending on it,
was gradually introduced; it has now become the
staple, and is carried on to a greater extent here,
than in any other town in Britain, if we except
Manchester.   In order to carry this manufacture
through in all its branches, cotton mills *, bleach-
fields, and. printfields have been erected, not
only on all the streams in the neighbourhood, but
even in situations more remote.   And such is its
prosperous state that though the number of these
mills have increased greatly of late, they are still
unable to supply the necessary quantity of yarn
which it requires; so that daily, that article, to
a considerable amount, is brought from England.
Neither is this trade altogether confined to the
workmen in the city, several thousand weavers
being employed by the manufacturers in Glasgow, who live in the district of the country a-
round, even to the distance of thirty or forty miles.

By a computation which was made in the year
1791,

* The most extensive cotton mills in Scotland, belonged lately to David Dale, Esq; an eminent manufacturer in this city;
now to Messrs. Owen and company, they are situated on the
banks of the Clyde, in the vicinity of Lanark.

1791, it was thought there were upwards of 15,000 looms employed in this branch; that each loom gave employment to nine persons at an average, in the various stages of the manufacture, including women and children, in all, 135,000 persons; and that each loom, at an average, produced goods to the value of L.100 per annum, making in whole the sum of L.1500,000 sterling. Since then the increase has been very great, but to what extent it is at present carried, it is impossible to determine with any degree of precision, for want of sufficient data. This manufacture is not only important of itself, but is productive of work to many thousands of bleachers, tambourers, calico printers, &c. many of whom being women and children, whose work was formerly unproductive, renders it of still more general importance.

The manufacture of ropes and cordage of all kinds; the making of soap and candles; and the refining of sugar, which appear to have been the first that were begun here, are still carried on to a great extent. There is also a very considerable manufacture of carpets and coarse woollens, for which, few places seem to be better adapted than Glasgow, from its neighbourhood to a country where wool is plentifully raised.

The Delft ware manufacture was first begun here before it was established in any place of Scotland, in the year 1749. About the year 1770 it was altered into the manufacture of stone or queen's ware; since which time, many improvements have been made, both in its quality, shape and colour. Queen's

china

china as it is called, plain and ornamented, is also manufactured at this pottery—as well as china, such as is manufactured in England, and which is reckoned of a very good quality. Egyptian black and brown China-ware is also made here in great perfection, no ways inferior to any in Britain. Another pottery, upon a very extensive scale, has been erected within these three years, upon the banks of the Monkland Canal, a little way to the north of the city, which likewise manufactures all the articles above mentioned, and in a very beautiful and tasteful manner. All the coarser kinds of pottery, together with bricks, tiles, &c. are made in abundance.

The incle manufactory is also carried on in Glasgow to a great extent. It was introduced about the year 1732 ¶, before any manufactory of the same kind was fixed in any other place in Britain. Hats to a very considerable amount, are likewise

¶ The Dutch before that time, were the only people in possession of these incle looms, the construction whereof they carefully kept secret. Mr. Alexander Harvie, of this city, was so zealous to introduce them into this country, that he went over to Holland, and in spite of the care and attention which the Dutch paid to concealing the proper methods of carrying on this manufacture, he was so fortunate, as to bring over with him from Haarlem two of their looms, and one of their workmen. This Dutchman remained some years in Glasgow, but upon some disgust he went to Manchester, and instructed the people there in the proper method of carrying on this manufacture.

wise manufactured, not only for homesale, but for exportation to America and the West Indies; together with nun's thread, silk, cotton, and worsted stockings, and gloves of all kinds. During the time of American trade, large quantities of tobacco were manufactured into snuff, &c. and immense quantities of shoes and saddles, made and exported to that country; for which purpose, very extensive works were erected for tanning leather. These manufactures still continue, though perhaps not to the extent that they did at that time.

The manufacture of bottles or green glass has been long established here, and is still upon the increase. The first glasshouse was erected about the year 1730. It began but upon a small scale, and continued to work for several years for only four months per annum, yet this was then sufficient to supply the demand. A glasshouse was thereafter erected at Leith, and to this place did the Glasgow workmen resort when unemployed at home. The manufacture of crown and window glass was also begun here, it, however, did not succeed. Another manufacture of the same material, has been more successful in Glasgow,—viz. that of crystal, or flint glass, begun in 1777, under the direction of Messrs. Cookson and company, of Newcastle, and Patrick Colquhoun, merchant in Glasgow. It thereafter came into the hands of the present proprietor, Mr. Geddes, by whom it is carried on upon a more extensive scale than any other work of the same kind in Scotland. Originally the cutting and engraving of glass was executed by foreigners,

reigners, it is now, however, equally well done by Scotchmen, who have been properly initiated into the art.

Another manufacture Glasgow has to boast of, which is not only superior to any in Scotland, but even in Britain, or perhaps in Europe: It is the art of type founding, carried on by Messrs. Wilson and Sons in the University.

Printing has likewise here attained to great celebrity*. That art was first put in practise in Glasgow about the year 1638, by one George Anderson, who afterwards settled in Edinburgh. To him succeeded Robert Saunders, in the year 1661, and by him and his son printing was carried on, till about the year 1730; when Robert Urie printed several books in a good taste and manner. He was, however, in a few years afterwards, outdone in his art by Robert and Andrew Foulis, printers to the Uni-

3 G   versity

---

* It may not be improper to mention here the different periodical publications at present existing in Glasgow;—The first newspaper printed in this city was the Glasgow Journal, it began in 1729, and still continues; then followed the Mercury, and Advertiser, which are now given up. To these last succeeded the Courier, and the Herald; these papers are published upon the following days, viz:—The Glasgow Journal, once a-week, upon Friday;—the Courier, established in 1791, three times a-week, upon Tuesday, Thursday, and Saturday;—and the Herald and Advertiser, begun in 1802, twice a-week, on Monday and Friday. No Magazine is printed here, one was begun in 1784, it, however, did not succeed; since then some other publications of a somewhat similar nature have appeared, they also have vanished.

versity, whose editions of the Greek, the Roman, and English classics, are known and admired through all Europe.

The introduction of the cotton manufacture, and the arts depending upon it has given rise to many new manufactures. Amongst these that are dependent upon the cotton manufacture, the staple of Glasgow, the art of printing upon cloths may be reckoned amongst the first; this art was first introduced into the neighbourhood, about the year 1742, by a company of merchants in the city, at the head of whom was Mr. Ingram. Their printfield was situated at Pollockshaws; for a considerable time the business was carried on with every disadvantage, the principal parts of the process having been gained at different times, and with difficulty, from the London printers; at length these obstacles to its success were overcome. The original purpose of this work was to furnish printed handkerchiefs, &c. for the English market, through the channel of a class of men, whose business was the buying of Scotch goods, and selling them in England; and above all, the supplying of our stores in Virginia, Maryland, and the West Indies. In a short time, the different processes of this manufacture became more generally known. Another company was formed, at the head of which was the late Mr. William Stirling. They erected a work on the banks of the Kelvin, at a place called Dalsholm, and began the printing of handkerchiefs with success. The printing of cloths for furniture, &c. was begun about the year 1771; in a

few

few years this company, from the high price of labour, at the situation they first had fixed upon, removed their works to the banks of the Leven, where they still continue, and where many others are now also situated. Previous to the year 1769, the printing of the figures upon the cloth had been done by wooden blocks; at that period copperplates were introduced, first at Pollockshaws, and thereafter at a printfield at Carmile, where the paste was invented and brought to perfection, which puts it in the power of the artist to print with the same plate which prints the red and black pattern, on the white ground, in the common way, to receive it and print the flower or pattern white on the red and black ground. The cylinder press, and several other improvements upon this manufacture, were also invented, and carried into practice here. This branch is now carried on to such an extent, that it employs upwards of thirty printfields, belonging to the merchants or manufacturers of the city, or with which they are one way or other connected.

The different methods of bleaching, a preparatory process to the printing, has also been carried on in the neighbourhood, for many years. The first bleachfield, we are informed, was that of Wellhouse, which, under the patronage of the trustees for manufactures, &c. began to bleach about the year 1730.

Oil of vitriol, an article reckoned requisite in the process of bleaching, is manufactured in a consid-

erable

erable quantity; before the year 1750, what was used, was brought from England and Holland.

The cudbear manufacture, as it is called, is also carried on in the vicinity; it was begun in the year 1777, under the firm of George Macintosh and company; this is a manufacture for making a dye-stuff, employed chiefly in the woollen and silk manufactures of Britain, and is made from an excrescence that grows upon rocks and stones, a species of the *lichen* or *rock moss*, which, with certain chemical preparations, makes a dye-stuff called cudbear. The process was first reduced into a regular system by Dr. Cuthbert Gordon, who, in conjunction with some others, erected a manufacture for it in Leith, which, however, did not succeed. Considerable improvements have been made since its establishment in Glasgow. This manufacture consumes a very considerable quantity of human urine, about 2000 gallons a day; the expence of collecting this is about L.800 per annum.

The dyeing of turkey red on cotton, was established here, earlier than in any part of great Britain. In the year 1785, Mr. George M'Intosh, being in London, fell in with, and engaged Monsieur Papillon, a turkey red dyer from Rouen, carried him with him to Glasgow, and in conjunction with Mr. David Dale, built an extensive dye-house at Dalmarnock, in the neighbourhood, where cotton is dyed a real turkey red, equal in beauty and solidity to East India colours. Since then, from the publication of the process, several other dye-hous-

es

es are erected for the same purpose. By means of these establishments, the manufactures are enabled to make cotton pullicate handkerchiefs, equal in beauty and quality to any in the known world.

Mr. Macintosh carries on another manufacture of a substitute for sugar of lead, in the dyeing and printing business, which answers completely the whole purposes intended by the use of that article in these branches.

The manufacture or brewing of ales and porter is carried on in Glasgow and its vicinity, to a great extent. Previous to the year 1745, there were, however, no works of this kind of any consequence; about that period, a brewery of some note was erected, to the west of Grahamston, which continued to do business with success for a considerable time. In 1762, another brewery, upon a still more extensive scale, was erected in the neighbourhood of the village of Anderston, called the new brewery, belonging to Messrs. Warroch and Co. which not only manufactured ales, but likewise began to brew porter, (though it required several years to establish its reputation); previous to this period, the porter consumed in Glasgow, was brought by way of Leith from London. In 1767, a third great brewery was built, adjoining to St. Mungo's lane, belonging to Mr. Struthers; a great number of others, (such as the brewery, the property of Messrs. Tennents, &c.) begun in 1780, have been since erected, from all of which, vast quantities of ales and porter are manufactured, not only for home consumpt, but exportation, insomuch, that

that it has been reckoned the produce of the Glasgow brewery may annually amount to betwixt L.50 and L.60,000 sterling. The distilling of spirits has never been carried on to any great extent in this city, though vast quantities are consumed.

Amongst the many arts that have owed their origin to the extension of the cotton manufacture, and that of printing, may be reckoned the manufacture of iron-liquor, which is carried on in Glasgow to a considerable extent. The stocking manufacture is also considerable; card-making was introduced here, within these 20 years, it employs a great number of children, that would otherwise be idle, and is of great service to the other manufactures, particularly the spinning of cotton yarn. In Glasgow and its vicinity, there are a great number of mills, as they are called, built for this last mentioned purpose, which it would be tedious to enumerate, they in general have constant employment, as may be expected, from being a principal branch of the staple manufacture of the city.

The making of soap and candle has been long carried on in Glasgow, as well as saddlery to a great amount, not only sufficient for home consumption, but also for exportation. The hardware manufacture, including founderies, of which there are many, both for brass or iron, and which carry on business, to a great extent, in making every kind of household utensil, commonly made of cast metals, as well as great guns, &c. There are others upon a smaller scale, for the making of files, locks, hinges, and many other articles, usually made of maleable iron.

We

We have thus enumerated the principal branches es of manufacture carried on here, there are, however, very many others, that it would be difficult, and perhaps uninteresting to enumerate; to ascertain to what extent these are carried at present, cannot be done with precision, and therefore, any thing upon that head would be mere conjecture. The consequence of these numerous works, however, has been, and still is, an accumulation of population and wealth, whereby not only the city is enlarged and beautified, but the country for many miles around, is improved and enriched, to an almost incredible degree.

From an event (the American war) which for a time diminished, and it was feared would ruin the trade of Glasgow, the most solid advantages have arisen to its inhabitants, by their industry being more especially directed than before, to the prosecution of manufactures. The effects of these, which of late years have made prodigious strides, combined with a foreign commerce, again increasing, and conducted in a less hazardous manner than before, are plainly discernable, in the rapid increase of inhabitants, of new streets, and elegant buildings, which still secure to Glasgow, the appellation of being the richest as well as the fairest city of the land.

MISCELLANEOUS OBSERVATIONS.

The climate of Glasgow, in general, like that of the other parts of the Island, is variable; there are
some

some circumstances in its local situation, however, which affect it more than other places, nearer the middle of the country. The lower extremity of the county, in which this city is placed, is situated nearly in the narrowest part of the island or isthmus, betwixt the Forth and Clyde, from which position, and no intervening high grounds of any consequence, the air is often refreshed by the temperate breath of the sea breeze. The wind blows here from S W and west, about two thirds of the year.; these winds, coming over the broad surface of the Atlantic, are saturated with vapour, which frequently overclouds the sky, and consequently renders the summer's heat less intense; these vapours are frequently arrested in their progress by the high grounds of Renfrewshire and Dumbarton, and consequently fall in heavy showers on all places in their vicinity; from this circumstance it is, that more rain†, in general, falls at Greenock than Glasgow, more at Glasgow than at Hamilton or Lanark, and so on. But if the rains are more frequent here than on the east coast, the weather certainly, in the winter season, is no colder, if indeed so cold *, being more sheltered from

the

---

† The quantity of rain annually is about 32 inches.

* The great cold in the year 1780 has been already mentioned; in the beginning of 1785, the frost was likewise uncommonly severe, yet the following summer was uncommonly warm, insomuch, that on the 27th of June, the mercury in the thermometer in the College garden, rose to 85°, the greatest degree of heat, it is believed, that has been yet felt in Scotland,

the chill easterly winds, which blowing over a narrow sea, from the cold countries of Lapland and Norway, often cover the east country with snow, while none is observable in the neighbourhood of Glasgow*. Fogs, which are in general driven before the same wind are also here more rare than in the vicinity of Edinburgh. Intense frost is of no long continuance, neither do snows lie long, nor are they deep.

The wind, which blows most frequently, as has been already mentioned, is the S. W. next to it is the N. E. which, for the most part, is accompanied with fair weather; the rain, which is the heaviest and most lasting, but not the most frequent, is from the S. E. The wind seldom blows long from the south,

3 H　　　　　　　　　without

land, at least for this century past. For these two last summers, the thermometer has once or oftener risen to 75°. The beginning of 1795, was extremely cold here, on the 6th of that month the thermometer stood at Zero or o. A still greater cold took place, 8th January last, when at eight in the morning, the thermometer stood at 3 degrees, which is lower than it has been since 1780.

* The most remarkable fall of snow for these many years, was in the end of January, 1794; from its obstructing the roads, five London mails were due on the 1st February. Another heavy snow took place here, and indeed throughout Britain, on the 8th and 9th February, 1799.

On January 24th, 1796, the tide in the river rose to an unusual height, at Greenock it was three feet higher than was ever known before, and did very considerable damage.

without bringing rain, and this rain is heavy, but of short continuance. The rain from the west and S.W. comes in repeated showers, between short intervals of fair weather, and the greatest quantity of rain here comes from the latter, which, as the wind blows much from that quarter in the beginning of the year, drenches the ground greatly before the sowing of the seed. Rains from the N.W.N. and N.E. are neither frequent nor heavy, but sullen and unnourishing. The N.E. wind is most frequent in the months of April and May; it sometimes, however, sets in in the month of March.

Thunder and lightning are not very frequent here, nor destructive *, at least for these several seasons by-past; with respect to meteors, they are observed here in common with the surrounding country.

The soil in the neighbourhood of the town is various—in some places it is a rich clay, in others a light sand; towards the N. and N.E. it is a cold clay, upon a till bottom, though now very much improved by cultivation. The quantity of grain raised around the city is not nearly equal to its support, so that immense quantities are imported from Ireland, Ayrshire,

* Sometimes, however, considerable damage has been done by this subtle fluid: in 1756, in the month of February, it struck and damaged the High Church steeple; it was repaired with much ingenuity, by a mason of the name of Naismyth. Slight shocks of an earthquake have been sometimes, though very rarely felt. A shock took place in August 1786, at two in the morning. Another slight one about three years ago, at six o'clock, A. M.

Ayrshire, and the east country §. The quality of the water has been taken notice of in another place.

The principal fossils are coal and lime-stone, both of these, in particular the last, having many different qualities. The best free-stone is produced from a quarry to the north of the city, the property of Robert Crawford, Esq; of Possil; the fronts of the principal buildings are in general constructed of this stone. There is likewise plenty of whin-stone in the neighbourhood, but no marble, lime-stone, or granite, in any quantity, within some miles. There is also plenty of clay, proper for making bricks, tiles, and the common kinds of pottery, but none of the finer kinds.

There is no uncommon natural productions of the soil in the neighbourhood, as far as the writer of these sheets knows; neither is there any thing meriting much notice in the other departments of natural history†. In the river sometimes there have appeared

3 H 2   very.

---

§ We have subjoined a list, more full than that mentioned in the preceding part of the work, of the prices of provisions during the scarcity in 1800 and 1801:—oat meal sold at 4s. 6d. and potatoes at 2s. 6d. per peck; eggs, 1s. 8d. per dozen; beef, 1s. 6d. per pound; salt butter, 1l. 4s. the stone; fresh butter, 1s. 8d. per pound; the quarter loaf at 1s. 8d. and other necessaries in proportion.

† According to the observations of a gentleman here, the swallow has never been observed earlier than the 23d of April, and at one time it did not appear before the 15th of May. Swans have been shot in the neighbourhood sometimes, though seldom.

very uncommon fish, such as the sturgeon ‡ and the porpoise, it is not, however, to be supposed that they are often to be met with in such a situation.

With respect to antiquities, the principal articles that come under this head have been mentioned in the body of the work, which renders any recapitulation unnecessary. A fact or two which has there been omitted, may here be taken notice of. In digging the foundation for the Tontine buildings, in the middle of the city, part of a boat was found many feet below the level of the ground, embedded in sand and gravel, where it must have lain for many ages. It would appear from this circumstance, that the bed of the river had once run in that direction.

In the month of August, 1801, in repairing the outer church, one of the divisions of the Cathedral, on lifting up the pavement opposite to the pulpit, there was found under a large stone, about two feet deep in the earth, part of a human skeleton, and a gold chain about 30 inches long, weighing about 11 drop, with circular rings soldered into each other. The chain was lying above the bones of the leg. The stone was inscribed with the date 1599, and

‡ About the year 1768, a sturgeon was caught in Carmile dam, about four miles above Glasgow, it measured about eight feet in length, and was shown in Glasgow for two or three days. Porpoises have been frequently caught: in May, 1801, five were killed at the Broomielaw; they afforded much sport to about 20 boats full of people, and many thousands on shore. Last year, in July 1803, a grampus of 28 feet in length, was towed up the Clyde to the Broomielaw.

and a number of old Saxon characters, but so indis-
tinct as to be perfectly unintelligible. The chain is
supposed to have served the purpose of supporting
the peaked shoe, which was generally worn from the
year 1382 to 1465.

Great numbers of ancient coins have frequently
been found in the city and its neighbourhood, mostly of the Scottish and English Kings, it would however be most likely uninteresting here, to particularize any more, as the most remarkable have already
been noticed in another place.

With respect to the manners of the people of
the city, a great change has taken place. Before
the war with America, when Glasgow was, in comparison, merely a commercial city, wealth was
the property only of a few individuals, the greatest part of the people being but in ordinary
circumstances; this naturally led to an apparent
difference of rank, as well as in the style of living and manners of the two classes. Upon the introduction of manufactures, however, a considerable change was produced; riches, by degrees became to be diffused more widely, and consequently
more general information and respectability. These
gradually filled up the chasm betwixt the merchant
and tradesman, so that that difference has now become less conspicuous, than at the former period.
The consequence is, that a great alteration has taken place in dress, houses, furniture, education,
and the amusements of the inhabitants in general,
every thing being now more shewy and elegant
than before; the mode of living has changed in a
similar

similar manner, many of the citizens, even not
of the first rank, living in a style of elegance,
which, within these twenty years would have
brought upon them the opprobrium of extravagance
and impolicy. The condition in the lower classes has in like manner been much meliorated.

The character of the people in general, is that
of being remarkable for industry and exertion in
their business, qualities which have secured
many of them independence, and the means of
rendering themselves otherwise highly useful to
the community. Glasgow was formerly said to
be remarkable for the severity, and apparent sanctity of manners; it is believed, that in this respect,
they are now pretty much upon a footing with
their neighbours. Some years ago the crimes of
housebreaking, robbery, &c. were much more frequent than at present, these were commonly com-
mited by such as were not natives of the city or
country, and consequently no blame on this head
can attach to the morals of the people; these exces-
ses have, however, been almost put a stop to by
those excellent regulations which have been framed, and are now in force, for preserving the order,
property, and comfort of the citizens.

THE ENVIRONS OF GLASGOW, &c.

AQUEDUCT BRIDGE AND CANALS.

Even as late as the beginning of the present century, the environs of this city were almost wholly
uninclosed,

uninclosed. Trees and hedges were then, in a manner, unknown in this quarter, and scanty crops were the only produce of a miserable mode of agriculture.

As the city began to increase in commerce and manufactures, their benign influence gradually diffused itself around. The landholder and the tenant saw a near and ready market for all their commodities; and therefore naturally turned their attention to every method whereby the produce of their farms could be augmented. A new and more skilful mode of husbandry was adopted, the grounds began gradually to be inclosed and planted, and their crops consequently increased. A consequent accumulation of more wealth than they formerly possessed, induced them to alter, in some respects, their mode of life. Instead of their former huts, new and neat farm houses arose, interspersed here and there with the more elegant or showy villa of the manufacturer or the merchant.

The spirit of improvement once begun, has since been carried on with a degree of ardour and effect, that reflects the highest honour upon the industry and taste of the inhabitants. The environs of Glasgow now present as rich and diversified a scene of rural beauty, as the vicinity of any city in Britain, whether we consider the many princely seats, the elegant villas, the plantations or well cultivated farms, with which they are adorned, or the happy situation of the ground, calculated in an eminent degree to set out these beauties to the greatest advantage.

To

To particularize every object worthy of attention in this neighbourhood, might perhaps appear tedious, we cannot, however, neglect one or two of the most conspicuous of these, situated at no great distance from the city, viz.

THE GREAT AQUEDUCT BRIDGE

over the deep valley and river of Kelvin, alongst which the Canal connecting the friths of Forth and Clyde is carried.

This magnificent bridge ranks among the first works of art in this country. The design and execution are equal to the grand idea of uniting the German and Atlantic oceans. This fabric is connected with a chain of masons' work, consisting of locks, basons, drydocks and road bridges, situated within a distance of half a mile, and lying as it were in a cluster, exhibit a most enteresting group of architecture. But, above all, the beautiful and romantic situation of the aqueduct, carrying a great artificial river over a deep valley, 400 feet in length, where square-rigged vessels are sometimes seen navigating at the height of 70 feet above the heads of spectators, affords such a striking instance of the power of human industry, as pleases every spectator, and gives it a pre-eminence over any thing of a similar nature in this kingdom.

It was founded in June, 1787, and finished in 1790, and consists of four arches, each 50 feet wide, and 37 feet high; the whole length is 275 feet, its height 63 feet, and its breadth 57 feet. This work
was

was designed by R. Whitworth, Esq; engineer. Under the foundation-stone was laid an engraved plate, with an inscription, of which the following is an accurate copy, and for which we are indebted to the politeness of a gentleman of the city.

In the year of our Lord Jesus Christ, One Thousand Seven
Hundred and Eighty Seven,
And
In the 27th year of the reign of GEORGE the Third,
King of Great Britain, &c. &c. &c.
And
In the first year of the Presidency of Sir Thomas Dundas of Kerse, Baronet, Governor of the Company of Proprietors of the Forth and Clyde Navigation; and of the Right Honourable Lord Frederick Campbell, Sir Archibald Edmonstone of Duntreath, Baronet, John Purling, and John Ingram, Esquires, Counsellors of the Company in London,
THE FOUNDATION STONE
of the Aqueduct Bridge, for carrying the Navigation betwixt
the FORTH and CLYDE,
of the depth of eight feet, the length of the Bridge two hundred and seventy-five feet, and sixty-eight feet in height,
over the Valley and River of KELVIN, in the County
of Lanark in North Britain,
as designed by ROBERT WHITWORTH, Esq; Engineer,
(Supposed the largest Fabric of the kind in the World.)
WAS LAID,
On the fifteenth day of the month of June,
By Archibald Speirs, Esquire, of Elderslie, Chairman of the
Committee of Management;
At a period when the direction of the affairs of the Company of Proprietors of the Forth and Clyde Navigation in Scotland, was committed to the care of the said Archibald Speirs, Esquire, in conjunction with the Right Honourable John Lord.
Elphinstone,

3 I

Elphinstone, the Right Honourable Ilay Campbell, Lord Advocate for Scotland, the Right Honourable John Grieve, Lord Provost of Edinburgh, the Honourable John Riddell, Lord Provost of Glasgow, Sir John Inglis of Cramond, Baronet, James Hopkirk, Esquire, of Dalbeth, Deputy Chairman, John Campbell, Esquire, of Clathick, Peter Speirs, Esquire, of Culcreuch, George Buchanan, Esquire, James Gordon, Esquire, both Merchants in Glasgow, and Patrick Colquhoun, Esquire, Superintendant of the Navigation, all Members of the Committee of Management.

N.B. William Gibb and John Moir, Undertakers in Falkirk, have contracted to finish this work in the year 1789.

The expence of this bridge when completed, amounted to the sum of L.8,509 sterling, and that of the whole canal above L.330,000. Some account of this canal* betwixt the Forth and Clyde, has been formerly given; it may, however, not be uninteresting, to mention two or three other particulars, not only with respect to it, but also the canal called the Monkland canal, and other projected cuts, which also terminate within the environs of the city.

The original stock by act of parliament of the Forth and Clyde canal, was declared to be L.150,000, divided into 1500 shares of L.100 each, with liberty to

---

* By a mistake, it is mentioned in the historical department of this work, that the canal was begun in 1755, it should have been 1768, that being the year the operations commenced, though no doubt it was projected long before that time.

to borrow L.50,000 more, and the subscibers for five shares were entitled to vote by themselves or proxies, and to be elected as managers of the company. On the 10th of July 1775, exactly seven years from the beginning of the work, the canal was rendered navigable as far as Stockingfield, from whence the side branch to Glasgow goes off. In November 1777, the side cut was brought forward to Hamilton-hill, where a large bason was built for the reception of of vessels, and granaries and other buildings erected. At this time the expence had exceeded by far the original estimate, while the tonnage dues did not exceed L.4000 annually. As there was, therefore, little probability that the canal would be carried forward to Clyde, the shares in the company's stock, frequently sold 50 per cent under par. An act, as has been mentioned, was obtained from government in 1784, upon which it was to draw proportional dividends with the proprietors, but the original subscribers were allowed to add the interest on their advances. In consequence of this assistance, the original design was completed, 28th July, 1790, by carrying the canal westward, from a place called Stockingfield, in the neighbourhood of Glasgow, to which it had been previously cut to the river Clyde.

From the trade of the canal increasing rapidly after the completion of the work, it was found that the bason at Hamilton-hill was too small for accommodating the great number of vessels daily resorting thither. In order to remedy this, a tract of about eight acres of ground was purchased by the company, within half a mile of the city of Glasgow, where a larger bason was formed, and likewise another for rafts of timber. A regular plan was also made out, for erecting the village of Port-Dundas, formerly mentioned, and which now contains many excellent houses. From this situation, a branch strikes towards the east to the western extremity of the Monkland canal, which has already been productive of a considerable increase of revenue.

This canal, which was 22 years in finishing, was one of the most arduous to execute in the kingdom. In its course, it passes over rocks, precipices, and quicksands; in some places it runs through a deep moss, and in others it is banked 20 feet high. In its course it crosses many rivulets and roads, as well as two considerable rivers, the Luggie and the Kelvin. This navigation is supplied with water by seven reservoirs, covering 409 acres of ground, and containing 12,679 lockfulls of water, and when necessary, the directors have it in their power to add two other reservoirs of very large dimensions.

The tonnage dues alongst the canal, are twopence per ton the mile, with exceptions in favour of lime, manure, and sundry other articles.

Tonnage dues from sea to sea, are,	L.o 5	10
From Grangemouth to Glasgow,	o 2	10
From Bowling-bay to Glasgow,	o 2	o

The most considerable part of the revenue arises from grain and timber.

That this canal has been of great service to the city, as well as the kingdom at large, needs no demonstration, and that its utility is still increasing, as well as the commerce of Glasgow and the other adjacent

jacent ports, will appear sufficiently evident from the advanced price of shares, and the increasing tonnage annually.

To give some better idea from whence the revenue is derived, as well as the expenditure, we have here presented an abstract of both for the year 1802.

REVENUE
Arising from

Grain,	L.3,471	2	0
Wood,	4,619	16	1
Coal,	1,801	11	11
Iron,	1,400	0	0
Salt and Herrings,	2,885	15	6
General Trade,	7,434	10	1
Rents, Feus, and Miscellaneous Revenue,	1,759	1	7
	23,371	17	2

EXPENDITURE.

General Expence of Works,	4,405	1	0
Contingent Expence,	620	1	6
Officers Salaries,	1,320	0	0
Lock, Bridge, and Reservoir Keepers Wages,	861	3	0
Ice-breaking,	171	19	5
Annual and Casual Damages,	97	13	6
Law Charges,	49	10	0
Interest Account,	687	10	4
	8,212	18	9

EXTRAORDINARY

EXTRAORDINARY EXPENCES.

New Houses, -	386	8	2
New Barge and House,	453	15	5
Hill-end Reservoir House, Furniture,	70	6	3
Steam Boat, -	298	17	9
	1,209	7	7
Dividends paid Proprietors, -	13,704	19	4
Balance in favour of the Revenue,	244	11	6
Revenue of 1802, -	L.23,371	17	2
Revenue of 1801, -	21,725	1	1
Increase in 1802, -	1646	16	1

The second canal in the environs of the city, is the
Monkland canal, which terminates in a bason to the
north of the Cathedral church. The design intended by this canal, was to open a free and easy communication with the interior parts of the country,
and likewise by transporting alongst it, coal from
the particular districts, to reduce the price of that
article in the city of Glasgow. An act of parliament was procured for making this cut in the year
1770, but owing to a deficiency in the original subscription, and a stagnation which took place in trade
about the beginning of the American war, the
scheme was interrupted. In 1782 the stock was sold.
The greatest part of the shares were then purchased
by Messrs. Stirlings, who ultimately became the sole
proprietors. These gentlemen finished the plan, having extended the navigation to the river Calder,

13

13 miles east of Glasgow, and formed a junction with the great canal at Port-Dundas.

This canal is 15 feet wide at the bottom, and 30 at the surface, and is capable of admitting vessels which draw 4½ feet water, equal to about 60 tons burden. Its greatest height above the level of the sea is 273 feet, the lowet at the bason, situated at the west end, 156 feet, the same height with the Forth and Clyde canal to which it is connected. The principal trade of this canal consists in the carriage of coals to the city, from the coaleries in the parish of Monkland.

Other canals besides these have been projected, to be carried from Glasgow to other places, particularly Edinburgh, and the Frith of Clyde near to Saltcoats or Irvine. With respect to the first of these, the subscription for carrying it into effect, was opened about twelve years ago, and a very considerable sum brought forward, in consequence of which, surveys of different tracts were made; these surveys have not, however, as yet been carried into execution. The principal tracts laid out for this canal are two, one runs to the city of Edinburgh from Glasgow, to the south of a high ridge of ground called the Shotts-hills, the distance betwixt the places in this direction is 50 miles, and the greatest height of the canal would be 522 feet above that of the Monkland canal, with which it was proposed to form a junction. The other tract lies to the north of the Shotts-hills, it does not rise so high as the south line by 140 feet, and is 10 miles shorter. The design of this canal is to afford a more steady

and

and cheap supply of coals to the cities of Edinburgh
and Glasgow, as well as for the purpose of conveying lime, iron-stone, and manufactured iron, &c.
to and from the different works and towns that are
situated in the vicinity of these tracts, and also to
convey at a cheaper rate, goods and merchandize
from one city to the other.

The second proposed canal is intended to form a
shorter communication betwixt the river Clyde and
the sea, at a place called Troon bay, or some other
situation in its vicinity, than the river by its present
course allows. The tract of this canal will be upwards of 20 miles. The grounds through which
it is proposed to run, however, appears, from the
report of the surveyor, to be uncommonly favourable, nature having pointed out the line through a
narrow strath, having no great elevation, and affording plenty of water for supplying it at all seasons.

TOUR

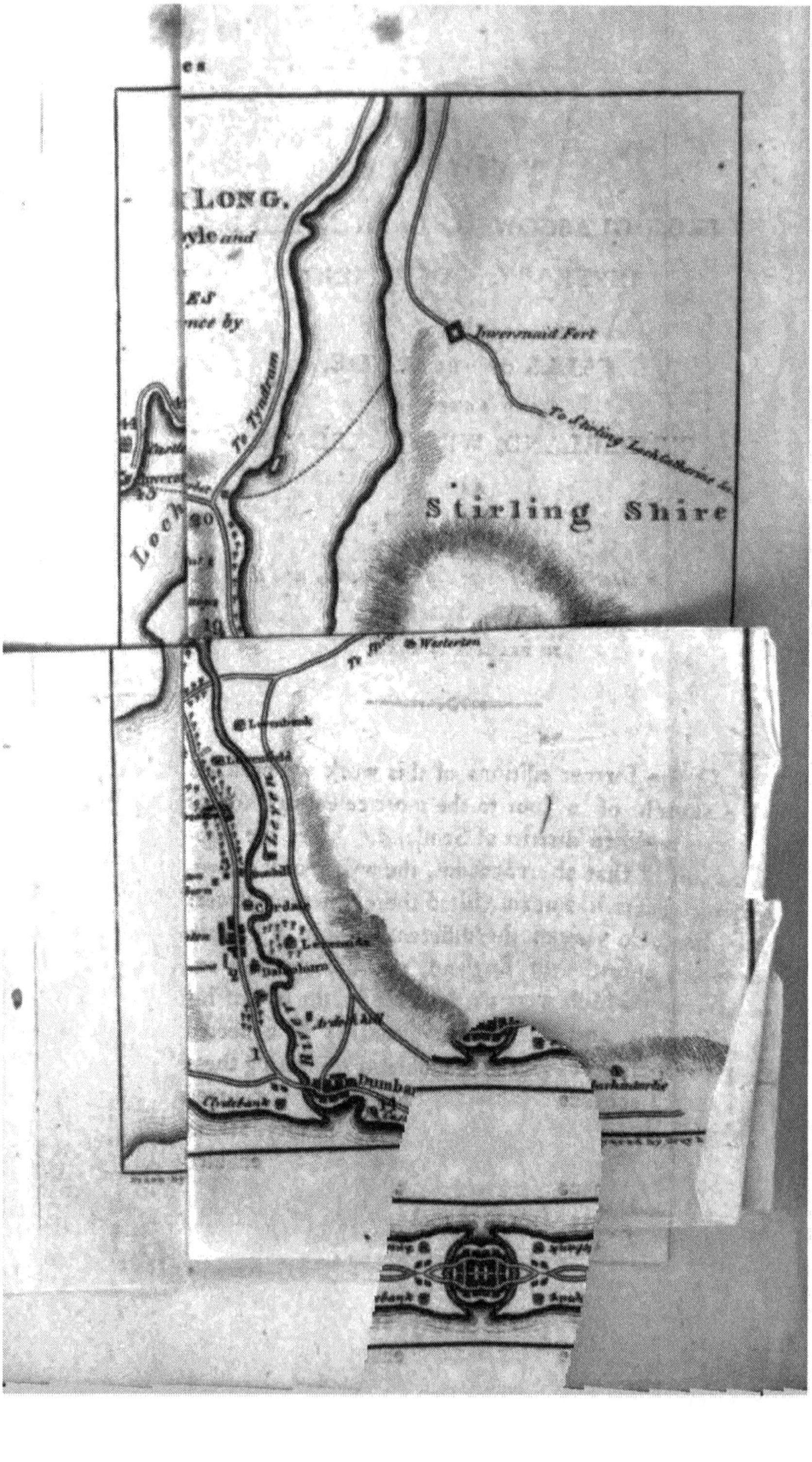
Stirling Shire
To Tyndrum

TOUR

FROM GLASGOW TO LOCH LOMOND,

INVERARY, LOCH LONG,

THE

FALLS of the CLYDE,

AND LAKES IN

CUMBERLAND, WESTMORELAND,

AND

LANCASHIRE;

With descriptions of these different scenes, and the
CHIEF TOWNS,

IN THE LINE OF ROAD.

————

To the former editions of this work we prefixed
the sketch of a tour to the most celebrated scenes
in the western district of Scotland. Since the publication of that short account, the writer of the foregoing sheets has again visited these different places;
he has also visited the different lakes in the north
western counties of England, and during these ex-
cursions (which were partly made in the line of his
profession, and partly from pleasure) he collected
such information as he could obtain, respecting these
beautiful scenes, and made such remarks as occurred
to him, respecting their picturesque beauty, as has

3 K   enabled

enabled him to enlarge considerably the descriptive part of the tour in this edition.

In describing these different objects, the most natural course appears to be, by setting out from Glasgow to proceed to Dumbarton, Loch Lomond, and Inverary, thence returning to the city by the banks of Loch Long, the Gair Loch, Greenock, Port-Glasgow, and Paisley; from Glasgow again proceeding by way of Hamilton, Lanark, and the Falls of the Clyde, to Moffat, Lockerbie, Gretna, Carlisle, Penrith, and so on to the lakes.

Leaving Glasgow at the west, and taking the high road to Dumbarton, passing through the extensive suburb of Anderston, and upon the left having the village of Finnieston, where the manufacture of crystal or flint-glass is carried on to a considerable extent, you shortly fall in with the banks of the Kelvin, a stream, which rising near the middle of the isthmus betwixt the Forth and Clyde, falls into the latter river, about two miles below the situation of the city of Glasgow. Its banks, in the latter part of its course, are picturesque and beautiful; many fine seats in different situations render them still more agreeable: upon the north, and situated in a commanding situation, is Gilmour-hill, lately erected, the residence of Robert Bogle, Esq; in its vicinity is also Kelvin Grove and some others.

Crossing the Kelvin by a new bridge, you fall in with the village of Partick, a place of considerable antiquity.

antiquity. Here the incorporation of bakers have some very extensive mills; these, or rather the ground upon which they were erected, were bestowed upon them, as has been already noticed, by the regent Murray, in the year 1568. In the same place, and to the left of the great road, are the ruins of a house, formerly used as a country residence, by one of the archbishops of Glasgow; it is, however, unpicturesque and uninteresting.

From this village the road continues through a level and fertile plain, having the Clyde at a short distance, upon the left, and gently swelling high grounds, studded with seats and cottages upon the right; amongst these may be mentioned Jordan-hill, the property of Archibald Smith, Esq; a gentleman, who from assiduity in business as a merchant, has realized a handsome fortune. This seat was once the property of a gentleman of the name of Crawford, who, by a singular stratagem, obtained possession of the Castle of Dumbarton, when it was held by the Lord Fleming for the Queen's party, against the Earl of Lennox, before the accession of James the VI. A little farther on, upon the left, and at the distance of about five miles from the city, is Scotstown, the residence of George Oswald, Esq; the head of a very respectable and ancient family.

The opposite banks of the Clyde now come more fully into the prospect; they are also richly cultivated, and are adorned by the residences of many families of rank. Amongst the most conspicuous appears El-

3 K 2   derslie,

deralie, the seat of Mr. Speirs, an elegant and modern house, surrounded with a pleasure-ground of considerable extent. Immediately adjacent, and to the west of this seat is Renfrew, afterwards to be more particularly noticed. The high road continues still westward, and passing the small village of Yocker, the house of Renfield, also upon the south side of the Clyde, presents itself to view; it is the seat of Mr. Campbell of Blythswood. Upon the north, at some distance, a romantic looking building is seen, called Garscadden Gate, the offspring of a very singular fancy. We now cross the great canal, at the distance of eight miles from Glasgow, the road still continuing level, and the face of the country rich and varied. Upon the right, a range of hills, far more lofty than the gently swelling knolls just now mentioned, appear to advance upon us; in proceeding to the west, the road also gradually begins to ascend, while the view to the westward appears more contracted, from the elevation of the objects in that direction. Nearly, in this situation, betwixt eight and nine miles from the city, and upon the south side of the Clyde is seen Semple House, the seat of Lord Semple.

The country, though thus rich, has as yet been unpicturesque, there now, however, bursts at once upon the sight, without your expectation of such a scene, one of the most beautiful views in Britain. It is first seen through trees, and produces the happiest effect from the aerial tints of the distance, and the local colouring and shade of of the foreground. You are now at Dalnotter hill, nine miles from the city. No traveller of taste, however, rests satisfied with the confined view which the prospect from the road affords him. He turns to the right or to the left, to enjoy more fully the treat which nature here so lavishly presents. The surface of the Clyde, swelled into a large river, moves with majesty along, bounded on the right by a ridge of lofty hills, called Kilpatrick-hills, which approach almost to the brink of the stream; these are terminated by the hill of Dumbuc, at no great distance westward, and are not only broken by the most picturesque outline, but have their verdant sides covered here and there with beautiful copses, and farther down, villages and seats. The bank of the river on this side, is also broken by many head-lands and capes, upon which are also placed several villas that produce a fine effect. Farther, and rising as it were from the bosom of the Clyde, is the rock or castle of Dumbarton, of a conical, or rather from this point of view, circular form, and far beyond, the mountains of Argyle, softened by distance into a-zure. On the opposite or south side of the Clyde, the surface is more level, though still finely broken. Amongst the most conspicuous objects here, are Erskine House, the seat of Lord Blantyre, and in the distance, the towns of Port-Glasgow and Greenock, with the numerous vessels upon the bosom of the river.

Neither is the foreground of this picture uninte-resting: the village of Kilpatrick with its ancient church,

church, the entrance of the great canal, and some
fine old trees, add a still greater effect to the other
parts of the scene. Leaving this sweet spot, we
gradually descend to the village just now mentioned,
which though ancient, claims in other respects, except its situation, little notice. In this neighbourhood have frequently been found many Roman antiquities, and at no great distance towards the right,*
is still to be seen a bridge, the work of that once
mighty people. The remains of that great wall
which began near Kilpatrick, and extended alongst
the isthmus to Abercorn on the Frith of Forth, a
distance of 36 miles and 877 paces, cannot now,
however, here be traced; though vestiges are still, in
other situations, particularly to the north of the city
of Glasgow, very apparent.

From Kilpatrick, the road continues westward,
bounded on the north by this range of hills, and on
the south by the Clyde. You now arrive at Bow-
ling-bay, 11 miles from Glasgow, from whence the
canal branches from Clyde. Opposite to this situation nearly, is a charming little seat, screened by the
mountains from the north, and surrounded by trees,
called Glenarbet, the residence of Gilbert Hamilton, Esq. Farther on, and on a point of land stretching into the Clyde, are situated the ruins of Dunglas Castle, a place of some note in the Scottish history. Mr. Pennant supposes it may have been a
Roman

* At Duntocher.

Roman station, and perhaps that, which was situated exactly at the termination of the wall. These ruins are, however, not very picturesque or interesting, except from their situation with respect to the surrounding objects. On the other hand, and rising from the woods on the brow of the hill, is Auchintorlie, the seat of Mr. Buchanan, a place which commands, in the most complete manner, the different objects we have just now been speaking of. A temple, as it is called, has lately been erected upon this property, somewhat farther west, in a very elevated situation, for a bird's eye prospect; its form, however, and its glaring whiteness, are by no means in unison with its situation, perched, as it were, upon a lofty summit, covered with shaggy wood, and environed by the most picturesque rocks and craggs.

Continuing still alongst the highway, the hill of Dumbuck appears directly in front, now very much elevated above the plain. It is composed principally, like the rest of that chain of mountains, which extend from Stirling to Dumbarton, with few interruptions of basaltic granite. The surface of this immense mass is much broken, by wood, moss, and rock intermingled; their various hues, particularly in the end of autumn, are beautiful in the extreme, and the effect of the whole rendered grand and sublime, if by chance, as is often the case, the summit should be hid in a fog, while the middle division of the hill, and the lower parts, remain clear and unobscured. To such as have leisure, the prospect from the top is deserving of attention. The best

path

path appears to be that which strikes off to the right from the great road, after passing Auchintorlie. In this ascent, you meet with an extensive printfield, called Milton, belonging to MacDowal and Co. from which government draws a revenue of from 8000 to L. 10,000 per annum. Passing this situation, and turning more to the left, while the hill increases in steepness, you at length reach its summit, upon which is a cairn, as it is called, or a collection of stones, a monument, perhaps, of some fallen hero; or collected, as some imagine, by the absurd regulations of the Roman see; or according to others, merely for the purpose of placing a beacon or alarm fire, in a still more conspicuous situation.

From the top of Dumbuck, the prospect in whatever way, except to the N. E. is extensive. Looking up the river, its various windings are traced to a great distance, the spires of Glasgow are also conspicuous, as well as the distant mountain of Tinto and other hills towards the south, the middle distance or side screen upon the left, is composed of the Kilpatrick-hills, the Milton printfields, the broken rocks and woods around. And upon the right, are the woods of Erskine, and the rich country around the towns of Paisley and Renfrew.

Turning to the west, the prospect is equally, if not more grand. The rock and castle of Dumbarton, sunk here as it were below the feet, the surface of the Clyde, forming to appearance an immense bason

son broken in its outline by numerons capes and fine retiring bays, the town of Dumbarton, which appears delineated as upon a map; its bridge, the Leven, and other objects present themselves to view. And at a more remote distance, the towns of Greenock and Port-Glasgow are distinctly visible. Towards the north, the rich vale of the Leven, its parent lake, at least a small portion of it, and the towering mountains in its vicinity, compose a landscape of a still more different kind. This last resembles the grand and striking productions of Salvator Rosa or Wilson, while the other two have more of the character of the soft and pleasing pictures of Claude.

Descending from Dumbuck, we again fall in with the highway, about thirteen miles from the city, alongst which, after winding around the base of the hill, which here threatens destruction to the traveller, we gradually approach through a level and fertile plain, the castle and town of Dumbarton. In this part of the ride, the castle appears more upon the left than heretofore, its form, as well as its apparent size differs. It now rears its head high above the horizon, and divides itself into two conical rocks, joined at their base, but whose summits are at a considerable distance; the outline as you advance nearer becomes more broken and more picturesque, and the whole from its consequent size, claims more of your attention and regard. A road branches from the highway, nearly about the fourteenth mile stone to the left, pursuing this road at a very trifling distance we find the object just now mentioned, the

CASTLE

CASTLE OF DUMBARTON.

The entry to this fortress is from the south, through an ancient and massy gate. Travellers are here shewn an armoury and several other curiosities, or rather antiquities, which are by no means undeserving of notice. The rock upon which the castle stands, or rather the castle itself, is composed of the same materials with the hill of Dumbuck, in its neighbourhood, with which, according to some, it has been originally connected, but disjoined by some dreadful convulsion of nature. Its form, as has been just now noticed, is biforked, the western rock being considerably more elevated than that upon the east; betwixt these two are situated the stairs, cut from the rock, which lead to the upper part of the fortress, from whence the prospect is extensive and varied, the same objects we have remarked as visible from the summit of Dumbuck, here presenting themselves to the eye, differently grouped, and situated, however, and consequently, forming new scenes. In particular, the view to the north, from the top of the rock, is admirable: the windings of the Leven, its rich vale, the numerous villages, its gently sloping hills; part of Loch Lomond and its guardian mountains, particularly, lofty Ben Lomond, and Benvoirlich; besides other objects, such as the town of Dumbarton in the foreground, present a rich and diversified scene.

This castle has a governor and a company of invalids, maintained by government. It formerly
made

made a conspicuous figure in the history of the country. In the early ages, according to Bede and Mr. Pinkerton, it formed the capital of the strath Clyde Britons, under the name of Alcluid. The neighbouring Caledonians gave it the name of Dunbriton, or the fort of the Britons, from lying within their territory, which, by an easy transposition, is now called Dumbarton.

The town of this name lies in the immediate vicinity.

DUMBARTON.

This town, which most likely owes its origin to the castle, is situated about 14$\frac{1}{2}$ miles from Glasgow. It was first erected into a royal burgh by Alexander the II. in 1221, and lies on the east side, and near the mouth of the river Leven. It is a town of no considerable size, or commercial eminence, though well situated for carrying on the coasting trade; the number of vessels belonging to the port are, however, believed to be rather upon the increase; its tonnage amounts to betwixt 2 and 3000 tons. Its principal manufacture is that of glass, which has been carried on here these several years, and to a considerable extent, insomuch that it pays annually to government about L.4000 sterling.

Proceeding on our ride, and leaving Dumbarton, the road crosses a handsome bridge, built over the Leven, immediately after which it strikes towards the north, a direction it keeps for many miles. Upon the left, from this situation a road branches to Helensburgh, a fishing village upon the Clyde, and to Arroquhar, by the way of Loch Long. You now direct your course alongst the vale of the Leven, a rich and diversified tract, every where presenting flourishing villages, elegant seats, and neat and comfortable cottages; it is also finely wooded with copses, hedge-rows, and other plantations; but its principal beauty is the Leven, which issues from Loch Lomond, and after a course of about nine miles, including all its windings and a fall of 22 feet, it empties itself into the Clyde. This stream, and the surrounding scenery, are finely painted by the able pen of a native of the vale, Dr. Smollett, in the beautiful ode:

> " On Leven's banks while free to rove,
> And tune the rural pipe to love," &c.

A little farther on, and at the distance of two miles from Dumbarton, you pass upon the right, an old mansion house, upon the verge of the river, in which this eminent and elegant writer was born. A monument to his memory is erected upon the left of the road, a little farther north; it was built by his relation, the late James Smollett, Esq; of Bonhill, and consists of a Tuscan column, terminated by a vase; on its pedestal is an elegant Latin inscription, of which the following is a translation:

Stop,

453

Stop, Traveller!
If humour, and a happy vein of wit;
If manners, painted by the most skilful hand,
Ever challenged your admiration,
Pause awhile, on the memory
Of TOBIAS SMOLLETT, M. D.
A person not slightly adorned with those virtues
Which deserve your praise and admiration,
As a man, and a citizen.
Conversant in various parts of literature,
After he had recommended his name to posterity,
By a happy exertion of original genius,
He was cruelly snatched away by death,
In the fifty-first year of his age.
Alas! far distant from his country,
Near Leghorn, a port of Italy,
Sleep his remains!
To such, and so great a man,
Was this column erected,
By his Cousin German, JAMES SMOLLETT, of Bonhill,
Who, in the decline of his life,
Might rather have resigned this office of piety,
To be performed towards his own remains,
By a relative so prematurely deceased.—
Unavailing monument of affection!
Placed on the banks of that Leven,
Which resounded the first cries of his infancy;
And not long before his departure,
Its own praises, the tribute of his muse,
Depart—but remember,
That this monument is not solely destined to the memory
Of the deceased,
But meant to shew to others, if they prove worthy,
That the same recompence may await
Their virtue.

Immediately after passing this monument to de-
parted genius, we enter the village of Renton, a
creation

creation of the numerous manufactures and bleach-
fields in the neighbourhood. The houses are modern, neat, and commodious. The village contains
upward of 1000 inhabitants, and these are rapidly
on the increase. In the same neighbourhood is
likewise the village of Alexandria, which owes its
existence to the same causes with that of Renton. Passing these places, upon the right is Cor-
dale, belonging to Messrs. Stirlings, who are likewise proprietors of the most extensive printfields on
the banks of the Leven. In this vale, these works
are more numerous than in any other tract of the
same extent in Britain; and to such an amount do
they carry on business, that it has been calculated,
they, together with one or two others in the neighbourhood, pay annually to government, upwards of
L.40,000 sterling of duties. These numerous manufactures have been drawn into this situation, principally from the excellency and pureness of the water of the Leven, at all seasons, for here,

"No torrents stain thy limpid source,
No rocks impede thy dimpling course,
That sweetly warbles o'er its bed,
With white round polish'd pebbles spread."

and likewise from labour, being considerably cheaper than nearer the great towns.

Proceeding towards the north, at the third mile-
stone upon the right, we pass Bonhill, the seat of
——— Smollett, Esq;. The beauty of this vale still
continues to enchant. You now pass in one situation

tion through a vista of trees of every diversity of foliage, at one place hiding every other object from the eye, and opening at another a delightful peep to the eastern banks of the river, with the fine plantations of Leven bank, the seat of Lord Stonefield, and the thriving, and even elegant village of Bonhill, upon the same side of the river, its neat church and picturesque spire.

Farther on, some beautiful hedges bound the road, which in the season of summer, are finely interwoven with the wild-rose, honey-suckle, and other sweet smelling plants. Upon the left you fall in with Broomley, a seat, the property of —— Carmichael, Esq; and upon the same side of the road, at the distance of betwixt four and five miles from Dumbarton, with Woodbank or Stockroger, belonging to Miss Scott. Opposite, or nearly so to this, is a road leading to a ferry over the Leven, called Balloch-ferry, a place upon the opposite bank, remarkable for a great fair of horses, held annually on the fifth of September. From this ferry a road leads to Buchanan, the residence of the Duke of Montrose, as well as to Killearn, the banks of the Endrick, and other places towards the east.

Continuing alongst the road from Dumbarton, after passing Woodbank, the prospect is more confined upon each hand, from intervening trees and hedges, affording a delightful shade in the heats of summer,

" 'Midst bowers of birch, and groves of pine,
And hedges flow'rd with eglantine."

Various

Various openings, however, present themselves, some of which afford fine peeps. The house of Cameron at the fifth mile stone, is thus seen, the seat of Alexander Smollett, Esq; and immediately thereafter, through a fine vista, appears the polished expanse of

LOCH LOMOND,

its large islands, and the soft hills in the distance; a view that at once arrests the attention of the traveller. The objects that compose the scene are so finely diversified in form, in situation, and in colour, as to compose a picture, at once beautiful and impressive. You now still approach nearer the shores of the lake, then recede, and at the sixth mile stone pass Belvidero, the seat of another gentleman of the name of Smollett, which also commands (as its name implies) a fine prospect of the surrounding scenery. At the seventh mile stone is Arden, upon the left, the property of H. Buchanan, Esq; environed in woods, and placed at the bottom of a lofty hill, called Dunfion, or the Hill of Fingal, tradition reporting it to have been one of the hunting seats of that supposed hero.

Somewhat farther on, and passing Nether Ross upon the left, you cross a small river called the water of Fruin, which falls into the lake. It rises in glen Fruin, or the Vale of Lamentation, so called, it is said, from a dreadful slaughter of the Colquhouns by the MacGrigors, a Highland clan, in 1602, and
on

on account of which the MacGrigors were ordained by law, to abjure their name, which for a century they dared not re-assume.

After passing the water of Fruin, the road is, for some considerable space, more open, whereby the lake upon the right is more completely seen, with its numerous islands, backed by the western extremity of the Grampians, and the towering summit of Ben Lomond. Upon the left, the mountains increase in height as you advance, and approach still nearer the brink of the lake. These hills are in general verdant, and in many places well wooded. In other situations, craggy rocks burst forth from their sides, interspersed with verdure, furze and heath.

Another glen opens amongst these hills to the left, at the distance of a mile from glen Fruin, it is named glen Finglas, from the streamlet that waters it. Near its opening, and at the ninth mile stone upon the right, is Rosslodge, the seat of Mr. Colquhoun. Proceeding towards the north, through a beautiful varied scene of mountains, cottages and trees, you come in sight of the finest situation on the Loch Lomond, Rosedoe, the seat of Sir James Colquhoun, Bart.

Rosedoe is a modern house, and stands upon a peninsula projecting into the lake, and in such a situation as to command a delightful prospect of the fairy scenes around. The pleasure grounds, though of no great extent, are planned and laid out with

3 M   taste;

taste; the trees are in general beautiful, as well as numerous, and together with a ruined tower of the old mansion house, add much to the beauty of the whole.

From Rosedoe, we continued on our course, through a well wooded tract, nearly parallel to the side of the lake. Many sweet little scenes here occur from the figure of some venerable trees, the picturesque appearance of the cottages, and the groupes of men and cattle, which are frequently to be met with in this situation.

About eleven miles from Dumbarton, we passed upon the right, Camstraddan, a seat of another gentleman of the name of Colquhoun. Opposite to this seat, and in the mountains to the left, is a slate quarry, which is wrought to considerable advantage; great quantities of these slates are annually sent hence by the way of the lake, to the towns upon the Clyde, and other places. Shortly after leaving Camstraddan, you cross by a bridge, the river of Luss, which descends through a valley of that name upon the left, and immediately after enter the village of

LUSS,

at the distance of 12 miles from Dumbarton. This village, is situated upon a tract of level and well cultivated land, though of no very great extent, stretching eastward into the lake. It is a very inconsiderable

inconsiderable place, and irregularly built, though placed in a most delightful situation.

To a native of England, or the Lowlands of Scotland, the houses in general appear exceedingly uncomfortable. They are mostly built of loose stones*, perhaps with a layer of turf betwixt each row, and are covered with rushes, the produce of the lake. they are likewise very low, and the door before, which is a thick layer of fern, so difficult of access, that a person must stoop considerably before he can enter. The interior in general corresponds to their outward appearance, being dark, and often full of smoke, which is discharged as plentifully at the window and the door, as at the ordinary aperture.

Notwithstanding these appearances, however, the people here, it would appear, find them sufficiently comfortable. They live contented and happy, and are commonly intelligent, polite, and obliging. The spinning of cotton has been introduced at Luss sometime ago, as well as the weaving of muslins; these manufactures have contributed to call forth, and stimulate the industry of the inhabitants, and are otherwise attended with beneficial effects.

Luss is the first Highland village we have yet met with on the road northwards; indeed, to use

3 M 2   the

* There are, however, some exceptions: the church and the manse are both modern houses; the inn may also be mentioned as far superior to the others in the village.

the expression of a late writer, it is situated at the very " portal of the Highlands," the inhabitants to the north using the Gaelic language and garb of the Highlanders, while those on the south side of this boundary, speak the English, and dress like the inhabitants of the Low country.

This village is much resorted to in the summer months, by the numerous parties that come from all parts of the empire to visit the lake, or in their way to Inverary, or other parts of the west Highlands, to which it is a great thoroughfare. The accommodations at the inn are, however, but indifferent, though superior to what has been often represented.

Luss is so finely situated, that every person who visits it upon a pleasure excursion should here spend a little time. He may navigate the lake, and visit the islands, from each of which he will find a rich and extensive prospect; or he may explore the glens amongst the mountains, where the man of taste, the painter, or the botanist, will equally find entertainment.

To many of these situations the writer of these sheets was conducted, by Dr. Stuart, the minister of Luss, (to whom he had letters of introduction) a gentleman of great learning, politeness, and taste. Amongst these pointed out to me may be reckoned Stronehill, to the north of the village, which commands a scene truly beautiful.

At

At this point, about one third of the way up the mountain, the whole breadth of the lake is spanned by the eye, including

> ———" All the fairy crowds
> Of islands, which together lie,
> As quietly as spots, to sky,
> Among the evening clouds."

These islands are of many different forms and magnitudes: some are covered with the most luxuriant wood, of every different tint; others shew a beautiful intermixture of rock and copses; some like plains of emerald, scarcely above the level of the water, are covered with grass; and others again are bare rocks, rising into precipices, sterile, and destitute of vegetation.

From this situation they also appear distinctly separated from each other, but not so much so as to present the idea of a map or bird's eye view, which a higher point of view would undoubtedly present to the imagination. The prospect is bounded on the south by the distant hills, betwixt and the Clyde, which here appear, in comparison to the mountains around, to be gentle swells; the Leven, its vale, the rock of Dumbarton, and even the surface of the Clyde, are in the same direction conspicuous. Towards the east, the vale of the Endrick, its principal seats, the obelisk erected to the memory of Buchanan, at Killearn, and the Lennox hills, are also distinctly visible.

Turning

Turning to the north, the lake is seen to wind
far amongst the mountains, which are finely broken
in their outline, and very lofty, particularly BEN
LOMOND, which, like Saul amongst his companions,
seems to tower to the heavens; the prospect here
has something in it more grand than that to the
south or east, and perhaps more picturesque and
better adapted to the pencil, though not nearly so
soft and pleasing in its aspect as the view in the opposite direction.

While viewing these different scenes, we were
still farther gratified, by the information respecting
them, with which the gentleman, just now mentioned, favoured me, and to whom I am much indebted, in the following short account of this fine
expanse of water, and its numerous islands.

Loch Lomond extends in a direction from north
to south, nearly thirty miles; its breadth, where
greatest, at the southern extremity, is betwixt eight
and ten miles; from this situation it gradually becomes narrower as you advance towards the north,
where it terminates amongst the mountains.

Its depth is very different: in the southern parts
of the lake, it measures twenty fathoms, and increases in depth towards the north, from sixty-six fathoms at the point of Farkin, to 100 fathoms, two
miles above Tarbet; from this place, however, the
depth begins again to diminish.

It is remarkable that the northern part of Loch
Lomond

Lomond never freezes, even in the most severe frosts, though the southern part of the lake is often covered with ice, so strong, as to render a communication betwixt the different islands alongst its surface, safe and easy.

The islands in Loch Lomond amount to about thirty in number, and are mostly situated to the south of the village of Luss, those to the north being very small and few in number; they are of various sizes, from the length of two miles, to a mere rocky point. The most remarkable are the following:

INCH MURRIN,

which first strikes the eye in coming from Dumbarton, is the largest island in the lake, extending from east to west about two miles. It is the property of the Duke of Montrose, and is kept as a deer-park, there being upwards of 200 deer, under the care of a game-keeper, who resides upon the island. The Earls of Lennox had here formerly a castle, where they resided; its ruins are still to be seen. A hunting lodge has been lately erected in this island by the proprietor.

To the north-east of Inch Murrin, is

GRANGE, OR CRAINGE, ?

well wooded with oaks, it measures about half a mile in length. The next is

INCH

INCH TORR,

about the same size with Grange, and like it, covered with woods of oak.

INCH CAILLAICH,

or, as the name is said to import, the Isle of Nuns, from its once having contained a nunnery, lies to the east of Inch Torr. It measures about a mile in length, and abounds in wood; it is the property of the Duke of Montrose, and is rented by some of his tenants, who reside here; it is said to produce good crops. In this island was formerly situated the parish church of Buchanan; its ruins still remain, and the cemetry surrounding them is still used as a place of burial by the neighbouring people.

INCH CLEAR AND INCH ABER

lie to the south-east of the last mentioned island; they are, however, comparatively small.

INCH FAD,

or the Long Island, lies to the north of Inch Caillaich; it measures about half a mile in length; it is inhabited, and produces good crops. To the south-west is

INCH GALBRAITH,

formerly the residence of a family of that name; the ruins of the castle are still seen.

INCH CONAGAN,

is about half a mile in length, and lies to the north of Inch Galbraith; it is covered with oak and fir.

INCH MOAN,

or the Moss Isle, is about three quarters of a mile in length, it is low and flat.

INCH CRUIN,

in which is an asylum for insane persons, lies to the east of the Moss Isle, and is about three quarters of a mile long.

To the west of Inch Moan, and to the south of the village of Luss, is,

INCH TAVANACH,

about three quarters of a mile long, and nearly half as broad. It is in general very rocky, and in other situations covered with wood. It derived its name, it is said, from having been formerly the residence of of a monk. Inch ta vanach signifying, the Island

3 N of

of the Monk's house. This island is the highest in the lake, and commands a beautiful prospect of the whole scenery around; upon which account it is often visited by strangers.

INCH LONAIG,

lies to the north of Inch Cruin, formerly mentioned, its length is about a mile, by a quarter of that space in breadth. It abounds in fine old yews, which were formerly, before the adoption of fire arms, in great request. This island belongs to Sir James Colquhoun, by whom it is used as a deer park.

These are the principal islands in the lake; the remainder are in general, much smaller: some of them produce excellent pasture, while others are little better than barren rocks. Amongst the second order may be reckoned, Fraoch Island, or the Prison of Luss, as it is called. Ton inch, Buck inch, Cardag Ross Isle, and Dergadunellan.

It would appear that the surface of the lake is now considerably higher than formerly; the ruins of houses and buildings being distinctly visible under water, particularly in Camstraddan bay; and somewhat farther south, are still to be seen near to the shore, a heap of stones, which are said to be the remains of a church, which formerly stood in that situation, but which is now overwhelmed with water.

To

To guard against future encroachments of this kind, the neighbouring proprietors advised with Mr. Golborne, an engineer, who deepened the Clyde, what was the best to be done: He advised the cutting through some necks of land formed by the Leven, the only outlet of the lake, and which, together with the deepening of the channel of that river, would allow the water to pass more quickly along. This, however, has never yet been done. Indeed, the rise of the water is so slow, as not to be perceptible in the course of an age; and at present, it is a question, whether it may, or may not, generally speaking, be stationary.

Great falls of rain, if long continued, as may naturally be imagined, raise the surface very considerably, insomuch, that after the droughts of summer, it has been raised higher by six feet; as the weather sets in fair again, however, it gradually falls to its former level.

This lake, like many others, is often violently disturbed by the wind rushing from amongst the mountains, its waves then swell and roll like those of the ocean, and like them, are often equally to be dreaded by the small skiffs that navigate its surface. Nay, even in a calm, and when every thing is hushed around, a swell is often perceived in the water, whence it is said, that Loch Lomond has waves without wind. This is, however, most likely owing to a breeze of wind sweeping alongst some part of this extensive sheet of water, and which agitates by de-

3 N 2

grees

grees the other parts of its surface, where a calm prevails.

But besides this motion of its waters, which is not unfrequent, Dr. Stewart mentions a still more remarkable agitation which took place at the time of the great earthquake at Lisbon, in 1755. At that period, its waters rose very suddenly above its ordinary level, then quickly retiring, it sunk as much below its usual height, and thus continued a vibratory motion for some considerable time; each tide of ebb and flow gradually diminishing, till it became perfectly serene.

In some places, where the face of the country was flat, it overflowed it to a considerable extent, and it is mentioned, that in one place, a boat was found at a distance of more than 40 yards from its former situation in the lake.

We have already mentioned, what is called one of the curiosities of Loch Lomond, "its waves without wind;" it is likewise, by the country people, said to possess other two, viz. a floating island, and fish without fins. From the natural propensity of mankind to magnify trifling, or perhaps, imaginary appearances into something striking or wonderful, arose, perhaps, these reports, for at present they are not strictly true. Indeed, one of the islands to the west of Inch Conagan, is called the floating island; it is, however, as stable as the others, though that it may have at one time possessed this property, is not improbable. It may have been a "mossy fragment," (according to the gentleman already mentioned)

tioned) detached by the waves from the island of
Inch Moan, which at length became fixed to the
bottom. To account for the other is not so easy,
unless we suppose, says Dr. Stuart, that the idea
has arisen from vipers, which abound in some of the
islands, having been observed swimming from the
one to the other.

Loch Lomond contains the finest fresh water fish
in abundance, particularly excellent trout, perch,
pike, and in the southern part of the lake, salmon.
Another fish, but more uncommon, called the pol-
lock, or fresh water herring, likewise abounds in the
lake, and during the summer months, is accounted
a delicacy.

Having seen whatever was remarkable at the village of Luss, we proceeded northwards, the road
still running parallel to the shore, alongst the
base of the mountains, which now become almost
precipitous, and alongst which it has been carried with incredible labour, at the expence of
government; the road being a military one, cut
by the soldiery since the year 1745. At the fifteenth mile stone, we are informed of this circumstance by an inscription cut on the rock upon the
left, mentioning that this part of the highway was
cut by the regiment under the command of Colonel
Lascelles.

The view northward becomes now more grand:
The mountains approach, as it were, nearer each o-
ther,

ther, and narrowing the lake, seem to terminate it no great distance. Amongst these mountains, that upon the right is so eminently conspicuous, as to lead our observation more and more from the others, and at length, from its immense magnitude, its towering height, and beautifully broken surface, it almost solely attracts the attention.

Proceeding on our course, while contemplating the scenery of Ben Lomond, we pass some cottages to the right, among the trees; the road then ascends a gentle eminence; a chasm or glen next appears in the mountains to the left, through which runs the Douglas—this river you cross by a bridge, and immediately arrive at the ferry-house of Inveruglas, sixteen miles from Dumbarton.

According to such as are conversant in the Gaelic language, the name of this river signifies the black grey water, and Inveruglas, its mouth or opening, terms very descriptive and just. The scenery up the glen is romantic and wild: Bleak and savage mountains, contrasted with the grey rocks, jutting out from their sides, the dark shades which these cast upon the pools, the bursting of the water from amongst the immense stones which threaten to obstruct its course, the weather-beaten and stunted birch on the sides of the hills, and the more luxuriant foliage upon the banks farther down, altogether unite in forming a variety of scenes, in which more of the terrible is combined, than the soft and beautiful.

Though

Though this is something like the character of the scenery far up the glen, it is more pleasing near its opening: the views here are formed by the bridge, the river finely fringed with trees, the cottages to left, the surface of the lake, and proudly pre-eminent above the rest, in the back ground, Ben Lomond. The effects of light and shade upon such a scene are captivating: Sometimes the upper part of the mountain is hid amongst the fogs, while a sunbeam strikes its middle distance or its base, and relieves it, as it were, from the objects in the foreground. At another time they are enlightened, while the mountain is obscured by the fine grey hues which form such a general tint in the colouring of nature, and so in succession do the effects continually shift.

The greatest part of travellers who visit Loch Lomond upon a pleasure excursion, in general take advantage of the ferry at Inveruglas, and cross the lake to ascend Ben Lomond; the breadth here is little more than a mile; it is narrowed in this situation by two peninsulas, approaching each other; that which you now pass through in walking to the boat, is level and fertile, the other upon the opposite side more craggy, and in some places covered with heath. Having crossed the lake, you find the neat and comfortable looking inn of Rowardennan, where in general a short stay is made before attempting the swelling mountain, and where a guide is at hand to conduct you, by the best and readiest tract, to the summit of

BEN

BEN LOMOND.

This mountain's perpendicular height is 3262 feet above the sea. At Rowardennan, when looking northwards, it almost completely fills up the view. It consists of three great stages, each rising above, and more distant than the other; these again are divided into a number of lesser swelling knolls, some of which are covered with heath and craggs, and others verdant and smooth. Betwixt these are formed many breaks, or gullies, as they are called, down each of which a stream pours with great rapidity, and when near, a deafening noise. At a greater distance, such a current is, however, more engaging: It looks like a white line on the face of the hill, while its noise is a gentle murmur that harmonizes with the stillness of the surrounding scenery.

The distance from the inn to the top of the mountain is reckoned six miles of a continued ascent, which in general requires about three hours. During the first part of the course the surface is rocky, and in many places covered with heath; by degrees you ascend a green ridge, alongst which the way is more plain and agreeable.

The view now becomes extensive as you advance, and the objects below, which lately so much engaged your attention, dwindle almost into nothing. You cross, in some situations, a mossy and spongy surface, where that water is received and deposited,
which

which gives birth to so many rills and cascades which
tumble down on every side. The ascent again becomes more steep, and the surface composed of a
slaty rock, while the temperature of the air feels very different from that upon the plain. At length,
after a toilsome ascent, you gain the summit, from
whence a varied and extensive prospect opens upon
the eye, in every direction, to an immense distance.
The lake, which you lately contemplated with so
much pleasure, now appears as a small pool, and its
rich and diversified islands as so many specks upon
its surface; beyond it, and to the left, appears the
vale of the Endrick—the distant county of Lanark,
its towns, and the mountain of Tinto, amongst the
highest of the southern hills. More to the right,
the outlet of the lake, the river Leven—its windings
and rich banks—the castle of Dumbarton—and
counties of Renfrew and Ayr. Nearly in the same
direction, the Frith of Clyde—the rock of Ailsa—
the islands of Arran and Bute, with the more distant Atlantic—the coasts of Ireland, and the Isle of
Man are, when the atmosphere is clear, within the
boundary of the view.

To the east from this point are seen, the counties
of Stirling and the Lothians, with the windings of the
Forth, and the castles of Stirling, and of Edinburgh.
The prospect to the north is, however, the most aw-
fully grand: Immense mountains, piled, as it were,
above each other, and extending from the borders of
Stirlingshire to the Western Ocean, with the indentations of the coast on one side, and the numerous

3 O

lakes

lakes on the right, particularly Loch Catherine, Loch Ard, and that of Monteith, reposing in the vallies, form a prospect, which may in some degree be conceived, but cannot be properly described.

Amongst the most conspicuous mountains in this direction appears Ben Artur or the Cobler, Cruachan, Benvoirlich, and Bennevis, the highest of the British hills; and still farther on, and in the south-west, the paps or mountains, in the island of Jura.

After surveying the extensive prospect around us, we naturally turn our attention to Ben Lomond itself, which appears as an immense cone, detached or insulated from the surrounding mountains. Towards the north, however, this figure is broken by an immense precipice of 2000 feet in height, conjectured by some to be the remains of an imperfect crater, with one side forcibly torn off. To look down this fearful steep requires a considerable resolution: you approach it with cautious step and a trembling nerve, clinging firm to the surface of the mountain, which even appears insecure; the view is terrific and grandly sublime, and such a one as the genius of our immortal bard had before his imagination, when describing the cliffs of Dover:

> " How fearful
> And dizzy 'tis, to cast one's eyes so low,
> The crows and choughs that wing the midway air,
> Show scarce so gross as beetles."
>
> SHAKESPEARE.

Upon

Upon the summit of this noble mountain, the air is, in general, even in the warmest months, chill and piercing, which indeed is not peculiar to Ben Lomond, but is felt in a like degree, on all high hills of a similar elevation; from this circumstance, snow lies on the northern side almost the whole year, and on other hills in that direction, it may be discerned in the middle of summer.

The attraction of Ben Lomond, and its great altitude, environ it almost every day in fogs and rains. Seldom, indeed, can you remain long upon the summit, without witnessing phenomena of this kind: sometimes a small cloud floating at a distance in a serene sky, and in a bright sunshine appears moving towards you, the current of air increases by degrees, as well as the apparent magnitude of the cloud, and all on a sudden, you find yourself involved in a thick mist, or perhaps a close rain, which continues a greater or lesser time, according to the dimensions of the cloud, or state of the atmosphere. It then passes on, and all is again serene and beautiful.

At other times, while on the top of the mountain, the clouds are seen to move far below you, sweeping over at one time the surface of the lake, at another winding down the vallies, and at a third, perhaps, environing Ben Lomond like a girdle, and insulating the spectator upon its top, as it were, from the world below.

Leaving this situation, after a descent of about an
hour

hour and a half in a zigzag direction, you again arrive at Rowardennan.

In order to pursue our route, it was necessary to re-cross the lake to Inveruglas. In this short voyage, Loch Lomond, and the surrounding scenery appear in many different points of view. From the want of a foreground, however, much of that beautiful effect is lost, which the contrast betwixt the objects near at hand and those more remote, when placed in another situation, never fail to present.

Proceeding from Inveruglas alongst the road to Inverary, you skirt the shores of the lake, and nearly upon the same level, opposite to you, in a short time appears a bold promontory covered with wood, and connected with the mountains upon the left, which, to appearance blocks up the passage. As you advance, and after passing a picturesque mill, and cottages upon the left, in some places overgrown with moss, and shadowed with trees, the road is perceived running up a steep ascent amongst the woods, into which you now enter. After winding through amongst the trees for sometime, you at length reach the top, or

POINT OF FIRKIN,

at the distance of 17 miles from Dumbarton. This eminence is noted for its beautiful prospect, either to the south or the opposite direction. To the south, the lake and its islands, with the hills betwixt and Renfrewshire

Renfrewshire, form the distance, they lie, as it were, near the boundary of the horizon, and consequently do not appear so distinctly separated as in the prospect from Stronehill. Upon each side of the lake are the sloping mountains, with their woody peninsulas, two of which, opposite Inveruglas, seem nearly to unite; and in the foreground, some broken rocks and trees finish the scene, which, though inferior to that from the situation just now mentioned, is still highly pleasing.

The prospect to the north, from the point of Firkin, differs much in its features from that to the south: Here the lake is seen, environed by mountains of the most picturesque outline, jagged, as it were, and broken in ten thousand shapes.

Upon the right hand, Ben Lomond washes its base in the water; its sides are covered for a great way up with copse-wood, betwixt the openings of which, are discerned here and there, a little patch of cultivated field, the labour of a few solitary beings, who live in that retired situation. In other points, there bursts forward from its surface, the most terrific precipices, crowned with wood, many of which advance into the water, like giants, threatening the opposite shore.

To the left of the view are the same chain of mountains that have accompanied us on that hand from glen Fruin; they are here, however, still
more

more broken, lofty, and picturesque, covered in some places with heath, intermixed with rocks and verdure; in other situations, particularly near their base, with wood, through which the road winds to Tarbet. In the back ground, another chain of mountains, which, as it were, hang over the place just now mentioned, retire behind each other in the most pleasing perspective.

The effect of this view, almost at all times, is grand and beautiful: We first saw it near to sunset, in the month of September; at that time the water was calm and serene, reflecting the figures of the mountains, and their various tints on its bosom; the hills to the left were in the shade, and of a warm and rich purple, gradually diminishing as they receded from the eye. A gleam of light struck through the glen that runs betwixt Tarbet and Arroquhar, and illuminated the lower parts of Ben Lomond, which, from its woods, heath, and verdure, and their different shades, appeared of the richest orange and green, contrasting finely with the hills on the opposite side. By degrees the appearance of the landscape changed: The sun sunk beneath the mountains, whose shades now became darker, and the objects on their surface more and more dim, till the whole melted into a soft, but sombre purple.

At another time we observed this scene in a storm —the effect was then still more grand: The drifting of the rain betwixt the distant mountains, the agitation of the water raised into waves, like those of the
ocean,

ocean, their lashing against the shore with unremitted noise, the sound of the wind amongst the
trees, bent by the force of the tempest, and the
grand and towering appearance of the mountains,
conspired to present a prospect, highly picturesque
and sublime.

Amongst these precipices at the base of Ben Lomond, is one, called Rob Roy's rock, from the name
of a famous free-booter, who, with his gang, took
up their residence in its vicinity, and for many years
plundered and harrassed the country far and wide,
about the beginning, and towards the middle of the
last century. This outlaw is reported at one time,
to have been the proprietor of the greatest part of
the lands on the side of Ben Lomond, called Craig-
rostan, of which he was legally dispossessed; being,
however, unwilling to leave the property, he retired
to a cave in the situation just now mentioned, with
a few followers, from whence he issued, for the purpose of plunder. Such a dread seized the people in
the country around, that to secure their property,
they often agreed to pay this horde and their successors a certain sum annually, called *black mail.*
So late as the year 1744, money under this name
was paid to M'Grigor, by the father of the present
minister of Campsie, for engaging to secure his property.

Leaving the point of Firkin, upon which we have,
perhaps, remained too long, the road winds, with a
rapid

rapid descent to the north, then ascends and so in succession continues to Tarbet. In this part of our route, you pass through several woods of oak, intermixed here and there with other trees. In some places you are completely overshadowed by the foliage, and all other objects at any distance hid; even the lake is only heard by the murmuring of its waves against the shore. But such a situation has likewise its beauties: The many ancient trees, their beautiful ramifications, the broken and moss grown fences upon the sides of the way, the foliage at a greater distance, and the plants and flowers upon the foreground, form a pleasing and a beautiful scene.

In this part of our course we likewise passed several cottages, some of which are situated in very solitary situations; they are constructed, as those at Luss, mostly with loose stones, covered with rushes, and are mostly inhabited by shepherds, who tend the flocks of the principal farmers on the adjacent mountains. You now arrive at

TARBET.

The inn of this name stands upon the right side of the road, going north, at the distance of twenty miles from Dumbarton; it is a neat modern house, when compared with those we have just now mentioned, and before Arroquhar was fitted up, as a place of accommodation for strangers, was the only one in this part of the road. Upon a pane of glass

in

in a window of this inn, are the following verses upon Ben Lomond, which, though often copied, we
cannot forbear again inserting, from their accuracy,
fidelity, and a considerable degree of beauty in the
composition. They are the production of an English gentleman, who visited the mountain and this
place upwards of 30 years ago.

Stranger, if o'er this pane of glass perchance
Thy roving eye should cast a casual glance:
If taste for grandeur, and the dread sublime,
Prompt thee BEN LOMOND's fearful height to climb:
Here gaze attentive, nor with scorn refuse,
The friendly rhyming of a tavern muse.
For thee that muse this rude inscription plann'd,
Prompted for thee her humble poet's hand.
Heed thou the poet; he thy steps shall lead,
Safe o'er yon tow'ring hills aspiring head;
Attentive then to this informing lay,
Read how he dictates, as he points the way:
Trust not at first a quick advent'rous pace,
SIX MILES its top points gradual from the base.
Up the high rise with panting haste I pass'd,
And gain'd the long laborious steep at last.
More prudent thou, when once you pass the deep,
With measur'd pace, and slow, ascend the steep.
Oft stay thy steps, oft taste the CORDIAL DROP,
And rest, oh rest, long, long, upon the top.
There hail the breezes, nor with toilsome haste,
Down the rough slope thy precious vigour waste:
So shall thy wond'ring sight at once survey,
Vales, lakes, woods, mountains, islands, rocks and sea,
Huge hills, that heap'd in crowded order stand,
Stretch'd o'er the northern and the western land;
Vast lumpy groups, while BEN, who often shrouds
His lofty summit in a veil of clouds,

High

High o'er the rest displays superior state,
In proud pre-eminence sublimely great.
One side, all awful to the astonish'd eye,
Presents a steep THREE HUNDRED FATHOMS high.
The scene tremendous, shocks the startled sense,
In all the pomp of dread magnificence:
All these and more, shalt thou transported see,
And own a faithful monitor in me.

THOMAS RUSSEL, *Oct. 3d, 1771.*

From Tarbet a road continues in a northerly direction, still alongst the border of the lake to Tyndrum. Loch Lomond, from Tarbet to its head at Stukin chapel, is very much contracted in breadth; the scenery is besides uninteresting, when compared with that we have lately passed; it exhibits, in general, a gloomy grandeur, from the immense height of the mountains, their sterility, the contraction of the glen, and the solitude which reigns every where throughout.

Instead of proceeding to Inverary from Tarbet, some prefer visiting the lakes in the western district of Perthshire, which abound with beautiful and highly varied scenery. The most direct road to these places from Tarbet, is to cross by water to Inversnaid, which lies upon the opposite shore of Loch Lomond, somewhat farther to the north. From this place, where a small garrison is kept, a road leads across the mountains, towards Stirling. After proceeding alongst it a very few miles, you turn to to the left, and fall in with Loch Catherine or Ketterin, a beautiful expanse of water, about

ten

ten miles and a half in length, by one and a half in
breadth, exhibiting the most romantic scenery that
imagination can suppose. It is formed by the river
Teath, in its passage amongst those rugged masses
called the *Trosachs*, some of which appear on its
surface, in the form of bold and rugged islands
and promontories. The scenery is uncommonly
sublime on the northern bank, where the road
from Callander is cut with great labour. Farther
on, towards the east is Loch Achray, and still farther, Loch Vennachar, all connected with each o-
ther by the Teath. From this last lake, a road proceeds to Callander, a village about ten miles farther,
from which is an excellent road to Stirling.

These lakes, as has been just now mentioned, lie in
the very bosom of the Trosachs. As some further account of the nature of the scenery may be interesting
to some, (although a digression from our subject,) I
have inserted the following short description, the production of Dr. Robertson of Callander.

" When you enter the *Trosachs*, there is such
" an assemblage of wildness and of rude gran-
" deur, as beggars all description, and fills the
" mind with the most sublime conceptions. It
" seems as if a whole mountain had been torn in
" pieces, and frittered down by a convulsion of the
" earth, and the huge fragments of rocks, and
" woods, and hills, scattered in confusion into the
" E. end and on the sides of *Loch Catherine*. The
" access to the lake is through a narrow pass of half
" a mile in length, such as *Æneas* had in his drea-

3 P 2   " ry

" ry passage to visit his father's home; *vastoque im-*
" *manis hiatu.*

" The rocks are of stupendous height, and seem
" ready to close above the traveller's head, and
" to fall down and bury him in their ruins. A
" huge column of these rocks was some years a-
" go torn with thunder, and lies in very large blocks
" near the road, which must have been a tremen-
" dous scene to passengers at that time. Where
" there is any soil, their sides are covered with a-
" ged weeping birches, which hang down their vene-
" rable locks in waving ringlets, as if to cover the
" nakedness of the rocks. The sensible horizon is
" bounded by these weeping birches on the summit
" of every hill, through which are seen the motion
" of the clouds as they shoot across behind them.

" The travellers, who wish to see all they can of
" this singular phenomenon, generally sail W. on
" the S. side of the lake, to the *rock* and *den* of the
" *ghost,* whose dark recesses, from their gloomy
" appearance, the imagination of superstition con-
" ceived to be the habitation of supernatural beings.
" In sailing, you discover many arms of the lake.
" Here, a bold head-land, where black rocks dip in
" unfathomable water; there, the white sand in the
" bottom of the bay, bleached for ages by the
" waves.

" In walking on the N. side, the road is some-
" times cut through the face of the solid rock,
" which rises upwards of 200 feet perpendicular a-
" bove the lake; sometimes the view of the lake is
" lost;

" lost; then it bursts suddenly on the eye; and a
" cluster of islands and capes appear, at different
" distances, which give them an apparent motion of
" different degrees of velocity, as the spectator rides
" along the opposite beach; at other times, his road
" is at the foot of rugged and stupendous cliffs; and
" trees are growing where no earth is to be seen.

" Every rock has its echo; every grove is vocal,
" by the melodious harmony of birds, or by the
" sweet airs of women and children gathering fil-
" berts in their season. Down the side of the op-
" posite mountain, after a shower of rain, flow a
" hundred white streams, which rush with incredi-
" ble velocity and noise into the lake, and spread
" their froth upon its surface. On one side, the
" water eagle sits in majesty undisturbed, on his
" well-known rock, in sight of his nest on the top
" of *Ben-venu*; the heron stalks among the reeds in
" search of his prey; and the sportive ducks gam-
" bol on the waters, or dive below. On the other,
" the wild goats climb, where they have scarce
" ground for the soles of their feet; and the wild
" fowls perched on trees, or on the pinnacle of a
" rock, look down with composed defiance at man.

" (In one of the defiles of the Trosachs, two or
" three of the natives met a band of Cromwell's sol-
" diers, and forced them to return, after leaving one
" of their comrades dead on the spot, whose grave
" marks the scene of action, and gives name to the
" pass. In one or other of the chasms of this sin-
" gular place, there lived, for many years, a distiller
" of

" of smuggled spirits, who eluded the most diligent
" search of the officers of the revenue, although
" they knew perfectly he was there; because a
" guide could not be bribed to discover his retreat.)
" In a word, both by land and water, there are so
" many turnings and windings, so many heights
" and hollows, so many glens, and capes, and bays,
" that one cannot advance 20 yards without having
" his prospect changed by the continual appearan-
" ces of new objects, while others are constantly re-
" tiring out of sight.

" This scene is closed by a W. view of the lake, for
" several miles, having its sides lined with alternate
" clumps of wood and arable fields, and the smoke
" rising in spiral columns through the air, from vil-
" lages which are concealed by the intervening
" woods; and the prospect is bounded by the tow-
" ering Alps of Arroquhar, which are chequered
" with snow, or hide their heads in the clouds."

Instead, therefore, of continuing from Tarbet, towards the north or Tyndrum road, which leads to
these scenes, we turned to the left at the inn, alongst
the road to Inverary, which is carried through a
glen or break in that chain of mountains we have had
so long upon our left. The highway is also shaded
with trees upon each side, and enlivened here and
there with cottages. At the distance of two miles
from Tarbet, you spy directly before you, the surface
of

LOCH

environed by lofty mountains. Before reaching the lake, we turned down a road to the left, which conducted us to the inn of Arroquhar, at the distance of twenty-two miles from Dumbarton, or thirty-seven from Glasgow.

Arroquhar, according to those conversant with the Gaelic language, derives its name from the words *ard* and *tir*, signifying a high country, terms truly descriptive of its situation, it being placed in the very bosom of the Scottish Alps. The country here originally belonged to the chief of the clan, MacFarlane, whose residence is now converted into the inn, the property having been acquired by purchase from the last proprietor of the name, by —— Ferguson, Esq; of Raith; this gentleman let the mansion house to the Duke of Argyle for a term of years, which his Grace enlarged and repaired, for the purpose of accommodating such as visit the romantic scenery of the country, or travel through it from other motives.

The situation of Arroquhar is beautiful and romantic: The mountains on every side, are in general covered with verdure, intermixed with rock and wood; the heath, which formerly abounded, being not now near so plentiful, since the more general introduction of sheep into the country. The scene is farther enlivened

livened by Loch Long, an arm of the sea, signifying, according to some, the Lake of Ships.

To a stranger unaccustomed to Highland scenery, and who has perhaps arrived at Arroquhar in
the evening, the prospect in the morning is delightful in the highest degree: The reflected rays of the sun
upon the rocky precipices of the mountains—the fine
purplish tint of their surface—the " lazy mists" hanging upon their sides—the smooth surface of the
lake, enlivened by the boats of the fishermen, and
the gentle sound produced by the tide on the shore,
aided by the fine trees surrounding the house of Arroquhar, and through which this prospect is first
seen, produce a view, very uncommon and captivating.

Amongst the many mountains in this vicinity is
one, which strikes every traveller, from the rugged
outline of its summit. It lies directly opposite to
the windows of the inn, and is called Ben Artur, or
more commonly the *Cobler*, from a rock upon its
top having some fancied resemblance to a shoemak-
er at work.

Ben Artur is the most elevated mountain in this situation, and to all appearance is an extinguished volcano, if we allow that they ever existed in Britain,
and that the common indications of a mountain having
been once a volcano are to be trusted. The crater
here is almost complete, of immense dimensions, and
bounded

bounded upon three sides by the most stupendous rocks.

The ascent of this mountain for a great way, is not attended with much difficulty—the views from it, particularly down Loch Long, are very fine—the the lake stretching like an immense river betwixt the mountains which bound its course almost to the sea from which it issues. In a short time, however, and in particular after crossing a deep valley which lies in your way, about the second stage of the hill, it becomes precipitous and rocky, and the ascent is not only attended with difficulty, but danger; very few, therefore, chuse to scale its summit, and the more especially, as Ben Lomond commands all the objects that can be seen from the top of this mountain.

In this part of the country it is said, that at one period, when Ben Artur was reckoned the highest mountain in the domain of the Campbells, the heir of that house, upon succeeding to the lands, was obliged to ascend the Cobler, and seat himself upon the highest pinnacle, in token of his having taken possession, which, if he did not perform, he lost his right, which devolved to the nearest relation, sufficiently adventrous.

Leaving Arroquhar, the road winds round the head of the lake, crossing a small river by a bridge of two arches, at the distance of one mile from the inn. To the north of this bridge is situated a district called Glen Tian, whose scenery, however, is

3 Q   inferior

inferior in point of beauty to that in the situations
we have just now left. This part of the vale of
Loch Long, and in the neighbourhood of Arroquhar,
contains a considerable number of cottages and farm
houses, the inhabitants whereof are mostly shepherds
and fishermen, living a simple, retired life, from being almost secluded, or at least at a distance from a-
ny populous part of the country.

After passing this bridge, the road strikes to the
south-west, alongst the side of the lake, which it
accompanies for two miles; it then turns to the right,
upon coming within view of Ardgarton, a seat of
———— Campbell, Esq; of Ormadale, situated on a
fine wooded plain, betwixt the mountains and the
lake, and enters the celebrated

VALE OF GLENCROE,

near the situation of a small farm house upon the
left, called Strongarton.

Glencroe is next to Glencoe, on the borders of
Inverness-shire, the most singularly romantic of all
the Highland passes. To a native of the Low country, its aspect for the first time is almost terrific.

Its entrance is guarded by two high mountains,
of the most bleak, sterile, and rugged appearance,
particularly that to the right, which we have already
mentioned, (Ben Artur). Betwixt these two, an
immense chasm yawns, into which we now entered.

ed. This glen is watered by a small river, formed by the streams which incessantly pour from the
sides of the mountains, and nearly parallel to this is
the highway carried in a very irregular line, as may
be imagined in such a situation, from the interruption of rocks and promontories, around which it
winds. This, however, is compensated by the variety
of prospects, which a more rectilinear course could
not have afforded, and which in some degree com-
pensates for the irregularity of its direction. It is
also far from being horizontal: At one time you
are carried up a steep ascent, and in a few minutes
descend, almost in a perpendicular direction.

The aspect of Glencroe is very different from the
environs of Loch Lomond, which we have lately left:
No beautiful copses or groupes of trees are here to
be seen creeping up the mountain sides. In place of
these lie thick around, immense fragments of rocks,
grey with age, and covered with moss, seemingly detached from the summits of the hills, whose
sharp and craggy points rear themselves, as it were,
to the sky. Many of these rocks have fallen into
the bed of the stream, and by being piled upon each
other, form very singular and romantic caverns,
through which the obstructed water rushes with
great force, often forming many fine cascades.

In travelling through this valley, few human habitations are to be seen; such as are in this situation appear to be very uncomfortable, being in ge-

neral

neral very low, and commonly built of stone and turf, without cement. They are mostly inhabited by shepherds, the servants of the great farmers, who, in this part of the country, rent immense tracts of land, which formerly were occupied by many families. In consequence of this engrossing of farms, Glencroe now contains but a very few inhabitants, although before this plan was adopted, it was much more populous, as the ruinous vestiges of houses, in different situations, too obviously show.

This evil is, however, in some parts of the Highlands, still increasing; and though the ill consequences of it to society, and even ultimately to the landholders themselves, are sufficiently obvious, it is still persisted in, without regard to these bad effects which such a system must bring about at length, and that in the course of no very distant period.

After traversing this valley for about three miles, during which we meet with all possible inequalities of surface, as well as change of appearance in the aspect of the rocky desert around us, the highway crosses the current just now taken notice of, and ascends, first by a gradual, then a more steep ascent, the side of the hill which seems to block or shut up the vale, in the direction in which we are proceeding. It thus continues for near a mile, till you arrive at the summit of the eminence, called, with great propriety, " Rest and be thankful," at the distance of 29 miles from Dumbarton.

At

At this situation is a seat formed, and a stone inscribed with the words just now mentioned, by the twenty-second regiment, who made this part of the road, and here in general a pause is commonly made before going farther.

Though we have thus ascended to a very great height above the level of Loch Long, we are still at the bottom of another valley, environed by mountains of rock of a most stupendous height.

This glen, which turns to the right, and alongst which the road leads, is watered by a small lake upon the left, called Loch Restal. The appearance of this place is equally, if not more striking and impressive than even Glencroe: No house is here to be met with, and neither tree nor shrub attracts the eye, all is a barren dismal waste of precipitous rocks and mountains, and every where the most gloomy silence prevails, except where the distant sound of a cataract, rushing from the mountains, or the bleating of a solitary sheep upon the hills, in some particular situations, strikes the ear.

Continuing our route through this solitude, alongst a road descending very quickly, and running parallel to a stream issuing from Loch Restal, which, about the 30th mile stone, forms a very fine cascade, we at length, at 31 miles from Dumbarton, cross the water or river of Kinlass by a bridge, turn to the left, and enter the valley of

GLEN

equally cheerless, for great part of the road, with
that we have just now left; the mountains here,
however, are not in general so precipitous, and are
more verdant, though less picturesque, than those
of Glencroe.

After travelling alongst this glen for about four
miles, in anxious expectation of the opening of some
more engaging scene, we at length caught a
glimpse through the opening of the mountains, of
Loch Fyne, seemingly at some distance, and far below the situation of the eye. By degrees as we advanced upon a descent, straggling, and at first,
stunted bushes and trees, began to be scattered a-
longst the sides of the hills—the number of these
gradually increased, forming copses and tufts—the
view continued to open, and at the 35 mile stone
we left this dreary waste.

In this situation you command a beautiful stretch
of Loch Fyne—its opposite banks—and part of the
woods and policy of Ardkinlass, the seat of Sir A-
lexander Campbell, Bart. situated betwixt you and
the lake.

Such a scene, upon emerging from these gloomy
vallies, as it were, into open space, fills the mind
with the most agreeable sensations. To enjoy it,
however, in a more perfect manner, it is requisite
to

to make a small deviation from the line of road: You ascend the hill to the right, called the Stroan of Glen Kinlas, till such time as the farm house of Stroan appears to the left, and the inn of Cairndow immediately below. In this situation, Loch Fyne is seen in all its grandeur, almost rivalling Loch Lomond, from its great extent—the fine indentations of its coasts, by the many head-lands—the mountains that bound it on either hand—the town and house of Inverary in the distance—and that of Ardkinlass, with its fine woods and venerable trees in the foreground.

From this situation you in a few minutes reach the inn of

CAIRNDOW,

35¼ miles from Dumbarton. Cairndow stands upon the east shore of Loch Fyne, in the parish of Ardkinlass, and is a neat and comfortable inn.

The house of Ardkinlass, as has been already mentioned, is situated in its immediate vicinity: This building is a large modern house, with a pavilion roof, and contains some spacious and elegant rooms. It is surrounded by a policy, containing many very fine trees, particularly upon the banks of the river Kinlas, that runs through it, with a fine broken stream. This river is crossed by a bridge within the pleasure grounds, which, with the surrounding objects,

objects, afford, in different situations, many subjects well adapted for the pencil.

Proceeding from Cairndow, we shortly fall in with the church of Ardkinlas, situated upon the right, a small building, and though to appearance of some antiquity, no way interesting. A mile farther, you arrive at the head, or northern extremity of

LOCH FYNE,

around which, after passing by a bridge, a small rivulet issuing from Glen Fyne, you turn to the left, and skirt the shores of this estuary.

Loch Fyne issues from the northern extremity of the Frith of Clyde, to the west of the island of Bute. It stretches from that point to its head, 32 miles, nearly in a north-east direction. Its breadth is various, in some places measuring 12 miles, and again in others, not more than three. Its coasts are in general flat and sandy, and contain some large and spacious bays; the mountains that environ it, at least near its northern extremity are, in general, lofty and verdant, but mostly bare of wood, excepting near the brink of the Loch; they are, however, from their form, sufficiently engaging, especially when aided with the accompaniment of the lake, its indented coast, and other objects.

Loch Fyne has, from time immemorial, been noted for its excellent herrings, which are here caught

of

of a larger size and better quality, than any where else in the British seas. They arrive annually in immense shoals, pushing up to the very head of the lake. The fishery begins generally in July, and continues to the month of January; during which time the surface of the Loch is, as it were, crowded with fishing boats, many of whom come from places at a very great distance. These boats, of whom 5 or 600 will be sometimes employed in one bay, generally return home with as many fish as yields a profit of L.50 or L.60, and even L.100 each. The quantity of fish thus caught, must consequently be very great: It is estimated by some at 20,000 barrels annually, which, at 25s. per barrel, produces the sum of L.25,000 sterling.

The extension of this fishery, however, has been greatly hindered by the heavy duties upon salt, which in this part of the country, as well as in other situations alongst the west coast, forms the subject of very general complaint; and deserves that immediate attention and redress, which it is hoped the legislature will ere long give; convinced as it must be, of the great national advantages accruing from these fisheries, by enriching the empire, and in particular, this district of the west Highlands, and thereby preventing a diminution of the population by emigration: While, at the same time, by taking off this restriction, they further contribute to our safety and protection, by rearing up a race of hardy, intelligent, and enterprising seamen, who

3 R
have

have long been regarded as the bulwark of the British islands.

In proceeding from the bridge at the head of the loch,. the road is carried generally in a level direction, and in many places upon the brink of the lake. Many neat and pleasantly situated houses now begin to appear upon the right, while you, at another time, are carried through vistas of natural wood; then the road is open, and so on alternately, till you approach a venerable looking house, with castlelated turrets, and surrounded with lofty trees, situated, upon a peninsula, jutting out into the water, called Dundurraw, the property of Sir Alexander Campbell, Bart.

The name of this house is said to signify the fort of the two oars; alluding, as some conjecture, to its situation upon the lake; or from a pair of oars, which may have been erected as a trophy near it. It is a place of considerable antiquity, though the present building is of no older a date than 1596—that year being marked above the gate. In the same situation there is the following inscription, which has already, however, been several times copied:

MAN BEHALD THE END BE NOCHT,
VISER NOR THE HIESTES HOIP IN GOD.

Dundurraw is distant 41 miles from Dumbarton. After leaving this place, we still continued through a pleasant road, alongst the shores of the loch, in

anxious

anxious expectation of obtaining, at every turn, a
view of one of the principal objects of our journey,
the castle and scenery of Inverary: After being
disappointed thus once or twice, we at length obtained our wish, near the 43 mile stone. In this
situation, the road ascends a gentle eminence, turns
suddenly to the right, around the base of a steep
hill, and all at once, there opens up one of the most
beautiful scenes in the island.

The lake here spreads out to the north, into the
form of a deep semi-circular bay, upon the opposite side of which, and situated on a beautiful lawn,
besprinkled with fine trees, appears the Castle of
Inverary, with its circular towers, giving dignity and
an air of majesty to the scenery around. A little
to the right, and somewhat farther on, is the conical hill of Dunicoich, covered with wood, and rising
from the plain. Towards the left appears the town
of Inverary, with its spire, and neat looking houses,
and in the distance, beyond all these objects, a range
of broken mountains, betwixt and the western
coast.

Though this view never fails to arrest the attention of the stranger, from the beauty and grandeur
of its composition, there are yet other situations in
which these different objects still appeared, at least
in our opinion, to greater advantage. One of
these points of view is situated about a mile farther
to the north, beyond the head of the bay, where the
river Shira enters it, and upon the declivity of the

3 R 2   hill.

hill. In this situation the prospect is inimitably grand and beautiful: The principal object is here, Loch Fyne, which stretches out to the horizon, bounded by mountains of every gradation of tint, according to their distance; upon the right of the lake, a plain stretches to the base of the hills, which, as it were, retire in the opposite direction, and on this plain stands the castle, and farther on, alongst the lake, is the town of Inverary, upon a projecting point of land.

The hill of Dunicoich is situated more to the right than the castle, part of which its trees hide from the eye, but in such a manner, as rather to add to than impair the effect. This singular hill has its outline and surface here better broken than in the former situation: It loses the formal appearance of a cone, divides itself into two stages, and stretches its irregular summit towards the north. A beautiful bridge at the head of the bay, across the Shira, forms one of the finest objects in the foreground, and, with the broken surface, covered with trees and brush-wood, amongst which you now stand, and which relieve every formal or continued line, altogether constitute a view of the very first class.

Descending from this point, which is situated in what is called the Deer-park, we crossed the bridge just now mentioned, and entered shortly a vista, formed by some fine trees—then approached nearer the lake and the castle—crossed another bridge over the

the Aray, a river which waters the pleasure grounds
—left the castle upon the right—approached, and
in a few minutes arrived at the town of

INVERARY,

where we proposed to make a short stay; the inn
here is large and spacious, and the accommodations
in general good.

This town is, though small, well built, and some
of the houses, particularly the inn, in a style even
approaching to elegance; they are covered with
slate, and some of them white-washed, which adds
very much to their agreeable appearance. It consists principally of one street, running towards the
south, and contains about 1100 inhabitants.

Not far from the centre of the town is a monument with an inscription, mentioning, that nearly in
that situation, 17 gentlemen of the name of Campbell were barbarously massacred at one time, by a
neighbouring clan, in consequence of a writ of *fire*
and *sword*, issued by government against the Campbells. The cause of this order was attributed to
the unfortunate Earl of Argyle's having been concerned in the Duke of Monmouth's rebellion, in
1685.

The principal public buildings are the town-
house and the church, the former of which also contains the jail, is immediately in the vicinity of the
inn,

inn, and consists of three stories of ashler work; here the county courts are held, and the assizes kept. The latter edifice is but lately erected; it also is a handsome building, erected of a reddish stone, extremely hard and durable. This house is divided into two places of worship, in one of which it is performed (it is believed) in English, and in the other, in the Gaelic language, for the accommodation of such part of the inhabitants as do not understand the language of the low country. This church is crowned with a neat spire, which contributes to enliven, in some degree, the surrounding scenery.

The old town of Inverary stood rather in a different situation, being built on the lawn before the front of the castle, whose appearance was thereby very much injured. The present town was an erection of the present Duke of Argyle, to whom it principally belongs.

Inverary is a place of some antiquity, though prior to the beginning of the 14th century, about which time the family of Argyle fixed their residence here, it is most likely that it consisted of a few huts, inhabited by fishermen, who subsisted upon the produce of the lake. After that period, under the benign influence of this potent family, it appears to have increased; the inhabitants exerted themselves in the fishery, and gradually brought merchants to their

their doors, who, particularly the French *, exchanged wines for their herrings. Thus it gradually came more and more into notice, and about the year 1648, when it was erected into a royal burgh by Charles the I. came to be considered as the capital of Argyleshire, and where the Courts of Justice were and are still held, and the principal business of the country transacted.

Inverary carries on a small coasting trade, but it is believed, has no vessels at present of any considerable burden. The manufacture of linens is here carried on, and in 1776, a manufacture of woollens, upon a large scale, was attempted, under the protection of the present Duke, by whom the works were erected· it, however, did not meet with success, or rather, the business was not carried on with that advantage which was expected at its commencement.

The manufacture of iron from the ore, is carried on in the neighbourhood of the town, somewhat farther down the lake to a considerable extent. These works were first erected in the year 1754, by an English company, who were, it is believed, induced to settle here by the plenty and cheapness of charcoal, produced from the timber of the adjoining woods.

But the chief dependence of the inhabitants of Inverary,

* A point of land here is still called the Frenchman's point.

verary, is still upon the fishery‡ of the herrings,
which, as has been already mentioned, annually visit the Loch in immense shoals; and from which, if
unrestricted by the excise duties upon salt, and
vigorously prosecuted, a certain and lasting source
of wealth must undoubtedly be derived.

In order to visit the Castle of Inverary, it is requisite first to leave the names of the party at the
inn, which are transmitted to the castle, and an answer mentioning a time, very politely returned. In
walking thither, you cross the park through a path
leading in a serpentine direction to the house, passing many beautiful and lofty trees, which are disposed, not in regular lines and stiff vistas, but disposed
in the most natural and agreeable manner.

The castle itself, is a large square building of the
Gothic style of architecture, flanked with circular
towers, and crowned, as it were, with a square embattled pavilion, rising from the middle. It consists
of three stories, one whereof is partly below the level of the park. It is built of a dark greyish stone,
finely harmonizing with the surrounding scenery,
and which is brought from the opposite banks of the
lake.

The

‡ That this has all along been their principal dependence, appears from the arms of the burgh, representing
a net with a herring, and this motto. *Semper tibi pendeat halec.*
Inverary is governed by a provost, two baillies, and a council,
nominated by the Duke.

The principal entrance into this noble mansion is from the west, when ascending a flight of stairs, you are conducted into a spacious and lofty saloon, hung round with arms and armour, disposed in a great variety of figures. This saloon is also furnished with a gallery and an organ, and otherwise ornamented with great taste. From it branch the different apartments, which are by far too numerous to be particularized. Many of these are spacious and elegant in the highest degree. In particular, the great drawing-room may be mentioned, it is hung around with beautiful tapestry, and otherwise ornamented in the newest and most superb manner.

The number of pictures are, however, not considerable, though such as are here, are the production of very able masters. They are mostly portraits of members of the family, or their relations; amongst the best, may be reckoned that of the Duke of Hamilton, by Battoni, the late Duke of Argyle and the present Lord Frederick Campbell, very spirited portraits by Gainsborough. Amongst the old portraits, those most worthy of notice, appear to be the unfortunate Marquis of Argyle and his son, who both perished on the scaffold, in consequence of sentences which will leave a lasting stain upon the memory of those who inflicted them.

There are none of the old landscapes very remarkable for excellence; here are, however, some by

3 S   Nasmyth

Nasmyth and Williams, highly creditable to the taste of these artists. Amongst those by the former gentleman, we noticed a view of Inverary from Loch Fyne, very warm and rich; another view by the same master of a waterfall, at no great distance from Inverary, a scene very picturesque and beautiful. The landscapes by Williams, are in the Duke's sitting room. One represents another view of the castle and scenery adjacent, and a second, a rural scene somewhere in the neighbourhood, both executed with a breadth of light and shade, and a warm and sweet effect, for which the productions of Mr. Williams are so much valued. There are also a number of other drawings, particularly by De Croc, and a great collection of very fine prints, in many of the rooms throughout the house.

After having seen the castle, we walked through the park, which is crossed by the river Arey. Amongst the most conspicuous objects here, are the elegant bridge over that river, within the pleasure grounds, and the insulated hill of Dunicoich, which, in coming from the inn, appears directly behind the castle, and above which it seems to rise in an almost perpendicular direction.

The height of this hill is about 750 feet, it is mostly covered with wood, except upon its summit, where is erected a small square tower, noted for its extensive prospect. From this situation, a beautiful panorama spreads before the eye: Below, when looking to the south, is the castle, and part of the

pleasure

pleasure grounds adjacent; the town of Inverary, Loch Fyne, and its surrounding mountains, and many other objects, which united, form a prospect, highly gratifying, but upon too broad a scale, and in too high a situation, to be reckoned e-qually picturesque with the views we have lately noticed. Nearer to the base of these hills, however, the view, though not so extensive, is more engaging, and in many different situations in the park, the prospects are fine and varied.

Amongst the other interesting scenes in the environs of Inverary, must be reckoned those around the Dubh Loch, so called, from the darkness of its bottom, or the depth of the water. It lies at the bottom of a very picturesque glen, called Glen Shiray, and communicates with Loch Fyne by a small river, the Shiray, of about a quarter of a mile in length. This lake is stored with excellent fish, and it is no uncommon circumstance, even for herrings, sometimes, to be caught in the same net with fresh water fish—the waters of the sea in high tides, often reaching to Loch Dubh, and carrying their fish into the lake. In Glen Shiray are, likewise, the Duke of Argyle's drying barns, which have been found very useful for drying grain after reaping, in the time of unsettled weather.

Essachosen, a romantic vale, about two miles distant from Inverary, and to which the road leads from the neighbourhood of the inn, through a long and dark avenue of aged elms, is also worthy of at-

3 S 2   tention:

tention: At its upper extremity is a fine cascade, surrounded by hills, covered with wood, and broken here and there by rocks and verdure.

The bridge of Douglas, upon the small river of that name, entering the lake about three miles below the town, may also be reckoned amongst the objects deserving of notice. It lies up the river, near the situation of the woollen manufactory of Clunery, is said to be of Roman structure, and is very picturesque, from its form, and the pendant weeds, foliage and ivy, which enrich it. Scenes of the same kind may likewise be found, by tracing the river Arey, upwards from the park: The first you meet with is Carlonan linn, a fall of the river just now mentioned, in the neighbourhood of a mill, and surrounded by woods; still farther is a second fall, at the distance of about $2\frac{1}{2}$ miles from the town; the most beautiful is, however, more than half a mile higher up the stream—it is called Lenach Gluthin.

Here the river rushes down a precipice, broken by fragments of rocks, with a considerable noise, and dashing with fury, from one to the other. Immediately above this fall, is a rude wooden bridge, which, together with the surrounding rocks and trees, form a simple, but highly pleasing view.

Inverary, at least its vicinity, is much indebted for the beauty of its scenery, to the good taste of the late and present Dukes; particularly since the year 1745, when the castle was begun, immense sums,

sums, to the amount of L 250,000 it is said, having
been expended in planting, improving, making roads,
and other works of utility and decoration. Still
these improvements are by no means at a stand, the
present Duke expending annually in this way, upwards of L.3000 sterling.

In the summer season, the fine scenery of Inverary is much enlivened by the vast number of small
vessels which come to Loch Fyne, on the herring
fishery. These, and their different operations, gratify the curiosity of a stranger, in no small degree,
while they add life and motion to the landscape.
The night is the time devoted for fishing:—during
the day they lie at anchor, and in the evening again
begin the fishery. These boats, at this time, form
a line almost across the loch, and uniting their nets,
produce a chain of perhaps a hundred or even more
fathoms long.

The herrings swim at very uncertain depths, so
that it is necessary to sink their nets, or raise them
accordingly: To ascertain the exact situation of the
shoal, with respect to depth, requires much experience, as well as a considerable acuteness of observation, for it will frequently happen that the nets of
one boat, which is properly managed, will be full of
herrings, while those of the others have caught nothing. The nets are kept up by buoys, consisting
of blown bladders, or bags of leather, fastened to
the ropes at certain distances, and are, previously to
their being used, soaked a considerable time in a
decoction

decoction of oak bark, which tends much to preserve them from putrefaction.

Having seen the principal scenes at Inverary, we left it on our return to the low country, retracing the road back the length of Arroquhar *, and having consequently a reversed prospect of the objects, which we before saw in another direction.

After spending some time at Arroquhar, we left the road which leads to Loch Lomond and which we had formerly journeyed, and took that which runs to the south, alongst the east side of Loch Long.

Proceeding in this direction, you pass upon the left, the church and manse of Arroquhar, sweetly situated upon the side of the lake, and shortly thereafter, the road enters a woody tract of land, sometimes leading alongst the summit of high precipices, hanging over the water; and at other times, retreating at a greater distance; thus it continues for near seven miles, till you reach a few houses called Finart. The highway then bends to the left, while it ascends a steep hill, from the summit of which, the prospect

* Some, instead of returning the same road to Arroquhar, cross Loch Fyne to St. Catherine's inn—thence proceed through Hellsgate to Loch Goyle head—coast alongst that lake to its mouth—take a boat there, and ferry over Loch Long, to Portincaple, and so proceed by way of the Gair Loch, to Ardiscaple, Dumbarton, &c.

prospect is open and extensive, commanding the stretch of road you have passed—Loch Long, and the mountains upon the opposite side, (with some straggling cottages, corn-fields, and wood near their base) called Argyle's Bowling-green, of the most irregular and grotesque outline.

The road continues still to ascend, but less so than formerly. At the distance of 8½ miles from Arroquhar, Loch Goyle begins to open upon the eye, branching from Loch Long, amongst the mountains towards the north-west. By deviating a little from the highway towards the right, a fine prospect of this arm of the sea is obtained, with Castle Carrick near its opening upon the south, and the houses of Portincaple on the side of Loch Long, in the foreground.

Castle Carrick appears here most romantically situated, surrounded by mountains, and shut out as it were, from a communication with the rest of the world. This castle is of great antiquity. According to tradition, it is said to have been built by the Danes, and in after periods was used by some of the Scottish monarchs as a hunting-seat. Its dimensions are very considerable, and its walls upwards of seven feet thick. Of this castle, nothing of which now remains but the walls, the family of Argyle are heritable keepers.

Attaining the high road, you shortly arrive at the greatest height of its elevation, near the 9th mile

stone,

stone, and immediately thereafter, a soft and beautiful prospect opens to the south upon the eye, consisting of the Gair Loch, another arm of the sea, issuing from the Frith of Clyde, with the mountains
upon each side—the distant castle of Roseneath—
and the hills of Renfrewshire in the distance.

You now arrive at the borders of the Low country, and leave the Highlands, with all their grand
and romantic scenes;—scenes, which in point of su-
blimity and grandeur, can scarcely be any where
surpassed—whether we consider their particular
parts, or the effect of the whole, when combined.

The road then begins to descend: For some distance
before you arrive at this point, it has run through a
barren tract, mostly covered with heath, and destitute
of trees. The aspect around you in this situation,
however, becomes somewhat more agreeable: Cottages, trees, and farms, enliven the prospect, and
proclaim our approach to a better cultivated country. In this part of the ride, the Gair Loch appears in many fine points of view, particularly
when seen through the trees, near its head or northern extremity. A road here strikes down its
western bank to Roseneath, a parish lying in a
peninsula, betwixt this lake and Loch Long; that
which we followed, turns more to the left, skirting the eastern shores of

LOCH GAIR.

This lake communicates with, or rather branches

es from the Clyde, in a north westerly direction; its length is about six miles; its breadth very various, from near one mile to not above the eighth of that space; it abounds with excellent fish, such as mackarel, salmon, cod, whitings, herrings, &c. which are often caught in great plenty.

At somewhat more than ten miles from Arroquhar, we passed upon the left, Faslane, a pleasantly situated seat of Sir James Colquhoun, and nearly in the same situation, the ruins of an old church or chapel, rendered particularly engaging, from its accompaniments of brushwood and trees, many of which grow from the moss-covered walls, and others arise even in the very centre of the building; when this was founded, or by whom, we could not learn.

Continuing upon the banks of the lake, the country still improves: The rough hills begin to soften off into gentle declivities, and are, in many places, covered with wood and corn-fields; the scenery upon the opposite bank of the loch, appears also rural and pleasing, consisting of many neat houses, surrounded with trees and plantations, before which a level lawn, in general well cultivated, stretches to the lake.

In a short time, you pass upon the left, a picturesque mill and cottages, and immediately thereafter, Ardenconnel, the seat of Andrew Buchanan, Esq; situated on the sloping side of the hill, in a

3 T ! very

very commanding situation; almost immediately below, is the church of Row, surrounded by trees.

At this place the lake is very much contracted, by a peninsula upon the east, so that its breadth appears quite inconsiderable; owing to this, a very strict current sets southward at the tide of ebb, which causes the water, in some places, to assume a boiling and threatening appearance.

About one mile farther, skirting alongst a pleasant bay, decorated with wood upon the left, and having a beautiful view of the castle of Roseneath and its plantations, directly before you, you arrive at the inn of Ardincaple, at the distance of about 15 miles from Arroquhar, and 9½ from Dumbarton.

From the neighbourhood of this place, we crossed over Loch Gair to Roseneath, a seat of the Duke of Argyle. At this time, great part of it had been destroyed by a recent fire which broke out accidentally on the 30th of May, 1802, about six in the evening, and in the course of seven hours, entirely consumed the principal part of the edifice. The damage sustained was estimated at L. 18,000 sterling. It appeared, therefore, in a state of ruin, but even in this situation, it was majestic and engaging, from its dimensions—its lofty and embattled towers—its broken arches and windows, contrasted with the many fine trees around; time was only wanting, to cover with its mosses and shrubs, the walls and crevices, to vary the tints, and harmonize the whole,

to

to render it one of the finest and most picturesque ruins.

Since that period, however, the whole has been removed, in order to make way for a castle, upon a more modern plan. This is at present erecting from an elegant design by Mr. Bonomis of London, an architect of great eminence.

This palace, for so it may be called, was founded in March, 1803, and is now the height of one storey from the basement. It is of the Grecian style of architecture, of the Ionic order. It lies in an east and west direction, presenting a front to the south of 189 feet; its depth is 80. From the south and north fronts project three porticoes: those in the middle are semi-circular, and very magnificent; the others square, and constructed in a chaste, but elegant style. This building is also to have a highly ornamented cupola, and other decorations suited to the grandeur of the design.

Its situation is finely chosen with respect to prospect, a very delightful one lying on every hand. The scite for the building was fixed by Mr. Nasmyth of Edinburgh, whom we already have had occasion to mention as an eminent landscape painter. The same gentleman was employed to give a design for a court of farm offices, which has been carried into execution: These are crowned by a lofty prospect tower, which rises from the centre to the height of 90 feet, and commands an extensive range

of

of view; they extend 280 feet, and are designed and constructed with that fine taste, which Mr. Nasmyth has been so long known to possess.

The pleasure grounds around are much varied in their surface, swelling into hills in one situation, and in another, stretching into a plain. A great number of trees are every where interspersed, which, together with the adjacent lake, the village of Roseneath, its church, and the other objects, render it a spot highly pleasing and beautiful.

Amongst the objects pointed out here, is a rock, 34 feet in height, called Wallace Leap, from the top of which, it is said, that patriot leaped upon horseback to the plain below, at a time when he had no other resource than either by making this desperate attempt, or falling into the hands of his enemies— he escaped unhurt, tradition says, but his horse was killed.

A short ride from Ardincaple inn, now conducts you, after passing upon the left Ardincaple house, the property, like Roseneath, of the Duke of Argyle, and leaving the entrance into the Gair Loch to

HELENSBURGH.

Helensburgh stands upon the north shore of the Clyde, which here is expanded into a great breadth.

It

It is a modern village, well built, and rapidly increasing in size and population. It is much frequented during the summer season, by the citizens of Glasgow and their families, for the purpose of bathing, and enjoying the free air of the country *.

From this place you cross the Clyde, by a ferry, which conducts you to Greenock, a town of great commercial eminence; as such, and from its consequent importance, requiring a more particular description than those places we have already passed.

GREENOCK.

* From Helensburgh an excellent road leads alongst the shore eastward to Dumbarton, which is distant eight miles, passing in its course, a number of seats, plantations, and villas, and on the right, the river, enlivened by the numerous sails that continually skim its surface, and the opposite coast of Renfrewshire. Upon the left, the principal places are Drumfork, the seat of ——— Laird, Esq; Cambus Erskine, ——— Denniston, Esq; Keppoch, ——— Ewing, Esq; Lileston, ——— Donald, Esq; On the right, the hill of Ardmore, stretching into the river in a peninsular form, Captain Noble; farther on, Ardarden, belonging to the same gentleman; then upon the left, Gileston, ——— Lennox, Esq. At six miles from Dumbarton, you pass the church of Cardross, and upon the same side, or the north, Ardoch, a seat of Robert Graham, Esq; of Gartmore. Farther on upon the left, some trees distinguish the spot where formerly stood a seat of Robert the Bruce, in which he died. At a short distance beyond this point is Dumbarton.

GREENOCK †.

Greenock is situated at the north west corner of the county of Renfrew, at the distance of 22 miles from Glasgow, and upon the west side of the united bays of Greenock and Crawfordsdyke, anciently called the bay of St. Lawrence.

The town principally lies betwixt the base of a chain of hills, which run parallel to the Clyde, and that river, which is its northern boundary, and extends in a direction from east to west, alongst the coast.

As late as the beginning of the last century, Greenock consisted only of a few mean houses covered with thatch, and inhabited mostly by fishermen, without any harbour, or even trade of any consequence. At this time, and even for many years thereafter, it had no existence as a separate parish, being included in the united parishes of Houstoun and Innerkip.

In the year 1636, from its increased population, and an application of the proprietors, the town and the neighbouring district, was erected into a separate

† The name of this town is said to be derived from the Gaelic *Grianeg*, signifying, according to etymologists in that language, the *Bay of the Sun*.

rate parish, which again, in the year 1745, was divided into two, called the Old and New parishes of Greenock. In the year 1757, the town was erected into a burgh of barony by Sir John Shaw, the superior. At this period, the population of the two parishes, including the country district, did not amount to more than 3,900 inhabitants.

From the year 1760, the town began to increase rapidly in size and population; and so continued till the breaking out of the war with America; a circumstance that almost entirely ruined the trade of Greenock. It, however, began gradually to revive, and the town to enlarge, though slowly, till the termination of the contest with the colonies; when commerce was again carried on with spirit.

In 1792, so much had it increased in population, that by an accurate account taken up of the number of inhabitants, it was found they amounted to 14,299, in both parishes; exclusive of those on board coasting vessels.

The increase of Greenock has however, since been still more rapid, insomuch, that it appears, from the report lately made to government, it contains at present, upwards of 20,000 souls; and these, as well as the size of the town itself, from the flourishing state of its commerce, are still increasing.

The town of Greenock is governed by two magistrates

gistrates or baillies, a treasurer, and six counsellors.
In the election, every feuar and sub-feuar, by the
charter of erection, is entitled to vote; so that they
are very numerous. One magistrate goes out of office every second year, and the treasurer and three
counsellors annually; while others are at the same
time elected to supply their place. In the election
of a magistrate, the feuars are not restricted to a
member of the council, but may nominate any of
their own number they think proper. A town clerk
is also appointed by the magistrates and council, for
managing such business as falls within his province.

The town, as has been lately mentioned, lies upon the south side of the river Clyde, and, together
with the village of Crawfordsdyke, with which it is
now connected, stretches alongst the river, upwards
of a mile. Its breadth may be about one eighth of
that space *.

.The

* By act of Parliament obtained in 1801, the limits of the
town are exactly defined, " extending from Crawfordsdyke
burn on the east, to Jerdan's burn on the west; and 2000
yards in breadth, from the low water mark southward, reserving therefrom the mansion house, garden, and policy of the e-
state of Greenock." The mansion house of Greenock, as it is
called, is situated upon a high bank, immediately south of the
town, and in a very commanding situation; it was formerly the
residence of the family of Shaw Stewart, the proprietors of the
estate or barony of Greenock. At present they are still su-
periors of the town.

The principal street, running the whole length of the town, has its direction from east to west; smaller streets run parallel to this; these again are intersected at right angles by others.

The street just now mentioned is in general well built: in some parts of its course the houses are elegant, and demonstrative of much good taste; but more particularly is this the case at its eastern and western extremities. In the middle of its course, it spreads out into a square, which is reckoned the centre or cross of the town, and from this square runs a street down towards the north, being the principal avenue to the harbour, or one of the quays, called the mid-quay.

The new streets to the west, are composed of modern houses, many of them in the first style of of architectural beauty—these streets are spacious and airy, and are mostly inhabited by the more wealthy part of the community.

Greenock owes much for its improvements to the public-spirited gentlemen, who have been from time to time in the magistracy, particularly of late years. During their administration, they procured a bill to be brought into parliament, for paving the streets—for bringing in water to the town—for enlarging the harbour—and for other beneficial purposes. In consequence of this, the streets are now well paved, a foot pavement of cut stone is laid upon the sides; they are likewise well lighted, kept free from ob-

3 U

structions

structions and nuisances, and regularly swept once a day; so that a new and agreeable appearance is given to the town, and the health, safety, and comfort of the inhabitants thereby better secured.

In speaking of these improvements, it would be injustice not to mention the name of Hugh Crawford, Esq; the present chief magistrate, a gentleman who has done much to promote them, to whose good taste and exertion Greenock owes much, and to whose politeness the writer of these sheets is indebted for many of the facts stated in this short account of that thriving sea-port.

With respect to public buildings: Greenock has two churches upon the establishment of the church of Scotland. The new church stands in the centre of the town, upon the south side of the square, looking down toward the harbour. It is a large and stately building, of cut stone, with a portico, supported by a range of columns, to which you ascend by a flight of steps; it has also a neat spire, of a considerable height, with a clock and dial plate. This church was built in the year 1759.

The old or first church is also a large building, though in point of architecture, inferior to that just now mentioned. Besides these, there is another, called the chapel of ease, erected about thirty years ago; and a large, elegant, and commodious church or chapel, in which the service is per-

formed

formed in Gaelic, for the benefit of such of the inhabitants as are Highlanders, and who are partial to their native tongue. To these may be added, two burgher, and one antiburgher meeting houses, making in whole, seven churches or places of worship, within the town or suburbs.

The town-house of Greenock stands upon the south side of the principal street, to the west of the cross or the square, lately mentioned. It is appropriated by the magistrates and council for the discussion of public business, and is also, for the accommodation of the merchants, used as a newsroom and change; in adjoining apartments are the offices for the town clerk, a coffee-room, guardhouse, and prison; in another situation are the public markets, in point of appearance, however, no way remarkable.

But the finest public building, is undoubtedly (next to the church) the new inn or tontine. This elegant house stands upon the north side of Cathcart street, and to the east of the cross; it is of ashler work, and in its architecture, very chaste and beautiful. It was founded about two years ago, and is expected, when finished, to equal, in point of accommodation, any other in this part of the kingdom. In order to carry it into execution, a subscription was set on foot, on the principle of a tontine, and in two days it was filled, to the amount of L. 10,000 sterling.

3 U 2   A

A bridewell and work-house, for which the town have an act of parliament, is also intended to be immediately built. A coffee-room, and ball or assembly room are also expected soon to be erected; at least they are in contemplation, designs having been already made out for the purpose.

A very considerable sum was a short time ago subscribed, for the erection of a theatre, upon an extensive and elegant plan, but from some misunderstanding, the design is, at least for the present, given up.

From the great increase of the town of late years, and the demand for houses, many new streets and buildings have been projected. That situation which appears, however, to have the preference, is a tract of land, called the Minister's Glebe. This, by an act of parliament, obtained in 1801, was feued out for this purpose *, at no less than an average annual rent of L.100 sterling per acre. Several new and spacious streets have been traced, and buildings already erected, which, together with the restriction put upon the feuars, with respect to the value of the houses which they shall place in that situation, promise, when completed, to render this part of
the

* By obtaining this liberty to feu, the minister has now, from a stipend of L.200 or less, acquired one of L.700 annually, and has consequently, the richest charge of any clergyman in Scotland.

the town, at once elegant, healthful, and convenient.

In other parts of Greenock, the price of property is now very high, the surest criterion of an increasing trade. In centrical situations, areas have
sold from L.3 to L.4 per square yard, and in places
somewhat more remote, it has been feued at different prices, from L.200 to the rate of L.3,500 per
acre, besides a perpetuity annually of L.24 sterling.

The origin of this town and its persent prosperity, has arisen from its situation upon the coast, and
its excellent road and harbour—respecting which,
it may not be improper to say a few words.

The river, or Frith of Clyde, runs in a direction
near W. N. W. and E. S. E. in that place on
which the town and harbour of Greenock are situated; but about four miles to the W. it bends to
the S. and becomes nearly due S. and N. The
breadth of the river here is four miles—it gradually
narrows towards the east, and at Port Glasgow,
is not above two miles in breadth.

In the river, from the situation of Dumbarton, to
a little below the town, a sand-bank runs along, having, however, channels across it, these divide it
into two great divisions; the one opposite Port-Glasgow is called the Cockle-bank, and the other opposite Greenock, called Greenock-bank, both of which
are dry at low water spring tides.

By

By these banks, two channels are formed in the river, the one to the north, through which the flowing tide, from the particular direction of the river runs, and the other to the south, through which the tide of ebb makes its way, and by whose force, aided by the current of the river, which moves in this direction, the channel upon this side is always kept deep and navigable. These banks, besides keeping the channel deep, by confining the ebbs and currents just now mentioned into a narrow compass, serve essentially in breaking the force of the waves, insomuch, that there is here never any heavy swell of sea, which materially affects the harbour; so that for the greatest part of the year, vessels can load and discharge their cargoes outside of the piers.

Previous to the commencement of last century, the inhabitants of Greenock were without any proper harbour. About that period, however, they petitioned the Scotch parliament for a fund to build one; but for some reason which does not appear, this application was refused.

Sometime afterwards they entered into a contract with the lord of the manor for this purpose; in consequence of which, the harbour was begun in 1707. The expences amounted to upwards of 100,000 merks Scots; in order to defray which, a voluntary assessment of 1s. 4d. was laid on each sack of malt brewed within the limits of the town, but this proving inadequate to the debt incurred, so far alarmed the

the inhabitants, that they resigned the harbour and assessments into the hands of Sir John Shaw.

After the Union, the trade of the port increased so rapidly, that in the year 1740, the whole debt was extinguished, and there remained a surplus of 27,000 merks; the foundation of the town's funds. From the great increase of shipping after this period, application was made to parliament in 1768, for liberty to extend the harbour *, and for other purposes, and in consequence of an act, an addition was made to it, by building what was called the new quay; which rendered it still more extensive and commodious than formerly.

The trade of the port still advancing, and likely still further to increase, another act of parliament was obtained in 1801, for enlarging the old harbour, and building new piers, quays, &c. on any part of the shore, from a place called the Deling burn on the east, to the White Farland point on the west.

In 1803, application was again made to the legislature, and an act obtained enlarging the powers of the former act, and impowering the trustees to embank the shore ground, to build warehouses thereon, and a dry dock, for the graving and repairing of vessels, within the limits of the new harbour.

The

* This harbour is situated between two circular quays, with a tongue or mid quay, inclosing a space of near ten acres.

The trustees, in consequence of these acts, employed an eminent engineer, Mr. Rennie, to make surveys, and give in an estimate of the expence, of making new harbours and enlarging the old. Mr. Rennie accordingly gave in his report, relative to the mode and expence of carrying these works into execution.

In this report, he states the expence of the works for the new harbour, at L.35,392. For enlarging the east quay of the present harbour, and what is called the new quay, L.8,444, and for the western quay, L.14,731, making in all, L51,567.

In the same report he estimates the expence of the proposed tide harbour at the Bay of Quick, with wet docks upon each side, capable of containing 120 square rigged vessels, and for a bason, dry docks, and ground for ship building, at L.121,975, making in whole, the expence of the alterations and improvements upon the port, the sum of L.173,542 sterling.

That these improvements might be carried into execution, the trustees or commissioners appointed by the act of parliament, were authorised to borrow money, upon the rates or duties to be levied from the vessels entering the harbour, a sum not exceeding at any one time, L.50,000 sterling.

Having thus obtained the requisite authority, and removed such obstacles as lay in the way, there remain

main now few circumstances to prevent the necessary operations from being begun. These, when carried into effect, will render Greenock one of the completest harbours in the united kingdom; and of a consequence, when joined with the other advantages of situation, must tend to its farther advancement, wealth and population.

With respect to the trade of Greenock, the herring fishery seems first to have occupied the attention of the inhabitants. A society of fishers was established towards the end of the last century. The merchants of Glasgow first, and afterwards the merchants here, were the exporters of this produce: They received in exchange, timber from the Baltic, and from France, Spain, and other parts of Europe, the respective productions of these countries.

Commerce continuing to increase, in 1714 a custom-house was established here as a branch of that of Port-Glasgow. From this time an extensive trade was carried on from Greenock by the merchants of Glasgow, particularly to America, until the unhappy contest with that country gave a severe shock to the commerce of this port; and it was not till after peace was concluded that it began to revive: Since then it has yearly increased, and of late years in an almost unprecedented manner. Indeed there is every reason to think, that Greenock will become the chief port for the produce of the West Indies, destined for the Baltic and the north of Europe,

3 X

rope, as it lies in the vicinity of the Forth and Clyde canal, which opens a ready communication with the German ocean, and therefore has much the advantage of Liverpool, whose situation for traffic to the continent is by no means so favourable.

That a better idea may be formed of the extent of the commerce of Greenock, at the present and former periods; we have presented the following account from the custom-house, with which we have been favoured through the politeness of Hugh Crawford, Esq.

This account contains the total number of ships and vessels, with their tonnage, which entered inwards and cleared outwards from Greenock, to and from foreign ports, in the years 1773, 1776, 1783, 1789, 1800, 1801, and 1802, including their repeated voyages.

Years.	Employed in Foreign Trade.		Employed in Coasting Trade.		Total.	
	Ships.	Tons.	Ships.	Tons.	Ships.	Tons.
1773	604	44,148	651	21,715	1255	65,863
1776	413	30,963	825	30,765	1238	61,728
1783	377	26,114	661	19,849	1038	45,963
1789	595	60,755	832	36,125	1427	96,880
1800	659	80,393	2021	95,158	2680	175,551
1801	735	103,069	2134	108,843	2869	211,912
1802	882	111,717	2006	88,032	2888	199,749

A source of considerable wealth to the merchants in Greenock, arises from the prosecution of the fisheries, which, as has been already mentioned, have been long, in a greater or lesser degree attended to.
The

The herring fishery, in particular, is often prosecuted with great success; for its encouragement there is a bounty of 30s. per ton; on this bounty, in the year 1791, there were cleared at the custom-house, Greenock, and out-ports, 129 busses, on board of which were 938 men, and in the same year, besides what were sold for immediate consumption, there were entered 45,054 barrels.

The whale fishery has not been attended with the same success, at least from this port. It was first attempted in the year 1752, but from some unfortunate circumstances, given up. In 1786 it was again revived, at which time, five large ships, three from Greenock, and two from Port-Glasgow, well equipped, and commanded by men of experience in the business, sailed for Greenland. Neither did this adventure answer the expectations that had been formed of it, and consequently any further prosecution of this fishery at the time was dropped.

The merchants of Greenock carry on, to a considerable extent, the cod and ling fisheries upon the coasts of Newfoundland and Nova Scotia, which have hitherto, it is believed, been prosecuted with advantage.

The principal imports into Greenock from the West Indies, are rum, sugar, cotton, coffee, and mahogany; from America, rice, naval stores, pot-ash, oil, timber, &c.; and from France, Spain, Portugal, and the Mediterranean, wines, fruits, &c. To the

3 X 2

ports

ports on the Continent of Europe, and in the Baltic, are sent the commodities of the West Indies and America, and in return are imported timber and naval stores. The coasting trade is carried on to all the ports of Ireland, and to the west of England, for grain, &c. and the canal between the Forth and the Clyde has opened an extensive trade to the east coast of Scotland and England, particularly with Leith, Dundee, Aberdeen, Montrose, Berwick, Hull, Newcastle, and London.

In regard to manufactures, rope-making is carried on to a great extent. The making of sail-cloth also employs a great number of people, and these, with the making of nets for the fishery, form the chief stationary manufactures. There are, however, others, which carry on business to a great annual amount, such as the refining of sugar, the making of soap and candle, and of shoes and saddles, great quantities of each of which are annually exported.

The building of vessels was formerly little attended to, all the large vessels belonging to Clyde being built in America. Since the year 1783, at the termination of the war with that country, shipbuilding has been a branch of business here, as well as in all the other ports of Clyde, and indeed at present, at Greenock in particular, it is carried on to a very great extent; vessels of great burden, constructed upon the best principles, and of the most excellent workmanship, are often built.

For

For the defence of the town and harbour of Greenock, a fort was erected many years ago, mounting
twelve 24-pounders, and flanked by several field-
pieces. It has now obtained the name of Fort-Jer-
vis, and is at present capable of making a most vigorous resistance against such vessels of the enemy
as may attempt to sail farther up the river.

To this short account of Greenock it may be added, that the great body of the inhabitants are noted
for industry, which has secured to many of them,
wealth and its consequent enjoyments. The higher
orders are in general polite and intelligent, and with
respect to the female sex, it is believed, no place in
Scotland of the same size can, in point of beauty,
and every elegant and polite accomplishment, vie
with the ladies of Greenock.

Leaving this town, and proceeding towards the
east, you immediately fall in with the village of
Crawfordsdyke, which may be considered as a
suburb of Greenock. It was erected into a
burgh of barony in 1633, by Charles I. The street
through which the highway leads is narrow, and the
houses old, and no way remarkable for their appearance. To the east of this place, you shortly enter
upon a beautiful extent of level ground, lying betwixt the base of a chain of hills upon the right, and
the river. This range of hills add a principal fea-
ture to the prospects on this side of the Clyde: They
are lofty, in many situations well wooded, and in o-
ther places covered with verdure, affording excellent
                                                    pasturage

pasturage. To such as have leisure, the view from the summit (which, in one situation, is near 800 feet above the level of the sea,) cannot fail to be particularly agreeable. At this point, a very rich and varied prospect presents itself: Below are the towns of Greenock and Port-Glasgow, with their crowded harbours, and the number of vessels sailing to and from the port. On the opposite side of the frith are in view the parishes of West Kilpatrick, Dumbarton, with its rock and castle, and the peninsular parish of Roseneath, on the south-east part of which, amidst flourishing plantations, stands the castle of that name, lately mentioned.

The prospect still opens more extensively upon ascending to the summit of the Greenock hills, and from Corlic, the highest ground in the parish of Greenock, may be seen, besides that of Renfrew, the counties of Bute, Arran and Argyll, with the lofty hills of Cowal, the most western of the Scottish Alps, the Grampian mountains, and part of the counties of Perth, Stirling, Lanark and Air.

Two miles eastward from Greenock, along the banks of the Clyde, is situated

NEW PORT-GLASGOW.

This town, as has been already noticed, was a creation of Glasgow. The magistrates and council of that city, in the year 1668, feued its scite from Sir Patrick Maxwell of Newark, and began to build

the

the town and harbour, which was, with some adjoining farms, erected into a separate parish in 1695, by the name of New Port-Glasgow.

Upon the application of the inhabitants, it was, about the year 1775, erected into a burgh of barony, with a council of thirteen persons to regulate and manage its police. These counsellors must each be possessed of at least L.10 sterling a-year, of heritable property within the town. They were chosen for the first time, by a general poll of all the feuers, and have been since elected by themselves; four of them are disqualified yearly by a plurality of votes, and four others who have not been in the council for three years before, are chosen to fill up the vacant places. Of these counsellors, two are baillies, the one called the oldest baillie, is chosen annually by the town council of Glasgow, and the other, who is the youngest baillie, is elected by the counsellors themselves.

Port-Glasgow, though inferior to Greenock in point of situation, population, or trade, is yet a very considerable town, adorned with many handsome houses and well paved streets. Its population, since the year 1755, when Dr. Webster made up his account of the number of inhabitants in each parish of Scotland, has been greatly on the increase; the number at that time being 1695, whereas, at present, they amount to about 5,000 souls. From the last mentioned year to 1775, the town had made a very rapid increase both in extent and population, chief-

ly

ly owing to the trade carried on from the port during that period. From 1775 to 1783, the population of the town continued stationary. The cause of this was undoubtedly the American war, which, by un-hinging those springs of commerce upon which Glasgow depended, consequently struck at the pros-perity of this place: But since the conclusion of that unhappy contest, the town has been gradually in-creasing in size and commercial importance.

At Port-Glasgow is established the head custom-house for the trade of Clyde. The officers employ-ed in it having the King's commission, or rather a Treasury warrant, are a collector, a comptroller, a land-surveyor, a tide-surveyor, a weigher, six land-waiters, seventeen tide-waiters, and six boatmen.

Beside its parish church, it contains a chapel of ease, built about the year 1774, according to an elegant plan, which is capable of containing upwards of 1800 people. A town-house, according to a design by Mr. Hamilton of Glasgow, is also about to be erect-ed, in a centrical and well chosen situation.

The revenue of Port-Glasgow amounts to about L.500 sterling yearly. It arises chiefly from a tax of 2¼ sterling per cent. upon house rents; from another tax of two pennies Scots upon every pint of ale, ei-ther brewed in the town, or brought into it; from the rents of the kirk seats and flesh market, and from the harbour dues. This revenue is expended in pay-ing the minister's stipends, the different schoolmasters'

ters' salaries, in keeping the streets and quays in repair, and other public purposes.

The Clyde, opposite to the town, is near two miles in breadth, though there is only a small part of it that is navigable by vessels of burden. This part, commonly called the channel, and which has formerly been noticed, lies along the new Port-Glasgow shore, is about 200 yards broad at an average, and every where so deep at high water, that the largest vessels which enter the frith of Clyde can easily be moored in the harbour without discharging any part of their cargoes. The tide rises here about nine feet.

The foreign imports of this port, consist chiefly of tobacco, sugar, rum, cotton, mahogany, logwood, and staves, together with timber, iron and hemp, from the Baltic; and the exports are such goods as suit the American and West India markets. The coasters are chiefly employed in carrying coals and merchant goods upon the river, and in bringing grain and other provisions from Dumfriesshire and Ireland.

Contiguous to Port-Glasgow on the east, and upon a prominent neck of land overhanging the river, is situated the old castle of Newark, which formerly gave name to a village upon the seite of the present town of Port-Glasgow. This castle was long in the possession of the Maxwells, a very ancient family in Renfrewshire, and now belongs to Lord Belhaven. In former times, it served

as

as a mansion-house to the barony of **Newark,** and from its castelated form and situation, it appears to have been a place of great strength. By an inscription upon one corner, it would seem to have been built in the year 1599, though another part of it, from its mode of architecture, and present state of its decay, appears to be of a much more ancient date.

Proceeding eastward in the former direction, the road, for several miles, continues nearly parallel with the river, passing several seats; the principal of these, Finlayston, a seat of the Earl of Glencairn, is finely situated upon the brow of the high ground to the right; it then, by a gradual ascent gains the summit of the ridge, in the neighbourhood of Bishoptown (a seat anciently the property of the family of Brisbane, now belonging W. Gillespie, Esq.) In this situation, the landscape to the north well merits attention: In the fore-ground the Clyde moves majestically along towards the west. Arising from its flood, and near to its opposite bank, is the picturesque rock of Dumbarton, the town of that name, its bridge, glasshouses and spire; beyond, the rich vale of the Leven opens to the eye, studded with numerous seats, villas, and the busy scenes of manufacturing industry; and farther on, the summit of Ben Lomond, towering above his kindred hills, closes upon the north, the back ground of a very fine prospect.

You then pass the inn of Bishoptown, at the distance

tance of thirteen miles from Glasgow, travel through a rich and variegated country, adorned with numerous seats; of these, North-Bar, the property of Boyd Alexander, Esq; and Walkinshaw, belonging to D. H. M‘Dowal, Esq; are the most conspicuous.

Not far eastward is the bridge of Inchinnan, of a beautiful and very uncommon structure. It was built in the year 1759, and stands immediately over the conflux of the Carts, and the Gryffe, which at this place form a body of water betwixt 5 and 600 feet in breadth. From the centre of the bridge, towards the south, a transverse arch is cast over to the angle of ground called the Abbot's Inch, formed by the junction of these two rivers. Along the summit of this arch runs the high road to Paisley, forming a right angle with the longitudinal direction of the bridge, by which particular construction, either or both of those rivers may be passed over as may suit the purpose of the traveller*. In this neighbourhood formerly stood a noble palace, one of the seats of the illustrious family of Lennox. It was built by Matthew, Earl of Lennox, in the year 1506, and its vestiges, till within these few years, were sufficiently visible, though they are now entirely obliterated by the plough; but some

3 Y 2

stones

---

* This bridge consists of nine arches, four upon one side of the transverse arch, and five upon the other; it is 775 feet long, and 19-broad, and is ornamented with two turrets or watch towers, rising above the center arches. Upon the west end are erected two handsome dials cut in marble.

stones with inscriptions belonging to that edifice, may yet be seen in the wall of an adjoining barn.

In this neighbourhood also, is situated the royal burgh of

RENFREW,

a place of very considerable antiquity, and which, as the county town, gives name to the shire. It was erected into a royalty by Robert the II. who used often to reside here in a palace which stood upon the banks of the Clyde, at a place still called the Castle-hill. This monarch first erected Renfrew into an independent sheriffdom,—preceding his reign, it belonged to that of Lanark:

Renfrew, in the course of last century, stood upon the immediate banks of the Clyde, and vessels of considerable burden were built close to the town; but the river having left its ancient bed, at some distance above, took its present course by a semicircular sweep to the north of what is called the King's Inch, and thereby left the town at a greater distance from its banks. In the old bed of the river there is cut a canal from the Clyde to the town, by which even large vessels can come up and unload at spring tides. Renfrew is but an inconsiderable place, in regard either to trade or population, when compared with the thriving towns around. The principal branch of trade here is the weaving of muslins for the manufacturers of Glasgow

gow and Paisley. It is governed by a provost, two ballies and sixteen counsellors.

Near to this place was defeated and slain, Sumerled, thane of Argyle, who, 1164, with a great army of banditti, collected from Ireland and other parts, landed in the bay of St. Laurence, and led them in rebellion against Malcolm III.—The brave, but unfortunate Marquis of Argyle, was also taken in this neighbourhood, towards the end of the last century, made a prisoner by the Laird of Greenock, and carried to Edinburgh, where he suffered.

Betwixt Renfrew and Paisley the country assumes the form of a beautiful plain, subdivided in every direction with hedges and belts of planting, and in the highest state of culture. Every where are scattered in this fertile tract, the seats of the landholder, the habitations of the farmer or manufacturer.

PAISLEY.

at the distance of seven miles from Glasgow. This town is of very great antiquity, and according to the best antiquaries, is supposed to have been the Vanduara of Ptolemy. It was erected into a burgh of barony in the year 1488, upon the application of the abbot of the monastery which had been established here for several ages preceding. Yet still at the beginning of this century, it appears to have been but an inconsiderable place. Crawford, who wrote his history of Renfrewshire about that time, describes it as consisting of one principal street, a-

bout

bout half a mile in length, and containing only be-twixt two and three thousand souls.

Paisley now contains above 23,000 inhabitants, is pleasantly situated upon the banks of the White Cart, over which it has three stone bridges. Its principal street, which runs from east to west, is of a great length, and contains a number of handsome and well finished houses. The other streets, which in general branch from this main stem, have likewise many good buildings.

Of the public edifices in this town, the old Abbey* is the chief. Though not entire, its remains still demonstrate

---

* A particular history of this abbey would fill many pages. It was founded as a priory for monks of the order of Clugni, a-bout the year 1160, by Walter, Great Steward of Scotland. It was afterwards raised to the rank of an abbey, and the lands belonging to it were, by Robert the II. erected into a regality, under the jurisdiction of the Abbot. After the Reformation, the Abbey was secularized by the Pope, in favour of Lord Claud Hamilton, third son of the Duke of Chatlerault, as a re-ward for his steady adherence to the cause of Queen Mary; and in 1588, it was, by the King and Parliament, erected into a temporal lordship, and Lord Claud was created Lord Paisley. It continued in possession of that family till 1653, when Lord Claud's grandson, James, Earl of Abercorn, sold the lordship of Paisley to the Earl of Angus, who, next year, sold it to Wil-liam, Lord Cochrane.—Great part of the lordship was, at dif-ferent times, sold off by the family of Dundonald, and what remained of it was, in 1764, re-purchased by the late Earl of Abercorn.

The

demonstrate its former magnificence. It has originally been in the form of a cross. The great north
window is of beautiful workmanship, and as such,
stands high in the estimation of the connoisseurs of
Gothic architecture. Only the chancel of this abbey now remains. It is divided into a middle and
two side aisles, by lofty columns, whose capitals are
ornamented by grotesque figures, and supporting
Gothic or pointed arches. Above these is another
range of pillars much larger, being the segment of
a circle, and above these again, a row of arched niches from end to end, over which is the roof, terminating in an angle. Both the west and north doors
are highly decorated with sculpture; indeed, the
whole outside has been profusely ornamented, than
which scarce any thing lighter or richer can be imagined. About the year 1789, this building was begun to be fitted up of new for a place of worship,
and now that it is finished, no town, it is believed,
in Scotland, can boast of a more elegant church.

The Earl of Abercorn's burial place is also well
deserving of attention. It is an old Gothic chapel,
without pulpit or pew, or any ornament whatever,
but

The monks of this abbey are supposed to have written a
chronicle of the affairs of Scotland, called, the Black Book of
Paisley, from the colour of its cover. This curious monument
of antiquity, cited frequently by Buchanan, belonged to the
President Spottiswoode, and after his death, was carried into
England by General Lambert, and is now in the King's Library, at St. James's.——*Pennant.*

but has the finest echo perhaps in the world: When
the end door, the only one it has, is shut, the noise
is equal to a loud and distant clap of thunder; if a
good voice sings, or if a musical instrument is played upon, the effect is inexpressibly agreeable. In
this chapel is the monument of Marjory Bruce,
daughter of Robert the Bruce, wife of Walter, Great
Steward of Scotland, and mother of Robert the II.
Her story is singular: In the year 1317, when she
was big with child, she broke her neck while hunting in this neighbourhood; the Cæsarian operation
was instantly performed, and the child taken out a-
live; but the operator chancing to hurt one eye with
his instrument, occasioned the blemish that gave
Robert II. afterwards the epithet of *Blear eye*, and
the monument is also styled that of *Queen Bleary*.
In the same chapel were interred Elizabeth Muir,
and Euphemia Ross, both consorts to the same
monarch.

Beside the Abbey Church, which, till the year
1738, was the only place of worship in Paisley, there
are now three others belonging to the Establishment,
viz. the Laigh or Low Church, the High and Middle Churches.—The Laigh Church was built about
the year 1733, is in the form of a Greek cross, and
very well laid out.—The High Church was erected
in the year 1756. It is a handsome building, of
the form of an oblong square of 82 feet by 62, and
capable of containing upwards of 3000 people. It
has a beautiful and lofty spire, which, from its situation, commands a very extensive and variegated
prospect.

prospect.—The Middle church was erected in the year 1781 : It is not so large as the High church, but is well built and handsomely finished. The same year this church was erected, the town was divided into three separate parishes, called after the names of these respective churches.

The Town-house of Paisley is a fine edifice, with a spire and clock; it stands at the cross, in the centre of the town, and contains a prison, court-hall, and a set of other apartments, which are now let for an inn. The Town's hospital is a large building, with a garden behind, situated opposite to the quay, in that district called the New-Sneddon. It was erected in the year 1752, for the support of poor and destitute children, and as an asylum for the aged.

The height of this house is three stories; it will accommodate 200 people. The expence of the erection and of fitting it up was L.584; some additional buildings and cells have since been added, in 1781. This house is supported by a tax laid on the inhabitants. It is under the management of fifteen directors, ten of whom are chosen by the magistrates and council, three by the kirk session, and two by the company or society of Taylors.

The flesh market is also a neat and commodious building; it stands in the neighbourhood of the cross, having a front of ashler work, extending about 70 feet; it was built in 1766, and cost the community L.1200 sterling.

Paisley

Paisley has also an Assembly-hall, in the vicinity of the Town-hall; a Grammar school, and Meal market, built in 1665, with the arms of the town cut upon the front. The Paisley bank and Abercorn inn likewise deserve notice: They are handsome buildings in the modern taste, situated near the eastern extremity of the town. Paisley contains also several meeting-houses for dissenters of different denominations, particularly chapels for the Antiburghers, Burghers, and those of the Relief communion.

The river Cart, upon which the town stands, is crossed by three bridges: The oldest was taken down in 1782, and the same year rebuilt; the second bridge, called the Sneddon bridge, was erected in 1760, and the third, or Abbey bridge, in 1763. Besides these buildings there are some others, the property of the community, which the limits prescribed to this account, will not allow us to take notice of.

To its manufactures is Paisley indebted for its present importance; these may be traced from very small beginnings. Not long after the Union, when a free trade was opened with England, the spirit of manufacture began to shew itself here, and the fabrics produced were made upon such just and economical principles, and with so much taste and judgment, that they found a ready market not only at home, but likewise in the neighbouring kingdom. The trade of Paisley at that period, owed its chief encouragement to a number of of itinerant merchants, many of whom having frequented Paisley as their staple, came afterwards to settle in it, and bought up large quantities of its manufactures, which they vended amongst their friends and correspondents in England. The merchants of Glasgow afterwards found their account in purchasing these goods, which they chiefly exported to the London or foreign markets.

Such was the state of trade and manufactures in Paisley, from a short time after the Union till about the year 1760.—The different articles fabricated during that period, were at first coarse chequered linen cloth, and Bengals, afterwards chequered coloured handkerchiefs, some of them fine and beautifully variegated. These were succeeded by manufactures of a more light and fanciful kind, such as plain, striped and ornamented lawns, and linen gauze.

The making of white sewing thread was early introduced at Paisley, principally through the exertions of a Mrs. Hamilton of Bargarran, who, about the year 1725, found means to procure from Holland, the machinery necessary for this purpose. It has had here its principal seat ever since, and is now carried on to a very considerable extent.

About the year 1760 the making of silk gauze was first attempted at Paisley, in imitation of that of Spittalfields in London. The success was beyond the most sanguine expectations of those who

3 Z 2   engaged

engaged in it. The inventive genius, the patient application of the workmen, and the cheapness of labour at that time, gave it every advantage for being naturalized here. The consequence was, that by the superiority of the Paisley manufacture, Spittalfields was obliged to relinquish this branch. Companies came down from London to carry it on here, where it prospered and increased, and not only became the great distinguishing manufacture of this town, but occupied the country round to the distance of twenty miles.

To give some idea of the extent to which it was carried, in conjunction with the thread manufacture, we have presented the following account, drawn up, of its state in the year 1784. In this year the number of weavers employed in that branch, were not under - - - -   5000
These gave employment to winders, warpers, and others necessary in the various parts of the silk manufacture, -   5000
                           10,000

At an average, these 10,000 people earned 5s. per week; the sum paid for wages therefore will be - - - L.130,000
Every silk loom produces in value yearly, upon an average, L.70; the whole amount then will be - - - L.350,000
Value of Paisley manufactures in 1784, viz.
Silk gauze, - - L.350,000
Lawns and thread gauze, - - 164,385
Thread,

| Thread, | - | - | - | - | - | 64,800 |

L. 579,185

The different descriptions of people employed in these manufactures, amounted then to the following numbers, viz.

Weavers employed in the linen branch,	2400
Spinners, - - -	7384
Winders, warpers, &c. - -	1000
Overseers, · - - - -	100
Makers of machinery and implements,	800

11,684

Thread Spinners, winders, bleachers, &c. &c.	4000
Silk weavers, as above, -	5000
Warpers, winders, clippers, &c.	5000

14,000

| Total number employed, | 25,684 |

The change of fashion has been, for these several years past, unfavourable to the silk manufacture. That of muslin has succeeded, and is now carried on with a degree of ardour which has hitherto insured it complete success. Every where in the neighbourhood of this town, are mills erected for spinning cotton yarn, and though a vast quantity is prepared, they are yet insufficient to supply the demands, so that it continues to be imported from England and other parts.

Besides

Besides these principal manufactures, here are tanneries, two soap and candle works, a ribbon manufacture, and another of incle and tapes, in each of which business is carried on to a very considerable extent¶.

Paisley derives great advantage to her trade and manufactures from the navigation of the Cart, which having been deepened some years ago, now admits vessels drawing seven feet of water from the Clyde to the quay, and this, even in ordinary tides; so that an easy communication is opened by water from Paisley, not only with the city of Glasgow, the towns of Greenock and Port-Glasgow, and the west of England, but also through the channel of the Great canal with Leith, London, and the Continent of Europe.

With respect to the political constitution of this town, it is governed by three magistrates and seventeen counsellors, chosen annually upon the first Monday after Michaelmas, the term at which similar elections take place in general throughout Scotland.

About two miles eastward from Paisley, and at a short distance to the right from the great road to Glasgow, stands in a most charming situation, the ruins of

CRUICKSTONE

¶ The total value annually of the Paisley manufactures was calculated, some years ago, at L.700,000 sterling.

CRUICKSTONE CASTLE.

It is now a mere fragment, only part of a square tower remaining of a place of much magnificence, when in its full glory. This was originally the property of the Crocs, a potent family in this county; but in the reign of Malcolm the II. it was conveyed by the marriage of the heiress-daughter of Robert de Croc into the family of the Stewarts, in after times Earls and Dukes of Lennox, who had great possessions in this neighbourhood. To this place, Henry Darnly retired with his beautiful queen; and here, according to tradition, the yew tree still exists that witnessed their fond endearments. To perpetuate their remembrance, while her love for Darnly intermingled itself in all her thoughts, Mary had the figure of this tree impressed upon her coins.

Not far distant from Cruickstone is the Halket, or Hawkhead, an elegant seat of the Earl of Glasgow, surrounded with a beautiful pleasure ground and thriving plantations. Proceeding alongst the highway towards the east, you pass upon the right, Ralston, an elegant modern house, the property of —— Orr, Esq; and at the distance of about three miles from Paisley, Cardonnel, an old family seat surrounded by some venerable trees. This was formerly the property of a branch of the family of Darnly, it belongs at present to Lord Blantyre. Farther upon the left is Craigton; a fine seat, with extensive pleasure grounds, belonging to James Ritchie, Esq. You are now come within view of the city of Glasgow, which,

which, from its numerous spires, its extent, and the richness of the surrounding country, cannot fail to convey a favourable idea of its opulence and population.

The seats and villas now increase in number on every hand; to particularize them all would be tedious and uninteresting; it may not, however; be improper to mention one, Plantation, a sweet and highly ornamented spot, the property of John Mair, Esq; a gentleman of distinguished taste. Mr. Mair possesses a number of fine paintings in every branch of the art, in particular, the principal productions of the late Mr. Allan, of Edinburgh; whose skill in pourtraying Scotch characters, particuly in the lower scenes of life, has never yet been surpassed. Amongst these pictures by Allan, is the resignation of the crown by Queen Mary, and her flight from Loch Leven—the Highland family— Highland reel—John Anderson my Joe—and the Cottar's Saturday night, from that celebrated poem by Burns. Prints are at present publishing of the last picture, engraved in London. The profits arising from the publication, Mr. Mair means to dedicate to the assistance of the widows of the poet and painter.

After leaving Plantation you shortly fall in with

TRADESTOWN,

a modern and even elegant village, with many good streets. The principal one of these conducts you by the new bridge, across the Clyde to the city, of Glasgow.

Having finished the first part of this tour, and described as concisely as possible the most interesting objects that occur in the course of the road from Glasgow to Loch Lomond, and in the return by the way of Loch Long, Greenock, &c. we now proceeded southwards, and in the direction formerly mentioned, to

THE FALLS OF THE CLYDE, &c.

Proceeding eastward from Glasgow, and passing the villages of Camlachie and Tolcross, the first object that merits attention is the extensive iron works in the neighbourhood of the latter village. These works are the property of Messrs. Outram and Co. and were begun to be erected in 1786. Their situation is exceedingly favourable; abundance of coal is obtained within 200 yards of their scite, and iron stone of a very rich quality is in great plenty in the neighbourhood. Upwards of 30,000 tons of coal are consumed at these works annually, and betwixt 4 and 500 mechanics and labourers find employment. Here are not only manufactured all kinds of cast iron goods, but maleable iron is made from the pig, cannon are cast and bored by a very ingenious machine, and a vast quantity of balls, bombs, and other engines of destruction, are the daily produce of this manufacture.

4 A   At

At the distance of about six miles from Glasgow, the Clydesdale road branches to the right from the great road to Edinburgh. A short way farther, the former road crosses the river North Calder by a bridge, and immediately thereafter you fall in with the banks of the Clyde. The country from Glasgow to this point, though rich and well cultivated, has nothing in its appearance either very picturesque or interesting. But here the scenery begins to change; objects both picturesque and interesting are scattered around as you advance, and by a continued variety create these ideas which are so highly gratifying to every mind susceptible of the beauties of nature.

From the bridge over the Calder the road runs parallel to the banks of the Clyde, through a beautiful plain, till it arrives in the neighbourhood of the village of Uddingstone. This village, which is situated in an elevated situation, commands towards the west, an extensive and highly diversified prospect:—The Clyde—the city of Glasgow—the numerous seats around, and the distant hills of Stirling, Dumbarton, and Argyllshire, lie extended before the eye. A short way from Uddingstone is the village of Bothwell, in the vicinity of which is the ancient and modern castles of that name, the property of Lord Douglas.

BOTHWELL CASTLE.

The old castle of Bothwell is most enchantingly
situated,

situated, upon an elevated bank of the Clyde, which here makes a noble sweep.

" Where towering high in stately pride,
" Thy walls frown awful o'er the flood†."

Though it has been long in ruins, it still exhibits striking remains of its ancient grandeur, and of the power of its possessors.

Two of its towers are nearly entire; in the highest is still a stair which conducts to the top, from whence a beautiful and extensive view is obtained, and, in the corner of another, is to be seen the well which supplied its inhabitants with water. The whole building has been very extensive, when entire; what remains, still occupies a space of about 234 feet in length, by 100 in breadth; its walls are upwards of 15 feet in thickness, and in some places 60 feet high, built of a beautiful red coloured stone.

This castle once made a conspicuous figure in the history of Scotland: Its history is curious and interesting, but our limits will not allow us to enter into a very particular detail*.—It appears to have
4 A 2 been

---

† Bothwell Castle. By Mr. Finlay, Author of Wallace, or the Vale of Ellerslie, *an original poem.*

* From the castle of Bothwell, Edward III. published a writ requiring his Parliament to assemble for concerting
means .

been about the beginning of the 13th century, the property of Sir David Oliphant. His daughter, who was heiress of Bothwell, having married Sir William de Moray, the castle and lordship came into the family of that name. From the Morays it was wrested by Edward the I. of England, and given to Aimer de Valence, Earl of Pembroke, Governor of Scotland, and thither he fled ‡ upon his defeat by Bruce at the battle of Loudon-hill in 1307. Upon the forfeiture of Pembroke it was bestowed by King Robert the Bruce upon Andrew Murray, a brave and intrepid warrior, and lineally descended of its former possessors. With his granddaughter it came to Archibald the Grim, Earl of Douglas, by marriage, and continued one of the chief seats of that powerful family, till their forfeiture by King James II. in the year 1445. It was by that monarch given to Lord Chrichton, son to Chancellor Chrichton. Chrichton was forfeited in 1485. It was then given by James III. to the Lord Monipenny, from whom it was retaken, upon pretence that it had been given by the King in his minority, and was thereafter bestowed by him upon John Ramsay, his favourite, who enjoyed it till the year 1488, when he was forfeited

for

means of defence against the Scots in the year 1336.—In the following year it was besieged by the Scots, taken and dismantled. In this castle were imprisoned many of the English nobility taken at the battle of Bannockburn.

‡ Douglas's Peerage.—Guthrie's History of Scotland.

for counterfeiting a commission under the great
seal to the Earl of Northumberland.

It having again reverted to the crown, James IV.
granted the castle and lordship to Patrick Hepburn,
third Lord Hailes, whom he created Earl of Bothwell, a young nobleman of a great fortune, and no
less ambition, who was one of the chief ringleaders
in that horrid rebellion against James III. which
proved so fatal to that monarch. In his line it continued till the year 1567, when James, fifth and last
Earl of Bothwell, who married the unfortunate Mary Stewart, was forfeited for the murder of her former husband, Henry Darnly, father of King James
VI.

It was afterwards given by that King to Francis
Stuart, son of John, Prior of Coldingham, natural
son of King James V.; and he being forfeited, the
estate was gifted to the lairds of Buccleugh and
Roxburgh, from whom the Marquis of Hamilton
acquired the superiority of the lordship of Bothwell.

The property, which was less than the third of
that lordship, with the castle of Bothwell, was disponed, by Hepburn, Earl of Bothwell, to Douglas,
Earl of Angus, in exchange for the lordship of Lid-
disdale, the patrimonial portion of his son the Earl
of Forfar. By the death of Archibald, Earl of Forfar, in the year 1715, the noble family of Douglas,
as nearest heirs, came again into the possession of
the castle of Bothwell, and with them it still remains.

The

The modern castle of Bothwell, which stands in a beautiful lawn, in the neighbourhood of these magnificent ruins, is an elegant structure, containing many handsome and princely apartments. It was erected by its present noble owner, Lord Douglas, nearly in the situation where formerly stood another mansion-house of this fair barony, built by one of the Earls of Forfar. But to its pleasure-ground is Bothwell chiefly indebted for its fame. It lies principally upon the sloping banks of the Clyde, and around the ruins of the old castle, which forms one of its most striking features—the beautiful and variegated woods which clothe the banks; the disposition of the walks, which at every turn present some new or interesting prospect; the Clyde, which here makes a noble sweep, deep ingulphed amidst rock and copses, and the ivy-clad and mouldering towers of the old castle, proudly situated upon a lofty bank, conspire to render Bothwell a paradisical spot, well deserving the eulogium in that beautiful Scotch air,

" O Bothwell banks thou bloometh fair."

On the opposite side of the river, and perched upon the summit of a lofty rock, are the ruins of Blantyre priory, the property of Lord Blantyre. This priory appears from history, to have been founded before the end of the thirteenth century, and was dependent upon the monastery of Jedburgh. Upon the abolition of the Romish religion in Scotland in the sixteenth century, it fell into the hands of a Walter Stewart, Lord Privy Seal, who was afterwards

terwards created Lord Blantyre *. On the same
side of the river with these ruins, and a little way
to the east, are situated some extensive cotton works,
the property of Mr. Monteith of Glasgow.

Neither is the church of Bothwell undeserving of
notice. It was founded by Archibald the Grim,
Earl of Douglas, in 1398, and munificently endowed for a provost and eight prebendaries, by a grant
of many lands in the neighbourhood, and others at
a greater distance. It is built in the Gothic style,
of excellent workmanship. The roof is arched,
lofty, and has a very fine appearance. The whole
area is enlightened by a tier of large windows on
each side, and a great window in the east end, in
the upper part of which are cut the Douglas arms.
The noble founder, according to tradition, lies interred here. The same year that he died, viz. 1400,
his daughter, Marjory Douglas, was married in this
church to David, Prince of Scotland.

About a mile to the east of the village of Bothwell, is Bothwell bridge, celebrated for the battle
fought near it on the south bank of the Clyde in
1679, between the Covenanters and the King's
troops, the event of which was fatal to the affairs of
the

* Between the old castle and this priory, tradition informs
us, there formerly existed a subterraneous passage under the
Clyde, by which the more tender part of its inhabitants fled in
the time of danger, to the protection which a monastery, in
those barbarous times afforded.

the former. The same bridge, celebrated in the
story of that battle, still stands.

Two miles farther on, lies

HAMILTON,

one of the handsomest of the smaller towns in Scotland, situated in a beautiful, populous, and highly
cultivated country, and in the neighbourhood of
two fine rivers, Clyde and Avon, which unite their
waters in its vicinity.

Hamilton contains 3600 inhabitants, and owes its
existence to the noble family of that name, who have
had their principal residence here, since the time of
Robert the Bruce. The original name of the lands
or barony around, appears to have been Cadzow, or
Cadow. This barony was granted to an ancestor of
the noble owner, on the following occasion: In the
time of Edward II. lived *Sir Gilbert de Hambleton*, or
Hampton *, an Englishman of rank, who happening
at Court to speak in praise of Robert the Bruce,
received, on that account, an insult from John De
Spenser, chamberlain to the King, whom he fought
and slew. Dreading the resentment of that potent
family, he fled to the Scottish monarch, who received him with open arms, and established him at the
place the family now possesses, whose name, in after

* Camden.

ter times, was changed from that of Cadzow to Hamilton; and in 1445, the lands were erected into a lordship, and the then owner, Sir James, sat in Parliament as Lord Hamilton.

The same nobleman founded the collegiate church at Hamilton, in 1451, for a provost and several prebendaries, and in five years thereafter, Hamilton was erected into a free burgh of barony. In 1548, Mary, Queen of Scotland, created this town a free royal burgh; but the rights and privileges thus acquired, were, after the Restoration, resigned into the hands of William and Ann, Duke and Duchess of Hamilton, who, in 1670, restored to the community its former possessions, and erected it into a burgh of regality, dependent on them and their successors, and thus it has continued, after some ineffectual struggles, to the present time.

Hamilton formerly stood clustered around the residence of the family, or Hamilton house. By degrees, the lower part of the town was purchased and pulled down; it then stretched itself towards the south and west, and the palace is now almost left standing detached. Beside some handsome private houses, there are several public buildings deserving of notice. Amongst these, the Town-house appears to be one of the most ancient; it was erected in 1643, and contains a court-hall, prison, &c. —The parish church is an elegant building, and from its situation, on an elevated piece of ground, is seen to much advantage. It was erected in 1732,

4 B

after a design of the elder Adams. Here are also two
meeting-houses for dissenters, one near the west
end of the town, built in 1776, the other at the opposite point, built in 1761.

The public markets are neat and commodious.
Near to the Town-house stands an hospital, built
instead of one which stood in the lower part of the
town. This was endowed by the noble family of
Hamilton, and other pious donors. It contains lodgings for eight poor men, and a hall for morning and
evening prayers. Farther to the west, there is another for four old men and their families, built and
endowed in the year 1775, by a Mr. William Aik-
man, a neighbouring proprietor. In the neighbourhood have also lately been erected, handsome and
commodious barracks, for the reception of horse and
foot.

Hamilton has several manufactures: That which
is carried on to the greatest extent, is the weaving
of cotton stuffs for the manufacturers of Glasgow.
The tanning and dressing of leather is also no inconsiderable branch of trade here. A manufacture of
thread lace has long been established, but, from
the fluctuation of fashion, it is now on the decline.
Saddlery, and the manufacture of candles, are also
carried on to some extent. The latter manufacture
is in much estimation.

Hamilton palace well merits attention: It
seems to have been built at different periods; that
part which is most ancient, was erected in the year
1591;

1591; the more modern, and most considerable part, was built in the latter end of the 17th century. The buildings of the palace form three sides of a quadrangle; several of the rooms are spacious, and elegantly finished. But the paintings of Hamilton house constitute its principal ornaments; these are indeed worthy of admiration, and several of the rooms are well furnished with them, but particularly the gallery. The most remarkable piece is *Daniel in the Lion's Den*, by Rubens. The prophet is represented sitting naked in a cave, surrounded by lions; an opening at the top, through which he had been let down, affords light to the picture. The face of Daniel is most inimitably painted. The hands are clasped; agony appears in every muscle, and in the whole contracted form. In a word, nothing can be more strongly conceived, more thoroughly understood, more delightfully coloured, or more delicately touched, than the whole figure; it appears, indeed, all glowing over with beauties, without one defect. The lions, of which there are six, with two lionesses, are well disposed, and stand round the prophet with that indifference which seems to have arisen from a satiety of food: One is yawning, another stretching, and a third lying down. Of these last figures, as well as upon the general distribution of the light, some criticisms have been made; if, however, they have any foundation, they are more than counterbalanced by the grand effect of the whole, which is allowed by judges, to be not only the best picture in Scotland, but the master-piece of the immortal Rubens.

4 B 2   The

The *Marriage Feast*, by Paul Veronese, and the portrait of the *Earl of Denbigh*, by Rubens, are also distinguished paintings. In the former, the obstinacy and resistance of the intruder, who came without the wedding garment, is strongly expressed; and in the latter, the countenance is so full of nature and character, that you are amazed the power of colours can express life so strongly. Besides these, there are a very numerous collection of others, many of whom are inimitably fine. This collection has lately received an addition, from a considerable number of paintings brought from England by the present Duke, principally the productions of the foreign schools.

About a mile to the eastward of Hamilton, you fall in with the Avon, a beautiful stream, which gives name to Avondale, a tract of country lying alongst its banks, rich in the produce of the dairy. The bridge *, which crosses the river here, is of considerable antiquity. It was erected before the year 1500, and consists of three arches, built in the manner peculiar to such edifices of that age. The view from this situation is deservedly esteemed—the banks of the river are high, precipitous in some places, and in others beautifully diversified with

stately

* This bridge, tradition informs us, was built by a wealthy priest, who having been stopped from proceeding to a meeting of his brethren at Hamilton, by the swelling of the river, was so provoked, that he immediately ordered the present bridge to be erected at his own expence.

stately woods of oak, ash, and horn-beam—Barn-
cluth, a pleasant spot, formerly belonging to the
Hamiltons of Pencaitland, composes one of the
objects of the landscape. It is situated upon a lofty bank, on the west of the river, and is much resorted to by strangers, for its beautiful situation,
terrace walks, and picturesque views.

Farther up the Avon, and seated upon the summit of a rock, overhanging the river, are the ruins
of Cadzow castle, the ancient seat of the family of
Hamilton. It was plundered, and partly demolished by the Regent Murray's soldiers in the reign of
Queen Mary; since then it has continued in a state
of desolation and ruin. In the park, near these ruins, are some of the stateliest oaks in Scotland, the
only remains of that great forest, which, at one time,
nearly covered Clydesdale. Within the present century, the number of these noble trees have been
greatly diminished, some having fallen through decay, others have been cut down, and of those that
remain, many are now only mutilated trunks, some
of which measure in circumference, upwards of
twenty-seven feet. Here, so late as the year 1760,
were a few of those white cattle, with black or
brown ears and muzzles, once so common in Scotland. Their shyness and ferocity of temper rendered them troublesome, and of little use, they were
therefore exterminated in the year above mentioned.

On the opposite bank of the Avon, and at no
great

great distance, in a most commanding situation, is Chatlerault, an elegant summer house belonging to the family of Hamilton. It was built about the year 1730, from a design of the elder Adams, and is intended for an imitation of the castle of Chatlerault in France, of which the chief of this family is duke. It is surrounded with a fine park, well well stocked with fallow deer.

From the bridge of the Avon, the great park of Hamilton accompanies you for some considerable way upon the right, and from the height of its inclosures, precludes the possibility of any view in that direction. On the other hand, from the gentle decline of the ground to the Clyde, the prospect is more open; a beautiful strath of country lying alongst its banks, is immediately under the eye, full of objects both picturesque and beautiful. The house of Dalziel, surrounded with fine plantations, appears here to much advantage, on the opposite side of the river. It is an ancient and strong built fabric, the mansion of a once extensive barony, formerly the property of the ancestors of the Dalziels †, Earls of Carnwath, from whom it was purchased

---

† This ancient family, if we can credit tradition, obtained at once their name and these lands from a very singular circumstance, not unworthy of notice. In the reign of Kenneth II. a kinsman and favourite of that king was taken prisoner by the Picts, put to death, and hung upon a gibbet, in view of the Scottish camp. This so provoked Kenneth, that he
offered

chased in the last century, by a progenitor of Mr. Hamilton, its present possessor.

Farther to the west, and upon the summit of a beautiful bank overhanging the Clyde, is a summer house belonging to Mr. Hamilton, situated in the same spot where formerly stood a *Castellum*, or Roman outpost. In this neighbourhood also, and built across the river East Calder, at no great distance from its junction with the Clyde, is a semicircular arch or bridge, the work of that great people. Alongst this bridge the Roman road, or Watling-street, as it was called, ran westward to Dunglass. Its vestiges, in many places, are still sufficiently visible.

At the distance of about one mile from the bridge of Avon, a gradual descent carries you to the more immediate banks of the Clyde, nearly opposite to the house of Cambusnethan, the seat of Mr. Lockhart of Castlehill.—Cambusnethan is most beautifully situated. Its charming lawn betwixt and the river, its aged limes, terrace walks, and

offered a considerable reward to any of his subjects who would take down and carry off the body. For some time none would undertake the task. At last a gentleman came forward to the king, and in the old Scottish or Celtic tongue, said, *Dal zell*, signifying, *I dare*. He accordingly performed the dangerous enterprize, for which he was rewarded with these lands upon the banks of the Clyde, and from this circumstance he acquired his name, which was thereafter given to the estate.

and the surrounding scenery, sweet beyond description, attract and rivet as it were the attention and admiration of every stranger.

From this situation, as you proceed eastward, the beauties of the Vale of Clyde open still more fully into view; the banks, on every hand, are diversified with copse-wood, with corn fields, or with seats; in some places they are more precipitous, in others less inclined. Numbers of rivulets, descending from the high grounds, through picturesque glens, furnish many beautiful cascades, and contribute to heighten and diversify the features of the landscape. In this part of the road, before reaching Dalserf, you pass upon the left, and upon the north side of the river, an old mansion house, called *Garren;* and upon a high and beautifully wooded bank, on the same side, Brownlee, belonging to William Harvie, Esq. Upon the right, and looking down upon the village, Broomhill. Thus the country continues to

DALSERF,

a village embowered amongst orchards, the property of Miss Hamilton, whose fine seat stands upon an eminence to the east of the village.—Ascending the summit of a gentle rise of ground, all at once bursts upon the sight the princely towers of Mauldslie castle, situated in a most beautiful lawn, diversified with trees and watered by the Clyde, which, by a noble sweep, encircles its southern extremity.

MAULDSLIE

MAULDSLIE CASTLE.

This elegant mansion, the seat of the Earl of Hyndford, was begun to be built in the year 1792, from a design of Robert Adams, Esq; and is but lately finished. Its length is about 104 by 58 feet over the walls. It is flanked by circular towers a-rising from the base, and terminating in a cone. The south front is likewise decorated with a circular and two square projections in the centre, and is otherwise beautifully ornamented and proportioned. The north front is one storey higher, and is equally deserving of praise. Its roof is also of a very singular, though beautiful construction, of which it is impossible to give an adequate idea of by any description. From the situation at which the first sight of Mauldslie is seen, when coming from the west, in the immediate vicinity of Dalserf house, is one of the richest and most charming prospects in Scotland.—Your situation is upon a bold headland, jutting out from the west, which nature seems to have designed as the grand point from which are to be seen to most advantage the beauties of the Vale of Clyde.

Figure to yourself an extensive valley, whose sloping banks are beautifully diversified with woods, elegant seats and cottages, with the Clyde running in many beautiful meanders through its bottom; here, winding to the north, round the base of a proud promontory; there, it runs to the south, encircling some extensive lawn, covered with orchards

4 C   or

or yellow corn fields, and level as the unruffled surface of the ocean; take into view the soft distance to the west, of the ærial tinted hills of Argyleshire, or the lofty mountain of Tinto in the opposite direction : Paint all these objects in the most favourable situations, and with the most delicate tints which your imagination can fancy, and then you may have some idea of the beauties of this charming Valley.

From Dalserf† to the bridge of Nethan foot, a distance of between two and three miles, a succession of objects equally beautiful with those farther to the west, present themselves to view. In some places you pass through extensive orchards, laden with fruit, or in the opposite season, perfuming the air with their odoriferous blossoms, and giving the landscape

" The bloom of blowing Eden fair."

The banks of the river of Nethan, which is crossed by the bridge above-mentioned, near its conflux with the Clyde, abound for some miles upwards from that point, with many picturesque scenes.
Amidst

† A short distance above the village of Dalserf is still to be seen the ruins of a Romish chapel, dedicated to St. Patrick, and from whence this lovely vale has sometimes got the name of Dalpatrick. On the opposite bank, to the east of Mauldslie, is Milton, a delightful seat, belonging to Robert Brisbane, Esq; then Waygateshaw, Mr. Thomas Steel, somewhat fartheron.

Amidst the most romantic of these, and upon a lofty promontory, surrounded on three sides by the river, stand the ruins of the

CASTLE OF CRAIGNETHAN, OR DRAFFAN

formerly a place of great strength. It was anciently a seat of the family of Hamilton, whose arms are still visible above the gateway. Here the unfortunate Mary Stuart abode for a few days, after her flight from Lochleven. The castle of Draffan has sustained several sieges, as Buchanan and other historians relate; and during the 17th century it was the scene where some important transactions took place between the then chief of the family of Hamilton and the Covenanters. In the beginning of the last, it appears to have been the property of a family of the name of Hay. By them this castle and barony was disponed to the house of Douglas.

In this neighbourhood, and opposite to the deep dell formed by the Nethan, is the village of Crossford, situated on a plain upon the banks of the Clyde. On the north side of that river opens a picturesque vale, finely wooded, and abounding in cottages, and in one situation, a ruined castle or tower, called Habar, which adds much to the beauty of the scenery. Farther up, and embosomed in wood, is the house of Lee, at the distance of two miles from Lanark, the seat of Lockhart M'Donald, Esq; the representative of a very ancient family. Here is kept what is called, the

Lee penny, far famed for its medicinal virtues; some particulars in the history of which, it may not be improper to mention: It is a stone of a dark red colour, set in a shilling of Edward I. and has been in the possession of the family since the year 1320, that is, a little after the death of Robert the Bruce.

That monarch having ordered his heart to be carried and buried in the Holy Land, one of the noble family of Douglas, after the death of the king, was commissioned; the person, however, who carried the heart, was Simon Locard, of Lee, who, from this circumstance, changed his name to *Lockheart*, or *Lockhart*, and got a heart within a lock for part of his arms, with the motto *Corda serata pando*. Having taken prisoner a Saracen prince, his wife came to pay the ransom, and on counting out the money or jewels, this stone fell out of her purse, which she hastily snatched up: this inciting the curiosity of Lockhart, he insisted, that without its being given him, the captive prince should not be relieved.

Finding Lockhart determined, she at last consented, yeilded up the stone, and told him many of its virtues: viz. That it cured all diseases, in cattle, and the bite of a mad dog, both in man and beast †. Many are the cures which are said to be performed

† It is used by dipping the stone in water, which is given to

performed by it, and people used to come from all parts of Scotland, and even as far in England as Yorkshire, to get the water in which the stone is dipped.

It is said, that when the plague was last at New-castle, the inhabitants sent for the Lee penny, and gave a bond for a large sum in trust for the loan. And so confident were they of its supposed virtues, that they offered to pay the money, and keep the penny, which, however, the proprietor refused.

The most remarkable cure said to be performed upon any person, was the restoring to health, Lady Baird of Sauchtonhall, near Edinburgh, who having been bit by a mad dog, had all the alarming symptoms of the hydrophobia. The loan of this famous penny having been asked, it was sent, and used for a few weeks; the lady daily drinking and bathing in the water it was dipped in, till she was recovered. This happened 90 years ago, but the circumstance is very well attested, though we should rather be inclined to suppose that its virtues, in this case, as well as every other, are more imaginary than real ‡.

Leaving

to the diseased men or cattle to drink; the wound, sore, or bite, is also, at the same time, washed. Sir James Lockhart, one of the Lairds of Lee, in consequence of using this stone, was complained upon many years ago for using *Witch-craft.*

‡ At Lee is a remarkable large oak, perhaps unequalled in Scotland. It is called the Pease tree.

574

Leaving the bridge of Nethan, and continuing the route eastward, after passing Carfin, upon the left, the seat of —— Nisbet, Esq; the vale begins to contract, the banks of the river on either hand become more steep and precipitous, rocks of a considerable height bound the river's course, which now rushes with impetuosity through a broken channel, auguring the approach to scenes of still greater grandeur.

You now enter the wood of Stonebyres, the property of Daniel Vere, Esq; a forest of considerable extent. A hollow murmuring sound first strikes the ear; as you proceed, the noise increases, and the attention is more engaged. At last, having cleared the wood, a foot path to the left conducts to the verge of a tremendous precipice, from which you have a full view of the

FALL OF STONEBYRES,

a most beautiful cataract, of three successive falls, over which the whole body of water in the Clyde rushes with a prodigious fury into a deep chasm below *. The ear-stunning noise, the lofty rocks which surround the water-fall, the variegated copse-wood which covers their brow, and the effect produced from the grand combination of the whole, renders the fall of Stonebyres a scene wonderfully grand and sublime.

At

* The height of the fall is about 60 feet.

At no great distance from the Fall of Stonebyres the road crosses the Clyde to the northern side, by the bridge of Lanark, after passing the new village of Kirkfield bank. This bridge, which consists of three arches, was erected towards the end of the 16th century. Before that time, all communication with Lanark and the country to the south, was carried on across the river by a ford and ferry boat.

From this bridge * the high road leads you by a gradual ascent, alongst the side of a wooded hill, towards the town of

LANARK.

This is one of the most ancient towns in Scotland. According to the best antiquaries, it is the Colania of Ptolemy, a supposition by no means improbable, as it is certain that the Romans had in the neighbourhood several stations or camps, and that it lay nearly in the line of the great Roman road, called Watling-street, which extended from Carlisle to the western boundary of the wall of Severus.—The Castle-hill of Lanark appears to have been a Roman station, many monuments of antiquity having been found here, the vestiges of that once mighty people.

Lanark

---

* Within view of this bridge, a number of seats and villas, present themselves. These are Braxfield, Castlebank, Kirkfield, Baronald, Sunnyside; the seats of Robert Dundas M'Queen, John Bannatyne, James Cochran, William Lockhart, and John Walkinshaw, Esqs.

Lanark most probably had its existence at the early period alluded to. In some centuries after, it seems to have been a place of some importance. Here, according to Buchanan, Kenneth II. in the year 978, called a Parliament, or meeting of the Estates of the realm, the first we meet with on record. It was erected into a royal burgh by Alexander I. whose charter, together with those granted by Robert the Bruce and James V. were confirmed by Charles I. in the year 1632. At what time Lanark became the county town, it is now impossible to determine. It is, however, probable, that as soon as the division of Scotland into shires took place, Lanark obtained this destinction, not only from its centrical situation, but also from its being the most considerable town in the district.

Several important transactions related in the Scottish history have occurred at Lanark, which our limits will not allow us to particularize †.—This

town

† We may, however, mention, that here the gallant Wallace made his first effort to redeem his country from the tyranny of the English, taking the place, and killing the Governor or Sheriff, a man of rank.—The castle of Lanark, which stood upon the scite of the old Roman fort, has also undergone several sieges. It was first erected by David I. and at times, we are informed, was the residence of that monarch. From this castle, in the year 1197, is dated the charter, granted by William the Lion to the town of Ayr, erecting it into a royal burgh. In the negotiation which took place between Philip of France and John Baliol, relative to the marriage of

Philip's

town is finely situated upon the south side of a rising ground, and upon the northern banks of the Clyde, from which it is at no great distance. It is built nearly in the figure of the letter K, at least its principal streets resemble that particular form more nearly than any other. These streets are the High-street, which runs in a line with the Bloomgate, east and west, and terminates at the cross, a little below which the Bloomgate begins, and runs west to the extremity of the town; the Wellgate, which strikes

4 D   off

Philip's niece to Baliol's son, Baliol, in security of the lady's jointure, mortgaged this castle, alongst with his estates in France, and some other lands.

Before the present Convention of Royal Burghs in Scotland had existence, it appears that the affairs relative to them, now under the cognizance of that Assembly, were committed to what was called the Court of the Four Burghs.—these burghs were Stirling, Linlithgow, Edinburgh, and Roxburgh. When-ever this last town happened to be in possession of the English, Lanark was the burgh that filled up the vacancy.

Lanark has likewise, from a very remote period, had the privilege of keeping the standard for all weights that are used in Scotland, which appears from several acts of Parliament. This privilege it still retains. At the Union, a new set of standard weights were transmitted by Government from Lon-don to Lanark, where they still remain.—The writer of the Statistical Account of Lanark seems to think it dubious whe-ther or not they exist, which is indeed truly astonishing, con-sidering his acquaintance with the place, and accuracy in nar-rating most other facts. The writer of these sheets can affirm that they do exist, and are used often for regulating the weights.

off from the cross, in a south-east direction, and represents the upper branch of the letter above alluded to; and the Castlegate and Broomgate, which likewise run off from the same point, towards the south-west, and fill up the remaining part of the figure.

The town of Lanark is governed by a provost, two baillies, a dean of guild, and thirteen counsellors. It has seven incorporations, viz. the smiths, shoemakers, wrights, taylors, weavers, dyers, and skinners. The deacons of these incorporations form what is called the Seat of Deacons, which is the representative body of the craftsmen. Lanark is classed with Linlithgow, Selkirk and Peebles, in sending a member to the British Senate.

The number of inhabitants in this town have been rapidly increasing since the introduction of the cotton manufacture, they are at present betwixt 2 and 3000. The general aspect of the place has also been much changed for the better, the houses of late having been erected in a more elegant and shewy manner than formerly. With regard to the public buildings, Lanark contains a handsome town house, near the centre of the town, built within these twenty years. In it is an elegant and large hall for county meetings, a council room, court-hall and weigh-house. Immediately adjoining is the prison, which has been lately enlarged by the addition of some apartments. This modern part also contains the office of the town clerk.

The

The parochial church, which stands directly in the centre of the town, is a large modern building, nearly square, and well lighted. At the east end is a lofty steeple, containing two bells, terminated by a dome. The grammar school is also a modern edifice. It stands in the Broomgate-street, and has an excellent school-room, above which is another apartment, containing a library for the use of the inhabitants, bequeathed by the late William Smellie, D. M. a gentleman who also contributed to erect the building. In the same room is a very fine portrait of a late most respectable rector of this school, Mr. Robert Thomson, brother-in-law to the immortal author of the Seasons. His memory will long be held dear. His reputation as a teacher was great;—many, now eminent in the learned professions, as well as in other departments, have benefited by his instructions. The writer of these sheets owes this small tribute in gratitude to his memory.

The public markets are large and convenient. The meal market stands near the west end of the town in Bloomgate-street.—The flesh market is a modern building, erected upon the demolition of the old; it is situated in the Castlegate. In the old market, cattle used to be killed, as well as sold, a nuisance which is now removed by the erection of a slaughter-house in a convenient situation.

In Lanark is also built by subscription of the magistrates and freeholders of the county, an elegant

and

and excellent inn, with every requisite accommodation. It is situated on the south side of Bloomgate-
street, a little below the church. Nearly opposite is
the Black Bull inn, which formerly was the principal one in the town. There are also here two meeting-houses for dissenters, lately erected. The first
built, stands at the western extremity of the town,
and belongs to the Burghers; the other is at the south
end of the Broomgate, and pertains to a Relief congregation.

As to manufactures, the weaving of muslins appears to be the principal. Formerly, a very great
quantity of shoes were manufactured here, and exported to America during the late war; this manufacture is now, however, on the decline. The manufacture of stockings is not inconsiderable, upwards of sixty frames are employed; a few years a-
go there was not above four or five of these machines in the town. Cabinet work, the making of
candles, and tanning of leather, are also carried on.
The public fairs are of great service to the trade
here; there are no fewer than seven held annually,
at each of which a considerable deal of business is
transacted.

Lanark is now much resorted to by strangers,
more especially in the summer season. The beautiful and romantic scenery—the celebrated falls of
the river Clyde in the neighbourhood—the great
cotton manufactures—and the opening of the new
Clydesdale road, are the causes which occasion these
visits.

We

Engraved for the History of Glasgow

CORRA LINN, on the River CLYDE

We have already mentioned the fall of Stonebyres, which is the lowest upon the Clyde. Besides
it, there are two others, higher up the river, viz.
the Corra and Bonnington Linns. The first of
these is about a mile and a half distant from Lanark, in a southerly direction. In the immediate
neighbourhood of this fall stands the elegant seat of
Lady Ross Baillie, relict of the late gallant Admiral
Lockhart Ross, whose actions as a commander, will
long stand conspicuous in the naval history of this
country.

This seat, which is a modern building, of beautiful architecture, is surrounded with a fine park full
of waving swells, diversified with trees, and laid out,
like the other parts of the policy, in a style that does
honour to the taste of the proprietor.—In crossing
this park by a handsome carriage road, the turbulent
noise of the cataracts first strike the ear—the
sound gradually increases—you arrive at the
wooded banks of the Clyde—pass two venerable
and lofty chesnuts, which guard the entry to these
scenes, and after doubling a copse, arrive in full
view of the

CORRA LINN,

the most picturesque and sublime of the falls of
the Clyde.

The Corra Linn is composed of two separate falls
at an inconsiderable distance from each other, over
which

which the vast body of water in the Clyde, rushes
with impetuous fury into a deep abyss, eighty feet
below its former level.　On every side the course
of the river is environed with lofty rocks of the
most romantic forms, and covered with trees of every diversity of foliage.　Upon the summit of one
of the highest, and directly above the upper fall,
stands the ruinous castle of Corra, formerly the residence of a family of the name of Somerville.
More to the right, and environed amongst trees, is
the modern mansion of that name, the seat of Miss
Edmonstones.　Between these, and situated in a
most singular situation, immediately on the verge of
the fall, is a picturesque mill, which with the other
objects just now mentioned, add still farther to the
grandeur of the prospect.—To paint, however, in
adequate language, the beauties of the scene, is a
difficult, if not impossible task.—The mighty rolling
of the waters, dashing from rock to rock, as if they
would pierce the earth to the centre—the thundering noise occasioned by these concussions—the lofty rocks, the ivy-clad and mouldering castle of Corra,
shaking from its base *—and the thick clouds of mist
arising from the deep abyss below, and towering towards heaven above the stately woods, form such a
scene, and produce such effects upon the mind, as
must certainly baffle the utmost powers of description.

From

*

* In great floods, the castle of Corra is sometimes so violently shaken, as to spill water in a glass.

From the Corra Linn, the same walk which conducted you thither, leads upward to the fall of Bonnington, at the distance of somewhat more than half
a mile. This walk is beautifully picturesque; it
here leads through groves of lofty trees, intermixed
with the honey-suckle, the wild-rose, or other flow-
ering shrubs; there, it approaches the brink of some
tremendous precipice, from which the Clyde appears
deep ingulphed amongst rocks, thundering and boiling through a broken and narrowed channel. In
other situations, from the casual opening of the
woods, more distant prospects are obtained, which,
from the chasteness of the composition, and richness of the foreground, compose unrivalled landscapes.

From the summit of a lofty promontory, overhanging the Clyde, to which the foot-path leads,
you obtain the first and best view of the

FALL OF BONNINGTON,

consisting of one single cascade of about thirty
feet in height. Like to the other falls, this is environed with rocks, covered with wood. The scenery is, however, of a softer kind than around these
we have already mentioned; and those ideas of
grandeur and magnificence which had been raised
before, are now supplanted by others of a more
tranquil, though perhaps, no less pleasing kind.—
From the situation at which the first view of the
fall of Bonnington is seen, a similar foot-path conducts

ducts to its vicinity, where the view is more contracted, from the relative position of the surrounding objects, than at the station just now mentioned,

Returning about half way alongst the same walk
which conducted you thither, another strikes off to
the right. This conducts, by the summit of the
banks, to a pavilion, placed in a delightful situation,
directly in front of the Corra fall. In this pavilion, some mirrors are so placed, that they reflect
the magnificent fall, as if pouring directly downward upon the spectator. From the west window
is a beautiful view down the river, of its finely variegated banks, the cotton manufactures, the town
of Lanark, and the distant hills of Stirling and
Argyle-shire.

Leaving these sublime scenes ‡, and proceeding
westward alongst the banks of the Clyde, by a
winding walk, cut through the woods, you shortly
arrive in view of the

GREAT COTTON MANUFACTURES.

and village of New Lanark, lately belonging to David
Dale, Esq; and now to Messrs. Owen and Co.
                                             The

‡ Immediately above the situation of the cotton manufactures, is another fall of the Clyde, called, Dundaff Linn, about
ten feet in height, which, from its comparative insignificance
with respect to the others, is not more particularly taken notice of.

The situation of these works is singular and romantic, they are surrounded on all sides, except towards the Clyde, by high grounds, rising in the form of an amphitheatre, which effectually screen them from view, till such time as you are in their immediate vicinity; when all at once, as if by enchantment, they burst upon the sight, and from the magnitude and grandeur of their appearance, produce the happiest effect.

The great command of water * which could be obtained, was the principal inducement to erect a manufacture of that kind in this place. The first mill was built in the year 1785, and since then, three others have been successively erected, nearly adjoining. At these mills, the spinning of cotton yarn is carried on to a greater extent, than at any other place in Scotland, or probably in Britain. Upwards of 400 children are here employed for that purpose, the greatest part of whom are indented for a certain number of years, and receive their lodging, victuals, &c. from the proprietors. The remainder lodge with their parents, mostly at the village of New Lanark, adjoining. Neither are they neglected with regard to their education, or morals, every exertion being used for the accomplishment of these purposes, which, as yet, has been

4 E   attended

---

* The water from the Clyde which drives the great body of machinery here, is for many hundred yards carried through a subterraneous aqueduct, cut for the purpose out of the solid rock, at a very great expence.

attended with the most beneficial and happy effects.

From the excellent system likewise that has been adopted at this manufacture, the children and others employed, have been uncommonly healthy, much more so it is said, than at any other works of this kind upon the same scale in Britain: The principal regulations follow: The spinning rooms are of the whole extent of the buildings without any sub-divisions, and are from 120 to 150 feet long, from 26 to 30 feet wide, and all of them in height 10 feet from floor to floor, or 9 feet clear of the beams.

These rooms, which contain each, about 2000 spindles, are carefully ventilated, by regularly opening the windows at top at both sides, and to increase the circulation of air still more, air holes 6 inches square on a level with the floor, are opened below every other window through the walls, at the distance of 14 feet from each other, but these are only of advantage in summer, as the cold of winter precludes the use of them. The means of purification in use, are washing the walls and ceilings of the rooms at least once a year, with new slacked lime, and weekly washing of the floors and machinery with scalding water, and frequent and constant brushing of the walls, ceilings and floor.

The greatest number of persons in one room is 75, in some there are only 50. The hours of labour are 11½ each day, from 6 o'clock in the morning till
. 7 o'clock

7 o'clock at night, with half an hour of intermission for breakfast and a whole hour at dinner.

When fevers, or any epidemical disease appear in in boarding houses where the children are accommodated, the means used to prevent the infection, are the immediate removal of the sick to a detached part of the house, and frequent sprinkling and fumigating the bed rooms with vinegar.

In the sleeping rooms, which are six in number, and very large, three children are allowed to each bed. The ceilings and walls of these rooms are washed twice a-year with hot lime, and the floors with scalding water and sand. The children sleep on beds with frames of cast iron, with ticks filled with straw, which is changed once a month. The bed rooms are carefully swept, and the windows thrown open every morning, in which state they remain through the day.

The village of New Lanark owes its existence to the erection of this manufacture. It consists of neat substantial houses, of from one to five stories in height, covered with slate, and formed into regular streets. In this village, the people employed about the works, and their families reside; and according to the latest computation, this spot, which fourteen years ago, contained not a human being as an inhabitant, is now peopled with upwards of 1500 souls. Here also, one of the partners, and the principal manager have houses, fitted up in a more elegant style, and accommodated with gardens

4 E 2

in

in front. Besides these people who reside here, many more are employed in Lanark, and the adjacent country, as weavers, spinners, pickers, &c. It is to the establishment of this manufacture that we are to deduce the growing prosperity of the latter town. Money is now more frequent there, industry is awakened, and new branches of trade are carried on which had before no existence in the neighbourhood.

Not far towards the right, from the line of road betwixt the cotton mills and the town of Lanark, are the ruins of the old church of that burgh, in a most commanding situation. It has been long disused.—According to conjectures, founded upon its mode of architecture and appearance, it appears to be as old at least as the days of Robert the Bruce.

Beside the beautiful scenes about the falls of the Clyde, there are in this neighbourhood, a series of romantic and picturesque prospects upon the river Mouse, at no great distance above its junction with the Clyde, which are highly deserving of attention. The principal of these are situated at a place called

CARTLAND CRAIGS,

at the distance of somewhat less than a mile from Lanark.—This place which extends nearly half a mile on both sides of the river, is a most romantic dell, composed of lofty rocks, beautifully deversified with natural wood and planting. The approach from the north, which is the most common point

point of entry, is grand and striking.— A level piece of ground, around which the Mouse makes a sweep, conducts to the mouth of this great chasm. As you enter and through its whole extent, a succession of the most picturesque scenes, appear on every hand. Through the bottom runs the river Mouse, in a stream finely broken by the irregularity of the channel. In the most sequestered part of this dell, at some height above the river, and embowered in copses, is a natural chasm in the rock, called *Wallace's Cave*, which tradition and history both concur in telling us, was often resorted to by that hero.

Neither is this spot only valuable to the admirer of the romantic scenery of nature, the poet or the painter. The naturalist may also find ample scope for entertainment; He may, in many places, examine the different strata of earths or of fossils, which present themselves here in a wonderful variety, from the level of the river to the summit of the lofty rocks which surround him. Hundreds of rare and curious plants are also to be found, many of whom may yet have escaped the inquisitive eye of the botanist. Upon emerging from Cartland Craigs upon the south, you find yourself surrounded by a beautiful amphitheatre of high grounds, open towards the Clyde, and in the immediate vicinity of the bridge of Lanark.

Having thus taken notice of the principal scenes in this neighbourhood, we now proceed, as proposed,

to

to the counties of Cumberland, Westmoreland, &c.

Leaving Lanark, you cross the Clyde about two
miles from the town, by an elegant bridge, called
Hyndford bridge, turn to the right, and at the distance of about eleven miles from Lanark, arrive at
Douglas Mill, in Douglas-Dale, so called from a
tributary stream of the Clyde, which passes
through it.

Douglas Mill is situated on the great road from
Carlisle to Glasgow, from which, according to
the direct road leading by the villages of Lesma-
hagoe and Larkhall, it is distant 28 miles. Not
far from this stage, is placed the Castle of Douglas, the chief seat of the noble family of that name.
The present castle was built about 60 years ago;
it is, however, only part of the original design,
which has never yet been completed. In the neighbourhood of the castle, is the town of Douglas,
an ancient place, though of small extent.

The country, after passing Douglas Mill, becomes
bleak and dreary, without any object worthy of
notice. Elvanfoot is the first stage you meet with,
at the distance of 13 miles. The country that
lies farther on, after passing Elvanfoot, is equally
desert and gloomy, without any object, picturesque
or beautiful.

You are now nearly at the highest elevation,
betwixt the eastern and western seas, the three
principal

principal rivers of the south of Scotland, having
their sources from the opposite sides of the same
ridge of mountains in this district, viz. the Clyde,
the Tweed, and the Annan. After passing this
elevated ground, the country becomes more interesting, though still barren and mountainous, and
so continues nearly to Moffat, 13 miles from
Elvanfoot.

MOFFAT,

is pleasantly situated amongst the mountains, and
has long been famed for its mineral waters, as
well as the salubrity of the air. Its consists principally of one street, which is spacious, and in general neatly built. It has two good inns, and some
lodging houses for the accommodation of invalids;
the number of inhabitants are about 1000. You
are now at the head of a plain or valley, opening
towards the south, and extending upon both sides
of the Annan, and in this direction, upon the
east side of the river, the great road we
have been pursuing, leads through an improving
country, to

LOCKERBIE,

at the distance of 16 miles from Moffat, a considerable market and post town. It has several well
attended fairs, where vast quantities of linen
and woollen cloth are sold, principally to the
English merchants. Proceeding from Lockerbie, you enter a more level and fertile country, improving as you advance; at the distance of about
two

two miles, you pass through the village of Black-
ford; when in this situation, the lofty hill of Burns-
wark appears upon the left, noted for its extensive and variegated prospects, and the vestiges of
many Roman military works. At seven miles from
Lockerbie, you arrive at

ECCLESFECHAN,

in the parish of Hoddam, noted for its fairs, of
which there is 12 annually. Nine miles farther, you
arrive at the noted village of

GRETNA GREEN;

where you meet the road from Dumfries and Annan to Carlisle. Gretna, which contains one or
two good inns, is the last stage in Scotland, upon
this line of road; about half a mile farther, descending the slope of a hill, you cross the small river Sark
by a bridge of one arch, and enter

ENGLAND;

the road passing through an extensive morass, called
Solway Moss, remarkable for a dreadful eruption of
its waters, &c. which took place in 1771. Shortly
thereafter, you cross the Esk, and enter the neat
town of

LONGTOWN;

cross thereafter the river Line, turn directly south,
and at about seven miles distance, pass through the
village of Stanix, and obtain immediately a fine view
of the venerable cathedral and castle of Carlisle.

CARLISLE.

The city of Carlisle is one of the most ancient towns in Britain, though, like most others that claim any high degree of antiquity, its origin is now unknown. At an early period we find it a Roman station, under the name of Luguvallum.—After the departure of that people, it came again into the possession of the southern Britons, and in the reign of Egfrid, was fortified with a wall. It was afterwards burned by the Danes, and till the time of William the Conqueror, lay in ruins. That monarch seeing its importance as a western frontier, gave directions for rebuilding and fortifying it of new.

Since that period it has seen many changes of fortune, and sustained several sieges, being often in possession of the Scots, who, in their turn, were obliged to abandon it to the English. The last hostile act of which Carlisle was the scene, was in the rebellion of the year 1745, when it was taken possession of by the rebel army, and thereafter retaken by the King's forces under the Duke of Cumberland.

Carlisle is in general well built, with open and spacious streets; particularly the principal street, which runs north and south, in which is placed the Town-hall, Moot-hall, and Council Chamber. It is still surrounded by a wall, now in a state of de-

4 F

cay,

cay, and which, from preventing the free circulation of air, is more hurtful than otherwise. This wall has three gates: The Scotch, to the north of the Main-street;—the English at the end of English-street;—and the Irish towards the west.

The principal edifices are the cathedral, a fine Gothic structure, and the castle, situated upon an eminence in a beautiful and commanding situation; but now mouldering into ruin. The churches are St. Mary's and St. Cuthbert's, upon the establishment, and six dissenting chapels. The number of inhabitants amount to about 9000. These are principally engaged in the different manufactures carried on in the town; the staple manufacture appears to be that of cotton.

Carlisle is celebrated for its calicoe printers, who pay about L.20,000 annually to the revenue. Another manufacture carried on is that of malt liquor, which pays annually about L.6000 sterling; and a manufacture of soap, which yields about L.1500 annually of duty. For the encouragement of these manufactures, and others that may be established, there are two banks, which have been found of great service to the city.

Leaving Carlisle, you proceed to the south, alongst the great road to Penrith. For some distance the country is cultivated and beautiful; you thereafter enter a common called Inglewood Forest, which accompanies you to Penrith, distant 18 miles from Carlisle.

PENRITH

PENRITH

contains about 4000 inhabitants, and is a neat and well built town, having many houses that are even elegant. Its inns are excellent, and from being a great thoroughfare, numerous and well frequented.

You are now in the neighbourhood of one of the finest of the English Lakes, and to which a road leads from the town, towards the south-west, through a beautiful country, for five miles, when you find yourself at the village of Pooley, upon the banks of

ULLSWATER,

a beautiful sheet, extending about nine miles, and nearly of the form of the letter Z, but with less a-cute angles. Its breadth is not more than a mile.

On all sides except the eastern extremity, at which we first meet with it on the road from Penrith, it is surrounded with mountains, many of which are lofty, particularly at the western termination of the lake. Down the steep sides of these hills creep many beautiful copses. Nearer the base, in some situations, swelling fields, regularly inclosed, and in a high state of culture; these again interspersed with several cottages, add to the beauty of the scenery, by the contrast they afford with the rude grandeur of nature.

4 F 2   The

The best view of the lake is obtained from the summit of a hill, in the immediate vicinity of the village just now mentioned, called Dunmallet, and to which you ascend by a lane cut out of the wood. When in this situation, you command the first stretch of Ullswater, extending about three miles, with all its capes, bays, and promontories. The view is closed by a lofty mountain, called Placefell, which, to appearance, shuts up the vale. A number of other mountains are upon the left, presenting many awful precipices, interspersed with shaggy woods and spots of verdure. Upon the opposite side, the banks are more tame, rising gently from the lake; they are, however, in several situations, finely wooded, and are adorned with some neat houses.

A second view of this lake is obtained, about three miles from Dunmallet, at its first great bend to the north. In this situation, it appears much contracted in breadth, winding like a large river amongst the mountains. These, in this situation, are higher than those bounding the lake in the first point of the view ; that upon the left, in particular, exhibits a towering and rugged appearance, dipping its almost perpendicular side into the water, and destitute of wood or vegetation of any kind. The hills upon the right, though equally lofty, are more diversified with verdure, rock, and wood. Near the base of one of them is Gow-barrow-park, a summer-house, belonging to the Duke of Norfolk,

Norfolk, a modern edifice, built in the form of a Gothic castle.

A little farther, the lake turns round a lofty promontory, projecting from the barren side of Placefell, and stretches to its southern extremity at Patterdale. The scenery in this part of the lake, which is seen to most advantage in the neighbourhood of Gowbarrow park, is still more beautiful, grand, and picturesque, than at the stations we have just now mentioned; This arises from the increased height of the mountains, which seem to pierce the sky, and surround the lake like an amphitheatre, from the variety of their outline, the deep vales betwixt them—the rocks and woods that cover their sides—the cascades tumbling from the precipices, and a number of subordinate indescribable objects, which, all united, compose a picture, grand and sublime. From this station the road leads through the woods, sometimes on the brink of the water, and at other places at a considerable height above it, till you arrive at the sweetly secluded and retired village of Patterdale, at the head of the lake, and nine miles distant from Pooley, at its eastern extremity.

Returning from this place alongst the same road, you turn to the left, near to Gowbarrow park, ascend the slope of the mountain, enter an elevated valley, containing a small village, and many scattered cottages; continue a tedious ascent up the brow of a lofty hill; (Helvellin) gaining
the

the summit, you travel through a desert tract
for some time, till at length the road begins to
descend; you then obtain a view of the Vale
of Keswick, with the lofty mountains of Saddleback
and Skiddaw, upon the right. Shortly thereafter pass a well cultivated district, and at about ten
miles distance from where you left Ullswater, enter
Keswick, a small town, with many neat and pleasant houses. In its immediate vicinity, is

DERWENTWATER, OR KESWICK LAKE.

This beautiful expanse of water is about three
miles in length, and its greatest breadth measures
about half of that space. It is nearly of an ellipti-
cal form, contracting somewhat more than a true
figure of that kind allows at both extremities.
This lake is formed by the river Derwent, which
runs through it. Like most of the others in this
country, it is surrounded by mountains, with several
openings or vales betwixt them, leading into scenes
of a similar kind.

Derwentwater is adorned with four beautiful
islands, all finely wooded, though of no great extent: These are Pocklington's island, upon which is
a modern and elegant house with gardens and pleasure-grounds.—St. Herbert's island—Lord's island
—and Rampsholm.

The first station to which the guides in general
conduct

conduct you, is in the immediate vicinity of the village, at a place called Crow-park; the view here is, however, contracted, and every way inferior in point of grandeur to that from a conical wood-covered hill, called Castle-hill, about the 8th part of a mile farther to the east.

Upon its summit, the whole lake appears stretched before the eye, with its finely indented shore, and wooded isles. Two ranges of lofty hills bound it on each side, these approach nearer each other as the lake contracts at its farther extremity, leaving only a narrow pass betwixt them, which opens into a most romantic valley, watered by the Derwent, called Borrodale.

To such as incline to visit Borrodale, an excellent road leads up the eastern shore from Keswick, in the course of which, upon the left, you find a fine cataract, called Lowdore, one of the highest in Cumberland.

Returning to Keswick, you pursue the road to the N. W.—cross the Derwent by a bridge—pass through the village of Portinscale—gradually ascend, till near Tornthwaite; at the distance of about three miles from Keswick you obtain a view of

BASSENTHWAITE LAKE,

connected with that of Keswick by the Derwent; it is about four miles in length, and generally more than

than half a mile broad. This sheet of water, like the others, lies also in a vale; it is, however, broader than that in which Derwent water reposes, and the banks are finely cultivated, rich and fertile, every where adorned with fine white cottages, and more shewy mansions. In picturesque beauty it is reckoned, however, inferior to some of the other lakes; the mountains that form the vale wanting that fine and varied outline, that characterizes those in other situations; though in point of altitude, one of them, Skiddaw, which bounds the lake on the east, is superior to most of the guardians of Keswick or Ullswater *.

An excellent road leads also up the banks of this lake to Ousebridge, at its northern extremity from which a high road leads to Carlisle.

After passing Portinscale, the road ascends the sloping side of a mountain, and thus continues for some considerable space, presenting several fine views of Bassenthwaite lake, and Skiddaw. You then enter the elevated valley of Whinlatter, bounded on each side by the most stupendous mountains.

On emerging, at the west, from Whinlatter,

a

* Some visitors come direct from Carlisle to Ousebridge, and begin their tour with Bassenthwaite lake, then proceed to that of Keswick, &c.

a beautiful and extensive prospect opens upon the
eye, of a fine champaign country, richly cultivated,
betwixt and the Irish sea. The road now descends
the other side of this great ridge of mountains, passes the village of Lorton, through the vale of the
same name, and turns toward the south; you then
arrive at about 12 miles from Keswick, in the
neighbourhood of

LOWESWATER,

a view of which can, however, only be obtained by
deviating from the road to the right, and crossing
the small river Cocker.

Loweswater is about a mile in length, by a quarter of a mile in breadth. Upon the left or south side,
it is bounded by mountains, dropping down in a
quick descent to the water. Upon the north the
banks are less elevated, adorned with woods, inclosures, and many neat houses, tending to enliven
a scene of much beauty and simplicity.

Regaining the road, you enter a deep valley,
shooting out before you, and bounded by a chain
of very elevated hills. In the middle of this vale
lies

CRUMMOCK WATER,

about four miles in length, by half a mile broad,
ornamented by three beautiful little islands. Pas-

4 G

sing

sing through some fine woody lanes, at one place leading by the brink of the lake, and in other situations at a greater distance, you turn round a steep rock, hanging immediatey above the water, and enter the secluded, but sweet vale of

BUTTERMERE,

in which lies the lake of the same name, about about a mile and a half long, and a quarter of that space broad, connected with Crummock water, by the small river Cocker. The mountains, in this district, are still more lofty than these we have passed, in some parts they are clothed with wood, and in others entirely naked; some are covered with heath, and others with verdure. Several cataracts strike the ear and eye, in different situations, and contribute to the effect of the romantic scenery.

The principal fall of water here, is called the Milk-force, from the colour of the broken water, in falling over a succession of the precipitous rocks; it lies directly opposite the village of Buttermere.

From Buttermere, besides the road just now mentioned, by Whinlatter and Lorton, there are other two, one leading by Borrodale, and the other by Newlands vale to Keswick; that by Borrodale measures fourteen miles—the other only twelve.

Leaving

Leaving the secluded scenes of Buttermere, and returning by the vale of Newlands, you pass the Chapel of Buttermere, situated upon a small eminence above the village—ascend a steep hill, surpassed, however, by others of a much greater altitude—and continue through a solitude, without any object very interesting for some miles.—You then arrive at the greatest elevation, and descend gradually to the vale of Keswick.

. From Keswick an excellent road runs to the south, to the lakes in Lancashire and Westmoreland: Pursuing this direction, the highway leads up a steep ascent from the town, for nearly a mile, commanding a retrospective view, in many situations, of the vales of Derwentwater and Bassenthwaite. You turn then more to the right, descend the sloping side of a hill, and enter the pastoral valley of Legberthwaite, watered by a small rivulet running northwards.

The mountains which form this vale are lofty, though unpicturesque, adorned but in few situations with wood, and wanting that beautiful variety in their surface, which characterize those in some other situations. One of these, however, upon the left hand, is of a greater altitude, Helvellin, by some said to surpass Skiddaw. At the base of this mountain, and in the tract of the road you now pursue, lies

LEATHES WATER, OR THIRLMERE LAKE,

stretching in length about four miles, and of a very

4 G 2   irregular

irregular breadth. Coasting alongst its margin, the road presents nothing very interesting—pass the small village and chapel of Wythburn—ascend an eminence called *Dunmail Raise*, from which you have a view, though at some distance, of

GRASMERE LAKE,

surrounded by a spacious amphitheatre of mountains, different in their character from those just now mentioned, and from their relative situations with respect to each other and the lake, exhibiting many charming scenes. The lake itself is about 2¼ miles in length, and is adorned by a small island with a tuft of wood. Crossing an elevated, though narrow neck of land, you come in sight of another small lake:

RYDAL WATER.

This beautiful lake measures about a mile in length; its surface is enlivened by some small round islands, covered with elegant trees and shrubs, which, with the scenery around the margin, consisting of swelling fields, richly cultivated, and adorned with trees and cottages, compose a beautiful and harmonious landscape.

Passing Rydal hall upon the left, the seat of Sir Michael Le Fleming, commanding an extensive and rich prospect to the south, in which direction the country opens, you arrive at

AMBLESIDE,

AMBLESIDE,

16 miles from Keswick.

Ambleside is a small market town, finely situated; it is a place of considerable antiquity, and of much more note formerly than at present. In its neighbourhood are still to be seen the vestiges of a Roman station, supposed to be that called the *Dietis*, where a part of the Cohors *nerviorum dictentium* was stationed.

About a mile farther, travelling through shady lanes, we arrive at

WINDERMERE,

the largest of all the English lakes.

Windermere lies nearly north and south, extending about 10 miles; it is of very different breadths, though no where more than a mile; its depth is very various, but in general it measures 90 feet.

This lake is not surrounded with such rugged barriers as encompass the lake of Keswick or Ullswater. The banks are more humble, though still beautiful, from the distribution of the numerous woods, coppices, and fields, which every where enliven them. The surface of this fine sheet of water is broken by a number of islands, the largest of which contains about 27 acres.

The

608

The inn of Lowwood is situated about a mile farther on. Passing it, you leave the margin of the water, and travel through groves, secluded farms, and arable fields, scarcely gaining a glimpse of the lake, till we arrive opposite Colgarth, an elegant new mansion, the property and common place of residence of the Bishop of Landaff; it, in this situation, comes more fully into view, with its islands and other objects around, exhibiting a most beautiful, soft, and pleasing scene. You shortly thereafter arrive at

BOWNESS,

(6 miles from Ambleside) a small town upon the east bank of the lake, and nearly equi-distant betwixt its northern and southern extremities. Near to Bowness is a ferry across Windermere to the opposite side in the county of Lancaster. Crossing by this passage, you find upon the right a number of islands, decorated with wood. Of these the largest is called Curwen's island, containing an elegant house and pleasure-grounds, and commanding a general view of this fine expanse of water towards the north and south.

From the western shore of the lake you proceed to Hawkshead, alongst an excellent carriage road, 4 miles, in the course of which you fall in with

ESTHWAITE WATER,

about 2 miles in length by half a mile in breadth.
Like

Like Windermere, its banks are composed of gently swelling grounds, scattered with houses and villages, rising above the numerous woods and trees which lie around on every hand.

Hawkshead is a small market town, containing some good inns, and between 3 and 400 inhabitants; it is situated upon the declivity of a mountainous ridge, commanding an extensive prospect over the vale and lake below. Thence the road leads through some winding lanes, for some short distance, then ascends a barren heathy ridge, from the summit of which you catch another, though distant view of Windermere, and the hills near Ambleside. A little farther,

CONISTON LAKE

opens upon the eye, surrounded with the mountains, or, as they are called, the Fells of Furness.

This lake is about 6 miles in length, and three quarters of a mile in breadth. Its outline is finely broken by numerous bays and capes, while its banks, which swell from the side of the water, are covered with verdure, heath, and rocky fragments, interspersed with houses and corn-fields; presenting, in many situations, very soft and beautiful scenes, which, though not so strikingly grand or sublime as those around Ullswater or Keswick lake, are yet more engaging, in a picturesque point of view, than the environs of Windermere.

Alongst

Alongst the east side of this lake, the road leads to the Low country, and the towns of Ulverston, Lancaster, &c.

Leaving Coniston lake, which is the last in this district of country which claims particular notice, you take the road back to Hawkshead, then turn to the north, alongst the highway to Ambleside, near the head of Windermere— retrace the way to Keswick—thence by a road leading across an extensive common, having the mountain of Saddleback upon the left—to Penrith 17 miles, and so on to Carlisle, Moffat, and Glasgow.

Printed by R. Chapman, Trongate, Glasgow.

Lightning Source UK Ltd.
Milton Keynes UK
UKHW020930150822
407319UK00007B/1233